COMMUNISM IN
RURAL FRANCE

JOHN BULAITIS teaches at the University of Essex, specialising in twentieth-century French history. He obtained his PhD from Queen Mary, University of London. He has taught European history at Queen Mary, Royal Holloway and the Open University and translation at London South Bank University. He has also worked at Goldsmiths College, University of London, organising outreach work in schools and colleges. His forthcoming biography of Maurice Thorez will also be published by I.B.Tauris.

COMMUNISM IN RURAL FRANCE

French Agricultural Workers
and the Popular Front

JOHN BULAITIS

I.B. TAURIS

LONDON · NEW YORK

Published in 2008 by I.B.Tauris & Co Ltd
6 Salem Road, London W2 4BU
175 Fifth Avenue, New York NY 10010
www.ibtauris.com

In the United States of America and Canada distributed by Palgrave Macmillan
a division of St. Martin's Press, 175 Fifth Avenue, New York NY 10010

International Library of Historical Studies: Volume 55
ISBN: 978 1 84511 708 5

A full CIP record for this book is available from the British Library
A full CIP record is available from the Library of Congress

Library of Congress Catalog Card Number: available

Printed and bound in India by Thomson Press (India) Limited
From camera-ready copy edited and supplied by the author

To Stella and Vincent

CONTENTS

TABLES

MAPS & ILLUSTRATIONS

1. French Departments (1936): Percentage of agricultural workers employed on farms with over ten employees, p. 7.
2. A large farm in the Aisne (1920s), p. 48.
3. Industrialised farming in the Aisne (late 1920s), p. 65.
4. FUA poster advertising the Monster Rally held on 25 March 1935, p. 72.
5. On bicycles in the Artois, July 1936: a group of pickets responsible for communicating news of the strike to neighbouring villages and farms, p. 113.
6. FNTA strike poster during the conflict in the Artois (August 1936), p. 119.
7. FNTA fundraising event held in Melun (June 1937) as the strikes became increasingly bitter, p. 131.
8. Agricultural workers on strike in the village of Mory (Pas-de-Calais) in July 1936, p. 142.

Credits & References

1. Design by Patrick Minnikin.
2. Fonds André Vergnol (13Fi 922), Archives Départementales de l'Aisne.
3. Fonds André Vergnol (13Fi 966), Archives Départementales de l'Aisne.
4. Archives Départementales du Nord, M 149/86. Photo: Jean-Luc Thieffry.
5. *Le Grand Écho du Nord*, 30 July 1936.
6. Archives Départementales du Pas-de-Calais, M2386.
7. Archives Départementales, Seine-et-Marne, M4958. Service photographique de la Direction des Archives et du Patrimoine de Seine-et-Marne.
8. *Le Grand Écho du Nord*, 30 July 1936.

ACKNOWLEDGEMENTS

My thanks are due to all those whose help ensured this book was possible. I would particularly like to thank Donald Sassoon (Queen Mary, University of London), my doctoral supervisor. Others whose advice has been invaluable include Julian Jackson (Queen Mary), Kevin Passmore (University of Swansea), Matthew Worley (University of Reading) and Pamela Pilbeam (Royal Holloway, University of London). I am also grateful to everyone in the Department of History at the University of Essex, who have provided paid employment as well as a relaxed working environment conducive to transforming my thesis into this book. At I.B.Tauris, I am grateful for the support of Lester Crook and the assistance of Liz Friend-Smith.

In France, I received help from too many people to list. I was made to feel particularly welcome by staff at the departmental archives in the Aisne and Pas-de-Calais. The archivists at the French Communist Party were always willing to assist. Research was conducted in archives from the Aurillac in the south, Colmar in the East, Châteauroux in the Centre and others situated across the north-east of France. It would have been impossible without the existence of an efficient, reasonably priced, railway system.

The assistance of some individuals went well beyond expectations. I thank Jean-Pierre Besse (Creil), Jean-Claude Farcy (CNRS) and Gilbert Noël (University of Artois). I would not have survived Paris without André Strauss and Mémé for discussion, friendship and Algerian wine. I thank Claudine Eche for her hospitality. Most of all, my sincere gratitude goes to Guy Marival (Chambre d'Agriculture de l'Aisne), for not only sharing some of his expertise in French agricultural history but also for making me feel so much at home.

I would like to thank the Arts and Humanities Research Board for funding my research. I also received grants from the Royal Historical Society, the Central Research Fund of the University of London and the Stretton Fund at Queen Mary.

This work would have been unthinkable without Margaret's encouragement, support and patience. Not many would have been so forgiving about missing the ferry after a detour to visit rural cemeteries on the way back from holiday. I was often distracted from my writing by proud thoughts of Cheryl and Katy. Most of all, I will be eternally grateful for the support of my parents, to whom this book is dedicated.

INTRODUCTION

La-Ville-aux-Bois-lès-Dizy is a small village in northern France, close to the boundary between the Aisne and Ardennes departments. The layout of its streets, houses and farms remains, today, little different from the position in 1936. One main artery cuts through the village, from which a handful of side roads quickly peter out into seemingly never-ending fields of wheat and sugar beet. Despite its name, there are few trees surrounding La-Ville-aux-Bois. In 1936, the lives of the 390-strong population were dominated by six large farms (five averaging 200 hectares, the other just under 100 hectares); there were also three smaller holdings.[1] Two of the biggest farms were run by members of the Bertrand family, Pierre and André; other Bertrands ran the council: 68-year-old Henri was Mayor and Léopold, Deputy Mayor. Excluding a number of traders and craftsmen, most villagers were employed on the farms as agricultural workers.

On Monday 20 July, police in the nearby town of Montcornet received a phone call. The caller, Jules Drapier, a farmer in the village, reported a commotion outside *l'Économie moderne*, the café and convenience store run by Louis Marécal. Drapier explained that a strike of agricultural labourers, which had begun three days earlier, was turning nasty. Strikers were heading towards the fields in an attempt to halt the work of a group of Belgian seasonal workers. Police were quickly on the scene. As they arrived, 40 workers paraded through the main street, three-a-breast with red flowers in their caps. The demonstration stopped briefly outside the courtyard of each farm, before finishing at Marécal's café. After taking lunch, the participants, now on bicycles and encouraged by a boisterous crowd, including many women and children, left the village to spread the strike to other farms in the vicinity.[2]

Meeting in the mairie, the farming families were horrified by events. All agreed that relations with their workers had been poisoned by the activities of Marécal, who had established his business after moving to the village in 1932. A police inquiry into his background had found he was of previous good character, but farmers were worried by reports that he had recently joined the Communist Party. Although not part of the 'agricultural profession', the café owner was claiming to be president of the agricultural workers' union and was apparently orchestrating the strike from his premises. According to the mayor's wife, he had threatened that farm buildings would be set ablaze and livestock ill-treated, if farmers did not concede workers' demands within 48 hours.[3]

The following day, farmers agreed to make concessions to the workers and the stoppage was called off. But the dispute would continue in various forms over the next two years: union activists would be victimised, further strikes organised and farm property and crops burnt in suspicious circumstances. In 1937, the conflict gave rise to a legal case after farmers sued Marécal for damages. By 1938, it had become the central issue in village politics as workers attempted to wrestle control of the farmers' power-base on the village council.

*****

The drama at La-Ville-aux-Bois was one local element within a bitter struggle between agricultural workers and farmers that swept through large parts of the French countryside during 1936 and 1937. It introduces the two connected themes of this book. The first is the farm workers' movement, particularly in the Paris basin and northern France, as well as its characteristics and significance. The movement's evolution is traced from the early twentieth century through to the strike movement of 1936–37. The second is the relationship between that movement and the dominant political force within it, the Communist Party. This is placed within the context of a more general examination of the place of the agricultural worker within the agrarian strategy of the political left during the first half of the twentieth century.

The catalyst for the events described above was the victory of the Popular Front at the legislative elections in April–May 1936 and the subsequent form-ation of a government led by the socialist, Léon Blum. Emerging from an alliance of communists, socialists and radicals against the perceived threat of fascism, the Popular Front engendered hope, confidence and enthusiasm. The elections were followed by a festive manifestation of people power as two million workers staged strikes and workplace occupations. Panicking, the normally obdurate employers' association sought urgent talks and on 7 June an agreement between the trade unions represented by the Confédération générale du travail (CGT), employers and government was signed at the Prime Minister's Matignon residence. Workers secured wage increases of between 7 and 15 per cent, improved collective bargaining rights, together with promises of legislation to introduce a 40-hour working week and two weeks' paid holiday. The strike movement did not begin to ebb, however, until after 11 June, the day Communist

Party General Secretary, Maurice Thorez, famously declared: 'it is necessary to know how to end a strike.'

In France, the Popular Front has entered collective memory as the moment when society recognised working people's rights and dignity.[4] It has also been remembered as 'an essentially urban phenomenon', to quote a classic account.[5] Photographs in books and displays at commemorative exhibitions invariably depict strikers dancing inside occupied factories, sleeping next to machinery or parading through Paris streets. Cultural references draw attention to innovations in cinema, theatre and agitprop – phenomena also centred on the urban world. The archetypal rural image remains that of a young working-class couple venturing into the countryside on a tandem, taking advantage of their newly won holidays.[6] Even the best historical interpretation in English, Julian Jackson's *The Popular Front in France: Defending Democracy*, fails to mention the farm workers' movement and contains only a few, often indirect, references to the Popular Front's impact in rural society.[7]

The absence of the agricultural workers' movement in the historical memory is in stark contrast to the importance accorded to it at the time. A front-page editorial in *Le Temps* declared that the farm strikes posed 'extremely serious consequences for public order, the national economy and the republican regime'.[8] Well-publicised exchanges took place in parliament as opponents of the Popular Front found an issue around which to mobilise. In the Senate, on 7 July 1936, repeated heckling prompted the Interior Minister, Roger Salengro, to pledge that he would take action against attempts by strikers to occupy farms. The government and local administrations spent considerable time trying to resolve matters; at one stage, an attempt was made to organise an 'agricultural Matignon'.

The focal point of the strike movement was located in the wheat and sugar-beet fields of the Paris Basin and Northern France. Previously, agricultural workers' unionism had received its main support from vineyard workers (most notably in the Midi, but also to a more limited extent in the Champagne region) and forestry workers (particularly in the Cher and surrounding departments).[9] The conflict in the large-scale farming regions in the north of the country was considered to be the strikingly new feature of the Popular Front strike movement – and, for many, the most shocking. An outline of events in these regions provides the centrepiece of this book (Chapter 5).

Reverberations of the strikes and workers' unionisation campaign were felt elsewhere, however. Gordon Wright, in his classic work on the French peasantry, describes a 'small-scale repetition of the Great Fear of 1789 [as] smallowners in many villages gathered in the public square and swore to resist any workers who sought to occupy their farms'.[10] In Brittany, farmers' organisations were panicked into establishing their own workers' sections 'in order to get the workers in before they were grabbed up by the CGT'.[11] A farm occupation at Guebwiller in Alsace hit the front pages of the national press. The present study examines events in Guebwiller (Chapter 6) as well as the problems posed by the farm workers' movement in the Cantal and Calvados (Chapter 7).

*****

Agricultural workers have been described by Ronald Hubscher, one of France's leading rural historians, as '"the forgotten men". . . marginalised in rural studies and in the collective memory of the working class'.[12] Although the phrase is unfortunate – women made up a significant section of the agricultural labour force – the observation is extremely pertinent. The neglect of agricultural workers in labour and social history is, in fact, a general trend, not particular to France. In relation to Britain, Howard Newby notes how the interest of labour historians progressively declines 'the more one moves from the Captain Swing riots'.[13] David Pretty shows how in the historiography of rural Wales 'the movement of middle class farmers' has a 'place of honour', while 'the agricultural labourer could be virtually ignored by employer and historian alike'.[14] In France, however, an over-concentration on the small peasant and disregard for the position of the agricultural worker has been particularly marked. The literature has often viewed the peasantry homogeneously, failing to examine the contradictions and conflicts between its constituent groups. This trend reflects the pervasive ideology of agrarianism, which, though in different ways, profoundly influenced the thinking of both political right and left.[15]

'La France est, surtout, un pays de paysans' (France is, above all, a peasant country) was a phrase repeated so often by politicians, commentators and state officials during the Third Republic that it became almost a cliché.[16] But who, exactly, was a peasant? Literally, the word 'paysan' signifies 'someone from the country', covering the full spectrum of the rural population. In the first half of the nineteenth century it was employed primarily in a cultural sense – suggesting, often pejoratively, a way of life at variance to that of the towns. But during the latter part of the century its meaning changed. Not only did 'paysan' now take on positive connotations, it also became associated with a particular section of the rural population: self-employed farmers producing for the market. Rapid advances in commercial farming, the impact of the agricultural depression of the 1880s and a further shift in land ownership away from absentee landlords towards self-employed proprietors led to agricultural producers becoming increasingly conscious of their collective interests. After 1884, agricultural syndicates spread rapidly, drawing more than one million members into a network of co-operatives, insurance and credit facilities.[17] Dominated by the most prosperous farmers, the agricultural syndicates formed a powerful agrarian lobby to represent the interests of a 'peasant class'.[18]

Before the First World War, agrarianism provided firm ideological foundations for conservative republicanism – Jules Ferry and Jules Méline, amongst others, regarding the peasant as a bulwark against both monarchist reaction and a challenge from the left. Right-wing agrarianism championed supposed 'peasant values' – including individualism, defence of private property, the family and work ethic – as an alternative to the 'corrupting' effects of urban society. Agrarians argued that a supposed harmony of social relations was one of the distinguishing characteristics of rural society. A resolution passed at the first national congress of agricultural syndicates in 1894 declared: 'In agriculture, the line separating capitalist and worker does not exist as it does in industry. . . The interests of capital and labour are so closely intermingled that antagonism becomes impossible and the efforts of all are directed to the same end.'[19]

Right-wing agrarianism was reinforced by the experience of the war. A veritable cult of the peasant arose, venerating the sacrifice of the 'peasant-soldier' who had fused his blood with the land on which he had previously toiled. The crisis of the early 1930s acted as a further impetus. Perceiving a decline in the status of agriculture, agrarians advocated a peasant-based political economy, the corporate organisation of agriculture by the 'agricultural profession' and, rather contradictorily, a non-interventionist but authoritarian state, a programme that was adopted in its entirety by the Vichy government.[20]

The agrarian image of the French countryside as a collection of small, family proprietors was, however, a construct which, in many regions of France, had only a partial relationship with reality. French rural society was a much more complex world. As the rural specialist Michel Augé-Laribé noted, 'the share and influence of the *grands propriétaires* was greater than people wanted to admit'.[21] Landowners, including some remaining noble landlords, and big tenant farmers maintained significant social and economic power. Smallholdings (less than ten hectares) made up 75 per cent of the total number of holdings at the end of the nineteenth century and covered 23 per cent of cultivable land. But the *grandes cultures* (above 40 hectares) covered 46 per cent of total land whilst only making up 4 per cent of total holdings. And, as Augé-Laribé commented, these official statistics underestimated the real share of the larger concerns.[22]

The fact that peasant identity had become associated with that section of the peasant population linked to the commercial market helped to render invisible those with livelihoods linked to another type of market – the labour market. The contemporary literature focussing on rural life reveals the trend.[23] The central characters in Zola's masterpiece, *La Terre*, are property-owning farmers: in the background remain the carters, herdsmen, threshers, a shepherd and boy responsible for the pigs, in most cases nameless.[24] As Mark Cleary notes, agricultural workers represented 'an important part of the agricultural community. . . [but] they increasingly disappeared from view as statisticians and commentators sought to emphasise the emergence of a peasant France for political and social reasons'.[25] The government's agricultural enquiry in 1892 recorded 2,453,000 landless agricultural workers (37 per cent of the economically active agricultural population). Another 588,000 (8.8 per cent) were employed as day labourers while also working on their own plot of land.[26] By the Popular Front period, the number of agricultural workers had fallen, alongside the general decline of the rural population. But the 1936 census still recorded 1,852,504 wage workers employed in agriculture, 29.5 per cent of the active population.[27] In 1936, there were more agricultural workers than metal workers (1,179,020), textile and clothing workers (1,033,625) or miners (331,558).[28]

Most agricultural workers were employed on relatively small establishments. The 1936 census found that 86.4 per cent were occupied on farms with five or fewer permanent workers; only 6.2 per cent on concerns with more than ten.[29] The map indicates three zones with concentrations of agricultural workers. The first centres on the Paris basin, extending into Normandy, the Berry, the Champagne wine-producing region and the North. In four departments close to the capital, agricultural workers made up a clear majority within the active peasant population: 58 per cent in the Oise and Aisne, 55 per cent in the Seine-et-Oise and Seine-et-Marne. These large-scale farming regions were sections of the rural world closest to urban society in terms of dependence on the capitalist market and organisation of social relations. They were also geographically close to the country's industrial heartland – particularly, the engineering factories in the capital and the mining and textile industries of the north. The second zone runs through the vine-growing region along the Mediterranean Coast; the third smaller zone is based on the Bordelais. The map also shows the small-scale farming model dominating a large central belt, running from the Alps through the Massif Central, into Brittany. Here, less than 2 per cent of agricultural workers were occupied on farms with more than ten workers. It is important to note, however, that important variations existed not only between but within regions. Even where agriculture was most concentrated, there still remained a significant number of small and medium-sized farms. In the Aisne, 48 per cent of farms employed five workers or less and 42 per cent were cultivated by families without calling on outside labour. Although included in the small-scale farming belt, the Cantal was the home of profitable cheese-producing and cattle-rearing enterprises, occupying a significant number of wage workers. In Brittany, there was also a large presence of agricultural workers – making up around 37 per cent of the active agricultural population.

A number of factors explain why agricultural workers were slow to develop a collective identity. Chapter 1 outlines the way in which the workforce in large-scale farming regions was differentiated between domestics, day labourers, and seasonal workers and by hierarchies marked out in terms of gender, job specifications, age and origin.[30] Further obstacles arose from variations in agricultural type and diverse practices relating to geography and cultural tradition. Jean-Claude Farcy's study of the Beauce shows that at the beginning of the twentieth century many workers viewed their position as a temporary life stage: they were

FRENCH DEPARTMENTS (1936)

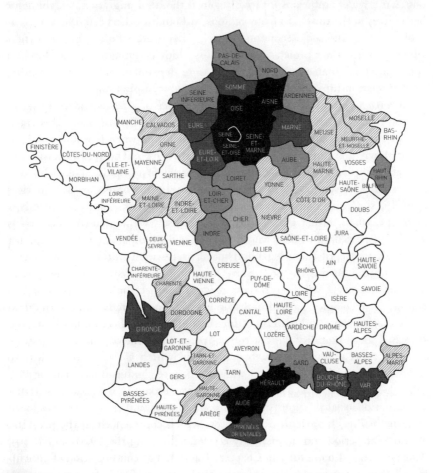

■ Departments with more than 20% of agricultural workers employed on farms with over 10 employees

■ Departments with between 10% and 20% of agricultural workers employed on farms with over 10 employees

■ Departments with between 5% and 10% of agricultural workers employed on farms with over 10 employees

▨ Departments with between 2% and 5% of agricultural workers employed on farms with over 10 employees

1. French Departments (1936): Percentage of agricultural workers
employed on farms with over ten employees

prepared to abide harsh working conditions and strict labour discipline before either inheriting the family farm or purchasing a small plot of their own.[31] Those possessing wider ambitions invariably joined the rural migration, searching for better lives in the towns. In many regions, although workers could be viewed as proletarian in the socio-economic sense – they were landless and sold their labour-power – their proletarian status was blunted through membership of a community of small proprietors. They were dependent on this community, formed relationships within it and, often, shared its aspirations.[32]

Nevertheless, and paradoxically, the emergence of a peasant identity set in motion the processes that provide the background to the themes of this book: the ways in which substantial numbers of agricultural workers would acquire – albeit slowly and unevenly – an identity of their own. The very association of 'paysan' exclusively with peasant producers was the first impulse. The inclination by agricultural syndicates to refer patronisingly to workers as 'nos ouvriers agricoles' suggested that wage workers were considered as second-class members of the peasantry, rather than authentic peasants.[33] While denied equal status within the peasantry, workers would also notice the campaign by farmers against proposals to accord them legal and social parity with workers in the towns. Another stimulus was the progressive loosening of the barriers between urban and rural society. While agrarians reacted against the influence of urban collectivist ideologies, agricultural workers were increasingly being introduced to alternative views and patterns of life through improved communications and increased social mobility. This factor was particularly the case in the large-scale farming areas of the Paris basin and north, which were not only close to industrial centres but a section of whose workforce combined farm labour with other economic activity. The final impulse was linked to the structural transformation of social relations in the most productive and technically developed sections of French agriculture, a process which commenced in the pre-First World War period and dramatically accelerated during the 1920s and 1930s. This is discussed more fully in Chapters 1 and 4. The concentration of agricultural holdings (particularly in the most fertile and profitable farming regions), structural changes within the workforce and the influx of propertyless immigrant workers helped to undermine former systems of dependency between farmers and workers. The wave of strikes and growth of workers' unionism during the Popular Front period were rooted in these processes.

*****

As at La-Ville-aux-Bois, opponents of the farm strikes in 1936–37 linked the movement to the activities of the Communist Party. According to the right-wing press, communists were recruiting agricultural workers 'with skilful propaganda' in order to prepare 'a vast offensive' at harvest time; the headline 'Le

Communisme aux champs' became almost ubiquitous.[34] The role played by communists in the conflict was, indeed, significant. The Central Committee passed resolutions 'saluting' strikers and the Political Bureau agreed to aid the work of the agricultural workers' union, the Fédération nationale des travailleurs de l'agriculture (FNTA).[35] Led by party members at a national level – the parliamentary deputy, André Parsal, and Michel Rius were its two most prominent leaders – and, in a majority of cases, at regional level, the FNTA swelled its ranks from 7000 in April 1936 to a claimed 180,000 at the end of the year. Some industrial trade unions grew faster in numerical terms but this was, by far, the biggest percentage increase in membership by any union during the period.[36]

Although today a marginal force, the Communist Party (PCF) was for thirty or so years, France's largest political party, influencing millions through propaganda, campaigns and associated movements. The party first emerged as a mass force at the 1936 elections; its role as principal animator of the Popular Front rewarded with 15 per cent of the popular vote and an increased parliamentary representation from 10 to 72 seats. One of the features of the breakthrough was the party's success in a number of rural constituencies, particularly on the western and northern fringes of the Massif Central. Communists had skilfully tapped into a tradition of radical republicanism amongst peasant smallholders in these regions. The party also benefited from a considerable shift in the voting patterns of agricultural workers in the large-scale farming regions.

The communists' Popular Front strategy was based on the building of an alliance between the working class and middle layers of society around a minimum political programme against fascism. At the behest of Moscow, communist leaders, remained outside Blum's government, for fear that participation would provide political ammunition for the Front's opponents.[37] For similar reasons, they took a cautious approach towards the 'social explosion'. The party identified with the strike movement, sought hegemony over it and successfully recruited amongst its activists. But simultaneously it attempted to restrain the movement and limit its objectives, fearing that its continuation and radicalisation would undermine the Popular Front's support within the middle class.

The strikes in agriculture posed problems for the communists beyond those arising from the conflict in the towns. Demographically, France remained a largely rural country – the 1936 census calculating the rural population as 47.6 per cent.[38] This meant that the most important proportion of the 'middle layers' to be allied with the working class was to found amongst the peasantry; in particular, amongst small and middling proprietors. Contrary to later impressions, the communists put great emphasis on the rural aspect of the Popular Front. Jean Renoir's celebrated film, La Vie est à nous, commissioned by the party and shown during the election campaign, begins with shots of wheat fields; its central section describes the impact of the economic crisis on the peasantry, while a final sequence depicts a child standing on a farm, staring longingly over fields and, optimistically, into the future.[39] The party championed the common interests of the entire peasantry and called for the formation of a 'Peasant Popular Front', uniting all political and professional organisations with support in the countryside. According to Daniel Brower, this was the 'most significant initiative' in communist policy during the Popular Front period.[40] The farm workers' movement was particularly problematic in that it brought to the fore not 'peasant unity' but social divisions amongst the agricultural population. It posed the dilemma of how to reconcile the demands of agricultural workers with the interests of the small and middling peasant employers that the party was attempting to win to the Peasant Popular Front.

The essential issues posed by the Popular Front farm strikes were, however, far from new. The position of agricultural workers within the agrarian strategy of the French left had proved a perennial problem since the emergence of socialism in its modern form towards the end of the nineteenth century. One difficulty arose from the left's concept of the 'central role' of the industrial working class, an outlook that downgraded the value of activity in the countryside and could lead activists to consider agricultural workers as just one component of a universally 'backward' peasantry. Another problem was rooted in the complex social organisation of French agriculture. In the towns, class relations could be viewed as relatively simple – Marx's idea of a polarisation between two main classes (proletariat, bourgeoisie), with an intermediary layer forced to take sides, appeared to be rooted in reality. The socialists and, later, communists could present themselves as the political representatives of the urban working class. In agriculture, production involved an array of social groups and sub-groups: tenant farmers, peasant proprietors, sharecroppers – categories which combined both relatively large employers and family farms producing barely above subsistence level. Moreover, the dividing line between categories could sometimes be blurred. Not only did wage workers form a minority of the working population but they contained a section of day labourers who were also part of the property-owning peasantry. Consequently, the question of which social forces socialists should principally target and aim to represent within agriculture was far from straightforward.

In response to these problems, two distinct trends emerged within French Marxism. The first argued that in the countryside, as in urban areas, priority should be accorded to activity amongst the proletariat. Marxists should, therefore, give unequivocal support to agricultural workers' demands and struggles, even if these were contrary to the interests of the small and middling peasant employers. The second trend was profoundly influenced by agrarianism. It considered the class struggle in the countryside as a movement of the 'peasant class' as a whole against big landed proprietors and/or capitalist influences. Differences between agricultural workers and peasant employers were, therefore, potentially disruptive to the necessary peasant unity. This 'peasantist' outlook also tended to view the self-employed smallholder as the most independently minded social group within the countryside, and consequently most open to revolutionary propaganda. These two trends were present within French communism throughout the inter-war period but their roots are found in pre-First World War socialism. These are examined in Chapter 1.

Until recently the historiography of French communism has neglected the party's peasant policy and strategy, despite the fact that the weight of the party's vote from the Popular Front period onwards was due to the significant level of support achieved in some rural regions. A series of studies have explained this phenomenon by showing how communists adapted their approach 'in a pragmatic manner' taking account of regional concerns and sensibilities.[41] Jean Vigreux has discussed the party's adoption of a 'progressive form of agrarianism', including its identification with the 'defence of peasant property'.[42] Laird Boswell's important account of the party's activity in Limousin and Dordogne also illustrates the significance of this slogan in establishing a base for rural communism.[43] An earlier tradition in the historiography had emphasised the party's support for collectivisation and, consequently, was unable to explain communist successes amongst sections of the smallholding peasantry.[44] The programmatic defence of private property was, however, only one aspect of communist agrarianism. The ideology also conditioned the party's characterisation of different social groups and underpinned its strategic aims in the countryside. In short, it had major implications for its approach towards agricultural workers. By focusing on the party's relationship with the property-owning peasantry, the literature has tended to ignore this aspect of the question and is, sometimes, prone to misunderstand the place of the agricultural worker within communist agrarian strategy.[45]

During the inter-war period, the agrarian policy of the Communist Party underwent a series of changes, each signalling a strategic reorientation in relation to agricultural workers. The different stages relate to the party's wider political evolution, itself reflecting the external influence of the Communist International. The process is traced in Chapters 2, 3 and 4. Broadly speaking, the years between 1921 and 1924 were characterised by a cohabitation between the two aforementioned trends – a reflection of the political confusion and factionalism that marked the party's early years. This was followed by a period (1924/5–28) during which stress was placed on reconciling the interests of agricultural workers with those of small and middling peasants. A major shift took place in 1929, coinciding with the Comintern's policy of 'class against class'. The 'agricultural proletariat' was placed at the centre of agrarian strategy and the work of the communist-controlled agricultural workers' union, La Fédération unitaire agricole (FUA), was prioritised. A turn away from this near-exclusive emphasis on agricultural workers began in 1933, culminating in 1935 with the adoption of the Peasant Popular Front. Whilst it is certainly true that the 'peasant question' was always secondary in the communist discourse, the argument that 'rural matters [were] left in the hands' of certain specialists (particularly Renaud Jean and Marius Vazeilles), who gradually helped communists become more conscious of the 'role of the peasantry', can underestimate the vibrancy of the debate over the agrarian question within inter-war communism and particularly the continuous tension between the two trends within the party.[46]

The Popular Front farm strikes have begun to emerge from the shadows during the last ten years. Jean-Claude Farcy has made important observations about the movement's character.[47] Édouard Lynch has explored its relationship with the agrarian policy pursued by the socialist Minister of Agriculture, Georges Monnet.[48] Robert Paxton has studied the way in which the 'peasant fascist' Greenshirts, led by Henri Dorgères, seized on farmers' opposition to the strikes and built significant support in the countryside.[49] All three studies raise questions about the nature of the conflict which will be discussed here. These include the extent to which the strikes were spontaneous or dependent on support from urban trade unionists (discussed in Chapter 5), the question of farm occupations and the level of participation by immigrant workers (discussed in Chapter 6). Chapter 7 explores, in more detail, the impact of the conflict on small employers and the difficulties posed for the communists' policy of 'peasant unity'.

Today, agricultural wage workers have almost disappeared from the French rural landscape.[50] Those who remain are no longer labourers, but tractor drivers and mechanics working farm machinery, though a super-exploited, largely migrant, seasonal workforce still exists primarily in the vineyards and fruit-growing sector. While the emphasis in the pages that follow is on political and social problems posed by the agricultural workers' movement during the first half of the twentieth century, I also attempt to voice the aspirations of men and women who were actors in this mostly forgotten piece of French rural history.

1

THE LEGACY OF
PRE-1914 FRENCH SOCIALISM

The Emergence of the 'Peasant Question'

The 'peasant question' emerged as a major issue for European socialist parties during the last decade of the nineteenth century. Whilst holding to the view that the urban proletariat was the key to social change and, therefore, the priority for propaganda and recruitment, socialists increasingly concluded that they would limit electoral progress if they could not extend their appeal amongst broader layers of the population and, particularly, into the countryside. With universal male suffrage and half the active population working on the land, the pressure to do so was particularly strong in France. Writing to Engels in 1893, the French Marxist, Paul Lafargue, announced that 'the conquest of the countryside' had become 'the socialists' great objective'.[1]

The Parti Ouvrier Français (POF), the most important section of the fragmented French socialist movement, had drawn the rural aspects of its 1880 programme from Marx's analysis that 'the desire for social changes, and the class antagonisms [were being] brought to the same level in the country as in the towns'.[2] Studying the English experience, Marx had believed that agriculture was following a parallel process of capitalist development to that of industry, albeit at a slower pace. Large farms were squeezing out the small and the class structure was becoming simplified as the peasant was 'annihilated' and replaced by the wage labourer. From this, socialists concluded that they should, in essence, follow the same policy in the countryside as that pursued in the towns. Their programme was based on the presumption that a trend towards technological advance and concentration of agricultural production would create support for a policy of collectivisation. Concerning strategy, the priority for propaganda would be the agricultural proletariat – the 'class nearest to the industrial workers in the towns', as Engels described it.[3] But as socialists attempted to win support in rural areas, it soon became clear that the smallholding peasantry was showing healthy signs of life and, although agricultural workers were present in considerable numbers, they represented a minority of the agricultural population and appeared reluctant to organise collectively. Socialists resolved that, if they were to make electoral headway in the countryside, it was necessary to target the broader layer of peasants rather than exclusively the agricultural wage workers and, consequently, they required a programme designed for the task.

Within the most influential European socialist party, the German SPD, these considerations prompted the first theoretical challenge to Marxist orthodoxy. Revisionists around the Bavarian socialist, Georg von Vollmar, questioned the thesis that peasant small holdings were doomed to disappear through the development of large-scale capitalist agriculture. They drew a number of practical conclusions: socialists should formulate demands linked to the defence of peasant property rather than highlighting collectivisation; they should appeal to the peasantry as a whole, instead of emphasising its social divisions and concentrating work on the agricultural proletariat and they should consider the urban working class and the peasantry as analogous, with socialists representing 'all working people', not exclusively the industrial proletariat.[4] A defence of orthodox Marxist theory was mounted by Karl Kautsky.[5] He argued that the continuation of small peasant property did not necessarily contradict the trend towards capitalist production and concentration in agriculture, though a series of countervailing tendencies was delaying the process and making it more complicated than envisaged by Marx. While Kautsky's analysis was officially accepted by European socialists, the functional aspects of the revisionists' argument penetrated deep into the socialist outlook.[6]

In France, a new agrarian programme was agreed by the POF in 1892 and amended at the Nantes congress in 1894. Although reiterating the orthodox position that small peasant property was 'inevitably bound to disappear', its conclusions were similar to those drawn by the German revisionists.[7] Socialists assured small peasants that they would not challenge their property rights and proposed a series of immediate reforms to improve their conditions. In addition, class differentiation within the peasantry was downplayed. One passage advocated the 'bringing together [of] all elements of rural production, all occupations which, by virtue of various rights and titles, utilise the national soil, to wage an identical struggle against the common foe: the feudality of landownership', an outlook remarkably close to that prevailing amongst right-wing agrarians. Another passage promised to 'protect' those peasants employing wage workers, arguing that 'while they exploit day labourers, they are forced to do so by the exploitation of which they are also victims'.[8] Within the programme, the interests of agricultural workers were relegated in importance: out of 18 proposed reforms, only 3 were specifically relevant to wage workers and, moreover, their nature was extremely limited.[9]

Famously, the Nantes programme received a severe rebuke from Friedrich Engels. While supporting attempts to win the small peasantry as a necessary socialist aim in 'the classical land of small peasant economy', he argued that French socialists were pandering to the peasantry's ideological attachment to private property, instead of advocating the advantages of co-operative practices and collective ownership of land. Engels' sharpest criticisms were, however, reserved, for the shifts in strategy. The justification of wage labour was 'bordering on treason', he declared: 'A workers' party has to fight, in the first place, on behalf of the wage workers – that is, for the male and female servantry and the day labourers.' No less scathing were his comments on the call for the unity 'of all elements' of agriculture: 'I flatly deny that the socialist workers' party of any country is charged with the task of taking into its fold, in addition to the rural proletarians and the small peasants, also the idle and big peasants and perhaps even the tenants of the big estates. . . and other capitalist exploiters of the national soil.' While accepting that the peasantry as a whole was exploited by the banks, capitalist supply and transformation industries, Engels insisted that socialists recognise the class divisions within it and prioritise the interests of agricultural workers and small peasants. He defined a 'small peasant' as 'an owner or tenant of a patch of land no bigger, as a rule, than he and his family can till, and no smaller than can sustain the family', specifically excluding those employing wage labour from the category.[10]

Socialist Agrarianism

After 1905, the Nantes programme became the basis of the unified Socialist Party's (SFIO) agrarian policy. Popularised by Jean Jaurès and, particularly, by Adéodat Compère-Morel, who became viewed as the party's agrarian specialist, policy remained a contradictory mix of orthodoxy and revisionism. Compère-Morel defended Kautsky's analysis of the concentration of agriculture, which, he argued, was preparing the long-term basis for its socialisation. Like Engels, he divided the peasant population between proprietors employing wage labour – whose land, he argued, should be socialised – and those who worked their own plot with their families. As the immediate impact of capitalism on agriculture was driving this section of the peasantry into poverty or away from the land, it was necessary to defend its interests, in the same way that socialists defended those of industrial workers facing negative effects of capitalist progress. Socialists tended, however, in practice to interpret this defence of the peasantry in a broader fashion. In 1907, for example, activists led by Ernest Ferroul helped to establish the Confédération générale des vignerons (CGV), an organisation claiming to represent the interests of all involved in wine production within a 'fraternal union of capital and labour'.[11]

In effect, while defending the livelihood of the small property-owning peasantry, socialist policy began to adopt elements of the prevalent agrarian outlook.[12] While right-wing agrarianism stressed the peasantry's social conservatism, the left-wing version viewed it as the inheritor of the revolutionary settlement, heir of the 1851 rebellion against Louis Napoleon and, in certain regions, upholder of anti-clerical tradition. Compère-Morel even argued that the peasantry's qualities offered a more solid support for socialism than those of the urban working class. In the towns, he maintained, the population tended to draw temporary political conclusions from the experience of sudden crises, but 'in the countryside, when an idea takes root, it takes deep roots, and nothing can unearth it'.[13]

Socialist agrarianism, while holding the small property-owning peasant in high esteem, simultaneously relegated the position accorded to the agricultural worker. Given the existence of regions with relatively small numbers of wage workers, geographical variations in propaganda would have been expected. But the disregard of issues relating to wage workers became a general feature, even in areas where they were present in considerable numbers. In the Languedoc wine-producing regions, social relations had been profoundly transformed by the phylloxera crisis. Although the biggest enterprises survived and rebuilt, many small producers were unable to recover and now found themselves working in teams of labourers on the large estates. Yet as Laura L. Frader notes: 'one looks in vain in the pages of *La République Sociale* or in socialist campaign speeches for references to the plight of agricultural workers, who suffered most from the phylloxera crisis.'[14] In the Paris basin, an examination of the socialist newspaper covering the Oise department, *Le Travailleur de l'Oise,* finds a similar neglect, despite the fact that the department contained belts of large-scale wheat and sugar-beet farming employing a significant labour force.[15] When reference was made to agricultural labourers it was to stress their 'individualism' and 'ignorance': they were the 'rough beasts of the land' [bêtes brutes de la terre] and the 'human packhorses' [chevaux humains], with whom it was impossible to have any serious conversation.[16] Compère-Morel advised socialist activists compiling information for a major party survey on agricultural conditions not to waste time talking to farm workers, but instead to seek information from their employers: 'the small, middling and large farmers. . . who love their profession and are happy to chat and speak about their land and agricultural activity.'[17]

Socialist agrarianism thus developed a view of worker-employer relations in the countryside markedly different to the approach taken in the towns. While in urban areas, socialists stressed the antagonisms between workers and employers, and viewed the industrial proletariat as the class most open to socialist ideas, in the countryside, they considered the agricultural proletariat as too brutalised and uneducated to understand socialist propaganda, or even to display the slightest independence from employers. Both Marx and Engels had emphasised the difficulties posed by the agricultural proletariat, 'the section of the working class which has most difficulty in understanding its own interests and its own social situation and is the last to do so'.[18] But socialist agrarianism viewed farm workers as virtually impenetrable. Compère-Morel argued:

> It is necessary to live amongst [them] to know how to evaluate them. The rural proletariat differs *far, far, far* too much [*beaucoup, beaucoup, beaucoup trop*] from the urban proletariat for it to give us solid and sufficient support. The working-class population of the provinces has been creamed off by the towns and, in the countryside, all that remains for us are the dregs!! [petit lait] [emphasis in original][19]

Flowing from this, socialist agrarianism began to change the concept of agricultural proletariat, extending it to include peasant proprietors who did not sell their labour. 'Small proprietors are for us similar to factory workers,' argued Compère-Morel, 'they are workers in every sense of the word.'[20] Agricultural workers were referred to as 'salariés' (rather than proletarians), just one section of a wider proletariat.

The French Agricultural Worker in the Early Twentieth Century

Domestics formed the section of agricultural workers viewed with particular disdain by socialist agrarians. Recorded as making up 75 per cent of the landless agricultural workforce in the 1892 agricultural survey, they were permanent workers, usually living on farms in accommodation provided by the employer. They included those responsible for horses, oxen and cows [charretiers, bouviers, vachers], general farmhands, shepherds and farm servants. Hours were not fixed and the needs of the animals usually meant duties seven days each week. In many regions, recruitment took place at hiring fairs [louées] held in market towns either once or twice a year. In the Beauce, workers from surrounding villages assembled on the market place – carters carrying whips, barn threshers wearing ears of corn and farm servants carrying a rose.[21] Employers would size up workers, approach them and negotiate an individual contract, a procedure that encouraged relationships more akin to those between masters and servants than employers and workers. These dependencies led Compère-Morel to describe domestics as 'enslaved. . . attached to the farm like a dog to his kennel' – an analogy particularly apposite given the fact that workers invariably slept on planks or wooden boxes in stables and cowsheds. Possessing a 'dubious mentality' and 'very low mental level', domestics were 'pathetic people soaked in ignorance and alcohol condemned to go from church to tavern and from tavern to church'.[22] Socialist agrarianism embraced, in fact, many of the themes and anxieties contained in the discourse of *dégénérescence* pervading French politics, philosophy and literature during this period.[23] Compère-Morel counter-posed the 'healthy' property-owning peasant to an almost sub-human agricultural domestic steeped

in 'alcoholism, criminality, ignorance and racial degeneration', all 'deadly consequences of rural impoverishment' arising from 'capitalist concentration'.[24]

Day labourers [journaliers] possessed greater independence from employers,
although they often faced a more precarious existence. At the turn of the century,
a significant number of day labourers combined wage labour with working on
their own plot.[25] Considered by Compère-Morel as part of the 'healthy' section
of the peasantry, this group, which was barely indistinguishable from the smallholding peasantry, was in rapid decline. Landless day labourers generally
possessed their own home and were not fixed to a single employer. They were
paid by the day, not the hour, which could mean working from sunrise to
nightfall. For certain work, such as that associated with the sugar-beet crop, they
were paid at piece rates. Often the agricultural cycle would guarantee a continuity of employment from spring through to autumn, as different crops
required work at varying times of the year. Day labourers would also possess
particular skills that farmers could call upon at other times. Sometimes, during
labour-intensive periods they would group into teams and work in a village for
a number of farmers in turn. One section of journaliers worked solely in agriculture, even if this meant periods of unemployment in the dead season. Others
combined agricultural work with employment in a range of industries, including
distilleries and dairies, or repairing the roads. In regions to the south of Paris,
day labourers often worked in the forests during the winter months. In north
Picardy and the Caux (Normandy), many combined agricultural work with
proto-industrial occupations, particularly home weaving; though this way of life
was in the process of dying out at the turn of the twentieth century.

Other categories of workers received little recognition in the socialist discourse. Migrant seasonal labour played an important role in many of the most
intensive farming regions. Bretons travelled to the Beauce for the wheat harvest
and to farms closer to Paris to pick fruit and vegetables. The grape harvest in
Languedoc recruited labour from the southern fringes of the Massif Central, as
well as attracting workers from the other side of the Pyrenees. In the north, home
weavers from villages in the Cambrai region (known as Camberlots) were
specialists in working sugar beet and, during spring and autumn, travelled into
the Paris Basin, Normandy and elsewhere. The migrant workforce was overwhelmingly young, and a significant part of it was female.

Despite the traditional portrait of an agricultural worker as 'a man in full physical
condition',[26] women formed an essential part of the paid labour force. Elements
of work on middling and large farms were strictly gendered and women per-
formed some of the most backbreaking tasks. Men supervised, drove and loaded
the carts, tended the horses, cut the crops and did the threshing; women bundled
up the harvest, spread manure, dug up potatoes, prepared and weeded fields.[27]
As the value of manual work was linked to men's assumed physical superiority,
women were paid at around half the male rate. Farm servants were particularly

exploited: the first to rise and last to bed, vulnerable to sexual harassment and deprived of any personal life. In an account of her experiences on a farm in the Beauce during the 1920s, Léonne reminisces about how employers frowned on her social life: 'I used to enjoy myself but I didn't dance. Going to a dance was, for my employers, well, rather indecent.'[28] Although working them to the limit, devoutly Catholic farmers were inclined to view their servants as unruly women in need of moral supervision.

On larger farms, servants were at the bottom of a strict hierarchy within the workforce.[29] Carters had the most privileged positions and were themselves ranked in order of seniority: first carter, second carter and so on. Next were shepherds, *vachers*, *bouviers* and general labourers. Léonne recalls the authority of the premier charretier: 'The other workers, including the second and third carters had to obey him. When workers were eating and he put down his knife, everyone had to get up from the table and leave to start work. . . Sometimes the young lad [p'tit commis] who was serving did not even have time to finish his meal.'[30] In effect, age played an important role in the hierarchy. Young workers could be treated almost as servants by the more senior employees. At the same time, it was not unusual for workers to face discrimination once past a certain age: at the beginning of the century in the Soissons region, farmers generally cut wages after men had turned forty five.[31]

Another factor in determining the hierarchy was origin. In the Paris basin, an influx of migrants, particularly to the Brie, Soissonais and Valois, was one of the social consequences of the agricultural crisis of the 1880s. Pressurised to sell up, many small farming families who had traditionally provided domestics and day labourers for the big farms moved to search for work in Paris, their plots integrated into the holdings of the large farmers.[32] Departing workers were replaced by migrants from other parts of France, particularly from areas of the Massif Central, as well as immigrants, notably from Belgium. By the time of the 1906 census, a significant proportion of agricultural workers in these regions had no attachment to the local area. For example, of the nineteen domestics working on the large Potel farm at Dammard, on the eastern fringe of the Valois, ten were from outside the department, including six from the Nièvre and one from the Haute-Garonne; and amongst sixteen day labourers, only five originated from families indigenous to the commune.[33]

The division of the agricultural labour force between indigenous and migrant workers had a contradictory effect. On one hand, the presence of the 'étranger' helped to reinforce a common identity between some local peasants and the large farmers. Better-paid and supervisory positions were recruited from amongst locals, who were encouraged to look down on outsiders filling less prestigious jobs. On the other hand, the shake up in social relations disturbed the equilibrium between farmers and workers that had previously guaranteed relative social peace. That there had been few open conflicts between agricultural workers and employers during the nineteenth century arose from the immense social and economic power of the large farmer over village society. A complex system of dependencies assured his hegemony.[34] The large farmer provided employment to young members of peasant families as domestics or farm servants and seasonal work to others in the community, particularly women. For small farmers, he provided produce, such as seeds, and sometimes hired out farm equipment and horses. As mayor of the administration, he represented the village and provided services to its community – a position of patronage tying him into the personal lives of inhabitants. But it would be wrong to see nineteenth-century agricultural workers in the large-scale farming regions as totally docile and deferential. Although strikes were virtually unknown, disputes between farmers and workers punctuated rural life. Sometimes frustrations would break into the open, with domestics suddenly breaking their contracts or, more drastically, engaging in attacks on farm property.[35] Most conflicts were settled after individual negotiations or, sometimes, through the involvement of the local magistrate [Juge du Paix]. By restricting labour supply, the rural exodus gave workers a certain bargaining leverage, as they possessed skills that could not be easily replaced. But this advantage was counterbalanced by workers' lack of mobility: they were tied to the locality through their family's possession of a small plot and could only effectively choose employment from a limited number of farmers. The new social organisation arising at the end of the nineteenth century initially loosened the power of the large farmer over his workers. It meant that farmers were increasingly reliant on workers without any ties to the land or local area – and therefore not bound by the system of dependencies – who could, moreover, quite easily leave the farm or village in the hunt for better wages and conditions.[36]

Consequently, from the beginning of the twentieth century, the question of agricultural labour became a major issue for the farmers' associations. Some began to lobby for governmental action, including the reintroduction of the *livret*, the method used under the Second Empire to restrict workers' mobility. Many farmers introduced a *retenue*, a deduction from wages that would be forfeited if domestics left the farm before the end of their contract. The principal strategy was the creation of dependency through tied housing and a small plot of land. In the Soissons region, an agricultural worker called Saphel commented on how farmers were buying up vacant houses and gardens in the villages: 'Who wouldn't expect a worker who has sown his patch of land to put up with all the injustices and moody outbursts of his employer, without daring to murmur the slightest protest? He knows that from one day to the next, he may not only lose his job, but could see himself, together with his family, thrown out on to the streets.'[37] As well as giving farmers greater control over their workforce, the arrangement had the advantage of attracting families, thus guaranteeing access to the labour of women and children. It also helped to maintain low wages as workers were effectively using their own time to produce part of their subsistence.[38]

In such regions of advanced agriculture, the renewed attempt by farmers to render the workforce deferential and dependent was only partially successful. The transformation of the agricultural workforce – more precisely, the process of differentiation between an agricultural proletariat and the small property-owning peasantry – was beginning to bring latent tensions to the surface. Socially, the gap between employers and workers on the big farms had widened. While agricultural wages and conditions had not picked up significantly from cuts imposed during the agricultural crisis, the biggest farmers had become pro-gressively detached from agricultural labour, some employing managers to run the farms and adopting the trappings of a bourgeois life-style. Discontent led to an increased propensity of individualistic actions by workers against farmers' produce and property. Three agricultural workers appeared before a sitting of the Court of Assize at Soissons in November 1906. Louis Eugene Duval, a 64-year-old day labourer, was sentenced to three years' imprisonment for setting fire to two haystacks belonging to a farmer at Vénizel. The farmer had sacked him but refused to return the 4 francs 50 centimes *retenue* on his wages. Next, Édouard Daussin, aged 35, was found guilty of an arson attack on farm buildings and received a seven-year sentence. The court heard that his actions were due to 'a grudge harboured against one of his former employers'. Shocked by the severity of the judge, the jury signed a plea for clemency, which perhaps explains why in the final case a 24-year-old worker, also charged with arson, was found not guilty.[39] As well as illustrating their frustrations, arson attacks on property symbolised agricultural workers' impotence as a social group. In the first decade of the twentieth century, however, such individualistic acts were combined with the first stirrings of a collective response to improve workers' conditions and social position.

Socialists and the Agricultural Strike Movement

Socialists responded sluggishly to the surge in agricultural workers' unionism and strike struggles during the first decade of the twentieth century. This was nothing new. When forestry workers in parts of the Massif Central had begun to organise during the 1890s, members of the POF failed to offer practical support. Despite resolutions stressing the importance of activity amongst the rural population, many militants remained either unconvinced or unable to make the necessary adjustments.[40] A decade later an explanation for the lack of socialist involvement relates, however, not to apathy but to the peasantist orientation of agrarian policy. When strikes broke out in the vineyards of Languedoc during 1904, socialists had little influence over events. As Laura L. Frader notes in relation to the Narbonne region, their 'careful avoid[ance] of references to the class struggle' and 'almost exclusive attention to the agricultural bourgeoisie' had eroded support amongst vine workers, many of whom were attracted instead towards the ideas of revolutionary syndicalism.[41] The application of the party's agrarian strategy also explains why socialists were slow to involve themselves in the strikes to hit the big farming regions to the north and east of Paris.

The movement in the Paris basin was significant in terms of numbers and breadth. Beginning in the spring of 1906 in the Brie (Seine-et-Marne), Multien (Seine-et-Oise) and Valois (Oise), it spread during 1907 and 1908 into the Soissonais and Vermandois (Aisne).[42] Further north, strikes took place during 1906 in some villages in the Cambrai region[43] and, during 1910, a conflict broke out in the countryside to the south of Arras (Pas-de-Calais).[44] In the Oise, the number of strikes by agricultural workers in the ten years before 1914 was only surpassed by stoppages involving building workers.[45] As would be the case during the Popular Front, the strikes unfolded against a background of political and social upheaval – the 1906 legislative elections marking an advance of the left and prompting a wave of unrest to sweep through industry and the public services.

The agricultural movement succeeded, at least partially, in unifying a section of workers around the idea that they possessed common interests despite their professional speciality or origin. All categories of farm workers participated: day labourers, local women and migrant seasonal workers. Significantly, it was the domestics, so frowned upon by the socialist agrarians, who often played the most prominent role. While the movement's principal demands related to wages, issues specific to domestics were always high on the list of priorities. In the Soissonnais, workers demanded the outlawing of the *retenue*;[46] at Provins (Seine-et-Marne), they called for improvements in the standard of food and an end to the practice of sleeping in stables and cowsheds.[47] At Macquigny, a small village near Guise (Aisne), workers drew up a proposed collective contract. Demands included: fixed working hours (6 a.m. to 6 p.m. in the winter; 5 a.m. to 7 p.m. in the summer); overtime payments for additional hours; a day off each week, though promising that workers would still attend the horses; provisions for drinks during the working day; an end to domestics having responsibility for damages arising from accidents or for the deterioration of their tools.[48]

Farmers claimed that the strikes had been stirred up by 'arrogant trouble-makers' with a political agenda. Denying workers' right of representation by independent unions, they simultaneously organised their own 'defence organ-isations' to ensure employers' resistance was 'more compact'.[49] Attempts were made to play on divisions between different groups of workers, with success in some regions. At Lizy-sur-Ourcq (Seine-et-Marne), indigenous workers refused to take part in the strike, which had been instigated by workers originating from the Morvan.[50] In the Soissonais, farmers launched a campaign to establish 'syndicats mixtes', grouping both workers and employers and dedicated to 'the union of all citizens'.[51] This type of phenomenon would be repeated in 1936 when some indigenous workers were recruited into the Syndicats professionnels français (SPF) linked to Colonel de la Rocque's extreme right-wing Parti social français (PSF). The main weapon used against the movement was, however, simple repression, including sackings of union activists.[52] After workers presented their demands at Confrécourt (Aisne), the farmer, Monsieur Ferté, retorted with threats whilst brandishing his revolver.[53]

As the conflict in the Paris basin developed, socialists began to participate more consistently, winning some influence amongst workers. At Mormant (Seine-et-Marne), the entire union committee joined the party; at Champeaux (Seine-et-Marne), the secretary of the socialist group led the union.[54] Compère-Morel was dispatched to the Brie to represent the party and spoke at a series of meetings. His reports in the party press remarked on the party's neglect of agricultural workers, though without a hint of self-criticism: 'The socialist message has never been delivered in these rural areas where the class struggle is asserting itself so violently! Our pamphlets? They have never been seen! Our newspapers? People are totally unaware of them, even of their titles! And this, only two hours from Paris!'[55] As well as highlighting the socialists' lack of attention towards agricultural workers, the conflicts in the Paris basin and Midi wine region posed the problem of the relationship between agricultural workers and peasant employers. The strike movements were centred on the big holdings; but they did not discriminate – many small and middling farms were also touched – and socialists began to debate the implications for agrarian policy.

At the 1909 SFIO Congress held in Saint-Étienne, Jean Longuet, delegate from the Aisne department and future leader of the party's left, commented on events at Macquigny. Starting on 25 March 1908 and involving around two hundred workers, the strike had been led by socialist activists, particularly the future deputy Ernest Ringuier, and an interesting local inhabitant called Auret, a former army sergeant with a penchant for wearing his military medals. It was an exceptionally bitter affair, with clashes between strikers and gendarmerie leading to complaints of police brutality.[56] From the outset, farmers were determined to break the movement by recruiting replacement labour, but workers were equally resolute. A soup kitchen was established in the village square and 150 of the strikers' children were evacuated from the commune, to be looked after by socialists and trade unionists in Guise.[57] The Police Commissioner reported that 'farmers are unable to bring outside workers into the village as the roads are guarded by the strikers and above all by their wives. . . An indication of the strict nature of this surveillance is that a farmer had to bring two workers he had recruited to his farm by hiding them in barrels'.[58] The strikers hoped that the movement would spread into neighbouring villages, but it remained isolated. Farmers in the region, while urging the Macquigny employers to stand firm, simultaneously conceded wage increases to their own workers to head off potential strikes. After a month, strikers began to seek work elsewhere, on neighbouring farms and in factories. Farmers responded by sacking the entire workforce – the outcome was a major and sudden transformation in the village's population.

Drawing lessons from the conflict, Longuet re-evaluated the party's approach towards agricultural workers.[59] Firstly, he criticised the view 'according to which we should have greater difficulties drawing the farm worker towards us. . . than the small peasant proprietor'. He noted that the Macquigny strike had involved 'agricultural proletarians' with 'qualities of tenacity, vigour and devotion to the common cause, equal if not superior to those we so admire amongst workers in the big industrial cities'. Then, he raised the essential problem: 'from the day we decided to organise these agricultural workers, we found ourselves confronted not only by the big proprietors, but also by the middling and even some of the small.' The socialists' orientation in the countryside, he implied, overlooked the fact that peasant interests would sometimes be contrary to those of the agricultural worker. Socialists would have to decide clearly which side of this antagonism they were on: 'The Socialist Party, while ready to support peasant proprietors in their struggle against the plutocracy, . . .has the duty to be always alongside the agricultural worker, even against the small peasant, because this conflict is still effectively a manifestation of the class struggle.'[60]

The Saint-Étienne debate was the only full discussion on the agrarian question held during a SFIO national congress. Compère-Morel's opening report repeated arguments against immediate collectivisation and re-emphasised that the party's priorities in the countryside should be amongst the small property-owning peasantry. While applauding the agricultural workers' movement, he attached little significance to it.[61] The gains won by workers during the conflict further highlighted the impoverished position of the small peasant, he explained. The interventions during the subsequent debate reveal, however, that despite the general drift towards socialist agrarianism, the peasant question had remained controversial within the party – and that there was considerable resistance to Compère-Morel's approach. A number of delegates expressed the same themes as Longuet. From the party's syndicalist wing, Gustave Hervé argued that socialists must be concerned with 'the most lowly, most trampled down peasants, that is, with the domestics and day labourers'. Openly criticising Compère-Morel, he announced to great applause that 'in the case of a conflict between the propertyless and proprietors in the countryside, we – the party of those without property – are firstly on the side of the propertyless, even against small peasant proprietors'.[62] Likewise, Ernest Tarbouriech explained:

> We do not say to workers employed by a small employer: 'Oh, be moderate with your demands and do not claim too high a wage in order not to ruin the employer.' No we say: 'Claim from the employers, both small and large, the wage that is necessary!' (*Applause*.) It is very important to say. . .

that we always defend the interests of wage workers against middling and small proprietors. (*More Applause.*)[63]

The conflict within the SFIO over agrarian policy is often presented as an argument over programmatic questions – one between a dominant trend advocating reforms to support peasant property and another, representing 'les plus doctrinaires', stressing the need to move as quickly as possible towards a system of collectivisation.[64] This was certainly one aspect of the debate. At the Saint-Étienne congress, some critics of Compère-Morel's position continued to advocate the socialisation of the entire 'agricultural means of production'. As one delegate argued, 'it is necessary to make clear that there cannot be two socialisms, one for the countryside and one for the towns'.[65] But alongside the exchanges over peasant property and collectivisation two strategic issues had also increasingly emerged. The first was the position socialists should take when antagonistic interests emerged between agricultural workers and small peasant employers. The second was whether socialists should principally target 'the peasantry' or, primarily, agricultural workers and the poorest peasants? Longuet's call for a reorientation was unambiguous. 'The agricultural proletariat in the literal sense,' he argued, represented an 'immense sphere of activity' with more fruitful opportunities for the party than those offered by small peasant property 'where the difficulties are often insurmountable'.[66]

The emergence of agricultural strike movements and workers' unionism influenced socialist activity in the countryside and in the succeeding period the trend arguing that more attention should be accorded to agricultural workers was strengthened. Though by 1908, the strike movement was on the wane, activists in a number of regions continued attempts to establish workers' unions.[67] There was also more open criticism of the party's dominant agrarian outlook. In Languedoc, controversy reigned over the participation of prominent members within the leadership of the CGV. The conference of the Hérault Federation in 1908 demanded that socialists 'resign from an organisation which subordinates the interests of small proprietors and workers to those of the big proprietors'.[68]

In effect, two political currents on strategic orientation in the countryside and, particularly, on the question of the agricultural proletariat had been established within French Marxism. Following the war, despite the varying political evolution of the principal protagonists, the two trends – socialist agrarianism and an orthodox Marxist approach – would pass into the Communist Party.

2

COMMUNIST AGRARIANISM, 1921–28

The French Communist Party emerged after a majority at the SFIO's Congress, held at Tours in December 1920, voted to affiliate to the Third International. As Annie Kriegel has noted, decisive for the outcome was the vote for affiliation by socialist federations in rural areas, particularly some on the fringes of the Massif Central.[1] The new party was far from homogeneous, possessing three distinct factions. Many amongst its leadership were unaware of the type of organisation expected by the Bolsheviks in Moscow, who criticised the French party for preserving 'survivals of its reformist and parliamentary past', for its lack of cohesion and particularly for its resistance to 'international discipline'.[2] Between 1921 and 1924, French communists lived through permanent crisis – factional disputes breaking out over trade union activity, internal party functioning, the tactic of the 'united front' and, finally, over the issue of 'Trotskyism'. The crisis had inevitable repercussions on the party's functioning and support, with membership falling from a claimed 130,000, following the split at Tours, to 55,000 five years later. A second phase in the party's history opened in 1925 and lasted until mid-1928. The process of 'bolshevisation' dictated by the Comintern transformed it into a tighter, more centralised, organisation pursuing the political and strategic directives of Moscow.

Both phases had important consequences for agrarian policy and strategy. During the first, the International's emphasis on building a revolutionary party rooted in the urban proletariat ensured that the peasant question was not a major concern for the French leadership. Responsibility for rural issues was placed in the hands of Renaud Jean, who was initially granted great latitude in determining policy. Nevertheless, the role of the peasantry became part of the factional debate over the united front. A public clash between Renaud Jean and Leon Trotsky (at that stage the member of the Comintern delegated 'to liaise' with the French party) reflected wider tensions on agrarian strategy amongst French communists.[3] The second phase was marked by a more unified approach which attached greater political importance to activity amongst the peasantry.

But, as in the previous period, the position of the agricultural worker remained a central and unresolved problem within communist agrarian strategy.

The Comintern and the Agricultural Proletariat

Renaud Jean was the obvious candidate to become the communists' spokesperson on agrarian matters. Born in 1887 at Samazan (Lot-et-Garonne) into a family of small peasant proprietors, he had joined the SFIO at the age of twenty but left after three years, disillusioned by the party's parliamentary reformism. Severely wounded during the Battle of the Marne, he rejoined in 1916 and, identifying with its most consistently anti-capitalist wing, quickly rose to become the party's departmental secretary. Easily recognisable by his injured leg, Renaud Jean's ability to express the anti-war sentiments of the local population with his staccato, high-pitched voice soon made him a popular figure. His prominence and reputation as a peasant leader grew further when he mobilised support for the sharecroppers' movement that swept the Landes and Lot-et-Garonne during 1919 and 1920. In the aftermath of this bitter conflict, he was elected in a by-election as deputy for the Lot-et-Garonne. At the Congress of Tours, Renaud Jean sided with the communists and was immediately appointed editor of *La Voix Paysanne*, a journal established by the SFIO in February 1920, formerly the responsibility of Compère-Morel. Renaud Jean would also lead the team that drafted the thesis on the agrarian question presented to the party's first congress held at Marseille in December 1921, at which his authoritative position amongst the peasantry was recognised by election to the *Comité Directeur*.[4] When, the following year, this was replaced by a Central Committee with proportional representation for the main factions within the party, he was assigned a position as representative of the 'Renaud Jean Minority'.[5]

The dispute with Trotsky broke out in January 1922 after Renaud Jean criticised the party's united front platform for its failure to propose 'demands common to both major fractions of the proletariat', the two fractions being the peasantry and industrial workers. Renaud Jean particularly singled out the eight-hour day and minimum wage as irrelevant for peasants. While applauding his 'revolutionary spirit', Trotsky described Renaud Jean's formulation as 'an abuse of sociological terminology' and accused him of wanting to 'curtail the demands of the proletariat' to conform to the views of the 'agrarian petit bourgeoisie'.[6] He situated Renaud Jean within a wider 'peasantist' tendency in the party, warning of dangers if it was allowed to develop.[7]

Trotsky's critique correlated with the position argued by many on the French party's left wing. In the period before the Congress of Tours, members of the 'Committee for the Third International' – the most enthusiastic protagonists of communism within the SFIO – had viewed the break with reformism as synonymous with a turn away from socialist agrarianism. During a series of articles entitled *Vers l'Internationale* in the socialist paper covering the central region, Maurice Boin argued:

> Despite the undeniable prosperity of the class of peasant proprietors, the number of agricultural wage workers is today still rising in France, reaching more than three million. It is this mass that we must reach, organise and educate. Dragging these deprived people out of their inertia is a particularly difficult task. . . Nevertheless, it is necessary to make them aware of the role that our revolution assigns to them.[8]

While Boin stressed that 'revolutionary action' would not 'attack, undermine or destroy' small rural propriety, he was nevertheless signalling that communist strategy meant an end to the preoccupation with the small peasantry and a renewed emphasis on agricultural workers.

In the immediate aftermath of the Tours Congress, this reorientation was made even more explicit in a major article covering the first two pages of *La Voix Paysanne*. Written by Amédée Dunois, soon to become a prominent member of the left faction, it argued:

> Up until now the Socialist Party has above all addressed the small rural proprietors that it seeks to attract at elections. . . Has not this glaring contradiction between the form socialism gives to its propaganda in the towns and that it gives in the countryside been one of the weaknesses of socialism? In the towns, it is the party of proletarians; in the country the party of small proprietors. . . [or] no more than a semi-proletarian, semi-small proprietor party, and consequently it spreads confusion. . . What we will be wanting, what we are entitled to demand, is for socialism to maintain its true face in the countryside; that it should not hesitate to show that it is the great party of the proletarians, the great party of the propertyless. . . So, it's towards agricultural workers, towards the domestics of large and small farmers, towards the day labourers in the villages, the forestry workers of the Centre, the vineyard workers in the Midi, the market gardeners of the suburbs, towards the carters; it's towards wage workers of all categories that socialism must turn from this point on.[9]

The article's contention that a 'revolutionary party' must base itself 'without compromise or deviation' on the class struggle of the proletariat in the countryside, as in the towns, was in the tradition of Engels' critique of the Nantes programme and Longuet's arguments at the 1909 SFIO congress. But the position of Dunois was also influenced by an important element in the post-war debate between communists and 'reformists' at a European level.

Agricultural workers became a key question for leaders of the Third International after strikes broke out in a number of European countries and opponents of communism within the socialist movement took an ambivalent, and sometimes hostile, attitude towards them. The two most important conflicts were in Italy, including a massive wave of strikes with farm occupations in the Po valley during 1919 and 1920,[10] and in Germany, where following the Revolution of 1918/19 the main agricultural workers' union grew from 10,000 to over 600,000 during the course of a year.[11] As thousands of troops were mobilised to break strikes to the east of the Elbe in the summer of 1919 and again in the spring of 1920,[12] Karl Kautsky, now a firm opponent of the Comintern, warned 'workers in the countryside' of the 'unspeakable havoc [that] would be caused if they were seized by strike fever'.[13]

Although less extensive, the strike movement in France involved vineyard workers in Languedoc (1919) and Gironde (1920), forestry workers in the central region and workers in market gardening, particularly touching some large concerns close to Paris (1920).[14] Two disputes also broke out during the summer of 1919 in large-scale cereal farming regions to the north and east of Paris, socialist activists participating in both. The first began in July 1919 at Gonesse (Seine-et-Oise), spreading to involve around two thousand workers, including many demobilised soldiers. Facing intransigence from employers, workers decided on a return to work after two weeks, though 'a large number left the region to seek jobs in Parisian factories'.[15] More successful was the strike beginning on 3 August, which spread throughout the Brie and Gâtinais, embracing around six thousand workers.[16] After a week, employers conceded increased wages, a weekly break, a pledge to phase out sleeping in stables, a commitment to implement future legislation relating to working hours and conditions, and an arbitration system to resolve differences. There would be no victimisation for the strike and immigrants would receive the same wages and conditions as French workers.[17] Although most of the promises would remain unfulfilled, the signing of a contract with employers was significant, its contents providing a benchmark for the agricultural workers' movement during the inter-war years.

The thesis on the agrarian question, drafted by Lenin for the Second Congress of the Communist International in August 1920, declared the farm workers' movement to be the key to 'rousing the countryside from its lethargy and awakening the class-consciousness of the exploited masses'. Communists were urged to 'devote special attention towards' and 'give greater support to mass strikes by the agricultural proletarians and semi-proletarians'. Those socialists ignoring or opposing such strikes were condemned as 'traitors and renegades'. In relation to France, and ironically in view of his previous position, the thesis criticised supporters of Longuet for 'remain[ing] indifferent to the strike struggle in the countryside'.[18] Socialists in the newly constituted agricultural workers' union had argued that the demands of the defeated Gonesse strike were too radical. By drawing up a claim that included the eight-hour day, an immediate improvement in accommodation and hygiene, recognition of union delegates with wide powers to oversee the agreement, the Gonesse strikers – who had been supported by advocates of affiliation to the Third International – were, they argued, proposing 'a social programme', rather than a series of realistic demands that could be accepted by employers.[19]

Lenin's thesis dealt with the same two fundamental questions raised in Engels' 1894 critique. In terms of programme, it signalled a distinct change, making the type of concession towards private property that Engels had censured. Not only did the thesis guarantee that peasants would keep their land but, by advocating abolition of mortgages and particularly rents, it also implied that the amount of land in private hands would be extended. Even 'large peasants' would be allowed to maintain their property, on condition they did not resist the revolution. Only the estates of large landowners – those who 'did not themselves engage in manual labour', but either directly or indirectly through tenant farmers exploited wage labour – would be expropriated. In the wake of the experience of the Russian Revolution, a future communist government's need to consolidate support amongst, or at least to 'neutralise', the middling peasantry was considered more important than a rapid move towards collectivisation.

But in relation to strategic orientation the thesis made no concessions. Priority was accorded to three social groups within the peasantry. Firstly, and singled out as the most important, the agricultural proletariat: organising, waging propaganda and agitation amongst which was declared one of 'the *fundamental* tasks of Communist parties in all countries' (emphasis in original). Secondly, the semi-proletariat, a term used to describe day labourers who obtained their livelihood partly as wage labourers and partly by working a small plot of land and, thirdly, the 'small peasantry' – defined as owners or tenants (including sharecroppers) of 'small plots enabling them to satisfy the needs of their families and their farms and who do not hire outside labour'. Reference was made to two other social groups. Firstly, the middling peasants – either tenants or proprietors able to produce a small surplus and who 'quite frequently resort[ed] to the employment of hired labour' – who because of their 'direct interest in profiteering' and 'direct antagonism to wage-workers' could at best be 'neutralised', rather than won to communism. The 'large peasants' made up the final group. Defined as capitalist entrepreneurs who generally employed 'several hired hands', they were 'determined enemies' against whom communists must struggle to break their 'ideological and political hold on the majority of the rural population'. In short, the thesis not only prioritised agricultural workers in terms of communist activity but also directly addressed the potential antagonism between peasant employers and agricultural workers by emphasising, without equivocation, the interests of the worker. Possible conflicts between small peasants and agricultural workers simply did not arise because, by definition, the category of *petit paysan* excluded – as in Engels' critique – those utilising wage labour.[20]

The Marseille Thesis: 'Nothing Has Changed'

The argument of Dunois for a reorientation towards the agricultural proletariat provoked an immediate challenge from within the French party. In the pages of *La Voix Paysanne* and the regional party press, articles and letters argued that peasant proprietors, rather than agricultural workers, would be the most receptive to communist ideas. 'Contrary to what A. Dunois has said,' wrote Louis Garnier, a farmer from Yonne, 'we can do more with the small peasant proprietors than with propertyless agricultural workers. . . In the Yonne, there are not ten farm domestics capable of reading and understanding *La Voix Paysanne*.'[21] The extent to which sections of the party were at variance with the position of the Third International is illustrated by the coverage of agrarian issues in the communist paper covering the central region. Articles described peasant employers as the 'eternally exploited', left with very little to live on after they had paid their 'two domestics, suppliers and for home maintenance'.[22] Noticeably absent was similar propaganda dealing with conditions experienced by the domestics in their employment.

A major article in *La Voix Paysanne*, written in response to criticisms from an agricultural worker from the Cantal, justified the preoccupation with the small and middling peasantry. Complaining that the paper only dealt with issues of concern to self-employed farmers and was neglecting agricultural workers, the correspondent had asked whether the editors 'thought they could draw the small and large capitalists of the land to communism'. The reply argued:

> Renaud Jean. . . and the Communist Party have never neglected the three million rural proletarians. . . but we know how difficult it is to reach them through oral propaganda. For many years, I have had cause to note that meetings are the least well-attended in regions of large-scale property where small proprietors represent a minority. . . because rural proletarians do not attend. In contrast, in regions dominated by small-scale property, the wage workers are more emancipated. They come to political meetings, organise unions. . . As a general rule. . . small proprietors are more advanced than the wage workers on the big estates, it is through them that the propagandists of the Party hope to instil revolutionary thought [in the countryside].[23]

Some important differences with the discourse of Compère-Morel and the pre-war socialists can be noted. Gone were the explicit allusions to degeneracy. Communists sometimes referred to the propensity of agricultural workers for alcohol. But difficulties in winning them were related to long working hours and a social relationship described as close to serfdom, rather than any intrinsically inferior behavioural quality. Nevertheless, the practical conclusion – that small peasant proprietors were the priority for communist activity in the countryside – was identical.

The primacy accorded to the small peasantry stemmed from the wider vision of rural relations held by Renaud Jean and the trend he represented. Rooted in the social relations and radical political traditions of Lot-et-Garonne, Renaud Jean's approach had been particularly shaped by the experience of the sharecroppers' movement of 1919–20. Working in forests extracting resin, the sharecroppers had demanded a reduction in the share of the produce handed to proprietors as well as the end of various vestiges of feudalism, such as the 'duty' to work on certain days for landlords. For Renaud Jean, the struggle posed the question of 'unity of the peasant world' against the rich 'idle' landed proprietors.[24]

This outlook was, however, also conditioned by the way in which agrarianism as an ideology had been strengthened by the experience of war. Right-wing agrarians would throughout the inter-war years seek to mobilise support by contrasting the martyrdom of the 'soldier-peasant' with the peasantry's betrayal by governments supposedly more preoccupied with the interests of industrial society. Renaud Jean would also place great stress on the trial of the trenches from which, he maintained, had emerged a new 'peasant class consciousness'. He advocated the creation of 'a bloc of peasants', further arguing that there was a general trend towards economic homogeneity within the peasant population.[25] Important differences remained, however, between the approach of the communist spokesperson and that of right-wing agrarianism. Firstly, Renaud Jean argued that peasant consciousness could be 'transformed into a formidable revolutionary lever' – the war reawakening the spirit of 1789, 'the Jacquerie. . . dormant for more than a century'. Secondly, the unity of the peasantry was necessary not to confront the impact of industrial society, but specifically to oppose 'the capitalist class', a task for which it should form an alliance with the urban working class. This aim was soon popularised under the slogan 'bloc ouvrier et paysan'. Thirdly, membership of the peasantry was open only to those personally involved in working the land; excluded were the 'idle large proprietors and large farmers engaged in industrialised agriculture'.[26] Nevertheless, an essential element of agrarianism – the idea of a peasantry possessing an organic unity and common interests – remained central to Renaud Jean's outlook. Often, he painted an almost idyllic picture of social relations in the countryside. One article described peasants at work on the harvest: a small proprietor, a young female domestic in his employment, a sharecropper together with his hired hand – 'in miniature, a scene representative of the entire French peasantry', suggested Renaud Jean. By sharing the work in the fields, the peasant proprietor and his wage worker acted as 'equal and happy collaborators' and thus 'created the unity of the *classe paysanne*'.[27] Marius Vazeilles, the communist leader of a peasant organisation in the Corrèze, made the point even more forcefully: 'There is no antagonism between peasants and agricultural workers', he argued, it was only when employed by the 'well-to-do, non-working landowner' that the worker 'descends from his role as collaborator'.[28] Communist agrarianism rejected, therefore, the argument in Lenin's thesis that there was an essential division in the countryside based on the employment of wage labour.

The contradiction between Renaud Jean's position and that held by Dunois and the Communist International inevitably presented difficulties for the drawing up of the party's agrarian programme. As Vigreux has noted, the Marseille thesis fused French republican and socialist traditions with the new communist policy disseminated by the Comintern.[29] In relation to peasant property and collectivisation, the thesis promised no immediate application of 'communist principles amongst an unprepared rural population', it proposed an 'intermediary' position that would attempt to draw the peasantry towards communism 'through education and example'. The party would popularise this position through the slogan 'la terre à ceux qui la travaillent' (the land to those who work it) – a slogan open to several interpretations but which protected the rights of peasant proprietors, and would be the key to the party's success in a number of important rural regions. Only large-scale industrialised farming would be socialised and run by co-operatives of agricultural workers. Property owned by capitalists and rented to tenant farmers would be distributed to the peasants, with agricultural workers employed on small farms also having right to a share if they so wished. Peasant holdings, however, would be indefinitely safeguarded.[30] During a lengthy debate, only a small number of delegates on the extreme left of the party opposed these concessions to private property.[31]

The significant point about the Marseille thesis concerns, however, not what it included, but what it left out. Firstly, it conspicuously evaded the question of class divisions within the peasantry in the manner of the Comintern thesis. Social relations in the countryside were defined on the basis of property, with three categories designated: a) capitalist property organised for large-scale industrialised farming; b) capitalist property divided into family holdings and farmed by tenants, sharecroppers or wageworkers and c) property owned by peasant families. This schema not only avoided any differentiation between agricultural workers and other landless peasants (tenant farmers and sharecroppers), some of whom would have utilised wage labour, it also placed poor peasant proprietors in the same category as large family-run enterprises employing considerable numbers of workers. Secondly, unlike the Second Congress thesis, there was no emphasis on activity amongst agricultural workers and the poorest peasants. The Marseille document was essentially a programme for the 'agrarian revolution' that would be carried through after a 'workers and peasants government' had come to power, but it ignored the question of what social groups in the countryside would be the motor forces of that revolution and how communists should work to win them. Its practical application was, therefore, deeply ambiguous. For some, its preoccupation with the issue of peasant property, avoiding questions of class differentiation and strategic orientation, provided justification for continuing the agrarian tradition of the pre-war SFIO. Socialist observers were quick to point this out: 'Nothing has changed', wrote a sarcastic Compère-Morel.[32] Other communists could, however, interpret the thesis as a programmatic supplement to the strategic direction agreed at the Second Congress and continue to argue a policy prioritising agricultural workers and the poorest sections of the peasantry.

Post-War Agricultural Workers' Unionism

The creation in April 1920 of a national workers' federation (FNTA) affiliated to the CGT signalled a major advance for agricultural unionism in France. After assembling 198 local sections at its founding conference in Limoges, the union made rapid progress – almost doubling the number of affiliates within a few months and reaching an estimated 30,000 members. But the FNTA's support remained extremely localised. Vineyard workers in Languedoc and Champagne, forestry workers in the Central region and the Landes and workers in market gardening close to Paris formed the main contingents represented at Limoges. In relation to cereal farming, while there were sixteen delegates from the Brie, most other important large-scale farming regions on the northern plains were either sparsely represented or absent altogether.[33]

Within a year, the FNTA had split as the political scission signalled at the Congress of Tours quickly engulfed the trade union movement. In July 1921, the communist- and anarchist-influenced wings were expelled from the CGT and established a new national federation, the CGTU. Simultaneously, communists and anarcho-syndicalists were excluded from the agricultural workers' federation and formed the Fédération nationale unitaire de travailleurs de l'agriculture (FUA). Between 1921 and 1935, the FUA would be the focal point for communists' activity amongst agricultural workers.[34]

At the outset, the FUA was miniscule and fragile. Only 19 affiliated sections were represented at its founding conference in October 1922.[35] Even some prominent sympathisers of the Russian Revolution, such as the forestry workers' leader, Jules Bornet, did not immediately join the new union – an indication of the demoralising effect of the split on activists for whom the creation of a national federation had been a long-term goal. In the Brie, most sections retained their links with the FNTA, following the example of the local leader, Arthur Chaussy, who in 1919 had been elected a socialist deputy.[36] Moreover, the FUA's leadership team was unstable and divided politically. The first national secretary, Jean-Baptiste Lacambre was a supporter of Pierre Monatte's Committee of

Revolutionary Syndicalists (CSR) – a trend which joined the communists (very temporarily) in 1923.[37] After only a year, Lacambre was replaced by the assistant secretary, Justin Olive, an adherent of anarcho-syndicalism, which had a certain following amongst activists in the Languedoc wine region. In early 1923, the union's lack of organisational and political cohesion prompted the CGTU executive to investigate complaints about its 'bad functioning'.[38]

Difficulties for the FUA were also posed by the social conjuncture. Militancy amongst agricultural workers in the aftermath of the war was short-lived and followed by a sharp downturn in the number of strikes. Most of the isolated disputes that broke out, mainly in the Brie and Languedoc, were defeated. The difficulty of maintaining organisation outside periods of conflict was a general feature of agricultural workers' unionism – a result of pressure from employers, the isolating nature of much of the work and the general mobility of the labour force.[39] Following 1918, increased agricultural prosperity served to reduce its potential even further.[40] Many agricultural workers witnessed an increase in living standards and, in certain regions, managed to improve their social status. In the Beauce, the Prefect reported: 'the agricultural worker is still well provided for. . . many have become small proprietors.'[41] In the aftermath of the war, a number of workers' unions had been established in the region, with the most prominent activists adhering to the communists. By October 1921 the local secretary was punctuating his reports with the words 'difficulties' and 'stagnation'.[42]

Workers' unionism in the large-scale farming belts to the north of Paris faced particular problems. Important regions that had known strikes before the war – for example, the Soissons region (1907 and 1908) and the Arras plain (1910) – were in or close to the 'Red Zone' of total devastation. Here, agriculture required complete renovation. Many agricultural workers did not wait to return to the farms but were attracted to reconstruction projects or factories in the urban centres. In the Brie and surrounding regions, the FUA lost much of its potential base amongst the migrants from the Massif Central. Sarcastically referred to by socialist activists as the 'Morvan reds',[43] they had proved during the post-war strikes to be, as pre-war, the most militant section of workers. As they moved off the land, they were replaced by external migrants, mainly from central Europe, who were initially prepared to tolerate poor wages and working conditions.[44]

Communist agrarianism also impacted on the FUA. As with the pre-war socialists, Renaud Jean viewed the 'agricultural proletariat' in an extremely broad sense: it included not only day labourers and domestics but sharecroppers, tenant farmers and small proprietors.[45] Consequently, he argued that 'trade unionism such as that emerging from the class struggle in industry does not correspond to the needs of revolutionary action in the countryside. . . [where] a broader and more flexible method is needed'.[46] The party should attempt to build agricultural workers' unions on the 'big capitalist farms'. These were defined as those where the employer was not personally involved in agricultural work – farms which were rare, even in the large-scale farming regions. In cases where workers and peasant employers worked alongside each other, argued Renaud Jean, their common interests demanded they should become members of the same organisation.

The proposed model was the Fédération des paysans travailleurs established in 1922 by Vazeilles in the Corrèze. The meaning of the term 'paysans travailleurs' would evolve during the various phases of agrarian policy but in the early 1920s Renaud Jean and Vazeilles employed it to describe peasant proprietors working their own land 'either alone, with the help of their family or with several domestics and day labourers'.[47] It covered, therefore, not only those the Comintern had described as small and middling peasants but also some of the 'big peasants' employing 'several hired workers'. In the autumn of 1922, negotiations were underway for the merger of the FUA with Vazeilles' federation and one similar in the Gironde.[48] The proposed national federation would have had 'revolutionary' aims, but its structure would have been hardly different from the type of 'mixed union' [syndicat mixte] advocated by right-wing agrarians.

Complaints by Renaud Jean and his supporters that the 'leading spheres' of the party 'hardly considered the peasants' should be viewed against this background.[49] It was certainly the case that the party's priority during these years was on conducting work in the towns – a position in accordance with the Comintern's argument that the precondition for winning a wide section of the peasantry was the unity of a majority of the urban working class around a revolutionary programme.[50] Moreover, as the party was enveloped by crisis and the effects of falling membership, activity in the countryside assumed even less significance. Nevertheless, it is important to recognise that the criticisms also related to the political approach adopted on those occasions when the party did take up issues facing the peasantry. One activist wrote: 'L'Humanité sometimes publishes information and gives examples of the capitalist exploitation of the peasantry, but more often than not it's only to come to the defence of agricultural workers. . . Yet the situation of small peasant farmers – their wages in relation to hours worked – is worse than that of an agricultural wage worker.'[51] Others complained about the party's advocacy of the eight-hour day for agricultural workers – viewed as a 'utopian demand', given the seasonal nature of agricultural work and the unpredictability of the weather.[52] By highlighting issues relating to wage workers rather than property owning peasants as well as insisting on the independent organisation of agricultural workers, the central propaganda of the party adopted a political approach in sharp variance to that proposed by communist agrarianism.

The differences within the party became even more explicit when in 1924 a long document prepared by Jean Castel was published as a series of articles in the regional party press.[53] Castel was not an unimportant figure. Originally a peasant from the Arriège, he became secretary of the FUA in early 1924 and in November was appointed as full-time official responsible for the party's agrarian work. His text was based on the decisions of the International Congress of the Red Trade Unions held in July 1924.[54] It affirmed that 'the first and principal task' in the countryside was 'the organisation of strong and numerous unions of agricultural workers' – only 'next' should communists turn their attention to the paysans travailleurs. Implicitly criticising the position of Renaud Jean, he argued that 'agricultural wage workers comprised. . . the most revolutionary element in the countryside' and must 'serve as the link between the union of town and country'.[55]

Castel went on to make the first serious attempt to develop communist strategy and tactics towards agricultural workers in France. Like the peasantry, agricultural workers, he argued, did not form a homogeneous group but possessed different degrees of 'combativity', determined by varying conditions of existence and work. Day labourers were considered the most class conscious, while domestics were less militant, despite experiencing inferior living conditions and extreme exploitation. This was put down to the fact that they were 'sometimes living and working with their employer [or] in continuous contact with him' and 'inevitably subjected to his influence'. Significantly, Castel here considers the relationship between worker and peasant employer in a fundamentally different manner to the trend represented by Renaud Jean. Rather than seeing the shared work of employer and worker as a positive source of peasant unity, Castel argued it was the foundation for a 'dependent' and 'submissive' bond in which workers 'progressively destroy their individuality and model their opinions on those of the master'.[56] Along with their general lack of education, these conditions made the recruitment of agricultural workers into unions particularly difficult. But rather than retreating in the face of the obstacles, or accepting that the greatest effort should be devoted to seemingly more fruitful work amongst peasant proprietors, Castel proposed that communists adopt special measures to organise and recruit agricultural workers: finances and other support should be made available by industrial unions and a specific programme established to train propagandists and organisers. Instead of advocating a 'broader and more flexible' type of trade unionism organising agricultural workers as part of the wider peasantry, Castel concluded that the 'special situation' of the agricultural proletariat meant that its organisation was 'one of the most urgent tasks' facing communists.[57]

Between 1921 and 1924, then, two distinct strategies towards the peasantry cohabited within the young Communist Party. Despite its revolutionary rhetoric, the first – that associated with Renaud Jean – represented a continuity of the agrarian heritage of the pre-war SFIO. The priorities of the second were different. Basing itself on the texts of the Communist International as well as the tradition of the opposition expressed at the SFIO's 1909 congress, it viewed the countryside as a theatre of class struggle, with agricultural labourers playing the 'leading role'. In 1925, elements of these two contrasting approaches would be fused to create a new and distinct phase in agrarian strategy.

The 'Absurdity' of the Class Struggle in the Countryside

The influence of the Comintern on agrarian policy during 1925 was contradictory. The instructions to 'bolshevise' the party encouraged the existing antipathy amongst communist members towards conducting activity in rural areas. Guidelines for the new organisational 'cell' structure stipulated that if a factory existed in a village or small town, a factory cell should be created and peasant party members placed within it – the cell taking the name of the factory not the village.[58] But, simultaneously, the Comintern entered, in the words of George Jackson, a 'peasantist phase'.[59] This was an international extension of Soviet economic policy's emphasis on an 'alliance with the peasantry' – including its most prosperous elements – in order to provision the towns and stimulate the domestic market. Nicholas Bukharin, the architect of the policy and soon to become head of the Comintern, declared that national parties could only really become Bolshevik 'by taking an interest above all in the agrarian and peasant question'.[60]

The French party was quick to take up the message.[61] An Agrarian Section had been established in 1924 and, in early 1925, the party launched the Conseil paysan français (CPF) – supposedly an independent peasant organisation, though effectively a party-controlled front. The 'turn' was emphasised when *Cahiers du Bolchevisme* published a long speech by Central Committee member, André Marty, which criticised the party's previous 'grave errors', 'laziness' and 'apathy' towards the peasantry.[62]

While Renaud Jean remained the party's public spokesperson on peasant matters, retaining his position on the Political Bureau, responsibility for agrarian policy was increasingly placed in the hands of Jean Desnots, who became the secretary of the Agrarian Section. Desnots argued that the dominant trend amongst the peasantry was one of greater class and political differentiation, rather than Renaud Jean's 'opportunist' view of a tendency towards economic homogeneity and peasant revolutionary consciousness. Desnots' analysis highlighted the concentration of farming, noting that banking and industrial capital was increasing its influence over agricultural production, particularly in regions such as the North, the Paris basin and the Midi. He contended that the self-sufficient peasant family farm was losing its independence and no longer constituted the main unit of agriculture. A polarisation was taking place. On the one hand, the middling peasants were consolidating their position and becoming more firmly tied to capitalist interests.[63] On the other, there was a mass of peasants who, while no longer subsistence farmers, were unable to produce sufficiently and efficiently enough to compete in the capitalist market. In the analysis of Desnots, the class struggle in the countryside arose from the contradictions between the interests of the agricultural sector and industrial and finance capital, as well as from an unequal commercial relationship between big producers and small peasants.

Activity in the countryside was aimed not towards winning a 'peasant revolutionary class' but more as an insurance policy to help ensure the victory of workers in the town. Desnots reminded party members that most of the police were recruited from the rural areas, that employers sought to hire peasants as docile workers without a tradition of labour protest, and that social crisis posed the danger that sections of the peasantry could be attracted to fascist organisations. A circular to party activists in the Paris region explained: 'Awakening the agricultural population to political life, giving it a trade union education reinforces the proletariat of the towns by removing those they count on the most from the influence of the bourgeoisie.'[64]

By stressing the primary role of the urban proletariat and drawing attention to differentiation within the peasantry, the new approach maintained many aspects of the orthodox trend on the agrarian question. Marty, for example, censured party members in Languedoc for maintaining illusions in the wine-producers' organisation, the CGV, an organisation 'in the hands of the big employers'. In a barely disguised swipe at supporters of Renaud Jean, he noted the refusal of 'our good comrades' in the CPF to combat such 'deviationism coming from social democracy'. Social antagonisms between different sections of the peasantry were also recognised. Marty declared: 'the class struggle really exists in the countryside. . . Agricultural workers have it in their blood; even the young farmhand who says very little, and who never reads, feels hatred for his master and mistress.' Nevertheless, the new policy drew from agrarianism in one important respect: its analysis of the nature of the class struggle in the countryside underpinned the argument that communists should work to show that every category of 'labourers of the soil' were 'partners' in a struggle against the 'big employers and bourgeois state'.[65] In other words, the policy continued to advocate a community of interests between peasant employers and their workers.

The first repercussion to arise from this was a problematic relationship between the two organisations that the party sought to build in the countryside: the CPF (to represent paysans travailleurs) and the FUA (to organise agricultural workers). Although the Communist International had reaffirmed in August 1924 that wage workers should be organised independently from self-employed peasants,[66] the draft of the CPF's constitution contained programmatic demands for farm workers, indicating that a section of French communists were still pursuing the aim of organising workers within a broader peasant organisation.[67] The clauses were removed from the final text but *l'Humanité* still reported 'confusion' over the 'relationship between agricultural workers and proprietors' at the CPF's first conference.[68] After the establishment of the CPF, the autonomy of the FUA became increasingly blurred. The two organisations were run out of the same office, effectively by the same officials. Castel became general secretary of the CPF and another communist Joseph Boisseau became general secretary of the FUA. But for a period, Castel remained 'secrétaire appointé' of the FUA, undertaking much of the union's administrative work. There was even a joint newspaper.[69] *La Voix Paysanne* became the newspaper of the CPF, while the FUA purchased a page within it, under the by-line *Le Travailleur Agricole*. Given his previous argument that the organisation of agricultural workers was the 'first and principal task' for communists, the evolution of Castel's responsibilities, from general secretary of the FUA to that of the CPF, is indicative of the party's shifting priorities. In terms of resources and publicity, the CPF was given a much higher profile than the FUA. The agricultural workers' union became effectively the junior partner of an organisation seeking to represent the broader peasantry, including peasant employers.

Not surprisingly, communist activity amongst agricultural workers remained inconsistent and loosely co-ordinated. The FUA made progress in some regions: in Cantal, a campaign led to the creation of, according to the police, a 'rather active' section of around a hundred members;[70] in Picardy, the union recruited amongst day labourers around Péronne (Somme), an area that would witness sharp struggles during the Popular Front period, and claimed responsibility for forcing an increase in wages for work on sugar beet.[71] But activity in the large-scale farming areas surrounding Paris remained negligible. After a number of farm strikes broke out in the Brie, party sections covering rural areas close to Paris were asked to assist in a union recruitment drive.[72] The request was universally ignored and branches received an admonishment for not understanding that 'union activity amongst agricultural workers [was] one of the permanent tasks incumbent on rank-and-file organisations of the party'.[73] Indifference amongst activists was, however, only part of the explanation for the campaign's failure. The FUA's links with the CPF helped to ensure that activities were not integrated within the communists' general union work – a situation that prompted the party's trade union commission to complain that the agricultural workers' union was 'working outside the control of the central organisations'.[74]

The revival of agricultural strikes in the mid-1920s was on a very small scale but posed immediate complications for the new agrarian strategy. At the 1926 congress, a thesis drawn up by Desnots noted that strikes were 'taking place in isolated pockets' around the country and, while they were often against 'large capitalist property', many involved 'the middling and small peasant'. These latter disputes were viewed in a wholly negative fashion. Not only were they a threat to the unity of the 'labouring classes' in the countryside, they were also an illustration of 'the absurdity of the system [that] frequently brings into conflict two social categories which should, on the contrary, be united'.[75] As well its ambivalent approach to conflicts between agricultural workers and peasant employers, it is also significant that the thesis redefined the meaning of 'petit paysan'. Contrary to the categorisation of the Comintern, the term was now used to describe peasants employing wage labour.

Another text outlining 'immediate tasks facing the party' (May 1928) gave activists more detailed tactical advice when dealing with strikes in agriculture:

> During the development of the class struggle in the countryside, it is possible that conflicts will also break out between paysans travailleurs and agricultural workers. . . Communists. . . while supporting the most proletarian section, should make every effort to *reconcile* the differences. . . in order always to achieve the united front of the entire rural labouring population against the landed proprietors and the capitalist system. In several countries, the bourgeoisie has exploited conflicts of this kind to recruit layers of the peasantry to its cause [emphasis in original].[76]

This reorientation towards peasant unity was consistent with the general direction of policy during 1926 and 1927. In order to reverse the fall in membership and re-establish its position in French politics, the party began to take a more 'open' approach, part of which involved aiming a section of its propaganda towards the middle class. It also posed for the first time – albeit in a confused manner – the question of broad unity against the threat of fascism.[77] The allusion to 'other countries' in the last line of the text is, above all, a reference to Italy. During the spring and summer of 1919, strikes by socialist-led farm labourers in the Po Valley won not only increases in wages and conditions but, in some cases, also forced farmers' associations to provide funds to build schools to be run by the trade unions for local farming communities. When the unions recommenced their campaign the following year, the farmers were, however, better prepared. As well as organising their own vigilante squads, they increasingly called on the support of Mussolini's fascists. Blackshirt expeditions into rural areas terrorised socialist and union activists and emboldened the farmers and their supporters. By early 1921 the workers' union was defeated and fascism had built a mass following in the countryside.[78] The lesson drawn by French communists was that similar conflicts between agricultural workers and employers would also drive sections of the small and middling peasantry towards fascist reaction. By urging conciliation between agricultural workers and peasant employers, the party was, in effect, anticipating one of the ideas that, eight years later, would provide the basis of the Popular Front in the countryside.

Relations between workers and employers in the large-scale farming regions of the Paris basin and northern France were specifically addressed by an article in *Cahiers du Bolchevisme*. It noted that the farm worker 'is, in a rather confused way, aware of the antagonism that separates him from his employer; but most often he submits in deference and resignation, enslaved to the rich farmer, and only dares to stand up to the middling peasant'. Such action, stressed the article, was not in the worker's best interests: 'It's our duty to show him that his social role lies in an alliance with the small farmers. . . for the bold struggle against the greats of the agricultural industry.' In effect, the communists were proposing a dual tactic dependant on the size of farm on which workers were employed. On large farms, the task was to make workers conscious of their class interests and to recruit them into unions; but on smaller farms, communists' role was 'to prepare and facilitate' unity between workers and employers 'for the defence of their common interests against the rich peasants'.[79]

One problem for this strategy was that in the Paris basin workers on smaller farms generally faced inferior conditions than encountered by those working on the larger establishments. Writing in 1932, the Director of Agricultural Services in the Oise reported that, since the war, there had been a tendency amongst big farmers to reduce working hours to an 11-hour working day during the summer. 'It is,' he commented, 'on the small and middling farms that the longest working days are found, the example being set by the employer himself.'[80] The communists' idealistic view of 'common interests' between the small peasant employer and his workers ignored the fact that many 'self-made' men who had built their businesses through hard work and self-sacrifice were unable to understand that workers had their own priorities and lives. Perhaps the biggest contrasts in conditions related to accommodation. A survey by the Director of Agricultural Services of the Seine-et-Oise found a recognisable improvement on the big farms as the 1920s progressed. But he noted: 'On small and also middling farms the situation seems not so good. . . Agricultural workers are no longer forced, as before, to sleep two in the same bed on straw in the stables or cowsheds. But, on far too many farms, there are still workers who sleep with the animals under the pretext that there is the need to keep watch over them.'[81]

In any case, as party members working in rural regions close to Paris often found, peasant employers possessed little enthusiasm for an alliance that took account of workers' specific interests. When, in September 1926, the Agrarian Section co-ordinated a propaganda campaign in villages close to the capital, farmers often turned up at the meetings. The report rather optimistically noted: 'Small peasants and middling farmers have been keenly interested in the communist project. . . They are becoming aware of the class struggle and are clearly at a disadvantage in relation to the large landed proprietor.' But very few agricultural workers were in attendance. 'Trade union propaganda for the FUA has faced numerous problems', noted the report, 'not the least of them is pressure from the employers.'[82] Other reports illustrate the nature of this pressure and the contradictory position in which the party sometimes found itself. After communists formed a union in the village of Montereau (Seine-et-Marne), an agricultural worker called Drouet-Vallier wrote: 'All the employers in the region. . . seeing that their workers are organising, are up in arms [en révolution]. I'm sorry to note that. . . a good number of small peasants are blaming us for all their problems.'[83] In other words, when it came to opposing agricultural workers' unionism, the smaller farmers were in solidarity with the large. They may well have been becoming 'conscious of the class struggle' *vis-à-vis* the 'large landed proprietor', but seemed equally conscious of their class interests in relation to their own workers.

During 1926 and 1927, many activists within the FUA became increasingly frustrated with the constraints the party's approach was putting on the functioning of agricultural workers' unionism. Complaints arose over the union's organisational subordination to the CPF and tensions between the two communist-led organisations began to develop. In late 1926, the union blamed its 'large financial difficulties', which meant that its full-time officer had not received wages for 'several months', on the CPF's decision to raise the charge for the union's page in *La Voix Paysanne*.[84] At the FUA conference in October 1927, Boisseau felt compelled to comment on the union's relationship with the CPF. While referring to it as a 'sister organisation', he explained that the CPF represented 'small farmers, facing a particular kind of exploitation. . . They sometimes employ wage workers and do not always get on well with agricultural workers. . . particularly in relation to the eight-hour day and wages'.[85] Other leading activists also commented on the contradictions between the interests of the broader peasantry and those of agricultural workers. These included Henri Roqueblave, a communist leader from Languedoc, who was elected general secretary at the FUA conference. Roqueblave had been involved in an important strike movement in the Béziers wine region in May 1927 and wrote a report drawing lessons from the movement. During the conflict, pickets around the villages had allowed small proprietors to continue working. But, he emphasised, these were specifically vine growers 'not employing any workers', some of them were even agricultural workers possessing small vines themselves. Roqueblave was explicit: 'I understand by *petite propriété* those peasants employing no full-time worker. . . Small or middling proprietors who employ one or several workers must be treated in the same way as the large.'[86] In other words, the Languedoc communists were adopting a position on social relations in the countryside that differed in major respects from that proposed by the Agrarian Section. It amounted to the same uncompromising approach to conflicts amongst the peasantry as that argued by Longuet in 1909 and outlined at the Comintern's Second Congress. The criticisms were an anticipation of the major shift in agrarian strategy that would take place during the 'class against class' period – a period during which the question of the agricultural proletariat and the functioning of the FUA would take centre stage.

3

'CLASS AGAINST CLASS' IN THE COUNTRYSIDE, 1928–34

The Communist International announced its policy of 'class against class' at the Sixth World Congress held in July–August 1928. It was underpinned by an analysis of what was described as capitalism's Third Period, with its supposed features of deepening economic and social crises, an increased threat of war against the Soviet Union and an upsurge in the revolutionary mobilisation of the working masses. Communist parties were instructed to draw the working masses to the banner of revolution by openly combating the socialists, viewed as the last prop of decaying capitalism and, from the summer of 1929, denounced as 'social fascists'. Coinciding with 'class against class' was the adoption by the Soviet Union of a policy of rapid industrialisation and the ending of the concessions towards the peasantry under the New Economic Policy. Politically, this represented a decisive victory for Stalin over his erstwhile ally, Bukharin. A programme of, firstly, voluntary and, from the end of 1929, forced collectiv-isation of agricultural production was set in motion, with catastrophic results for rural populations. As Moscow declared its intention of destroying the kulaks (richer peasants) as a social class, the Comintern simultaneously de-emphasised 'the role of the peasant in the international revolution' and stressed that com-munists' role in the countryside was now to 'intensify the class struggle'.[1] In accordance with the new line, the French party re-emphasised the central role of the agricultural proletariat within peasant strategy and designated the communist-controlled agricultural workers' union as the most important rural organisation, introducing organisational measures to strengthen its position.

Few historians have paid attention to French communist agrarian policy during this period, which is generally regarded as a Moscow-induced parenthesis within a general inter-war trend towards an increased understanding of the 'role of the peasantry'. Recently, however, historians of international communism have begun to move away from a Moscow-centric interpretation of 'third period' policy. An important collection of essays stresses the inter-relationship between

the influence of the Comintern and the varying national experiences of communist activists, emphasising the connections between 'class against class' and
previous as well as subsequent policies and strategies.[2] The agrarian policy of the
French communists at this time is best understood in this fashion. While pressure from the Comintern was decisive, the French roots of the reorientation
should not be ignored. In a distorted way, the Third Period brought to the surface the main elements of the long-term debate within French Marxism over
strategy in the countryside.

The Agricultural Proletariat at the Centre of Agrarian Strategy

The first repercussion of 'class against class' was a sharpening of the tensions
between Desnots, the secretary of the Agrarian Section, and the tendency
represented by Renaud Jean. Supporters of the latter were accused of having a
negative effect on the functioning of the communists' new peasant organisation,
the Confédération générale des paysans travailleurs (CGPT), which was launched
in January 1929 in an attempt to attract a broader layer of support than had
managed the CPF. Supposedly, the Renaud Jean trend was directing the CGPT
in a 'timorous, passive, mercenary and electoralist' manner, was too close to the
better-off peasants and was ignoring 'the most proletarianised elements of the
village'.[3] Perhaps most significantly, it was also failing to address the problem
of the relationship between, on the one hand, the small producer and, on the
other, the 'mixed proletariat' and agricultural wage workers.[4] Renaud Jean would
for the next four years criticise 'class against class' and particularly the party
leadership's failure to put forward practical policies – including the control of
the price of wheat – to alleviate the position of the small and middling peasantry.

While landing blows against Renaud Jean and the leadership of the CGPT,
Desnots was soon in the sights of another tendency. On return from a period at
the Lenin School in Moscow, André Parsal (also known as Puech), originally an
agricultural worker from Capestang, a small town in the Languedoc wine belt,
wrote a long critique of the party's agrarian policy and strategy in the party's
theoretical journal, *Cahiers du Bolchevisme*.[5] Born in 1900, Parsal had joined the
local agricultural workers' union at the age of 18 and the Communist Party at
22, after completing his military service. He rapidly rose through the party to
become the secretary of the Languedoc region in 1925.[6] As well as his energy,
police reports comment on his 'bony face and very pronounced midi accent'.[7]

In his article, Parsal lumped together the approaches of Renaud Jean and
Desnots, censoring both for blurring class divisions in the countryside: the first
through viewing the principal antagonism as a conflict between 'the peasantry'
and landed proprietors, the second through considering it, primarily, as a
struggle between the agricultural and industrial sectors of the economy. Both
outlooks, he argued, created an 'artificial community of interests' between, on

one hand, the capitalist farmers and 'kulaks' and, on the other, the poor peasantry and agricultural workers'.[8] Using arguments remarkably similar to those deployed by Longuet at the 1909 SFIO congress, Parsal criticised the resolution adopted at the 1926 Congress which, he claimed, had led to the 'absurd' position of the party refusing to give unqualified support to agricultural workers' strike movements. That agricultural workers were in conflict not only against 'gros capitalistes' but also 'frequently' against small and middling peasant employers was not 'an absurdity of the system', as the resolution had suggested, but 'a progressive phenomenon. . . that we should salute and to which we must contribute all our efforts and activity'.[9] Perhaps appropriately for someone soon to become the party's principal organiser amongst agricultural workers, Parsal argued that the struggle between workers and peasant employers should be placed at the centre of communist strategy in the countryside.

Desnots' initial response to this onslaught appeared in an article published in December 1929.[10] Utilising the 'third period' discourse, Desnots stressed the 'rising discontent in the villages', outlined 'irreconcilable class antagonisms within French agriculture', condemned attempts by 'kulaks and aspiring kulaks' to create a 'peasant bloc' against the proletariat' and attacked the socialists for being, along with fascism, a tool of the bourgeoisie. He also continued to criticise the Renaud Jean trend for denying the 'proletarianisation of sections of the peasantry', for its illusions in reformist solutions and for failing to clearly differentiate communist-controlled peasant organisations from those run by 'the bourgeois'. Desnots refused, however, to accept Parsal's argument about the centrality of work amongst the agricultural proletariat. 'The extreme diversity of conditions specific to each region makes any national directive illusory', he argued. It would, for example, be inappropriate to prioritise the agricultural proletariat in regions such as the Limousin, dominated by the small peasantry, and the Lot-et-Garonne, containing a large number of sharecroppers. Desnots made, nevertheless, a number of significant points in relation to the party's work amongst agricultural workers. Firstly, he highlighted the importance of the large-scale farming regions surrounding Paris, 'our most important region but also [in relation to support within the peasant population] our weakest'. He urged the regional party to reorganise its rural cells and where appropriate to create new ones in order 'to devote the totality of activity to the immediate task of developing a regional union of agricultural workers'.[11] Secondly, he theorised some of the difficulties in conducting activity amongst farm workers. Whilst the agricultural proletariat was 'an underprivileged class', the methods used to maintain its oppression were, he maintained, at variance with those experienced by the urban proletariat. The 'bourgeoisie' had succeeded through different means – including social insurance, tied-housing and family allowances – 'to create division amongst [agricultural] workers to make them impenetrable to propaganda as well as trade union and political organisation'.[12] Workers not only faced

2. A large farm in the Aisne (1920s)

repression, intimidation and isolation, but 'foreign Catholic immigration' had been used to remove the 'most combative elements from the villages'.[13] Moreover, the agricultural proletariat was increasingly becoming sub-divided: one section seduced by 'the mirage of acquiring a small plot of land; another seeking a way out by taking jobs in factories; a third dropping into an 'agricultural lumpen-proletariat'. Desnot's conclusion was that the position of agricultural workers 'necessitated particular methods of organisation' of a type that 'up to now have not been contemplated'.[14] Although he made little attempt to suggest what these methods might be, the article was, nonetheless, a serious attempt to develop a strategy that took into account the complexities of the French countryside, as well as a generally balanced assessment of the opportunities for trade unionists and communists amongst agricultural workers.

Subtleties were, however, hardly considered by those at the forefront of pushing 'class against class' in the countryside. In the spring of 1930, Parsal followed up his article with a long letter to the party leadership which, while explicitly targeting Renaud Jean, was a detailed critique of agrarian policy pursued by the party since its inception.[15] Drawing his arguments directly from Lenin's Second Congress thesis, he noted that the party had correctly prioritised work amongst three social groups: the agricultural proletariat, the semi-proletariat and the small peasants. The problem was, he argued, that the category of 'petit paysan' had been incorrectly defined: the party had used the term to characterise peasants permanently employing wage labour, who should have been, according to Lenin's thesis, categorised as either 'middling' or 'large peasants'. Linked to this point, was Parsal's criticism of the party's use of the term 'paysan travailleur'. The concept was inappropriate as it included not only 'poor peasants' but also a section employing wage labour – in other words, it described peasants on both sides of the class divide. In addition, Parsal criticised the use of the term 'middling peasants' to describe 'peasants taking part in physical labour while exploiting several wage workers'. In Lenin's definition, such peasants should be viewed as 'large peasants' or, in the new language, 'kulaks'. Referring to Renaud Jean – though the criticism was equally aimed at policymakers more generally – Parsal noted that 'in all his writings and speeches' there are references to 'the struggle against big capital' but never to the struggle against 'the large peasants (the kulaks) who are not big capitalists but who are, all the same, capitalists'.[16]

Parsal's organisational conclusions were considerable: the political reorientation of the CGPT, so it would primarily become an organisation of the poor peasantry; the 'role of the party' to be more explicitly highlighted during activity in the countryside; the restructuring of the Agrarian Section, with representatives of agricultural workers forming its majority and its work to be linked more closely to that of the party; and, most significantly, his contention that 'our party must start from the fundamental principle that the FUA *is the mass organisation on which we must base our essential efforts in the countryside*' (emphasis in original). Parsal argued for the activity of the FUA to be more integrated into the work of the CGTU, for more material resources to be allocated – at the very minimum a tripling – and for the establishment of a 'mass paper' for agricultural workers.

The attack in Parsal's letter was centred on Renaud Jean partly on account of the rapid political transformation undertaken by Desnots. By May 1930, the secretary of the Agrarian Section had dramatically modified his positions.[17] Agricultural workers were now 'the natural extension of the proletariat within the small peasantry', a situation 'giving them a strategic importance within the class struggle'. In a major speech at the October 1930 Central Committee, Desnots contended that any conclusion other than that 'the central figure of the peasantry is the agricultural proletariat would be a crass oversight of the revolutionary line'.[18] Rather than stressing objective difficulties to explain why attempts to organise workers had generally failed, as he had done in his December 1929 article, his emphasis was now on the 'lack of understanding', 'laziness' and 'indifference' of communist activists. 'This underestimation of the capacities of struggle within the agricultural proletariat must be ruthlessly driven out and eradicated', he declared.[19] The shift in Desnots' politics is an indication of the pressure within the party to refocus its peasant activity on to the agricultural worker. Even Renaud Jean, when counter-attacking against charges of opportunism, argued that 'the real opportunism in relation to the peasantry' resided in the party leadership's failure to allocate sufficient resources to the agricultural workers' union.[20]

Like others who broke with communism for one reason or another, Parsal has been effectively airbrushed out of the history of the French party, but in view of his leading role within the agricultural workers' movement, a comment on his political influence during this period is relevant.[21] Parsal's analysis was not accepted officially by the party or by the leadership of the agrarian section: both Desnots and Georges Fouilloux, who replaced the former as head of the Section Agraire in 1932, criticised him for 'failing to take account of concrete reality'.[22] But the differences amounted to nuances: between mid-1930 and the autumn of 1932, the points raised by Parsal provided the basis for the party's application of 'class against class' in the countryside. For communists the essential division within the peasantry was now based on the employment of wage labour. Writing in August 1932, Fouilloux divided the agricultural population into three categories: 40 per cent were proletarians or semi-proletarians, 32 per cent were paysans travailleurs and the remainder – those who employed wage labour – were 'capitalist elements'. Although he drew a difference between a peasant employing a single worker and one employing twenty, Fouilloux argued that all peasant employers 'possess this major common trait. . . they are fundamentally opposed to the demands of agricultural workers and resolutely resist every aspect of revolutionary politics'.[23] Such conclusions led to the adoption of extreme measures against rural 'capitalist elements' within the party. The March 1930 national conference demanded that the Languedoc region and the CGPT purge richer peasants from their ranks.[24] The party also redefined its terminology. When the now undisputed party leader, Maurice Thorez, outlined agrarian strategy in an article in *l'Humanité* in June 1931, he described paysans travailleurs as peasants 'farming their small holding with their family who in certain cases were also employed part-time as workers in neighbouring agricultural or industrial enterprises'.[25] In other words, Thorez had removed peasants employing wage labour from the category of paysans travailleurs and was now using the term to describe what the Comintern had defined as the peasantry's 'semi-proletariat'. The party's orientation, stressed the general secretary, was 'in the first place, towards the agricultural proletariat, then towards the poor peasants', which he defined as 'small farmers, sharecroppers and small proprietors not exploiting a salaried workforce'.[26] Alongside his political arguments, Parsal's organisation proposals were also largely adopted, particularly those concerned with the functioning of the agricultural workers' union.

The FUA during 'Class against Class'

The upheaval within the FUA prompted by 'class against class' began with a crisis over the union's relationship with the communists' broader peasant organisation (the CPF and, after January 1929, the CGTP). In July 1928, the FUA launched its own newspaper, *Le Travailleur Agricole*. While the step was announced as an indication of its progress, a more illuminating explanation was Roqueblave's statement that the union needed to possess its own independent paper in order to put a clear line of 'demarcation' between itself and the CPF.[27] Roqueblave made his point – which was similar to that raised by Boisseau at the 1927 conference – in a cautious fashion, without explicit criticism of the union's course during the previous period. The following spring, however, those responsible for the FUA's strategy were subjected to a ferocious and public censure. An article in *Le Travailleur Agricole* attacked 'comrades placed in the highest position. . . who have let us down through a false perspective of the development of the class struggle in the countryside'. The leadership's crime had been 'the aberration of neglecting the union organisation of agricultural workers' while devoting activity to the CPF, whose purpose though 'useful' did not compare with the revolutionary potential of the agricultural proletariat.[28] In terms of content and tone, the article was, of course, a reflection of the points raised almost simultaneously within the party by Parsal.

These criticisms were the signal for a major purge of the FUA's leadership. The previous November, Roqueblave had put forward a proposal to reorganise the union, arguing that its limited resources should be concentrated in its two strongest areas – amongst forestry workers in the Centre and vine workers in the

Midi.[29] The proposal was now adopted as a means of removing those associated with the previous strategy from the executive. All but two members were replaced. Bornet, the pioneer of the forestry workers' union movement who had joined the party in 1927, took over as general secretary and Benoît Durandeu, based in Béziers, became the assistant secretary. The union's headquarters was transferred to Bornet's base at La Guerche (Cher).[30]

A campaign was launched to put the union on to a much firmer footing. Four CGTU regional secretaries were designated to attend the union's leadership meetings and CGTU resources were mobilised to support the preparation of a representative national conference.[31] Six regional conferences and 300 local meetings were organised, all well published in party and CGTU journals. Particular emphasis was placed on activity in farming regions in the Paris basin and north. The violent hostility towards the socialists helped to ensure priority for work in the Brie, the 'fief' of Arthur Chaussy, socialist leader of the FNTA. After reports reached communists of a socialist campaign amongst farm workers, the Agrarian Section passed a resolution 'to alert militants. . . of the urgency of propaganda for the party and FUA in the region'.[32] As a result, a union section of around forty members was established at Mormant and a 200-strong meeting organised in Brie-Compte-Robert, Chaussy's main base.[33] Some successes were registered elsewhere. In the Gâtinais, the union was involved in a number of small strikes.[34] Activity also began around hiring fairs in the Beauce: agitating against wage reductions, communists organised meetings in market places, sometimes prompting rowdy scenes when farmers tried to shout them down.[35] At Bonneval (Eure-et-Loir) in 1930, 500 workers refused collectively to accept the rates on offer, while in November the following year at Patay (Loiret) 'a spontaneous demonstration of 300 workers was formed on the market place', leading to an intervention by police.[36] In June 1931, *Le Travailleur Agricole* reported that the union in the Beauce and Gâtinais had built 'a strong base', although admitting that it possessed 'insufficient means to break the resistance of the employers'.[37] In the Paris basin, the most significant conflict unfolded in the Multien, a region on the fringe of the 'red belt' that now surrounded the capital. Workers at Mitry-Mory organised a strike in May 1932 and, supported by the communist-controlled municipality, won important concessions from farmers. The movement spread to neighbouring Tremblay-lès-Gonesse, where 110 workers on four farms walked out after employers tried to impose wage reductions. After the right-wing controlled municipality assisted with the recruitment of replacement labour and a large police presence was mobilised, the strike was defeated.[38] Nevertheless, a union was constituted in the region and managed to maintain a relatively high level of activity.[39]

To the north of Paris, FUA sections were established in six villages surrounding Rosières (Somme), an area that would witness a heated conflict during 1936. The union reported that 'collective action' had repelled farmers' attempts to cut wages for sugar-beet weeding and hoeing, although the character of the action was not specified.[40] Not all strikes were due to the union's intervention. In autumn 1932, Parsal reported a successful campaign against wage cuts by seasonal sugar-beet workers at Cattenières (Nord), despite the fact that activists had 'never been amongst them'.[41]

The period also saw a resurgence of strike movements in Languedoc. Clashes took place during the autumn of 1932 at Coursan (Aude) and Calvisson (Gard) after vine owners recruited replacement labour to break strikes provoked by wage reductions. The following spring a particularly violent conflict erupted at Capestang, Parsal's home town, during which disturbances led to the jailing of nine workers for up to eight months.[42] Although generally defeated, the strikes served to radicalise agricultural unionism in the region, helping communists to establish important points of support.

In general, however, the influence of communists and the FUA amongst agricultural workers remained extremely limited. Often, when union sections were established, communists were unable to consolidate them. Despite the successful strikes around Rosières, the union soon reported 'a certain loosening' of organisation and 'weakening' of workers' 'resistance' in the region.[43] A meeting to establish a union committee to cover the Seine-et-Marne, Seine-et-Oise and Oise departments, with representatives from the Brie, Beauce and the market gardening centre of Achères, spent most of the time discussing the 'difficulty of forming cadres' and the 'lack of solidity in organisation'.[44] The national conference, held on 13 April 1930 at Nevers, attracted only 41 delegates representing 44 unions.[45]

While the usual obstacles faced by agricultural workers' unionism explain the difficulties, they were reinforced by elements of the sectarian approach to politics inherent in 'class against class'. Agricultural workers were viewed simply as 'proletarians' facing essentially similar conditions to those experienced by workers in the towns. Little attempt was made to consider the sort of specificalities outlined by Desnots in his December 1929 article. Parsal insisted, for example, on campaigning for the eight-hour day, even though rank-and-file communist agricultural workers argued that the union should tactically fight for a more 'realistic' ten-hour day, given that the existing working day sometimes stretched to twelve or fourteen hours or beyond.[46] Propaganda often lacked concrete demands and was limited to general appeals: a police report of a meeting aimed at farm workers at Étréchy (Seine-et-Oise) noted that the speaker 'spoke at great length about the results obtained in Soviet Russia since the collectivisation of the farms', before 'asking the audience to campaign actively for farm workers to join the Communist Party'.[47] In the Midi, sectarianism helped socialists to win support for the idea of autonomous unions, independent of the two trade union centres.[48]

As with the results achieved, the extent of the communists' turn towards agricultural workers during the class against class period should not be exaggerated. Within the party, the policy was inconsistently pursued. The Agrarian Section in early 1932 was compelled to criticise 'a very large gap' in the draft thesis for the party congress on account of it containing 'not a word on our work amongst agricultural workers'.[49] Amongst large sections of activists, the traditional apathy towards work amongst the peasantry continued – although now transferred to the intervention amongst agricultural workers. 'Our first adversary,' declared Desnots, 'is the indifference and often hostility by comrades who have taken up the catechism of Compère-Morel: "Agricultural workers? A bunch of alcoholics and degenerates. Have nothing to do with them!".'[50]

The reference to Compère-Morel is an indication of a sharp difference in policy towards agricultural workers now existing between socialists and communists. Remaining the socialists' principal spokesperson on the agrarian question until he broke with the party in 1933, Compère-Morel maintained, in most fundamentals, the position he had adopted prior to the First World War. Despite attempts by Chaussy and others to organise workers' unionism, he continued to write articles in the socialist press describing the 'physical defects', 'indolent nature' and 'nonchalant disposition' of agricultural workers.[51] While communists orientated exclusively towards agricultural workers and small peasants (meaning those who did not employ wage workers), the socialists made further concessions under the 'weight of agrarianism' and became increasingly explicit in championing the interests of peasants employing agricultural workers.[52]

Nevertheless, the extent to which a left-agrarian outlook continued to be expressed within the Communist Party, even at the height of the 'class against class' period, is quite remarkable. An article published in *Cahiers du Bolchevisme* in September 1932 by a peasant activist from Saône-et-Loire questioned the revolutionary potential of agricultural workers and the landless peasantry:

> The middling peasants often make up the 'cadres' of the Communist Party cells. . . Why? 'Knackered by work' and threatened with dismissal by the big Catholic proprietor, agricultural domestics, tenant farmers and sharecroppers are not free. They only have time to read a single newspaper in the winter! The small and middling proprietors are a little more free. They can pay their party dues, become active.[53]

Some peasant activists continued attempts to recruit agricultural workers (along with their employers) to the CGPT rather than to the FUA, ignoring the party's stipulation of a strict line of demarcation between the two organisations.[54]

Communist activity amongst agricultural workers was further constrained by problems inherent in the functioning of the FUA. The purge of the old leadership had been carried through with the aim of ensuring the union was in the hands of those committed to the 'class against class' policy. But moving the headquarters to the Cher and centring activity on forestry and vineyard workers contradicted the goal of building a national union with a mass membership, which could only be achieved by prioritising the large-scale farming regions in the north. Moreover, the geographical centre of the union also meant that it was still 'escaping the control of the party and the CGTU', as an Agrarian Section report put it.[55] Other committees also complained about the functioning of the union. The trade union commission castigated the 'lack of activity by the leadership at a time when the discontent of the agricultural proletariat is growing following wage cuts. . . and the development of unemployment'.[56] The October 1930 Central Committee noted that the FUA was still dominated by forestry workers – who, it claimed, possessed elements of a craft mentality – rather than agricultural workers on the big capitalist farms.[57] The union's membership in the latter part of 1932 was only 3,500 – of which 73 per cent were forestry workers, 19 per cent vineyard workers and only 5 per cent farm workers – and financially it was in a 'disastrous' position, possessing only 43 francs in its funds.[58]

By 1932, the question of how to strengthen the FUA's apparatus was dominating discussions at the Agrarian Section.[59] From early 1930, Parsal had argued that the headquarters should be transferred back to Paris with additional personnel allocated to the union. But it was not until the Comintern promised financial assistance that this became a practical proposition. In May 1932, it was agreed that an 'instructor' should be employed to assist the union. Interestingly, given his later career as party general secretary, the first candidate was Waldeck Rochet, recently returned from the Lenin school in Moscow. He declined to take the position for reasons that are unclear.[60] In the summer of 1932, Parsal, at this time simultaneously party and CGTU organiser in Orléans, from where he had directed work amongst agricultural workers in the Beauce and Gâtinais, was appointed.[61]

The campaign directed by the party towards agricultural workers now became more co-ordinated and concentrated. Preparations for the FUA national congress held in Paris in January 1933 were given prominence. The party press was fully utilised – throughout November and December 1932, *l'Humanité* published a daily feature on the lives and conditions of agricultural workers. A 12-page article by the former general secretary, Pierre Semard, entitled 'La Conquête du prolétariat agricole' was published in *Cahiers du Bolchevisme*.[62] CGTU regions were allocated areas with important concentrations of agricultural workers in which to intervene; in Normandy, a special organiser for agricultural workers was appointed.[63] Party activists in the Paris region were mobilised to visit rural areas. A campaign in the Étampes region attracted 200 agricultural workers to meetings and recruited 20 new party members.[64] The Comintern financed an official to campaign amongst agricultural workers in the north, as well as funds to support the FUA congress.[65] A detailed programme of reforms for agricultural workers was drawn up. It included demands for wage increases, a shorter working week and weekly break, unemployment benefits, improvements in food, lodging and hygiene, 15 days' holiday each year, collective contracts, an extension of the Prud'hommes arbitration boards to agriculture, equality for immigrant workers and 'equal pay for equal work' regardless of sex.[66] More localised demands were agreed at regional meetings; for example, in the Beauce, where pork and lard formed agricultural workers' staple diet, the question of more varied, nutritious food was raised.[67] At the congress, Parsal was confirmed general secretary and it was agreed, not without opposition from representatives of the forestry workers, to rebase the union's headquarters and leadership in the Paris region. Significantly, the congress marked a shift in the centre of gravity of the union: 48 per cent of congress delegates came from the wheat and sugar-beet farming regions on the northern plains, including a number of immigrant workers. In the pre-congress period, the union had recruited over 1000 new members amongst sugar-beet workers in the Cambrai region and established 15 new union sections with 300 members amongst farm workers in regions close to Paris.[68] Claims that the congress represented 'a turning point in the development of the FUA' and for communists' work amongst the agricultural proletariat were not totally exaggerated.[69]

Winter 1932–33: a New Orientation

Although central aspects of the party's Third Period policy – particularly the refusal to make electoral alliances with the socialists – continued until the political turn towards the Popular Front during the summer of 1934, its most extreme excesses were moderated from mid-1932 onwards. Pressure for a more realistic approach emanated from a 40 per cent fall in membership over three years and the disastrous election results of March 1932. As in the mid-1920s, some elements of Popular Front policy were foreshadowed; for example, communists built the Amsterdam-Pleyel anti-war movement involving political forces broader than the party. Peasant policy also saw important modifications in the winter of 1932–33. During the subsequent eighteen months, emphasis remained on 'the central role of the agricultural proletariat', but new ambiguities over the party's orientation in the countryside began to appear.

The impetus for the shifts in agrarian policy was the rise of a peasant protest movement fuelled by the gathering agricultural crisis. The economic depression of the early 1930s had a devastating effect on French farming. Following the harvest of 1932, wheat prices, in steady decline since the mid-1920s, dived by 33 per cent – the beginning of a three-year collapse not only in the price of cereals but also in vegetables, dairy produce, meat and wine. During the latter part of 1932, peasants responded with large meetings, demonstrations and direct action, including tax strikes.[70] The movement had an overtly agrarian dimension and gave an impetus to the growth of both the Agrarian Party (Parti agraire et paysan français) led by the right-wing peasant populist, Fleurant Agricola, and the 'Peasant Defence Committees', organised by Henri Dorgères. As Robert Paxton has noted, the Dorgerist movement with its repertoire of direct peasant action can be firmly placed within the 'magnetic field' of fascism.[71] The extent of the agricultural crisis, the scale of the protest movement, its militant methods and political character, all took the communists by surprise.

During the previous four years, the party had refused to support immediate measures to alleviate the conditions of the broader peasantry, even describing the idea of cheap crisis credits as 'the politics of capitalism designed to produce the systematic indebtedness of poor peasants'.[72] This, together with the almost exclusive orientation towards the agricultural proletariat and poorest peasants, meant that communists stood aside from the protests, leaving the field open to the right-wing agrarians, as well as the socialists. In the Beauce, a coordinated campaign of resignations by local mayors against the fall in wheat prices was publicly attacked by Parsal. Agricultural workers and poor peasants 'should show no solidarity' with manoeuvres by rich farmers who had previously not thought twice about cutting agricultural workers' wages, he declared.[73] Large agrarian-inspired demonstrations at Chartres (14 January 1933) and in Paris (25 January 1933) were dismissed by Parsal and Desnots as 'only involving kulaks'.[74]

By November 1932, however, the party leadership had become alarmed by events. 'The most important demonstrations are taking place in the absence of communists', concluded a report drawn up for the Central Committee.[75] It seemed that right-wing agrarians were not only attracting support from better-off peasants but also drawing significant numbers of poor peasants and agricultural workers into the movement. Parsal was publicly censured for advocating a position that would isolate the party from peasants influenced by the agricultural syndicates and 'bourgeois' political parties. The communists now pledged support for the mayors' resignation campaigns and urged members to organise similar protests where they had influence on municipalities.[76] Other aspects of policy were also transformed. A package of reforms of the type previously attacked as 'reformist' was proposed, including demands for crisis payments, interest free credits and tax concessions. Discussion began over whether or not 'in some cases' communists should support price regulation for agricultural produce – recognition of the fact that the socialists' proposal for a Wheat Office was winning support within the peasantry, including amongst agricultural workers.[77] In addition, the isolation of Renaud Jean came to an end; his rehabilitation signalled when he gave the main report on the agrarian question at the February 1933 Central Committee.[78]

That this Central Committee discussion was the most extensive on the agrarian question in the party's inter-war history, with the exception of the debate around the 1921 Marseille thesis, illustrates the importance now placed on the peasantry. 'How great has been our neglect of peasant problems over the last months and years', declared Jacques Duclos, opening the session.[79] Directives were drawn up to reorganise the work of the party in rural areas. Emphasis was placed on the creation of farm and village cells to organise agricultural workers, paysans travailleurs and rural artisans.[80] Membership of the party was opened again to 'middling peasants sometimes employing agricultural workers', on condition that they pledged to 'work for the conquest of the poor peasantry'.[81]

This last decision is indicative of a more flexible approach in deciding strategic priorities in the countryside. The agricultural proletariat remained the declared priority for the party: even Renaud Jean felt obliged to declare in early 1934 that 'it should not be forgotten that while we must do everything to win non-wage-earning peasants, the conquest of agricultural wage workers must comprise our principal occupation'.[82] But voices began to be raised against a 'sectarian tendency to prioritise the work of the FUA'.[83] While, for example, communists in the Bordeaux region were censured for 'narrowly concentrating on the movement of sharecroppers and small farmers and neglecting any work amongst agricultural workers', activists in Languedoc were simultaneously criticised for 'exclusively working amongst agricultural workers and not at all amongst the small vine owners. . . [who] are up in arms and showing their willingness to struggle'.[84] The new balance was illustrated at the Central Committee when Renaud Jean's general report on the agrarian question was followed by an equally long supplementary report by Parsal, specifically dealing with the agricultural proletariat. The party adopted, in fact, a position broadly similar to that proposed by Desnots in his article of December 1929; an irony, as Desnots refused to associate himself with the new approach, moved into opposition and left the party in 1934.[85]

The declared aim of communist policy was to disrupt the formation of a 'rural bloc' in which the poorer peasantry and agricultural workers would come under the hegemony of the agrarians, representing the big property owners and rich farmers. Communists counter-posed a 'workers' and peasants' bloc', which meant 'the common struggle of the paysans travailleurs and agricultural workers along with the workers of the towns against their common enemy'.[86] Agricultural workers should not abandon the organisation of actions for their own specific demands but should also take the initiative in the building a 'united front in the countryside'.[87] Arising from this strategy were, however, two unresolved questions. Firstly, just how broad should the 'united front' be? Specifically, should it be limited to unity between agricultural workers and paysans travailleurs under the party's definition of the term during the 'class against class' period (in other words, excluding peasants employing wage labour)? Or should it include the important layers of 'middling and well-off' peasants that communists noted were involved in the protest movements? And, if so, how would the perennial problem be tackled – that, by raising their 'specific demands', common action between agricultural workers and peasants who would have to concede them (those employing wage labour) would be undermined? A lack of clarity or, probably more accurately, tensions and differences remained over these questions. Significantly, Parsal began his address to the February 1933 Central Committee by referring to Lenin's thesis to the Second Congress, as if making the point that peasant unity should be limited to agricultural workers and the section of the peasantry not employing wage labour. On the other hand, the emphasis in Semard's long document stressed the building of a movement involving 'the great mass' of those working on the land 'in direct struggle against the bourgeoisie and its state', thus ignoring the antagonisms between agricultural workers and peasant employers.[88] Perceptions of the class struggle in the countryside were, in fact, changing. Whereas, since mid-1929, the emphasis had been placed on the potential conflict between different sections of the peasantry, the approach now implicitly suggested the building of a movement of the entire peasantry, with the exception of the 'large proprietors'.

As communists began drawing on the logic of this position for their practical work, problems relating to the organisation of agricultural workers re-emerged. There were complaints that in the Seine-et-Marne 'some comrades have organised agricultural workers together with small peasants (even including small employers)'.[89] In the Loire, tensions developed between communists working amongst agricultural workers and members of the communist-controlled CGPT. A party Peasant Conference held in Tours heard how a 'young comrade' had begun work amongst agricultural workers. Yet the activity had not produced many results as the young activist had 'encountered the hostility of peasants belonging to the CGPT' who were employers of agricultural workers.[90]

Despite these contradictions in policy and practice, the party's discourse of relations in the countryside remained imbued with the language of class. In the large-scale farming regions of the Paris basin, propaganda continued against the 'kulaks', not only condemning their direct exploitation of agricultural workers but also their nefarious influence on rural society in general. The tone of an article by activists in Belle-Église (Oise) is typical. 'We have the sad privilege. . . of possessing in our village not one but several specimens of these long-eared individuals', it began, before cataloguing a list of claimed misdemeanours.[91] Farmers were accused of watering down milk – thus 'threatening the health of children' – imposing religious values on their workers and of damaging the rural environment through creating unhygienic cesspits of agricultural waste and churning up roads, making them impassable for workers on bicycles.[92]

Violent attacks continued against the socialists for proposing state-run 'offices' to regulate prices and notes sent to party 'agitators' emphasised the impossibility of resolving the growing agricultural crisis through 'bourgeois' policies.[93] Particularly condemned was a socialist proposal to establish departmental commissions to set a minimum wage for agricultural workers linked to the price of agricultural produce in the region. Communists attacked

the implicit suggestion that there existed a 'general interest' of French agriculture. The socialist approach would subordinate the interests of agricultural
workers and paysans travailleurs to those of the 'large landed proprietors' and
'capitalist farmers', they argued.[94]

'Class against class' was neither unimportant in the history of inter-war
communist agrarian politics nor a policy from outside the tradition of French
Marxism. Between 1929 and 1933, the party put into practice the arguments of
Longuet (1909), Dunois (1921) and those outlined by Castel (1924), albeit in a
inflexible and dogmatic manner. At its height, 'class against class' reduced the
conflict in the countryside to the struggle of agricultural workers against other
sections of the peasantry. In a fashion, it was a mirror image of the approach
previously adopted by Renaud Jean and the communist agrarians. The latter
attempted to generalise a social model rooted in the small-scale farming regions
on to a more complex national situation, including regions where class differentiation was apparent. 'Class against class' applied a model of social relations that
had some basis in reality in certain regions of *grande culture* on to a national
agriculture, in which personal and family ties made, in many regions, a deline-
ation between the 'peasantry' and agricultural workers extremely problematical.
Yet, whatever the detrimental impact of the policy for the position of the party
amongst the wider peasantry, the party undoubtedly reaped some positive
benefits for its relationship with agricultural workers.

4

COMMUNISTS AND THE AGRICULTURAL LABOUR FORCE, 1933–35

By the mid-1930s, communist activity amongst agricultural workers was provoking sufficient concern that the authorities placed the FUA under surveillance.[1] In April 1935, a 21-page police report appraised the history of the communist-controlled union, its strengths and weaknesses, and commented on its potential. Quite striking for its insight, the document noted that the union's influence during the 1920s had been 'almost nothing', explaining that 'generally, the activity of the Federation was subordinated to that of the CGPT. . . as a result of the same activists being placed on the leadership committees of the two organisations'. The economic crisis had, however, provided 'a more favourable terrain': prospects for the union were good; it had led a number of important strikes and was in the process of preparing others; its membership – estimated at 9000 – seemed to be 'making consistent progress'.[2]

The police linked the communists' relative success to the impact of the crisis on the living standards of farm workers. Alongside lower wages came longer hours, a feeling of increased insecurity and more frequent spells of unemployment. In the Paris basin and northern France, strikes – though still very isolated – became more common, with conflicts breaking out in the Multien, the Artois, the Vermandois, the Calais region and in market gardening around Achères. In itself, the economic conjuncture was, however, an insufficient explanation for the growth in workers' unionism and radicalisation towards the left by a significant section of agricultural workers. Some were radicalised in the opposite direction, attracted towards the agrarian movement after identifying their interests with those of the wider peasantry. The fact that the crisis acted as a catalyst for large numbers of workers to develop an identity separate from that of other sections of the peasantry was, in part, the outcome of the deeper structural transformation of social relations in the most advanced sections of agriculture, a process that dramatically speeded up during the 1920s.

'A Rural Proletariat Comparable to the Industrial Proletariat'

The First World War accelerated the trend towards concentration of agricultural holdings in the Paris basin and northern France. Plots of small farmers and agricultural day labourers heading for jobs in the towns were bought up by large proprietors and tenant farmers. Large farmers also benefited from generous compensation payments and the way in which 600,000 hectares of fertile but war-ravaged land were redivided into more compact packages.[3] It would be no accident that many centres of the strike movement in 1936 – such as the Santerre, Arras plain, Vermandois and Soissonnais – were situated on or adjacent to the classified red zone of wartime destruction.[4] Some large farms became more directly linked to industrial capital, particularly through the sugar industry. The company behind the Piot farm at Mitry-Mory, for example, also operated a sugar-processing plant and a brick works. In the Ainse and Somme departments, the Société industrielle et agricole de la Somme (SIAS), owned by the Belgian industrialist Baron Coppée, developed a formidable network of sugar processing plants and refineries supplied by 13 huge farms covering around five thousand hectares and employing hundreds of workers.[5] The tendency towards concentration of agricultural holdings is found in other regions: in the Berry, which was also touched by strikes and workers' unionism in 1936, the number of holdings of between five and ten hectares fell by 20 per cent after 1927 and the number above fifty hectares grew by 15 per cent.[6] While in many parts of France *petite culture* remained vibrant, the process in these most fertile and profitable farming regions indicates that, in the debate amongst French communists during the 1920s, reality was closer to the position outlined by Desnots than to Renaud Jean's suggestion of a general trend towards social homogeneity in the country-side.

An unpublished report drawn up in 1932 by the Director of Agricultural Services (DSA) in the Oise analysed trends in that department and drew conclusions that can be generalised for other large-scale farming regions.[7] His statistics (reproduced in Table 1) illustrate the substantial fall in the number of smallholdings and consequential concentration of agriculture. Although the comparison is with the position in 1892, the author noted that the trend was 'most noticeable between 1919 and 1930' (see Table 1.1).[8] The number of *petites exploitations* – farms of less than ten hectares that would not have usually employed wage labour – had collapsed to less than one-third the previous figure. There was a more stable position in relation to medium-sized farms (which would have generally employed a small number of workers) and an overall increase in the number of large farms, both numerically and in terms of percentage of the total. The growth in the importance of the big farms and the decline of the small is further indicated in Table 1.2, which shows the area of agricultural land covered by each category and the average size of holdings.

Table 1. Trends in the Social Structure of Agriculture in the Oise, 1892–1930

1.1 Comparison of Farm Sizes

Farm Size (hectares)	1892		1930	
	Number of Farms	%	Number of Farms	%
1–10	17,848	67.8%	5,188	39.3%
10–40	6,538	24.8%	5,019	38.0%
Above 40	2,083	7.4%	2,164	22.7%

1.2 Comparison of Agricultural Area Covered

Farm Size (hectares)	1892			1930		
	Area Covered	%	Average Farm Size	Area covered	%	Average Farm Size
1–10	78,200	17.4%	4 ha 36	16,890	4.2%	3 ha 25
10–40	121,000	27.0%	18 ha 50	109,863	27.1%	21 ha 8
Above 40	238,800	55.6%	114 ha 60	278,893	68.7%	128 ha 80

1.3 Make-up of Agricultural Labour Force

	1892	1912	1932
Domestics and Farm Servants	15,237 (51%)	14,970 (56%)	17,358 (65%)
Property-owning Day Labourers	6,641 (23%)	3,300 (12.5%)	1,047 (4%)
Day Labourers without Property	7,682 (26%)	8,460 (31.5%)	8,032 (31%)
Total	29,560	26,730	26,437

In addition to these figures, the 1932 survey counted 3,700 seasonal workers from outside the region and 2,500–3000 local seasonal workers (primarily wives of agricultural workers).

Source: Notes et rapports sur l'évolution de l'agriculture et sa situation en 1932, AD Oise, Mp4514

The impact of these changes on the category of agricultural worker is shown in Table 1.3. Although the size of the agricultural workforce had not significantly fallen from the pre-war situation, there was a marked change in its composition. While the category of landless day labourers had remained relatively constant, the number of small peasant proprietors working on larger farms as day labourers had collapsed from 23 per cent of the total workforce in 1892 to just 4 per cent in 1932. The decline of the small-peasant day labourer was offset by an increase in the number of domestics, either living on the farms or housed by farmers. In short, the importance of the domestic in the agricultural workforce had increased in both absolute and relative terms.

The raw figures hide, however, the transformation within the workforce, as many French domestics put life on the farms behind them and were replaced by immigrant labour – a process most pronounced in regions dominated by large holdings with good communication links to Paris. In 11 departments in northern France, the number of Polish workers in agriculture almost doubled between 1926 and 1936. In the Oise, in 1932, 51 per cent of agricultural workers in the Valois were of immigrant origin. Similar proportions were found in the Brie and Soissonnais. Dammard (Aisne), a village on the fringes of the Valois, has already been mentioned in Chapter 1. In the period before the war, a majority of domestics on the Potel farm were internal migrants, mostly from the Massif Central. By 1936, out of 56 agricultural workers in the commune, 30 were Polish, who together with their families formed 33 per cent of the commune's population.[9] The problems posed by immigrant labour for agricultural workers' unionism and the Communist Party will be returned to shortly.

The social consequences of the restructuring of the agricultural workforce did not go without comment from the DSA:

> [The class of property-owning day labourers] has almost completely disappeared in the large-scale farming regions. The small farms that still existed thirty years ago in our Valois villages have been gradually absorbed by neighbouring large farms. . . The evolution in these regions is clearly towards the composition of a rural proletariat comparable to the industrial proletariat, with all the associated negative consequences for social order. . . Strikes have broken out in the past, others are possible.[10]

Indeed the threat to 'social order' posed by the new relations became a constant preoccupation for the agricultural associations and public authorities. Many of the theses presented by farmers' sons attending the agricultural college at Beauvais are concerned with strategies to maintain a loyal, but low-paid, workforce. The practice of providing workers with small plots of land, which they could cultivate through borrowing equipment and horses, became more

3. Industrialised farming in the Aisne (late 1920s)

widespread. It was, according to one thesis, 'a means to fight against communism'.[11] Another declared that attaching workers to property 'secured good workers and was a means to struggle against the disruptive propaganda by a handful of "Moscowteers"'.[12] Many identified the advantages in recruiting immigrant labour 'to help control the level of wages and lower the exaggerated claims of local workers'.[13]

The impact of structural change was brought into sharper relief by the economic conjuncture of the early 1930s. The crisis ended any hope of social mobility for farm workers, not only on account of the virtual impossibility of raising capital to purchase or rent land, but also because the escape route into the towns had been blocked by urban unemployment. It also challenged many assumptions held by agricultural workers. The nature of farm labour can encourage the idea that the agricultural economy is governed solely by meteorological conditions. Indeed, in stable economic circumstances, this may largely be the case, with the weather being the predominant factor in determining success or failure. The economic crisis illustrated that nature was not the only determinant: the effects of an equally uncontrollable market could be just as important.

The outlook of farm workers was also shaped by the manner in which the economic crisis encouraged a section of urban workers to seek employment in the countryside. Farmers generally viewed the influence of such workers with trepidation. As the Director of Agricultural Services in the Pas-de-Calais noted: 'They fear they will end up with incapable people or disruptive elements who are difficult to supervise and capable of whipping up trouble amongst the existing personnel.'[14] Farmers were equally suspicious that government-sponsored campaigns to encourage French workers to 'return to the land' would lead to an increased number of socialist and communist influenced workers in the countryside.[15]

For agricultural workers, the crisis impacted on wage levels and prompted a rise in unemployment. In the Oise, rates paid during the sugar-beet harvest fell from 450 francs per hectare in 1929 to between 350 and 375 francs in 1932.[16] At Compans (Seine-et-Marne), the mayor reported that wages of '23 francs per day in 1930 have been reduced in 1935 to 16.50 francs for day labourers and to 20 or 21 francs for carters'.[17] Around Douai (Nord), an industrial region in which farms were generally small in size, the Sub-Prefect mused that 'wages of the agricultural labour force could hardly be lowered any further as they would be equivalent to unemployment allowances'. He noted 'a tendency towards extremist ideas in the countryside' and reported that 'communist representatives have not missed the opportunity to exploit the situation'.[18] Unemployment became an issue as farmers looked for further ways to reduce costs. The journal produced by the federation of agricultural associations covering northern France conceded that the position had become 'difficult' for many workers' families. 'Those agitating for the flag of revolution and proclaiming the dictatorship of the proletariat are going to have a field day', the paper warned. 'Most worrying is the rapidity with which peasant mentality is evolving towards extreme solutions.'[19] Such conclusions were not simply alarmist but based on firm impressions that left-wing ideas were making some headway amongst the region's agricultural workers.

Building the FUA in the Calais Region

The momentum of the communists' turn towards agricultural workers, initiated during the 'class against class' period and given renewed impetus by the campaign around the 1933 FUA Congress, continued into 1934 and 1935. A particularly good example of how communists built support against the background of the agricultural crisis is the party's activity in the countryside surrounding Calais. The first agricultural workers' union in the region was established at Marck in February 1933. Led by Charles Rome, a day labourer and secretary of the local communist cell, it claimed 86 members and provided the base for communists to extend their influence into other more outlying rural villages.[20]

If the small fishing industry is left aside, Marck was essentially an agricultural commune, with a few processing industries (a brewery, workshops to dry chicory and conserve vegetables, mills).[21] Agricultural production was intrinsically tied to the needs of the surrounding market: sugar beet for the processing plant operated by the Say company at Pont d'Ardres, peas and other vegetables for the canning factories at Gravelines and Petite-Synthe, flax for the Belgium textile industry, bundles of hay for the paper mills in the Aa valley, industrial chicory as a substitute by the Flanders coffee industry. In addition, vegetables, meat, butter and eggs had a substantial market amongst the population in Calais, only nine kilometres from Marck village, and milk was dispatched to two large dairies in the town. The 1929 agricultural survey registered 92 farms in the commune, most of a middling to small nature. One large farm covered more than 100 hectares, while eight others possessed a surface of between 50 and 100 hectares.[22]

The proximity to Calais had an important impact on the social composition of the commune. According to the 1936 census, 12 per cent of the economically active population were farmers, 27 per cent agricultural workers, but 25 per cent were either industrial workers, building workers, or employed on the railways.[23] In other words, a large percentage of Marck's working population commuted into Calais. Close to 300 agricultural workers lived in the commune; 90 were domestics living on the farms, which were, in the main, dispersed, some up to five kilometres from the village; the others sought work as day labourers, and were concentrated in the village or outlying hamlets. At times of *grands travaux*, they would often join *bandes* recruited by *bandiers* (in modern parlance, gangmasters) who then hired a team of workers to farmers. The agricultural day labourers generally worked the farms from April to November, when their situation became more precarious. Unable to find farm work, they sought employment in various industries, or attempted to survive the winter on proceeds earned during the rest of the year. Most owned small plots on which they grew vegetables and raised poultry. It was amongst the day labourers, who lived in proximity to socialist- and communist-influenced factory workers, that the agricultural union established its initial base of support.

The insertion of agriculture into the capitalist market had led to a relatively prosperous position for Marck's farmers, both large and small. By the same token, the collapse in industrial production in the early- to mid-1930s had a disastrous impact. The market relationship with Calais made the position particularly severe. Because of its dual role as an industrial and trading centre, the port town was particularly hit by the economic crisis, with unemployment provoking a 10 per cent absolute fall in its population. Farmers in Marck and other communes in the vicinity not only witnessed the collapse of prices for wheat, sugar beet and other industrial crops, but pressure on the market for their produce amongst the urban population.

The Marck agricultural workers' union built its reputation by highlighting the consequences of the resulting unemployment for workers and their families. It agitated for improved allowances for unemployed workers from the right-wing controlled municipal authority, assistance such as clothing and coal during the winter, and unemployment pay to continue during the period of the *grands travaux* (preventing farmers from paying rates not much higher than unemployment benefit for seasonal workers).[24] One high profile campaign during spring 1934 was against the conditions in which a convoy of unemployed young people (mainly children of agricultural workers, small farmers and unemployed workers) had been sent to farms in the Ain and Jura. The union circulated reports of how the young people were being forced to work 16 hours-a-day for extremely low return and were unable to return home without paying a fare equivalent to three months' wages.[25]

The campaign around unemployment enabled communists to penetrate other agricultural villages which, in the words of the local Police Commissioner were witnessing 'a level of unemployment unheard of up to now'.[26] One example is Campagne-lès-Guînes, a small community in which agricultural workers made up the largest social group. In 1936, 48 agricultural workers were counted on the census, out of an economically active population of 119. This was a decrease from 56, out of 133, five years earlier, and from 72 in 1926. Moreover, 9 of the 48 workers were recorded as unemployed. So the number of employed agricultural workers in the village had fallen from 72 to 39 in the course of ten years – a decrease of around 46 per cent. Women were particularly affected. In 1936, there is only one spouse of a male agricultural worker recorded as economically active, whereas the census in 1926 listed eleven wives employed full-time as agricultural labourers.[27] Together with other villages that witnessed farm strikes in 1936, Campagne-lès-Guînes sent delegates to a congress organised by communists in February 1935 to highlight rural unemployment.[28] In some communes the party helped to draw up lists of agricultural workers and small proprietors to contest the 1935 municipal elections. In most cases, the votes received were small; although at Saint-Tricat, a village in which agricultural workers formed 46.5 per cent of the active population, a communist-backed list secured 41 out of 109 votes cast.[29]

The union also attempted to resist reductions in wages. By 1934, traditional rates for hoeing, weeding and harvesting – paid as piecework – had been severely cut and farmers were sending workers home without pay if the weather was bad, when previously they would have allocated them work inside farm buildings.[30] In July 1934, the canning factories in Dunkerque and Gravelines cut the price paid to farmers for the harvest of *petits pois* and the decrease (around 15 per cent) was passed on to workers in reduced wages. In response, the union called a strike. The pea harvest was a major event in the region and each year a large seasonal labour force was mobilised. As well as recruiting available local agricultural labourers and their families, *bandes* of mainly women workers were assembled in Calais and Gravelines by gangmasters hired by the canning factories. In the mid-1930s, significant numbers of unemployed industrial workers were also seeking work on the harvest. The strike started on 7 July and involved 300 workers, 150 from Marck and 150 from Calais. Pickets were placed around the meeting points for the *bandes* in order to prevent the recruitment of replacement labour. In an attempt to spread the conflict, Rome led a group of 150 strikers across fields into the neighbouring commune of Oye-Plage, but police action dispersed them. With a large pool of labour to call upon and a big police intervention, the gangmasters were able to assemble additional labour and the strike was defeated.[31] Its ramifications continued into the autumn, however, when prominent farmers were hit by arson attacks on their harvests. During the night of 11 September 1934 at Oye-Plage, two stacks of wheat were destroyed in a fire put down by police to 'malicious intent'.[32] The communists' campaign amongst agricultural workers in the region continued into 1935 and 1936. Activists were regularly reminded of the importance of the work in the local party paper which, towards the end of 1935, also introduced a regular propaganda column aimed at farm workers.[33]

'Vive Marcel Cachin!', 'Vive Monsieur Béhin!'

The type of campaign waged by communists in the Calais countryside was repeated across northern France and the Paris Basin. Each Sunday, activists in Le Havre (Seine-Inférieure) visited villages in the Caux region.[34] In Saint-Quentin (Aisne), party cells were paired with agricultural villages with the aim of 'reaching our *frères de misère* tied the whole week to the plough or the hoe'.[35] Around Soissons, communists organised public meetings in villages and toured farms to agitate and carry out surveys of conditions.[36] A visit to a farm at Acy, an establishment that would be prominent in the strike movement of June 1936, met 'an old worker with tears in his eyes' pointing to a notice on the stable door announcing a 10 per cent cut in wages for all personnel.[37] In the Beauce and surrounding regions, systematic work continued around the hiring fairs with 'appreciable results'.[38]

One campaign, monitored closely by police, was conducted in the Étampes region with the direct involvement of Parsal and local communist leaders. During the autumn and early winter of 1933, an organising committee was established, meetings held at the hiring fairs and a local bulletin, *Le Travailleur des Champs*, produced.[39] Even an unsympathetic police observer noted the 'skill' with which communists conducted their propaganda over pay and food.[40] The campaign particularly won support from a layer of younger workers. Five people attended a local organising committee on 22 September 1933, including 'four kids under twenty'.[41] A public meeting signed up 11 new recruits, 'all youngsters between 16 and 18 at the most'.[42] Previously, many of these workers would have endured labouring in the fields as a temporary life-phase until undertaking their military service. Reduced job prospects elsewhere meant they had more to gain from making demands for improvements in wages and conditions in agriculture.

Compared with the approach taken during the height of the 'class against class' period, communists were now more adept at voicing grievances of agricultural workers. Propaganda concentrated on practical questions: demands that workers could present to employers and steps needed to build the union, instead of the previous 'grand speeches and general sloganeering', as *l'Humanité* admitted.[43] One adjustment concerned the length of the working day. Although Parsal had previously insisted that no compromise should be made over the demand for an eight-hour day, by 1935 he was describing the slogan as 'demagogic'.[44] The change reflected a shift in the way in which the party characterised agricultural workers. During the 'class against class' period, agricultural workers were considered as simply part of the proletariat and therefore subject to the same programme as workers in industry. While they were still viewed as 'proletarians', it was now recognised that they were proletarians 'living in particular conditions' because of their ties to the peasantry.[45]

Between 1933 and 1935, communist and union militants became increasingly involved in agricultural strike struggles. One conflict broke out in October 1934 in villages close to Arras after farmers reduced wage rates for the sugar-beet harvest by 17 per cent. At Pelves, a commune with a population of 545 and around thirty medium-sized farms, the dispute was led by Maurice Blampain, a factory worker and prominent local communist. At Quéant, where one of the leaders was a small farmer, police surprised two activists pinning a notice on a farm gate threatening severe action against strikebreakers, concluding with the slogan, 'Vive Marcel Cachin!'. Strikers were local agricultural day labourers, their families and a sprinkling of unemployed workers employed as seasonal labour. Women played a prominent role, organising into groups to confront those continuing to work. The fact that domestics were on the verge of joining the strike prompted farmers to settle.[46]

Isolated strikes also broke out in the Cambrai region where communists had built support amongst the day labourers in Avenes-lès-Aubert and surrounding villages.[47] In March 1933, they used this base to establish a union under the leadership of César Bavay, a communist municipal councillor at Avesnes-le-Sec, who would later be elected to the executive of the FNTA at the union's 1937 conference.[48] The union waged a campaign demanding the right of seasonal agricultural workers to draw unemployment benefit during the winter months, winning during November 1935 some concessions from the prefect.[49] It also tried to undermine the activities of the private recruitment offices that assembled teams of seasonal workers for farmers, charging a commission in the process. The union established six of its own offices, transferring the commission to workers through higher wages. After a conference of delegates in February, a 'monster rally' to mobilise support for a collective contract with local farmers was organised on 25 March, attracting 1300 people according to the police.[50] Strikes broke out at Avesnes-le-Sec during May and October 1935 as part of the campaign.[51] The statement agreed at the rally is a good example of communist propaganda amongst agricultural workers during this period. It proposed 'an alliance of struggle of small peasants and agricultural workers, together with the proletarians of the towns' and explicitly rejected any idea of a 'rural bloc. . . to unite exploiters and exploited'.[52]

In some regions, however, communists remained slow to engage in work amongst farm workers. In March 1934, a conflict broke out in market gardening at Montesson, west of Paris. The report to the regional party conference noted how 'the failure by local cells to support and organise the movement' meant workers were unable 'to extract a complete victory'.[53] Such complaints were not uncommon. At the East Paris conference (a region that covered the Brie) in March 1935, Hubert Chiquois, who would in August 1936 become the editor of the FNTA's newspaper, chastised the 'railway worker comrades [who] have stated they are unable to take responsibility for the organisation of meetings, due to the lack of comrades with close understanding of the situation of agricultural workers'.[54] For many activists, the idea that industrial workers formed the 'advanced guard' of the revolution and agricultural workers represented a more 'backward' section of the peasantry remained an unspoken truth.

One region in which party activists waged a consistent campaign with important repercussions was the Vermandois. In early October 1935, representatives

4. FUA poster advertising the Monster Rally held on 25 March 1935

of the Aisne CGTU were invited to attend a meeting at Prémont. When a communist militant from Saint-Quentin arrived, he was informed that workers on the sugar-beet harvest had been on strike for a week, refusing to accept wage reductions proposed by farmers. Fifty workers were present at the meeting, including day labourers, a large number of women, and domestics. Communists helped to establish a union and organise negotiations, during which farmers withdrew the wage cut and the strike was called off. The affair was announced in the local party press as a turning point: 'the first link in the chain that will be a regional union of agricultural workers.'[55]

An incident at the conclusion of the Prémont strike is revealing. At a meeting organised to announce the workers' victory, there was a cry by workers of 'Vive Monsieur Béhin!', a reference to the president of the local agricultural syndicate and one of the biggest farmers in the village.[56] Agriculture in this region was not particularly concentrated. A survey conducted in 1942 found that Prémont had 9 farms covering over 40 hectares (the largest was 90), 18 medium-sized farms of between 10 and 40 hectares and 22 small establishments under 10 hectares.[57] Although farm workers had been prepared to organise and take collective action, many still maintained a certain identity of interests with the employers.

Over the winter, however, relations in the region became more polarised. As the union grew in influence, a campaign of repression was waged by farmers.[58] The fact that the communists made repeated appeals that 'small farmers ought to be supporting the demands of agricultural workers' suggests that smaller employers were taking the same position as the large.[59] At Fonsommes, it was reported that 'all the farmers' had dispensed with their personnel over the winter months and announced that there would be no work until March.[60] At Gouy, one of the initial recruits to the union was sacked from a farm he had worked on for sixteen years.[61] At Fresnoy-le-Grand, farmers withdrew the coffee and beer that had traditionally been served during pauses in the working day.[62] In this way matured the conflict that would break out in the region on 16 May 1936, the first farm strikes following the election of Léon Blum's government.

Agricultural Workers' Unionism and the Immigrant Worker

Agriculture in the Vermandois and other parts of north Picardy was still largely reliant on indigenous workers. Closer to Paris, immigrant workers often formed an important proportion, sometimes a majority, of the labour force. Between 1921 and 1936, 49.5 per cent of the 2.1 million immigrant workers arriving in France were designated agricultural workers.[63] In the Paris basin and other regions of the north, agricultural associations and public authorities worked closely to oversee an organised programme of immigration from Poland and, to a lesser degree, from Czechoslovakia and Yugoslavia.[64] Farmers prioritised the recruitment of families, considered as providing greater worker stability as well as a readily available source of cheap female and child labour for seasonal work. The rationale was summarised in a report by the Société des Agriculteurs de France: 'The Polish woman is very hard-working. . . In her country, she carries out heavy labour in the fields: spreading manure, haymaking, the harvest. The children are also, from a very young age, accustomed to making themselves useful.'[65]

Considered 'étrangers' in every sense of the word, migrants from central Europe were not accepted as a legitimate part of French rural society. Before arriving in France, they had been subject to a strict screening and selection procedure. After a humiliating medical examination, which checked for deformations of hands and fingers as well as blemishes on the skin, 54 per cent of applicants were rejected as being of defective quality.[66] Tied to a particular farmer by a year-long contract, immigrants filled the most despised jobs, those previously occupied by internal migrants. 'Given the importance of the post of carter, preference is given to Frenchmen', noted a study of a big farm in the Soissonnais, 'on the other hand, the majority of cowhands are Polish.'[67] Former systems of division between indigenous and outside labour were now reinforced with sentiments of racism. 'In the Nord, the French use the familiar 'tu' as a sign of superiority when speaking to the Poles, but do not tolerate being addressed in the same manner by them', observed Georges Mauco in a survey of immigrant labour in French agriculture.[68] At the bottom of the hierarchy on the large farms, conditions for immigrants were probably worse on the small and middling farms, where they faced extreme isolation and were more directly under the surveillance of the farmer. A contemporary thesis discussing conditions of immigrant workers commented that 'the small French farmer is often a bad employer. . . abuses of all types, thefts, confiscation of identity papers, poor wages, and no shortage of unpaid wages'.[69] In 1930, the Polish authorities made an official complaint to the French government about such abuses.[70]

Farmers were quite explicit that they were recruiting immigrants as a form of social control. 'They are for the most part hardworking individuals, free from excess, thrifty. . . As a result, communist propaganda does not have a violent character in the Eure-et-Loir', commented the department's prefect.[71] On a number of occasions during the 1920s, Polish workers were used to undermine strike movements. Reporting a conflict on five large farms in the Brégny region in December 1927, the Oise Prefect noted that the movement had enjoyed 'no influence over the foreign workforce', while the socialist press explained its defeat because 'the Polish were there to maintain the work'.[72] A farmer's son explained: 'By their arrival, the Poles have stabilised the workforce and wages. They have returned authority to the farmers, who previously could not dare reprimand their workers, for fear they would depart and leave them without personnel.'[73]

The perceived threat to jobs and conditions of employment meant that French farm workers were generally hostile to the arrival of foreign workers. During the early and middle 1920s, both wings of the agricultural workers' union movement demanded controls on immigration.[74] The FNTA's paper, *Le Travailleur de la Terre*, addressed the question under headlines such as 'Le Menace' and 'L'Invasion', signalling that the function of the union was to defend exclusively indigenous workers.[75] The tone set by the communist-controlled FUA was similar. Evoking a 'véritable invasion', Jean Castel noted that immigrant workers were forming 'colonies' which were being 'actively worked by reactionary organisations'.[76] An article in *Le Travailleur Agricole* declared: 'Some talk of organising immigrants, as if that is possible in the countryside. . . if the CGTU does not raise its voice in protest against this invasion of foreigners into France, if we do not secure some control, the day is not long coming when Frenchmen will be out of work and will face the impossibility of defending themselves.'[77] The FUA National Council meeting in January 1926 agreed 'to organise a struggle' against further immigration.[78]

The position pursued by the agricultural workers' union was contrary to the official policy of both the CGTU and Communist Party, which often repeated that 'for us, the word *étranger* has no meaning'.[79] During the mid-1920s there was, however, a general trend amongst rank-and-file party and union activists to view the matter differently. Polish workers were, in particular, seen as politically 'backward' because of their attachment to catholicism. At the 1925 Communist Party National Congress, a Polish delegate criticised party members who were behaving 'under the pretext that nothing can be done from the communist viewpoint with Polish elements'.[80] These sentiments were particularly strong amongst activists working in the countryside. They gained sustenance from the deeper roots of racism in rural areas and the experience of immigrant labour being used by employers to undermine conditions of indigenous workers.

The problem of communist activists' relationship with immigrant workers was further complicated by the accommodating approach adopted by the party towards small and middling peasant employers. Immigrant labour tended to be concentrated on the largest farms, while small and medium farms employed a greater proportion of the indigenous population. By stressing a unity of interests between workers and employers on small and middling farms, rather than unity between French workers on smaller farms and immigrant workers on the large, communist policy served to deepen the isolation of immigrants from a section of indigenous agricultural workers.

By 1927 there were signs that immigrant workers were beginning to resist low wages, long hours, and unsanitary accommodation. A report drawn up by the Ministry of Agriculture described the increased propensity of Polish and Czechoslovakian workers to protest about their conditions: 'Sleeping in stables and cowsheds still goes on. . . and the workers find it very hard to accept. They complain of having to put up with the damp and not being able to dry either their clothes or bedding. The lodgings of the personnel not sleeping in the cow-sheds are also often poor.'[81] Most immigrants viewed farm work as a temporary sacrifice and planned to take jobs in industry after completing their contract.[82] Some did not wait: farmers would sometimes awaken to find a whole group of immigrant workers had disappeared overnight. As in the late nineteenth century, the agricultural associations demanded resolute action from the police 'to find workers who have broken their contracts', as well as further legislation to ensure labour was more securely fixed to the farms.[83]

While some immigrants resisted by escaping to the towns, others were begin-ning to attend union meetings and, in a few cases, to participate in strikes.[84] This was a significant step, as foreign workers possessed limited civil rights; although legally entitled to join a union or political party, they were subject to strict surveillance and effectively forbidden to be active members.[85] During the late 1920s, several FUA sections composed exclusively of Polish workers were created in the Paris basin and the union began to ensure that Polish orators and translators were present at its meetings. However, at the 1927 FUA conference in Bordeaux, Boisseau still found it necessary to criticise activists for displaying apathy for work amongst immigrant workers: 'The result is that our immigrant comrades, despite being well disposed towards organisation, feel themselves isolated and, abandoned by the French workers, allow their organisations to die.'[86]

The FUA's policy towards immigrant workers was effectively transformed during the 'class against class' period. The emphasis on 'class unity' encouraged a firm stance against immigration controls and highlighted the importance of recruiting immigrants to the union. The executive made uncompromising state-ments, promising that 'those amongst us who act as accomplices of the employers by struggling against our immigrant comrades' would be 'ruthlessly driven out of the leadership of our sections'.[87] The union's former leadership was attacked at the Central Committee for adopting the 'social-democratic viewpoint' by tolerating articles in the union's journal arguing for quotas on immigration.[88] Immigrants, it was stressed, should not only become members but also be encouraged to participate fully in the leadership of local sections, despite the legal obstacles.[89]

The communists' new approach helped to win support amongst Polish workers in parts of the Brie and Multien. The latter region had witnessed strikes in 1932 (see Chapter 3) and new conflicts broke out in 1934 on a number of big farms, including at Mitry-Mory.[90] The strikes were not solid, faced a large police intervention, and workers returned with only minor concessions.[91] Nevertheless, the communists viewed the conflict as extremely significant, partly because the party had recruited a significant section of strikers.[92] The following year, a new strike broke out involving 200 workers at Mitry-Mory, spreading also to a big farm in nearby Villeparisis. Better prepared, the movement won wage increases of around 15 per cent and a collective contract, granting a ten-hour day, a clause that wages would be increased in the event of inflation, no victimisation for the strike and equal pay and conditions for immigrant workers.[93] This last demand indicates the importance placed by communists on ensuring the participation of the immigrant workers, who were generally paid 2 francs less each day than the French. Farmers clearly expected immigrants to break the strike but Polish men and women were prominent, including during the conflict's key moment when demonstrators chased strikebreakers recruited from amongst local unemployed workers out of the fields.[94]

In contrast to the FUA, the socialist-influenced FNTA maintained its anti-immigrant position. Writing in the FNTA's newspaper, Chaussy complained of 'the harmful consequences of the excessive introduction of immigrant labour' which has meant that in many of the region's rural communes 'the majority of inhabitants are foreigners'.[95] Socialists argued that legislation introduced in August 1932, limiting migrant labour in industry and commerce, should be extended to agriculture. Statements by FNTA leaders and activists struck an implicitly racist tone, drawing a distinction between central European migrants and other workers of immigrant extraction. 'When speaking of the foreign labour force, we should not call into question our Belgian comrades, who have settled in the region with their families for many years', argued one report from the Brie.[96] During the early 1930s the French countryside witnessed 'a veritable wave of xenophobia', in the words of the government-sponsored l'Office central de la main d'oeuvre agricole.[97] While the Socialist Party and CGT were largely contaminated by this mood, communists were generally more immune. The ideology of 'class against class' – which stressed internationalism and the con-struction of a party of politically 'advanced' workers – counteracted temptations to adapt to 'backward' attitudes circulating amongst the mass.

Tensions between communists and socialists over the question of immigrant labour flared up at the FNTA reunification congress in February/March 1936. After Chaussy had insisted that the merged union adopt a policy of quotas, Parsal argued that limitation of immigration was 'a slippery slope' that would reinforce 'national chauvinism amongst the proletariat of the countryside. . . and go against the fundamental aims proclaimed by our movement'.[98] To prevent employers using immigrants to undermine conditions, the union should campaign for equal civil rights. 'If immigrant agricultural workers do not sense the solidarity and support of French workers. . . if they have the feeling that French workers are shunning or blacklisting them, then that's the best way to ensure they become a weapon in the hands of the employers', he declared.[99]

During the period leading up to the Popular Front, restrictions on the civil and employment rights of immigrants were progressively tightened. All immigrant workers in France had been required to carry an identity card granting them permission to work, indicating whether they were a 'travailleur industriel' or a 'travailleur agricole'. In 1933, the Ministry of Labour announced that all applications from immigrant agricultural workers to transfer to 'travailleur industriel' would be refused. Freedom of movement was further reduced by the decree of 6 February 1935 forbidding workers to move from one department to another without special authorisation from the Prefect.[100] These administrative measures only reinforced another reality: the escape route out of agriculture into the towns had, in effect, been blocked by the economic crisis – the trend was now in the opposite direction. Georges Mauco's survey notes that immigrants 'threatened by unemployment in the factories and mines' were moving into agricultural regions 'in order to avoid unemployment or repatriation'.[101] Indeed, throughout 1934, the mining regions of northern France witnessed some harrowing scenes as the authorities crowded immigrant workers and their families on to trains in order to transport them out of the country.[102] Tied economically and administratively to the farms, resistance through collective organisation and activity was, by the mid-1930s, the only practical course for immigrant agricultural workers seeking to improve their quality of life and to emerge from their position as an excluded underclass. Before that was to occur, however, communist agrarian strategy underwent another radical change.

The Peasant Popular Front

The development of the communists' Popular Front policy unfolded in a series of stages. The first was marked by Thorez's speech calling for 'unity at all costs' during the party's National Conference at Ivry in June 1934. Other landmarks included the agreement of a 'united front' with the socialists (July 1934), the extension of the pact to include the Radicals (July 1935), the adoption of a common Popular Front programme in January 1936 and the reunification of the two trade union federations in March 1936. The Popular Front would have been unthinkable without a turn in policy and strategy by the Communist International. The victory of Nazism in Germany encouraged Stalin to begin to search for alliances with remaining European liberal democracies. Negotiations began secretly with the French government in December 1933, culminating with the signing of a military assistance pact between the two countries in May 1935.[103] Simultaneously, the Comintern decreed a more open and collaborative approach towards the socialists and, later, 'democratic elements amongst the bourgeoisie'. But the Popular Front would have been equally unimaginable without social and political pressure emanating from within France, particularly the surge towards unity from rank-and-file trade unionists and left-wing activists after the riots instigated by the extreme right in Paris on 6 February 1934.[104]

The communists' Popular Front policy was motivated by the belief that in order to block the road to fascism the working class, together with its political representatives, should unite with the middle class and its representatives around a programme based on the defence of democracy. Within the context of France's social structure, this meant that great stress was placed on the position within the peasantry. The strategy posed the unity of the peasantry with the working class but also the unity of the disparate sections of the peasantry itself. The idea of a 'Peasant Popular Front' was, therefore, both a distinct and integral part of communist Popular Front policy.

Ideologically, the Popular Front represented a reconciliation of the Communist Party with the French nation, its traditions, myths and institutions. Given that an important element of French nationalism since the later part of the nineteenth century had been the idea of France 'as a peasant nation', this accommodation inevitably reinforced agrarian concepts within the party's thinking. The previous analysis of social relations in the countryside based on class was incrementally sidelined, culminating in the announcement in June 1935 of a project to unite all sections of the peasantry within a 'Peasant Popular Front'. The communists had implicitly posed the question of uniting different social groups within the peasantry when trying to connect with the developing peasant protest movement during the winter of 1932/33; but the question of how broad this 'united front' should become remained ambiguous. The Peasant Popular Front removed the ambiguity and posed the question of organising a movement of the entire peasantry around demands designed to represent its common interests.

The architect of the Peasant Popular Front was Waldeck Rochet who became secretary of the Agrarian Section in April 1934. Rochet's early working life as a market gardener meant that his peasant credentials were not in doubt. Born in 1905, he joined the communists in 1924, part of a generation of activists whose discipline and loyalty was shaped by the process of 'bolshevisation'. His eloquent oratory, often spiced with humour, was delivered with a rough and heavy regional accent once compared to 'certain wines of the Chalonnais'.[105] After a period as leader of the Lyon region, his accession to Agrarian Section brought Rochet on to the national stage and marked an important step on his career path, which would eventually lead him to the position of party general secretary in 1964. Rochet's approach to rural social relations was firmly rooted in the tradition of the trend represented by Renaud Jean. But the latter's opposition during the class against class period and, particularly, his association with the criticisms made by Jacques Doriot – who broke with the party in 1934 before moving towards fascism – would not be forgiven. For a period, Renaud Jean remained the party's peasant face, but Rochet became the key figure in communist agrarian policymaking and was consciously promoted to supplant Renaud Jean as the party's rural spokesperson.

Rochet's policy contained three distinct elements: an approach for united activity to other organisations with support amongst the peasantry, a revised agrarian programme and a re-emphasis in party propaganda away from agricultural workers towards issues relating to the peasantry as a whole. The initiative in relation to political organisation began in October 1934 with an appeal by Rochet for 'the widening of the united front' to include organisations with support amongst paysans travailleurs.[106] While party activists were directed to participate in a demonstration organised by the Front Paysan – an umbrella organisation of various right-wing agrarian movements – the concrete application of the idea, at this point, remained vague.[107] The policy was consolidated in June 1935 when the Agrarian Section agreed to launch a campaign for a peasant congress to form the basis of 'the Popular Front in the countryside'.[108] In an internal party document, Rochet outlined the aim 'to establish a Peasant Popular Front involving peasant organisations from across the political spectrum. It would be supported by elected representatives and activists of the various parties and groups claiming to represent the defence of the peasantry. . . even elements who are our enemies.'[109] The proposed alliance would involve 'Christian, republican, radical, socialist, communist, agrarian and independent peasants, all equally suffering from the impact of the crisis'.[110] Overtures were made through the auspices of the CGPT towards the Agrarian Party, the 'Committees of Peasant Defence' organised by Dorgères, as well as the socialist-inspired Comité national paysan (CNP). Although proposals for united activity were rejected by all three organisations, the communists maintained their basic orientation towards 'peasant unity'. The emphasis of activity was no longer placed on building the CGPT, but on working within 'agricultural syndicates with bourgeois leadership' and establishing 'peasant committees involving organisations of all political persuasions'.[111]

Rochet announced that the party's agrarian platform would be free from 'divisive political and doctrinal questions'.[112] Published in the autumn of 1935, the eight-page 'Programme to rescue French agriculture' [Programme de sauvetage de l'agriculture française] was, as its name suggests, designed to protect the interests of agriculture as an economic sector, rather than the interests of particular social groups within it.[113] Principal demands included a revaluation of agricultural products, relaxation of direct and indirect taxation on the peasantry, reduction of rents for tenant farmers, a moratorium on agricultural debts and the introduction of interest free credits. Despite a dose of rhetoric against 'trusts' and 'speculators' making vast profits in the agricultural supply and transformation industries, any references (as in the Marseille thesis) to the distribution of land held by capitalists and landlords and the socialisation of large farms under the control of workers' co-operatives had disappeared. The great advantage of the programme, underlined Rochet, was that it could be realised immediately 'within the framework of the present social system. . . It does not demand a change of regime, but simply the implementation of a genuine policy of peasant defence'.[114] He proudly announced that the communists had found common agreement on agrarian matters with the Radical Party.[115]

As the party moved towards the adoption of a reformist agrarian programme, so the idea of the primary role of the agricultural proletariat – a notion based on the concept of class struggle in the countryside – receded in importance. Writing in October 1934, Rochet still felt it necessary to cite Lenin's comment that agricultural workers are 'the group on which we must primarily base ourselves in the countryside'.[116] In March 1935, he severely criticised the Agrarian Party for dropping its demands for improvements in agricultural workers' wages and conditions for fear of 'displeasing the employers'.[117] Yet by August 1935, the position had changed dramatically: a full-page poster published in *l'Humanité*, summarising the main points of the new agricultural programme, failed to make any mention of issues specifically relating to agricultural workers.[118] The full version of the programme contained a number of reforms for wage workers, including better wages, reduction in the length of the working day, a weekly break, clean and hygienic lodging, better food, family allowances and the same rights in relation to social insurance as workers in industry.[119] But the fact that in a document of eight pages only one paragraph halfway through the text was devoted to matters relating to agricultural workers is indicative of the new priorities.

Rochet was acutely aware that the idea of peasant unity would resurrect the perennial problem of the relationship between workers and peasant employers. He directly addressed the issue in his speech outlining the new agrarian policy to the Seventh Congress of the Communist International in August 1935. The speech outlined the aim of creating 'committees of coordination and peasant defence' capable of mobilising the 'broad masses' of the peasantry. Such a movement, Rochet argued, should take action to satisfy the demands of the 'mass of agricultural workers [and] the small and middling peasants'.[120] Rochet, however, placed strict limits on the demands that should be raised by agricultural workers within this alliance. While a struggle should be waged 'to defend the wages and improve the working conditions of agricultural workers', it was necessary, he argued, 'to lead this action while taking into account that we must draw into the Popular Front not only the agricultural worker and small peasant but also the middling peasant'.[121] Communists should, therefore, 'support and organise the workers' struggle in defence of their class interests' against 'the capitalist proprietor and farmer employing a large agricultural workforce'. But they should simultaneously work to create 'une espèce d'entente' between 'middling peasants and their workers. . . for a common struggle against the common enemy – the large landowners, capitalist farmers and trusts, the bourgeois state and fascism'.[122] Rochet was, in effect, announcing a return to the position of the mid-1920s, that of 'reconciling' differences between workers and 'small and middling peasant employers'.

At the Comintern congress, Rochet defined the 'middling peasant' as someone 'employing one or two agricultural workers' but, in reality, a more fluid definition arose, one full of ambiguity. Firstly, the definition of the capitalist farmer 'employing a large workforce' was not quantified, which left a category of peasants whose social position was unclear. Should a peasant employing four or five permanent workers be defined as a 'middling peasant' or a 'capitaliste terrien'? Moreover, peasants employing one or two permanent agricultural workers would, in all likelihood, recruit several additional workers during the most intensive seasonal work. Were they still middling peasants, or should they now be regarded as capitalist farmers? Secondly, the definition of the term paysan travailleur changed once again, reverting to the sense in which Renaud Jean and Marius Vazeilles had employed it during the early 1920s. In other words, a farmer employing agricultural workers could be classified as a paysan travailleur, on condition that he was personally involved in the work of the farm.[123] This meant that this category – with which agricultural workers were urged to unite – included many of the relatively large-scale operators that Rochet appeared to be simultaneously defining as 'capitalist farmers'.

Examples of the application of the policy illustrate just how broad the peasant unity sought by the communists actually was. They also show that the new approach was far from understood at all levels of the party. In August 1935, a conference of 'Peasant Defence Committees' was organised in Amiens (Somme) by the Dorgerist sympathiser, Adolphe Pointier, a prominent sugar-beet and wheat farmer. The conference was an assembly of big tenant farmers along with regional representatives of right-wing agrarianism, many of whom would later become leading organisers of opposition to the agricultural workers' strike movement.[124] The initial report of the conference in *l'Humanité* was extremely hostile. Its decisions were denounced as 'a programme of fascist agitation. . . exactly the technique employed by the Croix de feu', the extreme right-wing league led by Colonel de la Rocque.[125] A similar article, also condemning the 'fascist demagogy' employed by the speakers, was printed a few days later in the regional communist press.[126] As it was published, however, a front-page article by Jacques Duclos, effectively the party's deputy leader, appeared in *l'Humanité*. It openly contradicted the conclusions of the original report and gave unqualified support to the decisions of the conference:

> he peasants assembled at Amiens are absolutely right. . . And these peasants do not speak without authority. They represent 500 agricultural associations in Picardy. . . Who could not see their anger. . . the desire to put an end to their wretched situation. . . ? The peasants must unify against their enemies. . . Some speak of a Peasant Front, others of a Peasant Bloc. What does it matter? The main thing is that the 'grand union of the land of France' is organised, that those who work the land are all united to defend themselves.[127]

Duclos' article, with its description of the big tenant farmers and notables leading the agricultural associations as 'paysans' and its sympathy towards the idea of a 'peasant bloc' indicates the extent to which the party had adapted itself to the politics of the right-wing agrarian movement. Previously, communists had excluded the type of gentleman-farmer represented at Amiens from their characterisation of the peasantry, and vehemently opposed the concept of a 'peasant bloc'.

Communists even supported much of the corporatist agenda pursued by the agrarians. In an article, Rochet argued against socialist proposals to establish 'offices' to regulate prices in the agricultural market. But unlike the party's position at the beginning of 'class against class', his opposition was not against the idea in principle but against an increase in the jurisdiction of the state over agriculture. Socialists were described as 'sectarian' for advocating measures towards which 'the peasants are generally rather hostile. . . because they fear being placed. . . under the supervision of state administrators'. Rochet supported the proposal for a Wheat Office but on condition that the institution be established under the control of the peasantry's 'qualified representatives'.[128] In addition, the socialists were attacked for balking at the idea of unity with extreme right-wing forces in the agrarian movement. At the January 1936 party congress, Rochet reported that 'the partisans of the Popular Front. . . are striving to find the path towards achieving the reconciliation of peasant society. Yet certain of our allies in the Popular Front do not want to understand this necessity'.[129]

The communists' view of the relationship between agricultural workers and peasant employers was also extremely close to that of the right-wing agrarians. In practice, communist policy made little differentiation between 'middling peasant' and 'capitalist farmers' but worked for a more general unity between workers and employers. At a large rally organised by right-wing agrarians in Saint-Quentin (Aisne) – which was dominated, as at Amiens, by big tenant farmers – the communists issued a leaflet entitled: 'We are with you, farmers and workers of the fields.' [Avec vous, Cultivateurs et ouvriers des champs.] Sympathising with the position of farmers who could 'no longer' pay their domestics and day labourers a 'sufficient wage' due to the low price of wheat, it called on 'all farming people, producers and workers, to unite for their just and legitimate demands'.[130] Right-wing agrarian propaganda was simultaneously deploying such arguments. In the Oise, the agricultural syndicates circulated petitions in August 1935 complaining that the government's deflationary measures were 'with great regret' going to 'force them to reduce their workers' wages and part with a section of the workforce'. Not without success, they sought the signatures of agricultural workers 'whose lot is intimately linked to that of the farmers'.[131] Dorgères also made an appeal for workers 'to unite with their employers to defend the rights of farmers and so improve their own immediate position' a more prominent part of his discourse.[132]

Communists recognised that this kind of propaganda was gaining an echo amongst a layer of farm workers and viewed the undermining of the influence of the Agrarian Party, the Dorgerists and the Croix de Feu (which in the countryside espoused an openly agrarian ideology) as an essential task in the struggle against fascism. The problem was, though, that many of the party's own arguments gave the agrarian agenda some credence. During a parliamentary by-election in autumn 1935 in an overwhelmingly rural constituency in the Oise, a party propagandist reported:

> At the meeting in Lassigny, two agricultural workers applauded our programme but reacted negatively when I denounced fascism. After the meeting, they approached me and posed me the question: 'You are Croix de Feu, you have the same programme as us.' I explained things to them and asked: 'But do you not fight against your employer (a large Croix de Feu farmer) for your demands?' They responded that he could not pay them more because of the prices at which he sells his produce. 'It's [not him but] capitalism that we are fighting', they replied.[133]

The position of the two Croix de Feu workers was, in effect, almost identical to that argued in the communist leaflet distributed at the Saint-Quentin rally.

Rochet and others in the leadership of the Agrarian Section attempted to redirect the activity of communists working in regions with large numbers of agricultural workers to concur with the new policy. At the Regional Committee of the Aude-Hérault region in February 1935, communists had set themselves the goal of preparing a major strike of vineyard workers in Languedoc. The minutes record: 'Agricultural workers and small wine producers are turning towards us. . . the struggle of agricultural workers is bound to break out this spring in April at the time of [crop] spraying. Close to 30–40,000 strikers can be anticipated. The party must be the guide, the driving force.'[134] During the subsequent months, communists in the region conducted a major propaganda campaign in support of demands submitted by the agricultural workers' union. Although a conflict did not occur in the spring, agitation continued with the target of organising a major strike to coincide with the grape harvest in September. As general secretary of the FUA, Parsal oversaw the project and made a number of visits to the region.[135] In June, however, Rochet proposed a major turn in the activity of the agricultural workers' union in Languedoc. The new task outlined was to reach 'an agreement between agricultural workers' unions, representatives of different political parties, and organisations of the CGV [the wine producers' federation]. . . to convene in the autumn the largest possible Congress for the Defence of the Wine Industry'.[136] To achieve this aim would mean, Rochet stressed, 'changing the methods of work employed up to now' by local activists and regional party organisations. He proposed that a member of the Agrarian Section should conduct an extended tour of the region to oversee the new strategy and to 'lay the foundations' for the congress. His choice of delegate is significant: 'I think that it would not be a bad thing to appoint Parsal.'[137] Rochet's proposal was, therefore, that Parsal's priorities should change from overseeing the preparations for a major strike movement to preparing the ground for united activity with an organisation (the CGV) described by the party only fifteen months earlier as representing 'the biggest exploiters of agricultural workers in the region'.[138]

The focus of the party's propaganda was once again centred on the problems faced by the small and middling peasantry. In certain regions, the reorientation was quite remarkable. The Nord-Pas-de-Calais regional party had been criticised at the Central Committee in January 1934 for possessing 'a quite pronounced sectarian tendency. . . to consider that nothing could be done amongst paysans travailleurs. . . [who] constitute a class bloc against the proletariat'.[139] By August 1935, the regional party newspaper was describing local sugar-beet farmers as the 'pariahs of the land' – a term previously reserved to describe agricultural workers.[140] Without a hint of criticism, the paper published statements by Pierre Leclercq, leader of the sugar-beet farmers' federation and prominent Dorgerist, who the following year would organise the strikebreaking operation against the agricultural workers' strike movement.[141] There were similar trends in other regions, even some in which communists had conducted important campaigns amongst agricultural workers during the preceding period. Between February and April 1936, the weekly paper covering Étampes carried ten articles on agriculture, without a single specific mention of agricultural workers.[142]

At national level, the situation in the countryside comprised an important aspect of communist propaganda during the Popular Front election campaign. In his celebrated radio address on the eve of the poll, published as 'For a Free, Strong and Happy France' [Pour une France libre, forte et heureuse], Maurice Thorez conjured up images of 'fertile soil raising beautiful harvests. . . a traditional country of rich arable land'. He spoke of 'small proprietors, farmers and sharecroppers. . . and the erosion and ruin of French agriculture'. But he made not a single reference to agricultural workers.[143] Similarly, the propaganda film, La Vie est à Nous opens with a sequence depicting wheat fields in a large-scale farming region, symbolising an element of the imagined majesty of modern France. But those employed on the farms are conspicuously absent, in contrast to an important section of the film highlighting the struggles of the self-employed peasantry.

The official position adopted by the party in 1935 was rooted in the tradition of the 'peasantist' trend on the agrarian question that first emerged in pre-1914 socialism. In this sense, there was nothing fundamentally new about the communists' Popular Front peasant policy. Arguments that the inadequate price of wheat did not 'permit' farmers to pay just wages to their workers were remarkably similar to one of the clauses in the 1894 Nantes programme singled out for censure by Engels; so too was the call for 'producers and workers' to unite around 'just and legitimate' demands. Yet, despite the prevalence of communist agrarianism, the second trend – that represented by Longuet in the pre-1914 SFIO and given expression by Dunois in the early Communist Party – also continued to manifest itself. For six years, between mid-1929 and mid-1935, the party had held that the principle activity in the countryside should be amongst agricultural workers. Not only had an important layer of activists been imbued with this idea, but the tendency amongst agricultural workers towards collective organisation and strike activity during 1934 and 1935 – albeit extremely limited – helped also to ensure that many communists continued to approach the 'peasant question' primarily from a class viewpoint.

The major conflict that broke out in the Midi during autumn 1935 would quickly illustrate the tensions between the two contradictory trends. Starting on 2 September with 4000 grape-pickers at Narbonne, the movement spread through the Languedoc wine-producing region from Perpignan to Arles, involving possibly 80,000 workers.[144] The strike's catalyst was an energetic series of meetings, conferences and demonstrations, organised by communist activists throughout Languedoc. Despite the proposal of Rochet that party members should adjust their political priorities towards a joint initiative with employers in defence of the wine industry, the emphasis of activity had remained on promoting a strike between workers and vine growers. This was one of the biggest conflicts involving any group of workers in the period preceding the election of the Popular Front government. Some of the methods of the May/June 1936 'social explosion' were even anticipated: l'Humanité reported that 'at Béziers, a large number of grape-pickers had taken part in a sit-down strike' [grève sur le tas].[145] Winning a series of concessions from vine growers, the strike not only consolidated the communists' position over the socialists as regional leaders of the agricultural workers, it also forged the partnership between Parsal and Michel Rius that would lead the FNTA at national level during the Popular Front period. Born in the Pyrenees in 1904, Rius joined the party at the age of 20. By the end of the 1920s, he had become a leader in the Perpignan region and in 1935 was the secretary of the Languedoc region of the CGTU. During the strike, he and Parsal toured the picket lines riding tandem on the back of a rickety motorcycle. At the national reunification conference the following year, Rius would become the FNTA's administrative secretary and effectively the union's second-in-command.[146]

Publicly, attempts were made by members of the Agrarian Section to reconcile the strike with the policy of 'peasant unity'. An article on the front page of 'l'Humanité highlighted the 'reciprocal solidarity' displayed between workers and small proprietors. 'Previously, grapepickers placed big landed proprietors and small producers on an equal footing. Times have changed. We live in the epoch of the Popular Front', it declared.[147] Privately, however, the position was not viewed so optimistically. At the October Central Committee, François Mioch, a member of the Agrarian Section, expressed concern at the 'sectarianism' adopted by strikers towards the 'middling peasantry': 'On that issue,' he observed, 'we still have much to do.'[148]

The frustrations of Mioch were partly due to the way in which communist activists within the agricultural workers' union had interpreted the issue of peasant unity during the conflict. At the end of September, Parsal reported on the strike in an address to the CGTU National Congress. He noted that small producers had supported the workers' movement, even participating in strike pickets: 'It's an indication that, as long as the issues are explained, workers and small peasants can march hand in hand.' Parsal, however, was employing the term 'petit paysan' in the sense it had been defined at the Comintern's Second Congress. In other words, his point was that unity had been achieved between workers and those peasants who did not employ wage labour and perhaps sometimes hired themselves out to work on the large estates. For Parsal, the important lesson of the conflict and the key to its success was that *vignerons* had rejected the idea that 'everyone had the same interests' and 'had realised that they could not hope of success through marching hand in hand with their employers'. Moreover, in his speech, Parsal associated the idea that 'workers should struggle together with their employers to defend the general interests of viticulture' with the arguments of Dorgères and the 'fascist Peasant Front'.[149] He would, of course, have been perfectly aware that Rochet and the party's Agrarian Section had been advocating exactly this aim since the previous summer.

On the eve of the Popular Front elections, communist policy in the countryside was, therefore, far from uniform. A large factor in determining the position adopted in different regions was the pressure emanating from the agricultural workers' movement. Where it was weakest – either because agricultural workers were few in number, or because they still largely viewed their interests as synonymous with peasant employers – communists effectuated a shift in strategy towards the wider peasantry without difficulty. But in regions where class differentiation was manifesting itself through agricultural workers' demands and organisation, the party's approach was often at variance to the national line. The Calais communists fell under the jurisdiction of the Nord-Pas-de-Calais regional committee which, as noted, made a quite dramatic reorientation towards the middling peasantry during the summer of 1935. But despite the fact that paysans travailleurs made up a large proportion of the rural population in the countryside around Calais, the local party maintained its prioritisation of agricultural workers, guided less by theoretical concerns than by practical successes. In the Beauce, the communist paper carried an article in March 1936 that argued: 'to form a bloc of the peasantry is a false position. . . it's an absurdity to want to group together the lord of the manor, big farmer, small peasant and carter. Their interests are opposed: some are wage workers, others exploiters.'[150]

Communists were in a large majority at the congress to reunify the two agricultural workers' unions held on 29 Feburary/1 March 1936, defeating the socialists on contentious issues by 243 votes to 25. Throughout the congress, they differentiated themselves from the leadership of the former FNTA by stressing their militant credentials. In his keynote speech, Arthur Chaussy urged moderation, arguing that 'the strike isn't the only weapon for workers. . . and must be used only when every possibility of conciliation has been exhausted'.[151] Parsal, in contrast, held up the strikes at Mitry-Mory in 1934 and 1935 as models to be followed by the new union. In contrast to his party's programme 'to save French agriculture', Parsal argued that 'French agriculture is a capitalist agriculture' and any notion that France is a 'country of small property. . . in which large farms comprise an exception. . . does not correspond to reality'.[152] His declaration was uncompromising:

> Our united Federation. . . will be a Federation of class struggle. We will repudiate any tactic of collaboration with the bourgeoisie. . . Our congress must raise the standard of struggle high and with confidence so that agricultural workers will no longer be the pariahs facing poverty and hunger on this rich land of France.[153]

It was this message, rather than the belief in an entente between employers and workers, that a considerable section of communist activists would take to agricultural workers during the events following the election of Léon Blum's Popular Front government.

5

REBELLION IN THE FIELDS, 1936–37

In terms of numbers involved, the rural conflict during the Popular Front period appears insignificant when compared with the eruption in the towns. But the 'powder trail' of strikes was, nonetheless, extraordinary.[1] Participants included vine workers in the Médoc, Champagne and Languedoc regions, forestry workers in the Nièvre, sharecroppers and labourers extracting resin in the forests of the Landes, workers employed on establishments supplying fruit and vegetables to major towns and cities (including Saint-Étienne) and labourers on farms on the Forez Plain in the Auvergne. Strikes broke out in Corsica and amongst indigenous workers employed on estates operated by colons in 'French Algeria'. The conflict's epicentre – in terms of intensity and scale – was situated in the farming regions of the Paris basin and northern France. Drawing a circle with a radius of 200 kilometres around the capital, farm strikes can be found in almost every direction: to the north and east, in the Brie, Soissonnais and Valois; further north, on the Picardy plain and its neighbouring regions surrounding Arras, Cambrai and Beauvais; along the coast around Calais and Dunkerque, looking north westerly, in the French and Normandy Vexin and the Caux; to the south of the capital, around Versailles, Pithiviers and in the Berry. The list is far from exhaustive.

The conflict in the Paris basin and north developed in a sequence of stages. An initial series of strikes in May-June 1936, which some have described as 'spontaneous', was followed by a more co-ordinated and broader movement beginning on 20 July. These two stages will be illustrated with examples drawn from the Calais region and Artois. There followed a third phase of more dispersed actions during the late summer and autumn.[2] The spring and summer of 1937 was marked by a series of sometimes long, bitter disputes, the outcome of which must be considered a major defeat for the agricultural workers' movement.

For the Communist Party, the farm strikes posed the same fundamental problems as previous movements of agricultural workers. But its relationship with the movement was now additionally conditioned by the party's new position within French politics and society. A major player in terms of votes and parliamentary representation, the party had abandoned its aim of a revolutionary transformation of society and, in face of the threat of fascism, was committed to the defence of 'national democratic unity' and republican institutions. The 'social explosion', however, expressed the desire of wide sections of the population for radical change, and many of its animators identified with the communists, not because of the party's apparent conversion to democracy but because of its revolutionary reputation.

Consequently, the Communist Party's position towards social conflicts had to balance two considerations. As Bertrand Badie has outlined, its intervention was, on the one hand, 'functional for the political system': working to preserve 'order', 'calm' and 'discipline', it 'contributed to the persistence of the French political system during a period in which it was marked by a strong loss of support and great instability'. On the other hand, the party sought to ensure that 'no aspect of its behaviour put into peril the symbiosis with its grassroots'.[3] So, while the Popular Front period saw the Communist Party emerge as a party rooted in and loyal to the French political system, it also introduced its role as a 'tribune party', to use the expression of Georges Lavau – one that gained its fundamental strength by voicing the demands of the working masses for improved conditions of life.[4] This led to contradictions. Party leaders sometimes urged prudence and restraint on to the social movement, while party activists were simultaneously encouraging or leading workers into action. In relation to the agricultural workers' movement, this paradox was personalised in the behaviour of Parsal, who was not only leader of the agricultural workers, whose demands and aspirations he would continue to reflect, but also now a deputy in parliament – more directly, therefore, under the influence and discipline of the party hierarchy.

The surge of unionism and outbreak of strikes amongst farm workers prompted a readjustment in communist priorities in the countryside. Although agricultural workers had been sidelined during the Popular Front election campaign, they featured prominently in the party's discourse during the summer of 1936. Leading party committees closely followed the conflict. On 13 June, the Central Committee 'saluted' the struggle of 'the agricultural workers of Seine-et-Marne'.[5] On 25 June, the Political Bureau agreed to 'assist the work' of the agricultural workers' union; further discussions about the strikes took place at the Secretariat on 20 July.[6] The FNTA was, in fact, the only union specifically recorded in the minutes of the Political Bureau and Secretariat during the Popular Front strike wave. The movement was regarded as an opportunity to extend influence over an important section of society – in terms of numbers and its social position within the peasantry – that was undergoing a process of radicalisation.

But the party's attention to the agricultural workers' movement was, of course, shaped by another consideration. The decision to propose Renaud Jean to become the President of the Commission of Agriculture in the Chamber of Deputies is another illustration of the significance of the peasantry within the Popular Front strategy. It is not surprising, therefore, that the impact of the strikes on peasant supporters of the Popular Front was closely monitored. In early July, Mioch reported that while increases in workers' wages and the proposed social reforms were provoking concern amongst small and middling proprietors, 'fascism in the countryside' was particularly 'taking advantage of agricultural workers' strikes and farm occupations'. When taking strike action, 'agricultural workers,' he argued, 'must be careful not to hamper in any way the work of small and middling farms'.[7] The repercussions of the strikes for the party's policy of peasant unity will be examined in Chapter 7, along with the contradictory ways in which communists sought to balance this aim with support for the workers' movement. This chapter traces the evolution of the movement, focusing primarily on the Paris basin and northern France.

'We will no longer be Common Bastards'

The farm strikes were anticipated by a major shift in voting behaviour by agricultural workers during the 1936 legislative elections. 'The countryside has voted red', headlined the local newspaper in Soissons, after the left parties polled 60–65 per cent in villages with large concentrations of farm workers.[8] 'Bravo. . . our sincere thanks are due to the proletariat of the fields', proclaimed the socialist paper in the Valois, after victories in Senlis and Nanteuil.[9] Similar articles appeared in the communist regional press. The front page of the paper covering Étampes declared: 'We honestly admit that the cause of Agricultural Workers was not sufficiently defended during the period of the election. . . On many occasions, meetings finished without us raising the important problem of the agricultural workforce. We must therefore pay an even more glowing tribute to this category of hearty workers. . . who have understood their class duty by voting for the Popular Front.'[10] Local studies have shown that farm workers' votes were decisive in winning seats for the left in rural constituencies centred on Laon and Arras.[11] In relation to the Brie, Philippe Bernard notes that 'the countryside was, taken as a whole, more to the left than the towns'.[12]

With confidence enhanced by the fact that its two principal leaders were now deputies,[13] the FNTA executive met on 11 May and formulated a nine-point programme to present to the incoming government. It centred on wages, the limitation of working hours and the extension of social reforms already acquired by workers in industry and commerce, including family allowances, health and safety inspections, social insurance, arbitration of disputes and the right to draw unemployment benefits.[14] At local level, the *cahiers* drawn up by ordinary agricultural workers were not only more eloquent but also sometimes dealt with wider issues. In the Caux, workers at Offranville (Seine-Inférieure) described themselves as 'the forgotten men' now demanding the right 'to enjoy the freedom accorded to all citizens':

> No more obligation to attend religious services, to accompany employers to their election meetings, no more votes with open ballot papers under the conniving eyes of certain mayors, compulsory passage to the polling booth. Confident in our just cause, we ask our employers to grant faithfully these modest demands; we ask the government to help us win them; so that in the French family we will no longer be the common bastards.[15]

Many farm workers thus viewed the election of the Popular Front as an opportunity to win an independent relationship with society. Alongside issues relating to wages and conditions arose the demand for the rights of citizenship: the right to vote privately, to practice or not to practice a religion, to socialise freely; in short, to live with dignity without intrusion from employers.

The first strikes unfolded in the Vermand region (north of Saint-Quentin) and in the Multien (north-east of Paris), starting on 16 and 18 May respectively – that is one week prior to the main strike movement in industry, which took off in a general fashion after the demonstration at the Mur des Fédérées on 24 May. The strike in the Vermandois was the culmination of the campaign waged by communists following events at Prémont in October 1935 (see Chapter 4). The impulse was a meeting organised at Beaurevoir (Aisne) on 29 March, at which workers from several villages drew up a programme and agreed to organise a regional congress of farm workers.[16] Over the next few weeks, twelve agricultural workers' unions were established.[17] When farmers rejected workers' demands, the congress, held on 10 May and attended by eighty delegates as well as national union officials (including Michel Rius), agreed the principle of strike action.[18] Communist activists toured the villages, addressing meetings and urging workers to join the stoppage.[19] The movement, which lasted until 26 May, took the authorities by surprise and has left only traces in the archives. L'Humanité reported that it covered 'around fifteen villages'; the regional public prosecutor mentions eight.[20] According to the local press, between 30 and 70 per cent of workers (depending on the village) joined the strike, both day labourers and domestics.[21] The outcome was mixed: in some villages, farmers agreed to raise wage rates for the impending work on sugar beet; in others, workers returned without concessions.[22] The movement in the Multien is better known as a result of a contemporary sociological study of events at Tremblay-lès-Gonesse (Seine-et-Oise).[23] Its roots can be traced to the dispute in the commune in 1932 and those in neighbouring Mitry-Mory during 1934 and 1935. The immediate catalyst was a major rally of agricultural workers held in Mitry-Mory on 17 May, addressed by Parsal.[24] Starting with 130 strikers at Tremblay,[25] the movement spread to other villages in the region a week later, including Le

Mesnil-Amelot and Villeneuve-Dammartin.[26] By the time workers returned to the farms on 15 June, it had involved over 1000 workers in the Seine-et-Oise department and 202 workers on eight farms in the Seine-et-Marne.[27]

The first two farm strikes had an immediate political impact: 'This agrarian movement of the extreme left. . . has worried political circles', commented a local newspaper.[28] Outgoing Prime Minister, Albert Sarraut, intervened personally in an attempt to resolve the dispute at Tremblay.[29] That the conflict could have such an effect at a time when a far more extensive movement was beginning to sweep through industry is another indication of the role of agriculture in the national psyche.

As workers in the Multien returned to the farms, strikes began to break out in departments across north-east France. In the Seine-et-Oise, the conflict was particularly sharp in the Magny-en-Vexin region, with the regional communist press reporting that 'certain big landlords. . . [were] threatening to open fire on anyone approaching their property'.[30] In the market gardening region centred on Achères, 1000 workers achieved most of their demands after a short strike on 9 June (there were other disputes in market gardening in the Paris suburbs at Gennevilliers, Maisons-Alfort, Créteil and around Versailles).[31] From 12 June, strikes broke out around Boissy-Saint-Léger and Corbeil. According to the communist press, '23 localities' were involved, although administrative sources mention only 9.[32] Strikes were also reported in the Montfort and Saint-Rémy-lès-Chevreuse regions.[33] In the Seine-et-Marne, 170 workers stopped work on 18 farms in the Brie (including at Fontenay-Tresigny, Roissy-en-Brie, Machault, Féricy) and a dispute involving 20 workers on a farm in Barbey on the Yonne river.[34] In the Aisne, the movement was more extensive. Strikes began to touch the countryside around Saint-Quentin from 13 June and farms around Soissons on 15 June, with reports of stoppages in eighteen communes. The Laon and Vervins regions were also touched.[35] A strike on 40–45 farms in fifteen communes in the Marle-Cilly region began on 17 July; reports indicating that between 600 and 740 workers were involved.[36] The movement in the Oise began on 12 June at Levignan, in the Valois.[37] From 15 June, ten localities surrounding Méru were affected, involving 340 workers on around 20 farms.[38] On 29 June, 644 workers stopped work on 145 farms in the Neuilly-en-Thelle canton.[39] There were also strikes in the Auneau, Chaumont-en-Vexin and Clermont regions, as well as on the giant Boullenger farm employing 107 workers at Moyenville.[40] In the Somme, the conflict was mainly centred on the Santerre region.[41] In the Caux (Seine-Inférieure), there were strikes in nine communes; the numbers involved are not known, though at Les Loges police reported 'around one hundred strikers'.[42] In the Nord, the movement swept the countryside around Dunkerque. It began amongst seasonal workers recruited by gangmasters and hired to farmers, many of whom ran relatively small concerns, and reached the Flemish villages of Quaëdypre and Ghyvelde on the Belgium border.[43] The

Cambrais region was hit from 10 June, including the Prouvy-Haspres area, Avesnes-le-Sec, Troisvilles, Rumilly, Beauvais, Caullery, Selvigny, Fontaine-au-Pire, Villers-Outréaux and Solesmes.[44] A settlement signed between the CGT and agricultural employers on 18 June, granting most of the workers' demands, provided the impetus for strikes to spread into the adjoining Pas-de-Calais department around Marquion. In the Marne, there were stoppages on a number of farms around Reims.[45] In the Champagne region, strikes began on 12 June and by 22 June there were 'at least 1000 vine workers on strike'.[46] In the Beauce and the Berry, agitation swept through hiring fairs taking place during the third week of June. With the participation of local communists, workers at Narcy (Nièvre) organised a meeting to establish common demands, forcing wage concessions of between 10 and 20 per cent.[47] At Auneau (Eure-et-Loir), a 400-strong meeting elected a committee to represent different categories of workers and to draw up a list of conditions to present to farmers. Workers then marched through the streets and established pickets outside the town's two hiring offices.[48]

The Communists and the Calais Strike Movement

The dynamic of this first stage of strikes can be illustrated by a regional case study. The farm conflict in the Pas-de-Calais has understandably been over-shadowed by the scales of the strikes in the department's mines, docks, engineering and other industries.[49] There are, however, reasons why a closer examination is appropriate. Firstly, the movement that swept the countryside surrounding Calais and Guînes was not only, in terms of numbers, the most important after those in the Vermand and Multien, but it was also the first to raise concretely for communists the problem of the impact of the strikes on small and middling farmers. Secondly, the strike movement that broke out in the Artois in late July was probably the sharpest confrontation, either industrial or agricultural, up to that point under the Popular Front government. It was the first systematic case of organised strikebreaking and served as a model for the 'revenge' of farmers' organisations during the summer of 1937.

Although primarily an industrial department, agriculture was an extremely important sector of the economy in the Pas-de-Calais — an illustration of the connection between a process of industrialisation and surrounding agricultural structures and methods. The Pas-de-Calais possessed only 1.6 per cent of French agricultural territory but, between 1930 and 1939, produced 4 per cent of the nation's wheat, 5 per cent of its oats, 12 per cent of its sugar beet, 3 per cent of its butter and 2 per cent of its milk.[50] The proximity to well-populated and easily accessible outlets for produce had led to the development of an 'intensive, highly commercialised agriculture, firmly inserted in the market economy'.[51] Agriculture was, however, less concentrated than in other strike-hit departments closer to Paris. Of 31,240 agricultural holdings, 13,448 (43 per cent) did not employ any workers, relying totally on family labour; 17,045 (54.6 per cent) employed between one and five workers, while 605 (1.9 per cent) employed between six and ten; 142 (0.5 per cent) farmers employed more than ten.

The above figures show the position at departmental level and, of course, hide local variations. In parts of the department's west, farming was primarily dedicated to rearing livestock, which was less labour intensive than crop production and did not involve recruiting large numbers of seasonal workers. Here, agricultural workers, whose isolation was increased by the generally dispersed nature of farming, found it hardest to find an independent voice. The west of the department was untouched by the strikes of 1936 but in some areas in which farming was more geared towards crop production, particularly around Montreuil, employers took the threat of one seriously enough, taking the precaution of raising wages in order diminish the likelihood.[52] The agricultural workers' movement did not reach Montreuil until July 1937, when a communist, Georges Darribère, organised a meeting of a thousand workers at Montreuil and another at Alette.[53] In the department's east, fields were cultivated with wheat, sugar beet and, nearer the coast, vegetables and chicory. These crops required a larger labour force and there were significant concentrations of both day labourers and domestics living on the farms. Agricultural areas were also nearer to the industrial centres and therefore closer to the influence of the political left. The predominant feature of the region to the south-east of Arras, one of the centres of the July-August strike, was that of small rural centres of 500 or so inhabitants surrounded by featureless open fields. Geological reasons (the need to create deep wells for water) had led to the concentration of farms in the villages, also concentrating the agricultural workers who were often the largest social group in the population.

A study of rural social relations in the Artois describes the big farmers as belonging to a 'farmocracy'.[54] Many were descendants of village lieutenants responsible for managing the estates and dispensing the authority of noble landlords under the *ancien regime* who, after the Revolution, continued to dominate village life by becoming important local employers as well as village mayors. However, the social structure of agriculture meant that the big farmer was generally surrounded by a large number of small and middling farmers, invariably identifying with him in a deferential manner. This meant that agricultural workers' strikes would potentially involve significant numbers of small and middling farmers and face, therefore, a group of employers with sufficient social reserves to organise serious resistance.

Deep rooted sentiments helped fuel farmers' belligerence in the face of workers' demands. The mentality of rural society in the Pas-de-Calais during the first part of the twentieth century has been described by Hubscher as a 'front du refus' in relation to the industrial world, its ideas and influences – the outcome of a contradictory relationship in which farmers had accepted the benefits of an agriculture linked into a huge exchange system, but rejected the economic subordination that accompanied it.[55] The 'social explosion' in the towns, coming in the wake of the agricultural crisis, reinforced this outlook. At markets, farmers faced action by groups of working-class women demanding reductions in prices. In Calais, on 13 June, for example, farmers were forced to mark down the prices of butter and eggs, later complaining that strikers' wives were 'helping themselves and only paying the prices they wanted to'.[56] Similar occurrences took place at Guînes, Saint-Pol, Bruay, Pont-à-Vendin and Pernes-en-Artois, where a 'demonstration of housewives led by a red flag paraded through the streets of the village demanding a freeze on the prices of butter and milk'.[57] The aggression was, however, not all in one direction. In the neighbouring Nord department, police marshalling a workers' demonstration through the village of Écaillon reported how 'several inhabitants were preparing to repel the demonstrators with pitch-folks and other weapons'.[58] In the Pas-de-Calais, as in other regions, there was, in effect, a certain urban-versus-rural aspect to the Popular Front conflict.[59]

The first farm strike in the department was initiated by the communist-controlled agricultural workers' union based at Marck (whose history has been traced in Chapter 4). Shortly after the Popular Front elections (14 May), a meeting agreed a *cahier* to present to local farmers. It specified wage increases for day labourers and domestics, a maximum ten-hour working with a day-off each week, healthy and plentiful food and drink for workers lodged on the farms, as well as hygienic living conditions and heating during the winter. Regarding women, it claimed 'equal pay for equal work'.[60]

The *cahier* formed the basis of the movement's demands as it spread to farms on the outskirts of Calais, before fanning out into the countryside around Marquise, Guînes, Ardres and Audruicq. There are also reports of strikes reaching the outskirts of Rinxent and the canton of Desvres; *L'Humanité* reported 'victories' in Tilques and Arques, near Saint-Omer.[61] All sections of the workforce were involved: at Nielles-lès-Calais the breakdown of strikers was 10 domestics, 10 male day labourers, 10 women and 5 children; at Saint-Tricat it was 58 men, 22 women and 14 children.[62] Table 2 details the position in 21 communes and indicates how the strike broadened in a 'snow-ball' fashion. At Guînes, according to the police, the strike began after 60 strikers arrived on bicycles: 'singing the Internationale, they continuously rode through the locality and its outskirts calling workers out on strike.'[63] The next day, the Guînes farm workers visited the nearby communes of Hames-Boucres and Andres, where 100 workers on 12 farms immediately stopped work.[64] The relation of strikers to farms shows an average of 4.8 workers on strike in each establishment, but hides big variations within and between communes. Amongst the first to join the strike were three farms employing a total of 35 workers at Sangatte and one employing 20 on the

Table 2. Strikes in the Calais/Guînes/Saint-Omer Region,
June–July 1936

Commune	Strike started	Strike settled	Strikers	Farms affected	Average strikers per farm
Marck	10 June	19 June	200	35	5.7
Calais	12 June	22 June	20	1	20.0
Sangatte	13 June	22 June	98	20	4.9
Fréthun	15 June	20 June	54	11	4.9
Guînes	15 June	8 July	80	6	13.3
Nielles-lès-Calais	16 June	20 June	35	3	11.7
Saint-Tricat	16 June	20 June	94	13	7.2
Coquelles	16 June	20 June	80	15	5.3
Ferques	17 June	18 June	(nk)	(nk)	
Campagnes-lès-Guînes	17 June	21 June	66	15	4.4
Andres	17 June	28 June	100	12	8.3
Landrethun	17 June	18 June	(nk)	(nk)	
Pihen-lès-Guînes	18 June	22 June	70	12	5.8
Hames-Boucres	18 June	22 June	100	15	6.7
Balinghem	18 June	18 June	9	2	4.5
Les Attaques	18 June	24 June	12	4	3.0
Oye-Plage	18 June	24 June	140	60	2.3
Bonnigues-lès-Calais	20 June	24 June	30	9	3.3
Peuplingues	20 June	24 June	40	9	4.4
Arques	(nk)	21 June	(nk)	(nk)	
Tilques	(nk)	22 June	(nk)	(nk)	
Vieille-Église	23 June	25 June	150	50	3.0
Nouvelle-Église	23 June	25 June	60	7	8.6
Quelmes	24 June	(nk)	20	7	2.9
Totals			1458	306	4.8

(nk = information not known)

Sources: AD Pas-de-Calais, M4456, 2Z93, 2Z152, M/DSA286, M2405.

outskirts of Calais. The six farms to join the movement at Guînes included two that employed 28 and 25 workers.[65] In every commune, however, both big and small farms were touched. As the strike spread, it drew in a larger proportion of smaller farmers, most particularly when it reached communes in the Saint-Omer arrondissement (including Oye-Plage, Vieille-Église and Quelmes).

Communists played an important role in escalating the conflict. Particularly prominent was Charles Roussel, a railway worker and Calais municipal councillor, who had directed the communist campaign amongst agricultural workers since 1935 and now emerged as their principal organiser and spokesperson. At the beginning of the third week of June, however, Roussel suddenly adopted a cautious approach to any further extension of the movement and proffered a conciliatory hand towards the farmers. His volte-face was fully consistent with directives arriving from the union leadership in Paris. Like Roussel, Parsal and Rius, the union's two most prominent figures, had taken an uncompromising position when helping to instigate and build the early strike movements, particularly in the Vermandois and Multien. But after Thorez's speech on 11 June, their approach softened. With emphasis now placed on restraint, the union issued statements expressing the desire to prevent 'the current agitation taking on an acute character' and instructing workers 'to launch new strikes only when the trade unions are in complete agreement and after referring the matter to the Federation'.[66]

The moderate approach was on display when negotiations to resolve the conflict in the Calais region opened on 18 June at the Bourgogne Sub-Prefecture. Present at the talks were the regional agricultural association, a CGT delegation led by Roussel, and the Boulogne Sub-Prefect. Immediately the parties issued a joint 'appeal to the agricultural population' urging that 'when demands of agricultural workers arise, it is in the interests of the two parties that work should not immediately stop'.[67] Agreement was then quickly reached on trade union rights, overtime payments, improved hygiene and paid holidays, though on this latter issue the accord amounted to a promise by farmers to implement future legislation rather than make immediate concessions.

The wages question, however, gave rise to 'stormy discussions', in the words of the Sub-Prefect who was presiding.[68] Initially, farmers' representatives proposed a sliding scale linking wages to the price of wheat. This was rejected resolutely by the CGT representatives, who demanded that wages should relate to the character of work carried out and its duration. Farmers then proposed an increase of 12 per cent on daily wages and 10 per cent for piecework – a settlement, they claimed, based on the Matignon accord. The offer fell far short of workers' demands: a daily wage of 25 francs for day labourers, which in percentage terms amounted to rises of up to 40 or 50 per cent. Moreover, a percentage increase was contrary to one of the central demands of the strike: a guaranteed minimum wage rate to remove the sometimes enormous discrepancies between wages paid in neighbouring communes, on neighbouring farms and even amongst workers on the same farm. The right to pay such differences was almost sacrosanct for many farmers. It symbolised a paternalistic relationship between employer and worker; while a regionally agreed minimum would acknowledge the collective rights of the workers. To the amazement of the Sub-Prefect, the CGT delegation accepted the farmers' offer. 'By accepting this last proposal the workers' delegates were really conciliatory', he remarked, 'but it did not occur to them that the application of these percentages to the excessively low wages found on many farms was not going to satisfy an important section of striking agricultural workers.'[69] Despite the Sub-Prefect's suggestion that a minimum wage rate be specified, on to which the proposed increases would apply, Roussel was not prepared to pursue the issue, signed the agreement and issued an instruction to end the strike.[70]

The following morning, strikers were furious that the farmers' offer had been accepted. 'Just as I feared', reported the Sub-Prefect, 'this morning despite the order for a return to work issued by the delegate of the agricultural workers' organisations, the striking workers have not returned to the farms: they have met and rejected the proposals, thus disowning their delegates.'[71] In Guînes, workers organised a new demonstration through the streets; at Saint-Tricat strikers occupied the *mairie*; at Oye-Plage, the authorities were astonished by the 'inflexibility' of local strike leaders, mostly Communist Party members or supporters.[72] New villages also now joined the stoppage, including Peuplingues and Bonnigues. In order to end the strike, farmers began to negotiate at village level. At Marck, the union won the majority of its claim, including 25 francs-a-day, and payment of strike days at unemployment rates.[73] The Guînes strikers stayed out longest and were rewarded with the highest wages, 26.66 francs-a-day.[74] By continuing the strike, most workers gained concessions far closer to their original demands than the accord negotiated by Roussel at the Sub-Prefecture.

The lessons of the agricultural movement dominated the agenda at the founding conference of the party's newly established Pas-de-Calais region on 28 June. In fact, the extent to which the problem of social relations in the countryside preoccupied communists in a predominantly industrial department is quite remarkable. Delegates were elated by the positive results of the farm strikes. But Léon Mauvais, the Central Committee representative, expressed unease in his report to party headquarters:

In the sector of St Omer there have been many movements involving agricultural workers led by comrades of our Party. Some very important victories have been achieved. However there has been some friction involving several small and middling peasants, whose situation is obviously difficult and who have been put into greater difficulty by certain of the workers' demands.[75]

Mauvais devoted the larger part of his closing speech to the peasant question. He stressed that party activists were obliged to work to 'unite the peasants' and 'protect them from the demagogy of the fascists'.[76]

In the aftermath of the strikes, many small and middling farmers in the region were, indeed, radicalised in a rightward direction. Two political trends were able to give expression to their mood: the Dorgerists and the Parti social français (PSF), the reincarnation of the Croix de feu, which had been banned by the Blum government.[77] Pascal Ory has noted how, during the Popular Front period, the centre of gravity of support for the Dorgerist movement shifted decisively from its heartland in the west of the country towards the Pas-de-Calais and Nord departments, as well as the Parisian 'green belt'.[78] The growth of Dorgerism in these regions can be directly related to its ability to mobilise farmers touched by, or in fear of being touched by, the agricultural strikes.[79] This required some rapid political readjustments by Dorgères. During the early days of the Popular Front government, he had presented a 'peasant programme' that included far-reaching reforms for agricultural workers; for example, a minimum wage and the extension of the law on holidays to agriculture. Immediately, after Matignon, he had even argued for the extension of the 40-hour week to agriculture.[80] But Dorgères quickly repositioned himself unequivocally on the side of farmers resisting such demands.

As the Pas-de-Calais strike movement developed, local Dorgerists within the region's agricultural associations warned farmers 'not to wait until the red flag is at their gate before taking a decision to organise'.[81] Events at Violaines are described in the council register: 'Towards half past eight, a demonstration starting at La Bassée (Nord) arrived at Violaines opposite the Mairie. . . A majority of demonstrators were armed with pitchforks, cudgels and shovels. There were more than 200 people, for the most part local farmers. . . threatening to use their weapons against potential strikers.'[82] Similar mobilisations broke strikes in other parts of the department. In early August, striking workers were gathered outside a large farm in Sangatte when 'an important procession of 50 motorcars stopped outside the farm. . . several hundred local farmers got out. . . [with] at their head M. Déclemy [a prominent local Dorgerist] who spoke to the strikers. In courteous but forceful terms, he asked them to return to work. . . if they refused, he was not lacking of "hands" to replace them. In the face of this attitude, the strikers capitulated'.[83] By far the biggest strikebreaking operation was during the dispute on the Arras plain, which will be returned to shortly.

Who Led the Farm Strikes?

There has been some discussion over where the stimulus for the farm strikes came from. Were they spontaneous or organised? The issue is linked to the debate in the literature over the spontaneity or otherwise of the wider Popular

Front strike movement. One camp has emphasised the importance of preparation and agitation by a 'pre-existing network', primarily Communist Party members and sympathisers.[84] Another has downplayed the role of political and union activists. According to Jacques Kergoat, 'none of the first strikes were provoked by a union decision' and, particularly, 'strikes in regions [outside Paris] reinforce the idea that "experience" and "organisation" did not play a major role in the chronology by which different groups of workers entered the struggle'.[85]

The limited discussion in relation to the farm strikes has mirrored this debate. It includes, however, an additional dimension. In her study of social relations in agriculture in the Brie, Danielle Ponchelet concludes that farm workers displayed a 'striking lack of autonomy': 'They responded. . . to calls by the trade unions of workers in the towns, but never took the initiative in organising the struggles and, worse still, they exercised no serious control over their newly-won conditions of work and life once the strikes were over.'[86] This argument echoes that of the sociologist Eric Wolf who, though in a different context, claimed that rural proletarians are 'unlikely to pursue the course of rebellion, unless they are able to rely on some external power to challenge the power that constrains them'.[87] In contrast, Lynch has characterised the first stage of agricultural workers' strikes as 'largely spontaneous' – in the sense that the strikes were organised by agricultural workers without the intervention of political or trade union activists. He quotes a worker's recollection of a strike near Soissons: 'It was a spontaneous movement. It wasn't led by the unions. . . on the farms, the lads weren't unionised. . . "that's it," they said, "we've had enough, we're also going to strike".'[88]

During the Popular Front period, the prevalent view amongst public officials, agrarians and other right-wing politicians and press was, in the words of the Oise Prefect, that the farm strikes 'do not have an absolutely spontaneous character'.[89] They were the result of agitation by 'des étrangers à la profession [outsiders of the farming profession]', a phrase that became almost a mantra of the farming associations. Press reports sometimes reached the point of absurdity. An article in the regional newspaper, La Somme, with the headline 'Le Communisme aux Champs', is typical: 'Suddenly, in peaceful villages, totally unknown, mysterious characters appear. They arouse the agricultural workers to make their demands and recruit them to the banner of the CGT.'[90] The authorities and farmers implied that every activist organising agricultural workers was from outside farming. After an 'inconnu' had recruited workers into the CGT and organised a work stoppage at a farm at Réez-Fosse-Martin, the Oise Prefect reported: 'I ordered an immediate and thorough enquiry. . . It seems certain. . . that elements from outside agriculture are seeking to provoke conflicts on the farms.'[91] The police enquiry into the incident soon discovered, however, that the activist concerned was a certain Jules Lahaye, a 57-year-old local man, 'literate, married and without a criminal record', an agricultural worker employed on a neighbouring farm.[92]

One of the problems with the spontaneity-versus-organisation debate, particularly the sharp manner in which it has developed in Popular Front historiography, is its premise that the two concepts are dichotomies, when in reality they are connected. 'Spontaneous' conflict of even an elementary form gives rise to some type of organisation, even if rudimentary or temporary. Historically, the tendency of workers engaged in 'spontaneous' class struggle, whether hidden or open, has been to seek allies amongst other workers and those claiming to represent their interests politically: this was, in essence, the basis for trade unions and political parties of the left. The farm workers' movement provides many examples of such a process. The strike movement in the Vermandois in May 1936 was clearly initiated by communist activists – as well as by a 'union decision' – and under the terms of the debate, could be described as 'organised' rather than 'spontaneous'. But, as has been noted (Chapter 4), the communists began their activity in the region only after workers 'spontaneously' organised a strike at Prémont in October 1935 and contacted local communist activists for assistance. Similarly, a strike developed in late 1932 at Cattenières in the Cambrai region without the knowledge of party and union activists (see Chapter 3). After comments on the significance of the dispute at the Central Committee, communists began a campaign to organise farm workers in the region.[93] It is also the case that 'organised' action, under certain political and social conditions, tends to prompt activity by other workers not yet organised, which is then considered 'spontaneous' action. This explains the snowball effect seen in the Calais strikes, a general feature of the agricultural movement. In short, rather than viewing 'organisation' and 'spontaneity' as mutually exclusive, it is necessary to recognise, in the words of Danielle Tartakowsky and Claude Willard, the 'ever complex relationship and shifting boundaries' of the two phenomena.[94]

Even accepting the concept as traditionally defined, there are several reasons why the description of the first stage of the farm strike movement as 'spontaneous' is misplaced. Lynch is correct to argue that farmers highlighted the role of 'outsiders' to deny recognition of the justifiable grievances of the farm workers.[95] But it would be a mistake to underestimate the impact of the call-to-arms issued by communists in large-scale farming regions during the days immediately following the victory of the Popular Front. 'A first step is imperative,' declared the Étampes communist paper, 'the establishment of workers' unions. . . the task is urgent, it is necessary to act and rapidly.'[96] Educated by the party from 1929 onwards that the struggle of the agricultural proletariat was a 'central question' and now impelled by the mass radicalisation and mobilisation around the Popular Front, many activists in rural and semi-rural areas perceived it a duty to assist agricultural workers in their attempts to organise. Paradoxically, an example offered by Lynch in support of his (undoubtedly correct) argument that the role of 'outsiders' was exaggerated by the right-wing press illustrates a good example of such activity. He believes Francis Gabriet, arrested after speaking at the hiring fair at Châteaudun and labelled as an outside 'agitator', to be a farm worker.[97] Yet, the regional communist paper makes clear that 'notre camarade' was an unemployed factory worker (dismissed for union activities) who had also helped to organise workers in engineering, building and transport.[98] Many other examples could be given. In the Berry, the strikes that broke out around Issoudun (Indre) towards the end of July can be directly linked to the establishment of agricultural workers' unions after a campaign around the hiring fair in mid-June led by Robert Habert, the local communist leader, assisted by striking building workers.[99] That there is a link between this type of agitation and the development of the agricultural workers' movement would seem incontestable.

Nevertheless, it would be wrong to conclude that, in general, agricultural workers' strikes were provoked by the direct intervention of 'outsiders'. Agricultural workers joined their own unions in considerable numbers, participated in their functioning, and as numerous examples can illustrate (including that of Jules Lahaye, above), took initiatives to organise strike action. The suggestion that the farm strikes arose 'spontaneously' – that is, without the intervention of political or union activists – underestimates the degree to which workers' unionism and the parties of the left, particularly the communists, had gained a foothold amongst agricultural workers in the period before the Popular Front elections. The geographical link between the areas in which the initial strikes broke out and those mentioned in the extensive police report of April 1935 on the activities of FUA, as well as the activities of communist militants amongst agricultural workers outlined in Chapter 4, is, indeed, quite remarkable.

There are, however, important regions where there would seem scant evidence of either communist or union activists initiating the conflict. A case in point is the Soissons region, cited as an example of spontaneity by Lynch (see above). Although communists had conducted some activity around the farms (Chapter 4), they had a negligible base in the region. Moreover, local socialists adopted a moderate position in relation to agricultural workers' wages, arguing for a minimum wage far below that proposed by the agricultural workers' union.[100] It would, therefore, seem possible to concur that the movement in the Soissons region was 'spontaneous'. But this would only illustrate another problem with the concept itself. Historical events do not combust automatically – they are set in motion by real human beings. In any social movement, such as a strike, certain individuals come to the fore, express the sentiments of others and make proposals for activity. Classifying the strikes in the region around Soissons as 'spontaneous' avoids an investigation into who these local leaders actually were.

In an interview given in 1996, Michel Leroux, a farmer at Dommiers, recalled the conflict on his farm that began on 20 June 1936. It was led by the 'mécanicien', a worker with a range of responsibilities, including some of a supervisory nature.[101] The reference was to Abel Lemaire, a 44-year-old local man, who became the farm's union delegate and assistant secretary of the local agricultural workers' union.[102] Although information about Lemaire is sketchy, it is known that he was a member of the secularist organisation, *Libre Pensée*, in Soissons. A skilled worker, he had standing in the community, some independence from his employer and authority amongst his fellow workers. Most significantly, he had previous experience of agricultural workers' unionism. As already noted (Chapter 1), the Soissons region had witnessed union organisation and strikes thirty years earlier. A 15-year-old in 1907, Lemaire had been working on local farms and could not have avoided the discussions and meetings about the unionisation campaign and strikes whilst helping in the village auberge kept by his mother. While not a communist or socialist activist, Abel Lemaire had a memory of agricultural workers' unionism and political experience of a broadly left-wing nature.[103] Others prominent in the Popular Front farm strikes around Soissons were also veterans of the earlier movement. At Saint-Pierre-Aigle, Louis Voiret was a delegate and treasurer of the union's local section. He had been 22 at the time of the previous movement and already working on the farms. Another delegate at Saint-Pierre-Aigle was Henri Lesueur, who had been brought up in the commune and was aged 21 at the time of the earlier strikes.[104]

The example of the Soissons region illustrates a factor that helps explain the 'chronology' of the farm strike movement. The agrarian outlook prevalent amongst farmers sought to deny any tradition of agricultural workers' organisation and struggle. The recruitment of immigrant labour was pursued partly with the aim of obliterating its memory. But in many villages a basic core of indigenous workers remained. In the Valois, the main base of the agricultural workers' union was at Silly-le-Long. In 1936, out of 121 agricultural workers on the local farms, 63 were French, of whom 37 had been born in the village.[105] Although the last strike at Silly-le-Long had been 30 years earlier, many of these workers would have been directly involved, given that it involved 'all the agricultural workers', around one hundred and twenty people, including '25 children'.[106] In the Marquion region (Pas-de-Calais), the Prefect noted that the conflict was 'particularly sharp' at Quéant,[107] a village that not only witnessed a strike in 1934 but had also seen bitter conflicts during 1910. The fact that 63 per cent of local agricultural workers in 1936 had been born in the village would have helped maintain the memory of earlier struggles.[108] In the Champagne region, where the communists in June 1936 had only a slender base amongst vine workers, the leader of the conflict's initial stages was Émile Moreau, a 61-year-old who had been a prominent leader of the 'revolt' that swept the region in 1911.[109] A police report dated 1921 described him as 'very violent, active and combative, he attends communist meetings at which he displays revolutionary sentiments, dangerous'.[110] The point should not be exaggerated: alongside this older layer of workers, a younger generation came to the fore during the June strike movement. For example, with Abel Lemaire on the union committee at Saint-Pierre-Aigle was Michel Cossin, a 16-year-old Polish *bouvier*.[111] Nevertheless, it would seem that the legacy of earlier agricultural conflicts helps to explain the timeline of the strike movement. While the first wave of workers' unionism had been unable to re-establish itself following the First World War, many older workers maintained a deep-rooted antagonism towards the employers – a conviction that the conjuncture of the Popular Front would translate into an opportunity for organisation and strike activity.

An Agricultural Matignon?

A main argument in Thorez's 11 June address was that, by continuing the strikes, workers would alienate the middle class and especially the peasantry, particularly as the movement's main demands had been conceded by the employers and government at Matignon. But agricultural workers had not been included in the Matignon accord or covered by the social legislation subsequently rushed through parliament: they were excluded from the agreements on wage increases of around 15 per cent, on union rights, and from the legislation introducing the 40-hour working week, two weeks' paid holiday and the extension of collective bargaining rights. No major political or trade union voices were raised in protest. 'We were eliminated without pain and without noise', Parsal would later complain, though he was silent at the time.[112]

Some historians have viewed the omission of agricultural workers from the Matignon reforms as 'incomprehensible'.[113] Part of the explanation was the urgent need of political and trade union leaders to resolve the conflict in industry and the fact that the agricultural workers' movement was in early June exerting minimal pressure – strikes had only touched the Multien and Vermandois at this stage. But the exclusion is also consistent with the entire history of social legislation in France. Agricultural workers had previously been left out of laws relating to accident insurance (1898), the Prud'hommes arbitration system (1907), limitations on working hours (1919) and family allowances (1932). Even when reforms reached the statute book, their implementation would be obstructed by filibustering in the Senate – as occurred with the legislation stipulating minimum sanitary standards for agricultural workers' lodgings.[114] The failure to extend legal and social rights to agricultural workers in June 1936 was a symptom of the left's reluctance to challenge the agrarian view that the social relationship between workers and employers in the countryside was fundamentally different to those in the towns.[115]

By mid-June, however, the momentum of the strike movement had encouraged a tripartite attempt to secure a version of Matignon appropriate to agriculture. With the harvest approaching, leaders of the agricultural associations became increasingly alarmed. In the Popular Front government, the Minister of

Agriculture, the socialist Georges Monnet, while concerned by the threat to 'order', was motivated by a genuine desire to secure reforms for farm workers. Leaders of the FNTA obviously shared this objective, but they also wished to channel the movement into safer social terrain. Hosted by Monnet, negotiations began between the federation representing farmers' associations in the Île-de-France region and the FNTA, with support from national leaders of the CGT. Both Monnet and the union hoped that the agricultural importance of the region (which covered the Seine-et-Oise, Seine-et-Marne and neighbouring cantons in the Aisne and Oise) would mean that a settlement could act as a model for elsewhere.

On 19 June, an accord was reached and the parties issued a statement. The conciliatory tone was very similar to that already noted in the Pas-de-Calais. A preamble described the 'significant harm' caused by the farm strikes to both employers and workers. It declared the 'impossibility of immediately establishing a collective contract' but promised 'a study of the issues' in order to 'conclude a final agreement before 31 August 1936'.[116] The significance of the date is that the FNTA leadership had accepted a postponement of any settlement until after the wheat harvest. Not surprisingly, employers' negotiators were quick to stress the 'considerable advantages' of the agreement, 'which [would] allow us to get calmly through July and August and consider the issues with the desirable equanimity'.[117]

The accord, however, quickly collapsed under the weight of two contending pressures. The first came from the growing belligerence amongst farmers in the face of workers' demands. The Île-de-France agricultural associations split into 'two clear tendencies'.[118] The first, more conciliatory, argued that the social and political climate necessitated compromise, even if temporary. This wing's agenda was for a settlement with workers that, while guaranteeing a minimum wage, would introduce a linkage between wages and the price of wheat and/or profits in order to tie workers' interests to the farmers.[119] The other wing, more openly confrontational, coalesced around a new organisation, l'Association Centrale des Employeurs Agricoles (ACEA). Under its influence, representatives of the Île-de-France agricultural associations vetoed the recommendations of their negotiators. The ACEA began to spread its tentacles across departments throughout northern France and was soon to become the principal co-ordinator of resistance to workers' demands.[120]

The second pressure was emitted by the farm workers' movement. The union was witnessing explosive growth. It claimed to be recruiting 2000 members each day throughout June, reaching a total of 120,000 by the end of July.[121] In the Aisne, it became the CGT's largest affiliate, forming 150 out of the 350 union sections in the department.[122] In the Oise, it became the second strongest in terms of numbers, after the metal workers' union, representing 22 per cent of union members.[123] Both existing militants and the new members pouring into the union were rejecting the idea of postponing a settlement until 31 August, the intransigence of farmers convincing them that giving up the bargaining weapon of the harvest would mean abandoning any prospect of significant reforms. The Oise Prefect remarked on 1 July that 'the movement of strikes and occupations, up to now localised, seems to be taking on a more general character'.[124] In the Beauce, the agricultural workers' union announced it would begin a strike and occupy farms from 14 July.[125] FNTA headquarters reported that throughout the country there was 'a very clear tendency pointing towards an outbreak of new strikes'.[126] Not prepared to jeopardise the 'symbiosis' with their base, the union's communist leaders changed their position and insisted that a collective contract be negotiated before the harvest, threatening a strike if an agreement was not forthcoming.[127]

The vigour generated by the workers' movement forced a resumption of talks at the Ministry of Agriculture and on 2 July the employers' negotiators agreed a collective contract with the FNTA.[128] The proposed settlement was an extensive range of important reforms, including trade union rights, a working year of 2845 hours (equivalent to an average working day of nine-and-a-half hours, six days a week), equal wages and conditions for immigrant workers, eight days' notice of dismissal and a commitment to introduce paid holidays when becoming a legal requirement. There was also agreement on a scale of wage rates, covering each category of worker and applicable across the Île-de-France region.[129] On 5 July, an exuberant conference of agricultural workers held in Paris ratified the deal and set a date of 18 July for it to be finalised.[130] But three days later, an assembly of farmers' associations took a jaundiced view of their representatives' recommendations and again overturned them. While opposition focused on the proposal to fix wage rates for agricultural workers across an entire region, the refusal equally reflected hostility that negotiations with the CGT were taking place at all. Farmers still defended their 'right' to set wage rates directly with 'their' workers. An ACEA communiqué declared: 'A Matignon-type accord is impossible in agriculture. . . What is true in one region is not in another, even a neighbouring one. Each farmer will deal directly with his own personnel, without going through third parties.'[131]

The government stepped up activity in an attempt to break the deadlock. Monnet circulated prefects asking them to organise negotiations between employers and union representatives in order to ensure that agricultural workers benefited from the reforms agreed at Matignon.[132] Léon Blum intervened directly, chairing negotiations at Matignon on 11 July and demanding that farmers 'decide their position without delay'.[133] Simultaneously, the government increased police surveillance of the farm workers' movement. Perhaps not coincidentaly, the same day on which he received a mauling in the Senate prompting him to condemn farm occupations, Roger Salengro, the Interior Minister, instructed prefects to draw up detailed reports of union activity in each department.[134]

Ministers meeting on 10 July agreed proposals from Monnet to extend social legislation and the law on collective bargaining to agriculture. Yet the government acted slowly and cautiously when compared with the speed with which changes were introduced for industrial workers. The issue of agricultural workers' holidays was put out to a consultation process, involving the agricultural associations and Chambers of Agriculture. This guaranteed it would be impossible for agricultural workers to receive paid holidays until winter at the earliest. There was no legislation either to limit working hours or to extend the legal recognition of collective contracts to agricultural workers. The hesitancy displayed in introducing reforms for agricultural workers was also in marked contrast to the determination of the government to push the Office du blé (to regulate the price of wheat) through the Chamber of Deputies and Senate during July. Although the Wheat Office was controversial, opposed by right-wing agrarians because it represented state interference in the running of agriculture, it could be presented as a measure to benefit small, middling and even richer farmers – in other words, the entire peasantry. On the other hand, improvements in agricultural workers' conditions only concerned one section of the peasantry, and were reforms that would have large, possibly negative, repercussions for another, the peasant employers.

While the government delayed over legislation, the communist parliamentary group sought to establish itself as the champion of the farm workers' movement and particularly to outmanoeuvre Chaussy, who had build a reputation as the parliamentary tribune of agricultural workers. Parsal introduced two proposals for legislation: firstly, the immediate extension of family allowances to agricultural workers and, secondly, the limitation and regulation of working hours and the legal entitlement to a weekly break. A pamphlet was rushed out publicising the initiatives.[135] Communists also promised to introduce legislation on other aspects of FNTA policy, including the extension of the Prud'hommes arbitration system to agriculture, legal requirements and inspections relating to hygiene and safety, equal rights with workers in industry regarding social insurance, an end to piece-working and the outlawing of gangmasters.[136]

Communists also attempted to outflank those socialists with influence in the agricultural workers' union at grassroots level. Throughout the Île-de-France, they rallied farm workers in support of the 2 July contract (which was printed and distributed in thousands), instructing them to await a signal for strike action. Socialists were attacked for their moderation and preparedness to accept a reduced offer. In the Valois, the deputy, Jean Vassal, together with a team of socialists, had played a significant role in organising farm workers during June.[137] In July, faced with defiance from farmers' associations, victimisation of union members and demands for a strike from union activists, his pleas for the arbitration of the Prefect became increasingly desperate: 'The agricultural workers are extremely agitated and a Jacquerie is to be feared', he wrote. 'It is urgent. If the public authorities do not help us the entire movement will fall into the hands of the communists and we can fear the worst.'[138] Vassal's fears were borne out: by the end of July, the majority of local leaders in the Valois were communists, the most prominent being Alexandre Baptiste, secretary of the agricultural workers' union based in Silly-le-Long.

The 20 July 'General Strike'

On 20 July, the biggest wave of strikes during the Popular Front period began to sweep through the large-scale farming regions of the Paris Basin. The decision to launch the movement was taken on the morning of Sunday 19 July at a conference in Paris of 150 agricultural workers' union secretaries and delegates. Organised by word of mouth, the meeting was dominated by communists; indeed, it is possible that Chaussy and other prominent socialists had not even been invited – the relationship between the two main political trends within the FNTA had become so strained that the two socialists in the leadership, Chaussy and Guillon, were no longer attending meetings of the Federal Bureau or Secretariat.[139] The strike, therefore, took socialist leaders of the CGT and the government by surprise.

There was particular astonishment as during the early hours of Saturday morning, the farmers' federation and a union negotiating team – including the CGT general secretary, Léon Jouhaux – had reached agreement at the Ministry of Agriculture on all issues except wages. And even on this issue, differences between the parties were minimal. Farmers' leaders remained hostile to a regional settlement, but were prepared to recommend a scale of increases that would be established through local negotiations.[140] During the talks, however, the communist FNTA leaders had expressed reservations, demanding that the suggested wage increases should be a minimum, with the possibility that higher increases could be agreed at local level. Farmers' representatives complained of the 'bad faith of Messieurs Ruys (sic) and Parsal, communist delegates of the CGT, whose position appeared quite different from that of Messieurs Jouhaux and Chaussy, who on several occasions intervened in an attempt at conciliation'.[141] Nevertheless on Monday 20 July, newspapers published a communiqué from the Ministry of Agriculture announcing that 'in principle, an entente had been reached in agriculture';[142] the Socialist daily, *Le Populaire*, applauded an agreement reached 'thanks to governmental arbitration and the conciliatory attitude of the workers' delegation'.[143] The ink, however, was barely dry as strike pickets assembled outside farms throughout the Paris basin urging their fellow workers not to start the day's work.

Detailed reports of the villages touched by the conflict and numbers of workers involved exist in departmental archives. In the Seine-et-Marne, the prefect recorded 4,317 workers participating on 320 farms.[144] It is a significant number, but an underestimate. By only counting permanent personnel, the authorities failed to record the large numbers of women and children taking part in the movement. At Chenoise, for example, the Prefect reported 158 strikers, yet the local Mayor gave the more accurate figure of 123 men, 58 women and 12 children (totalling 193). At Le Pin, the prefect reported 67 strikers, while the mayor indicated that 33 men and 70 women were involved.[145] In the Seine-et-Oise, there were strikes around Trappes and Crespières (west of Versailles) and renewed conflict in the region surrounding Tremblay-lès-Gonesse.[146] In the Oise, the movement was strongest in the Valois, where the Prefect reported 2,300 strikers. Other regions affected in the department were Chaumont-en-Vexin, Neuilly-en-Thelle, Bresles/La Rue Saint-Pierre, Bailleul-le-Soc, Attichy, Ognolles, Bailleval and Auneuil.[147] In the Somme, the movement touched primarily the countryside surrounding Péronne and Ham, though there are also traces of a strike in villages and hamlets close to Crécy-en-Ponthieu.[148] A number of villages in the Beauce were touched, with reports of strikes at Chatignonville and around Auneau (Ablis, Orsonville, and Béville-le-Comte).[149]

The position was particularly sensitive in the Aisne on account of the department containing Monnet's parliamentary constituency. Strikes were already underway in parts of the department prior to 20 July. Union representatives from a number of villages to the east of Laon, including Louis Marécal, the union president at La-Ville-aux-Bois-lès-Dizy, had presented a set of workers' demands to the prefecture on 10 July. Farmers refused even to consider them, announcing they would only deal with workers farm by farm. The mayor of La-Ville-aux-Bois declared that 'whatever happens [farmers] would have nothing to do with Marécal'. In response, workers began a strike on 17 July.[150] When two days later (19 July) a meeting of union delegates from across the Aisne heard from a communist activist that the Paris conference (taking place that same morning) had agreed to launch a strike, they enthusiastically voted to spread the action throughout the department.[151] The following day, workers walked off farms in regions surrounding Guise, Sains-Richaumont, Wassigny, Crécy-sur-Serre, Laon, Saint-Quentin, Chaourse, Soissons and Neuilly-Saint-Front.[152]

What then was the communists' motivation in launching the strikes? The Paris conference gave licence to union activists to organise localised conflicts, heading off the potential that conflicts would break out around the harvest outside the union's control. It was a classic example of a 'safety-valve strike', to borrow the term of George Ross.[153] While sanctioning strikes, the communists' approach was extremely cautious. Union activists were instructed that there were to be no farm occupations, animals should be cared for and there should be no obstruction to the distribution of milk.[154] As the conflict spread in the Aisne, Monnet contacted Léon Jouhaux, requesting him to instruct local unions to call off the strike.[155] Jouhaux duly dispatched a telegram to the Aisne CGT committee explaining that the strike call in Paris was not applicable to the department. Communist activists in the Aisne raised no objection and instructed workers to return to the farms. In regions covered by the Île-de-France negotiations, the strike was almost certain to achieve its demands within a short period of time, as all major questions, excluding wages, had been agreed during the negotiations at the Ministry of Agriculture. And, as noted, the difference between workers and employers concerning wages was not enormous (the employers were offering up to 24 francs daily, the communists demanding, in general, an extra 70 centimes). In most cases, strikes were settled after one, two or three days. In some regions, strikers won rates above those recommended by the farmers' federation, but in many cases the settlement was based on figures agreed the previous Saturday. It was, nevertheless, still possible for the communists to present the entire settlement as a 'victory' secured through strike action.[156]

The strike also served to hegemonise the fledgling FNTA membership around the communist faction in the union's regional and national leaderships. For new activists, communist 'militancy' could be contrasted with the more moderate approach adopted by the socialists. Events at Bailleul-le-Soc (Oise) illustrate the way in which the strike built the party's base. Union members in the village rejected the regional agreement that had been negotiated on their behalf by former-CGT representatives close to Vassal on 21 July. As the Sub-Prefect put it, 'the workers of the agricultural region of Bailleul-le-Soc, Choisy-la-Victoire, Avrigny have disowned their delegates and new delegates have submitted another set of demands to the employers'.[157] Four days later, after a visit from a communist propagandist, a new party cell was established in the village 'with 16 new recruits, the majority agricultural workers'.[158]

The 20 July strike call illustrates the contradiction at the heart of the Communist Party's approach towards the social movement during this period. Pursuing its political course linked to the Popular Front, the party sought a return to normality after the June explosion and was asking workers to temper their demands. Yet those joining the party were the most militant sections, many representing a younger generation of workers. At Bailleul-le-Soc, the local leader was the 25-year-old Abel Breton – in the words of the Sub-Prefect, 'clearly revolutionary'– who had been employed on the local farms with his parents since the age of fourteen.[159] This new layer merged with long-standing activists who, since the 'class against class' days, had devoted attention to the 'class struggle in the countryside' and who now viewed the strike movement as an opportunity to put theory into practice. In villages in the Caux (Seine-Inférieure), a particularly energetic propaganda campaign amongst agricultural workers was conducted by Joseph Féron, a communist activist based in Fécamp. Twelve hundred workers were quickly signed up into the union and a number of strikes organised. Feron's activities caused some consternation within the regional CGT. According to the Police Commissioner, 'the CGT has advised leaders of the union section at Fécamp to pursue a policy of calm and moderation in order to avoid any movement of agricultural workers'.[160] At national level, the communist FNTA leaders presented a reasonable face, suggesting that in order 'to avoid any extension of the strikes damaging to the national interests', workers would return to work on establishment of a 'commission of arbitration'.[161] But to the more radical elements, such statements could be presented as a 'tactic', the cover behind which militant action would be organised.

The strikes beginning on 20 July marked the high-water mark of the Popular Front agricultural workers' movement. In the Île-de-France, numerous collective contracts were agreed on a regional and local basis. The settlements gave an impulse to the signing of important accords between employers and workers in other departments, including the Aisne and the Nord (both on 29 July), and acted as a catalyst for demands by workers in other regions. From late July and throughout August, a series of disputes unfolded in more central regions, including around Pithiviers (Loiret) Issoudun (Indre), Charost (Cher) and in several villages north of Décize (Nièvre).[162] In many areas, the mere threat of a strike led to farmers agreeing a contract.[163]

The Île-de-France settlement also prompted the nearest equivalent of a Matignon conference for agriculture. At the 'invitation' of Léon Blum, a meeting of national and regional representatives of the main agricultural associations, the parliamentary agricultural commissions, the FNTA and the CGT was convened on 23 July with the aim of examining 'appropriate solutions' to the 'labour conflicts in agriculture'. As well as the Ministers of Agriculture and Labour, those in attendance included Henri Queuille, the former Minister of Agriculture, Léon Jouhaux and Renaud Jean, now President of the Chamber of Deputies' agricultural commission. The ACEA, however, refused to participate. It attacked the assembly as 'inopportune' and claimed that those taking part were not qualified to take decisions 'without consulting the diverse regions of France'.[164] Although the meeting ratified the Île-de-France agreement, farmers were already indicating their determination to roll it back.

The Battle of Arras

In the Artois, activists in the agricultural workers' union and leaders of the farmers' associations had been following events in the Paris basin with equal attention. During June and July, farm workers in the region swelled the FNTA to a claimed 5,724 members, around 50 per cent of the agricultural workforce.[165] This was a region of small agricultural villages of 500 or so inhabitants, but in relatively close proximity to industrial centres, such as Douai, and the mining region centred on Lens. Although communists possessed some important points of influence in the region, the Arras CGT was led by socialists, and Philibert Cléret, a Post Office employee who had been a socialist candidate at the legislative elections, emerged as regional representative of the agricultural workers' union.

5. On bicycles in the Artois, July 1936: a group of pickets responsible for communicating news of the strike to neighbouring villages and farms

The pattern of the strike movement in the Artois was initially similar to those in the Calais and Île-de-France regions. A strike broke out on 20 June amongst seasonal sugar-beet workers at Écourt-Saint-Quentin, a communist-controlled municipality with a sugar processing plant. It spread to Marquion, where, after a week's conflict, a regional agreement was signed (26 June) between the CGT and farmers.[166] Covering almost exclusively the issue of wage rates, specifically ruling out any changes in working hours and including a provision that higher wages were dependent on increases in the price of agricultural produce, the Marquion accord failed to pacify the conflict: further strikes broke out, including at Épinoy, Inchy-en-Artois, Quéant and Metz-en-Couture, in all cases winning new concessions from farmers. (This first wave of strikes in the Artois is charted in Table 3.) Agitation increased for a collective contract similar to that proposed in the Île-de-France region on 2 July.

As in the Île-de-France, the movement was marked by political rivalry between the two left parties. When communist-influenced farm workers at Roeux walked out on 20 July, socialist CGT officials urged workers 'to keep a cool head, observe the strictest discipline and. . . above all not launch a strike without formal instructions'.[167] Encouraged by Monnet's circular asking prefects to instigate settlements between the union and employers, as well as by events in the neighbouring Nord department where talks led by socialists showed signs of progress, the Arras CGT believed it could negotiate a collective contract to cover the region without recourse to a strike.[168]

This was, however, to underestimate seriously the determination of the Artois farmers' association to break the workers' movement. Rather than entering into talks, the agricultural syndicate prepared to resist and established an auxiliary wing, Le Groupement des Cultivateurs et Artisans de l'Arrondissement d'Arras, under the leadership of the militant Dorgerist, Pierre Leclercq, representative of the regional sugar-beet farmers' lobby. The minutes of the meeting on 18 July read like a war council. Under an item entitled 'Organisation et Résistance', a three-point plan was agreed: 'a) to recruit volunteers in each village, sons of farmers ready to go to striking communes; b) to plug gaps created by the strike through a public appeal (newspapers) for volunteers. . .; c) to keep workers staying at work under surveillance. . . and expel by force if necessary all outside agitators.'[169] A permanently staffed central office was established and a financial levy imposed on farmers, the amount linked to the number of workers employed. Leclercq also turned to the Dorgerist national network to ensure that he had a sufficient number of strikebreakers at his disposal. The Young Peasants [Jeunes Paysans] began mobilising in Montpellier to send members to Arras on 26 July.[170]

On Monday 27 July, the Arras CGT announced that a 'warning' strike would begin the following morning. The strike decision had in fact been taken the previous Friday by agricultural workers' delegates in the Croisilles and Vitry-en-Artois regions, after their patience had been exhausted by farmers' refusal to

Table 3. First Stage of the Strike Movement in the Artois,
June–July 1936.

Commune	Strike begins	Strike ends	Farms	Strikers	Average strikers to farm
Écourt-Saint-Quentin	20 June	nk	nk	nk	nk
Marquion	20 June	26 June	20	80	4.0
Buissy	22 June	26 June	15	26	1.7
Baralle	22 June	25 June	20	66	3.3
Cagnicourt	24 June	27 June	17	30	1.8
Villers-lès-Cagnicourt	25 June	27 June	12	23	1.9
Lagnicourt	27 June	30 June	6	20	3.3
Inchy-en-Artois	27 June	8 July	36	75	2.1
Quéant	29 June	9 July	20	60	3.0
Oisy-le-Verger	30 June	6 July	17	54	3.2
Épinoy	4 July	20 July	26	26	1.0
Metz-en-Couture	7 July	15 July	35	178	5.1
Totals			224	638	2.8

Sources: AD Pas-de-Calais, M4456, M2405, M2386.

negotiate. The rich documentation in the archives indicates that the strike involved over 1,200 workers and reached 32 communes (see Table 4). While the strike-hit region was marked by a significant number of large farms, the figures show that many small and middling farms were touched. Mobile pickets on bicycles toured the region keeping different villages informed of events and groups of pickets were formed to spread the strike into neighbouring communes. At Héninel, '100 strikers from Saint-Léger and Croissilles prevented one non-unionised worker from working. The group went to the farm to find him and brought him to the village square'.[171] A communication from Écoust-Saint-Mein reported that 'strikers have obstructed any work. Some small farmers who went into the fields with their parents were forced to withdraw in the face of threats'.[172]

The 'Groupement' now put its plans into operation: replacement workers were recruited, instructions issued to farmers, propaganda leaflets distributed to agricultural workers, press statements circulated and constant pressure placed on the public authorities. Mass assemblies were organised: the largest, on 2 August, mobilised between 2,500 and 3000 farmers and feted the recently arrived 'volunteers' as heroes.[173] Recalling the role of the peasantry in the Great War, Leclercq asked farmers 'if they were prepared once again to join a battle' containing 'perhaps fewer risks but more bitterness'.[174] Threats of violence were, indeed, endemic throughout the conflict. The Mayor of Hamélincourt reported: 'It is expected that strikers from Écourt-Saint-Mein will arrive this afternoon to spread the strike. . . Farmers have set out with their rifles to protect their workers.'[175] According to the Mayor of Boiry-Becquerelle, 'patrols of strikers are scouring the streets, going into the fields and even farms. . . there are 50 of them, equipped with butchers' knives. If this continues tomorrow, farmers are going to fetch their rifles. . . it can be expected blood will flow'.[176]

By the weekend, over 300 strikebreaking 'volunteers' had arrived from outside the region, lodged on a number of big farms and at the agricultural distillery at Vaulx-Vraucourt. There were contingents from the Hérault, the Somme, Alsace, Brittany and a large group from Paris. The Cambrai section of Colonel de la Rocque's PSF announced that it 'had served the country' by agreeing 'to send a busload of between 30 and 50' volunteers each day. Groups of strikebreakers were welcomed at Arras station by the local leader of the extreme-right *Action Française*.[177] The volunteers were not sufficiently numerous or adept at farm work to replace the strikers.[178] Their impact was primarily on morale: the fact that they were working in the fields, under police protection, was a major psychological blow for the strikers and, inversely, made the farmers more confident and resolute. Contingents of police were also lodged on the farms and intervened to ensure that strikebreakers could operate.

For a time, the conflict between the union and the 'volunteers' centred on Saint-Léger, a village (population 504) in which 50 per cent of the economically active population were agricultural workers. Most workers were employed on three large farms (with between 15 and 20 workers) and two medium-sized farms (with 7 and 8 workers). Around fifteen other holdings employed one or two workers and a number of small farmers worked their plot with family labour.[179] Opinions in the village were polarised and some small farmers in the village, including the socialist mayor, openly assisted the workers' union. On 2 August, word spread that Leclercq's volunteers would be arriving to work on the farm of Louis de Chérisey. For the union, this was an ideal target. As a member of the French nobility (he was one of seven children of the Marquis Gérard-Étienne-Sébastien-Louis-René de Chérisey), de Chérisey could be portrayed as a representative of the reactionary *hobereaux* [country squires] supposedly leading the resistance to farm workers' demands.

Table 4. Second stage of Strikes in Artois, July–August 1936

Commune	Farms	Strikers	Strike starts	Strike ends	Average strikers per farm
Roeux	15	22	20 July	23 July	1.5
Graincourt-lès-Havrincourt	35	60	21 July	22 July	1.7
Hamelincourt	6	15	28 July	5 August	2.5
Bullecourt	10	35	28 July	5 August	3.5
Adinfer	1	nk	28 July		
Boiry-Sainte-Rictrude	1	45	28 July	30 July	45.0
Boyelles	2	20	28 July	14 August	10.0
Avion	6	24	28 July	31 July	4.0
Écoust-Saint-Mein	25	100	28 July	4 August	4.0
Saint-Léger	10	80	28 July	8 August	8.0
Fontaine-lès-Croisilles	6	30	28 July	4 August	5.0
Croisilles	15	76	28 July	16 August	5.1
Hendecourt-lès-Cagnicourt	12	40	28 July	4 August	3.3
Mory	10	40	28 July	6 August	4.0
Hénin-sur-Cojeul	23	28	28 July	31 July	1.2
Feuchy	5	31	28 July	6 August	6.2
Vaulx-Vraucourt	30	150	28 July	5 August	5.0
(Writing illegible)	3	12	28 July	1 August	4.0
Rémy	1	4	29 July	29 July	4.0
Vis-en-Artois	9	13	29 July	3 August	1.4
Courcelles-le-Comte	5	20	29 July	31 July	4.0
Héninel	10	25	29 July	1 August	2.5
Beaumetz-lès-Cambrai	48	50	30 July	3 August	1.0
Brebières	53	60	30 July	5 August	1.1
La Herlière	1	6	30 July	31 July	6.0
Dury	7	15	30 July	31 July	2.1
Moyenneville	7	20	30 July	3 August	2.9
Neuville-Bourjonval	16	30	30 July	5 August	1.9
Roeux	15	15	31 July	2 August	1.0
Hermies	70	85	4 August	7 August	1.2
Achiet-le-Grand	3	15	11 August	18 August	5.0
Frémicourt	4	40	19 August	22 August	10.0
Totals	464	1206			2.6

Sources: AD Pas-de-Calais, M4456, M2405, M2386

On 3 August around two hundred workers, women and children blockaded the gate to the de Chérisey farm in an attempt to prevent 32 strikebreakers leaving for the fields. When asked to move by police, the demonstrators raised a chant of 'they shall not pass'. The police held demonstrators back and, after a series of skirmishes, cleared a path for the strikebreakers to leave for the fields.[180] After this initial victory, Leclercq quickly realised the importance of defeating the union's campaign at Saint-Léger and the following day provided an additional 70 volunteers to the de Chérisey farm. The union also realised that they were engaged in a trial of strength and organised a new demonstration on 5 August. According to the police, 'a group of 150 strikers from the locality marched in a column towards a group of around one hundred and fifty agricultural workers employed by M. de Cherisy (sic), who were working in a field about 800 metres outside the village. . .The strikers had a red flag and were led by several people from outside Saint-Léger. They were trying to prevent volunteer workers from working in the fields'.[181] Police reinforcements forced the strikers back on to the road and workers returned to the village where they dispersed.

The Artois conflict was not reported in *l'Humanité* until 5 August (ten days after it had begun), an indication of the difficulties, if not embarrassment, it posed for communists.[182] The movement contradicted the impression of strikes as disciplined, even joyous, events, without threat to public order. It undermined attempts by Waldeck Rochet to reassure the peasantry that the agricultural conflict had reached a 'speedy conclusion' following the settlement in Paris.[183] The scale of the resistance also contradicted his argument that only 'a small minority composed of big capitalist farmers were opposed to the agricultural workers' movement'.[184] To communist activists, it was difficult to explain the left's impotence in the face of organised strikebreaking and, particularly, the involvement of the recently banned extreme right-wing 'leagues'.

In response to the strikebreaking, CGT activists in the region began to mobilise in support of farm workers' demonstrations and pickets.[185] 'The unemployed and miners of Lens. . . on hearing of the presence of fascists on their patch immediately informed us that they were ready to come to help their comrades on the farms to drive out the fascist troublemakers', reported the FNTA.[186] But after the clashes on 5 August, the FNTA communist leaders drew back from further confrontation and cancelled another demonstration planned outside the de Chérisey farm. The national and regional party press published a statement declaring that 'the intervention of militants from the Federation. . . [had been] necessary to avoid regrettable conflicts between Frenchmen'.[187] The choice of words is revealing not only for its emphasis on 'calm' and 'discipline' but also for its moral neutrality when discussing conflict between strikers and fascist-inspired 'volunteers'.

Inevitably, the workers' movement started to weaken. With the harvest progressing, little prospect of halting the strikebreaking and with farmers

C.G.T. Fédération Nationale des TRAVAILLEURS de L'Agriculture F.S.I.
SYNDICATS DE L'ARRONDISSEMENT D'ARRAS

LA LUTTE POUR LE PAIN

Depuis 5 jours, **MILLE** ouvriers agricoles ont été acculés à la grève par suite de l'intransigeance patronale.

LES GROS PROPRIÉTAIRES TERRIENS qui ont toujours considéré les Travailleurs des champs comme des esclaves, se refusent de répondre à la convocation de M. le Préfet qui avait demandé qu'une entrevue ait lieu entre les ouvriers et patrons.

Ces mêmes patrons qui refusent aux ouvriers agricoles des salaires variant de 25 à 32 francs suivant les communes, font venir du Midi, d'Alsace et de Bretagne des hommes à qui ils assurent 21 jours de travail aux conditions suivantes :

Indemnité de Voyage : 375 fr. à 500 francs
Salaire journalier : 20 fr. plus le logement
la Nourriture et le lavage du linge

Ils ont en outre caché à ces ouvriers qu'ils les faisaient venir en briseurs de grève, aussi les Bretons d'Écoust-Saint-Mein se sont-ils solidarisés avec les grévistes dès leur arrivée.

Les autres suivront l'exemple des bretons d'Écoust-Saint-Mein.

QUE VEULENT LES PATRONS !!!

En se refusant à discuter avec les SEULS délégués ouvriers accompagnés du Secrétaire de la Fédération Nationale des Travailleurs de l'Agriculture, ils font la démonstration que leur objectif est comme LA VOTRE DORGÈRES de créer des incidents dans le pays, obéissant ainsi aux ordres des factieux, fauteurs de guerre civile.

LEUR PROVOCATION RÉVOLTANTE SERA DÉJOUÉE

Déjà un certain nombre de patrons ont manifesté leur désaccord total avec ceux qui obéissant à des objectifs UNIQUEMENT politiques font preuve d'une intransigeance absolue.

TRAVAILLEURS DES CHAMPS
Restez calmes ! Soyez disciplinés dans l'Action ! — ASSUREZ LE SUCCÈS DE LA GRÈVE
COURAGE, LA FÉDÉRATION COMPTE ACTUELLEMENT 135.000 OUVRIERS ET PETITS CULTIVATEURS

RÉPUBLICAINS ! DÉMOCRATES DE LA RÉGION
Soutenez vos Camarades en lutte ! AIDEZ-LES ! Leur Victoire Sera celle de TOUS LES TRAVAILLEURS

Pour que ceux qui toute leur vie font pousser le blé puissent donner du Pain à leurs enfants : TOUS UNIS.

Le Bureau de l'arrondissement d'Arras

DERNIÈRE HEURE — À FAMPOUX, le travail reprend Lundi: Nouveaux salaires 27 FR. 50 A 32 FR. À NEUVILLE-BOURJONVAL l'accord est conclu. Augmentation journalière de 7 FRANCS.

6. FNTA strike poster during the conflict in the Artois (August 1936)

offering local agreements on wages, negotiations at village level began to take place. Local agreements granted workers concessions, amounting in most cases to around 12 per cent on basic wage rates. But some workers returned for a wage increase as little as 4 per cent and were forced to accept that wages should be linked to the price of wheat.[188] Moreover, no concessions were granted on wider issues such as hours, holidays or trade union rights and differentials in wages between villages were maintained. In some cases farmers agreed improved conditions but refused to put pen to paper, leading to the bizarre position of contracts containing the clause: 'The farmers do not see the usefulness of signing the contract and would note that they have never gone back on their word.'[189]

The communists claimed a victory. 'Despite all the money spent by the Dorgerists. . . the volunteer harvesters have had to scarper! Almost everywhere the modest demands of the agricultural workers have been conceded', proclaimed an article in the regional communist press.[190] While such statements can be viewed as a device to keep up morale, they also ensured that no serious lessons from the conflict would be drawn. The attempt to avoid 'regrettable conflicts' had made a successful outcome less likely, but it had also failed to 'neutralise' the middling farmers, who continued to be radicalised in a rightward direction. By placing the blame for the conflict on a small 'band of Dorgerists', communists refused to recognise that the leader of the Greenshirts had gained widespread support and authority amongst the middling farmers in the region, and the policy of 'peasant unity' had suffered a serious blow.

The FNTA in face of a Counter-Offensive

The outcome of the Arras conflict emboldened farmers' resistance and strengthened the reputation of the PSF and Dorgerism. But the farm workers' movement was still in the ascendant, reaching new regions and consolidating its organisation. Throughout August and September, sporadic strikes continued even in regions where there had been settlements. To take the Nord department as an example, conflicts broke out in late July/early August at Clary, Auchy-lès-Orchies, Monchecourt, Armbouts-Cappel, Thumesnil and Flers-Lille. 400 workers employed on threshing wheat in the region surrounding Lille stopped work between 12 and 18 August.[191] The same day, workers in six villages in the Écaillon valley refused to continue the harvest. The fractious nature of the relationship between many farmers and workers was illustrated at Incy when, on 17 August, three workers stopped work after the farmer refused to 'deliver drink on top of the daily wage'.[192] The following day at Quaëdypre (south of Dunkerque) 80 striking workers tried 'to invade the mairie', after being refused a room for a meeting.[193]

A more extensive round of strikes took place during October to coincide with the sugar-beet harvest. Generally, the same regions were touched as in June and

July. Significant conflicts took place around Montdidier (Somme), around Saint-Quentin, Guise and Soissons (Aisne), in the Bailleul-le Soc, Choisy-la-Victoire and Saint-Just-en-Chaussée regions (Oise), in the Cambrésis, around Étampes (Seine-et-Oise) and in the Multien (based on Mitry-Mory and involving 1,250 workers).[194] The most important strike broke out on 5 October in the Normandy Vexin, touching primarily the region between Les Andelys and Gisors. Involving between 2000 and 2,500 workers, it secured the extension of a collective contract 'provisionally' agreed in July.[195] Although in most cases, workers won concessions, farmers' resistance was now more organised than during the spring and summer. An indication of the changed balance of forces in the Calais region was the defeat of a new strike at Marck (Pas-de-Calais).[196] Throughout the autumn and winter, an increasing number of conflicts were, in effect, becoming defensive struggles from the workers' point of view.

Besides direct attempts at strikebreaking of the kind witnessed in the Pas-de-Calais, farmers' resistance to the agricultural workers' movement took a number of forms. The first was victimisation of union activists. Sackings had taken place from the outset and would become more generalised as the pressure of the June/July movement receded. In the Caux, the 16-year-old René Gaston Vattement wrote to the Prefect: 'I am writing to inform you that I am an agricultural worker and have been a union member since 1 July. My employer having learnt that I was unionised has sacked me. Reason: I was talking too much politics.'[197] In the departmental archives in the Aisne, an entire dossier exists entitled: 'Dismissals of agricultural workers for union activities' [Licenciements d'ouvriers agricoles pour activités syndicales].[198] Persecution from farmers was in marked contrast to the public appeals for national solidarity from some communist leaders. During market day on 8 July at Coulommiers (Seine-et-Marne), Marius Vazeilles addressed a meeting of 200 people, the majority of whom were agricultural workers from surrounding villages. According to the police report, 'Vazeilles. . . explained the necessity of forming agricultural unions. . . [but] his speech displayed great moderation and exemplary correctness'.[199] Several days later, the Prefect received a letter from the secretary of the newly formed agricultural workers' union in the area. It protested that several workers had been sacked on their return from the meeting, including one man 'with 21 years' service'.[200] In this and most other cases, the union was powerless to defend sacked workers. One exception was at a large farm operated by the SIAS at Essigny-le-Grand (Aisne). After the foreman, a member of the PSF, sacked Paul Zwick 'for singing the Internationale while working in the fields', a walkout by workers forced the intervention of the Sub-Prefect and Zwick won his job back.[201] In general, strikes to reinstate victimised workers won, at best, some financial compensation for those who had been dismissed.

Secondly, farmers supported the setting up of 'unions' independent from the CGT. The first had been pioneered by Dorgerists during the Calais strike movement – workers joining a union established by farmers at Louches were immediately granted a wage increase of 12 per cent.[202] The biggest successes, however, were achieved by the trade union wing established by the PSF, the Syndicats professionnels français. Some large rallies were organised by Colonel de la Rocque in regions touched by the farm strike movement. In early August, he addressed an audience of farmers and not a few agricultural workers at Auffargis, near Rambouillet (Seine-et-Oise). 'The success of the meeting exceeded the hopes of the organisers', reported the Prefect. 'More than 2000 people. . . assembled in a huge barn, decorated with tied bundles [faisceaux] of pitchforks and tricolour flags.' Order was maintained by 'a large squad of stewards. . . commanded by the same former cavalry officer who had organised the self-defence groups in the Guyancourt region during the recent agricultural strikes'. Those present were asked 'to join the PSF in order to resist the revolutionary agitators of the CGT and Marxism'.[203] In the Aisne, the Syndicats professionnels claimed 1,500 members in 100 unions for the Soissons region and 900 members in 80 unions for the Laon region.[204] In the Oise, the list of registered unions in late 1936 indicates 23 SPF sections with a total of 1,379 members.[205] Support for the Syndicats professionnels was found amongst a layer of indigenous workers, usually with an elevated position on their farm's hierarchical ladder and often with some kinship or personal ties to the employer.[206]

Thirdly, farmers began to whittle away concessions granted in the collective contracts. At Brégy (Oise), the price of farm produce sold to workers was increased by 20 per cent and workers were asked to pay for straw and the use of the farmers' horses to work their own plots.[207] In the Aisne, the socialist deputy, Élie Bloncourt, complained that workers who were previously paid monthly were now paid by the day and 'consequently they earn less than in the past'.[208] In the Seine-et-Marne, the price of lodging was increased by 2 francs-a-day, despite an appeal to farmers for an 'esprit de conciliation' from the Prefect, who noted that 'sleeping arrangements are often. . . in conditions that leave much to be desired'.[209] When employers in the market gardening regions to the north of Paris (Pontoise and Achères) reduced the wages agreed in June from 4 francs per hour to 2 francs 80 towards the end of August 1936, a major strike involving between 5000 and 8000 workers forced a compromise rate of 3 francs 50.[210]

Encouraged by the fact that the government had not extended collective bargaining legislation to agriculture, some farmers simply refused to recognise the contracts. When the union secretary in Ognolles (Oise) was sacked after the 20 July strike and took his case to the local magistrate [Juge de Paix], the farmer's lawyer successfully argued that since 'legislation relating to trade unions and collective bargaining is not yet applicable to the countryside. . . the employer is able to apply the contract for certain workers, and not for all'.[211] Soon, other magistrates, many of whom were big farmers, were ruling that contracts signed in July had no legal status and dismissing complaints brought by agricultural workers. Dealing with a case involving workers sacked after a strike at Lesges (Aisne) in October 1936, the Juge de Paix at Braine ruled that the employer should be compensated by workers for 'losses resulting from their sudden withdrawal from work'. Permanent workers were ordered to pay a month's wages and day labourers a week's wages in damages. In addition, 'judging the motives of the strike as excessive, he ordered its organiser to pay 2000 francs damages and the other workers to pay supplementary damages of 300 or 500 francs'.[212] When it is considered that an agricultural worker's wage was in the region of 150 francs each week, the scale of the retribution is apparent.

By the end of 1936, the Popular Front government had extended only two pieces of social legislation to cover agricultural workers: family allowances and paid holidays. Both measures faced widespread obstruction from farmers. Family allowances were administered by the state but financed by contributions from employers to a local fund. For the large farmers, although they resented state interference, the principle was not particularly controversial: some had already introduced their own schemes, recognising that they would help tie large families to the land, accentuate the hierarchy in the workforce and, as Paul Dutton has noted, 'starve off general wages increases and pacify worker militancy'.[213] Amongst small and middling peasant employers, however, the introduction of compulsory payments 'triggered a revolt' – one eagerly encouraged by right-wing agrarians keen to land a blow on the government.[214] Some peasant members of the Communist Party were swept up in the disaffection. In April 1937, two members of the local cell at Mur-de-Sologne (Loir-et-Cher), including the secretary, resigned from the party. The report into the affair concluded that 'although they deny it, these comrades have been influenced by the arguments of Dorgères. . . In relation to family allowances, they consider that proprietors should not pay for their workers'.[215]

The biggest sabotage from farmers came over the introduction of paid holidays. On 7 October, following the consultation process, Monnet issued a decree granting agricultural workers' holiday entitlements.[216] Workers, however, had to wait a further period while prefects discussed with the Chambers of Agriculture and agricultural associations to decide the dates on which holidays would be permitted. When the details were announced, they contained major restrictions. In the Somme, holidays could not be taken from 15 March to 1 June, 15 June to 15 September and 1 October to 15 December.[217] The secretary of the agricultural workers' union at Proyart complained: 'It appears that workers. . . are only allowed to enjoy paid holidays during the rainy season.'[218] Many received no choice at all. At La-Ville-aux-Bois, Louis Marécal sent a three-page letter to the mayor complaining about the behaviour of one of his relatives, another farmer in the village. He outlined how each day Pierre Bertrand would allow workers to arrive at the farm, feed the animals, and begin tasks such as cleaning. But then he would survey weather conditions and in the likelihood of rain or snow would send his workers home, announcing that he was generously granting them part of their holiday entitlement.[219] One aspect of the Popular Front to remain in the popular memory has been the measures introduced by Léo Lagrange, the Minister of Sports and Leisure, enabling workers in the cities to experience the pleasures of the countryside, in many cases for the first time. Less known are the plans laid to introduce package holidays to allow agricultural workers to visit Paris. For a modest price, workers and their families were to have benefited from hotel accommodation, transport, theatre and sporting visits, as well as a trip to the Louvre.[220] The refusal by farmers to grant workers' holidays rendered the initiative a failure.[221]

The resistance from employers and the slow progress of reform provoked a mixed reaction from agricultural workers. For some, the mood was one of resignation or disillusionment in the Popular Front and trade unionism. But amongst union activists there was growing anger, not only aimed at farmers but also often at the government. As early as September 1936, Parsal claimed the Popular Front was letting down the 'great hopes' of agricultural workers:

> Except for the regulation concerning the application of family allowances. . . there have been no others. . . This unfortunate situation allows the employers systematically to refuse to honour the collective contracts and makes them unenforceable. . . Agricultural workers are worried. They are now wondering whether the Popular Front government is going to follow the same policies as the previous reactionary governments.[222]

Further criticisms arose in December 1936 after agriculture was excluded from proposed legislation to establish a compulsory arbitration process to resolve disputes in industry and commerce. In the Chamber of Deputies, Parsal introduced an amendment extending the proposed law, which if introduced would have implicitly recognised the legality of collective bargaining in agriculture. After initial reservations from Monnet, the amendment was supported by the Popular Front majority, but promptly blocked by the Senate.[223] With the situation at stalemate and threatening the introduction of the legislation as a whole, Blum intervened on 26 December and, not without some difficulty, convinced socialist senators to withdraw support from the sections on agriculture, while promising that the government would introduce further legislation at a later date.[224] FNTA activists were enraged. At the union's congress held in January 1937, Parsal accused Blum of accepting the arguments of the Dorgerists.[225] A socialist delegate was prompted to complain of the 'inappropriate applause' every time a speaker attacked the Popular Front government.[226]

Attended by 600 delegates, the FNTA congress displayed a confident mood. One report described 'several grey-haired experienced militants [amongst] a crowd of young delegates full of vigour and enthusiasm'.[227] The union had grown to a claimed 180,000 members in 2000 sections, with a regional structure, full-time workers and weekly newspaper. The communists had consolidated their position, dominating the Federal Bureau, the Executive, and most regional committees.[228] Alongside calls for government legislation to equalise the position of agricultural and industrial workers, the union signalled its intent to renegotiate the contracts with farmers' associations, seeking improved wages, guarantees in relation to holidays and, particularly, shorter hours. The claim for a 2,400-hour working year divided into 300 days was highlighted – the equivalent of an eight-hour day, six days a week. Following the congress, fifty 'grands rassemblements' were organised throughout the country 'to create the necessary atmosphere to achieve the demands'.[229] A further series of regional conferences was organised in the spring to finalise the new contracts to be presented to farmers.

1937: Radicalisation and Defeat

During 1937, the conflict in the Paris Basin and northern plains developed into a trial of strength between the FNTA and farmers' associations. The first skirmishes broke out at the end of March/beginning of April at Esquennoy (Oise) and on farms in the cantons of Montfort l'Amaury, La-Queue-les-Yvelines and Houdan (Seine-et-Oise), also touching Boutigny (Eure-et-Loir).[230] More generalised movements developed during May in the Caux and Cambrai, regions that had only witnessed isolated strikes the previous year.[231] During June, the union achieved some minor victories: at Dreux, it won the reinstatement of sacked activists and an agreement on wages to cover the entire Eure-et-Loir department.[232] Other movements went down to defeat: a stoppage in the Trumilly-Néry region (Oise) was broken by a mobilisation of strikebreakers by the local Dorgerist committee.[233] In the south of the country, strikes in the Languedoc wine region were met with similar resistance.[234]

As the summer progressed, workers' participation in the movement began to wane. In the Étampes region, a movement collapsed after only two days;[235] in the Oise, a strike called on 20 July was followed by little more than 500 workers in around twenty villages (notably, where the communists had a base), before disintegrating in less than three days.[236] By July, the agricultural conflict was characterised by long and sometimes violent struggles, during which employers gained the upper hand. In some villages around Cambrai, the strike lasted over a month, before going down to defeat; in the Brie and Multien, some workers stayed out for over two months. The final major strike unfolded in the Aisne during the height of the harvest (July and August) and was broken by the same type of mobilisation of 'volunteers' witnessed the previous summer in the Artois.[237]

The retreat of the movement is well illustrated by events at La-Ville-aux-Bois. On 24 May, a meeting held in the town hall was attended by almost every agricultural worker in the village, both unionised and non-unionised. Workers were aware that the intensity of the impending work on the sugar-beet crop [le binage] meant that farmers would be reliant on mobilising all available labour. The meeting rejected the wage rates on offer and, after a unanimous vote, agreed a proposal from Louis Marécal that work would only commence if an increase were forthcoming. But by the third morning of the strike (3 June), the village was split. Around forty strikers assembled at Marécal's café-épicerie; other workers made their way into the fields, under the watchful eye of a contingent of gendarmes. Throughout the morning, strikers toured the fields to remonstrate with those hoeing the sugar beet. Just after 10 a.m., a group of thirty entered a field to confront the 62-year-old Léontine Hubert who was working with two young lads, Jean Barrois, aged 19, and Albert Questroy, 16. Léontine Hubert had joined the farm workers' union the previous June but stopped paying her dues in early 1937; Jean Barrois had been an enthusiastic supporter of the strike in July 1936, to such an extent that his activity featured in police reports of the demonstration in the village.[238] Amongst the strikers was a married couple, Albert and Albertine Bricourt. They approached Léontine Hubert: 'Mum, come with me and join the others – don't work any more', pleaded Albert. Simultaneously, his wife approached her mother-in-law, beckoning her to put down her tools. Nearby, another striker, 23-year-old Marguerite Detouche, was arguing with Albert Questroy, one of the two lads. The quarrel, in this case, was between brother and sister. At La-Ville-aux-Bois, the movement had ebbed to such an extent that not only were participants in the strike of 1936 now on opposite sides, but the conflict's dividing line ran straight through families.[239]

In discussing the evolution and defeat of the farm workers' movement in 1937, it is appropriate to return to the debate over workers' autonomy. Already, in relation to 1936, the case studies in this chapter contradict a generalised view that agricultural workers could 'never take the initiative in organising the struggles'.[240] In the Artois (July 1936), the decision to strike came not from the CGT in Arras but from meetings of rank-and-file agricultural union activists. In the Calais region, the Sub-Prefect in Boulogne made a telling comment about the relationship between CGT delegate, Roussel, and workers in the Guînes region when in August they again ignored his recommendations and began a strike: 'I have the impression. . . that M Roussel who claims to be mandated by the agricultural workers is not at all so, unless he is totally lacking in authority over the troops of which he claims to be leader.'[241] The decision to launch strikes during the spring and summer of 1937 was taken primarily by assemblies of agricultural workers. National and regional FNTA officials often advised against action and sometimes complained that demands drawn up by local union activists were too far-reaching.[242] In the Caux, police reported that 'delegates of the CGT were not in favour of a strike during this period of the year. . . but they [have been] influenced by the pressure of the workers'.[243] In relation to a strike at Inchy-en-Artois at the end of May, the regional press stated that 'CGT officials were only informed later of the decision to strike'.[244] In the Aisne, *Le Populaire* noted that 'agricultural workers have commenced a strike . . . led exclusively by members of the local unions, without a delegate of the Federation of Agricultural Workers even being involved'.[245] During the summer of 1937, then, the impetus for the movement came primarily from the thousands of farm workers who had swelled the ranks of the union during the course of the previous year.

It is also necessary to question the conclusion that the movement's defeat arose from agricultural workers' supposed inability to 'exercise control' over conditions and rights. Compared with 1936, the conflict in 1937 unfolded within a markedly transformed political and social context. The heady anticipation of far-reaching change that marked the early weeks of the Popular Front government had long since evaporated – devaluation of the franc the previous autumn and the 'pause' in social reform announced by Léon Blum in February helping to fuel the disenchantment. In industry, employers were mounting a counter-offensive against the reforms conceded at Matignon, a war of attrition that would culminate in the defeat of the one-day general strike called by the CGT on 30 November 1938. Employers' confidence was further enhanced and workers' aspirations inversely frustrated when Blum resigned as Prime Minister in early June. While workers in industry and commerce found it difficult to defend their newly won gains, attempts by agricultural workers to protect or build on the achievements of the previous year started from a particularly disadvantageous position. Monnet had waited until 26 February 1937 to introduce a bill granting collective bargaining to farm workers but the legislation was again blocked by the Senate (which referred it back to the Chamber of Deputies on 6 July). As well as the absence of legal bargaining rights, agricultural workers lacked the same rights as industrial workers in regard to compulsory arbitration of conflicts, the right to call factory inspectors to investigate complaints over working conditions and access to the Prud'hommes committees to arbitrate local disputes.

In addition, farmers had made thorough preparations in anticipation of a conflict. A report from the Compiègne Sub-Prefect commented:

A good number of employers have taken advantage of the slowdown in agricultural work this winter in order to sack the ring leaders. Either because of the fear this has created, or through personal attachment, they have a group of workers who will remain loyal. . . The small farmers maintain they will be able to cope even if it means helping each other out.

> The big farmers have this winter bought combined harvesters and tractors, replacing the workforce.[246]

The farmers' campaign was now co-ordinated by the ACEA and was able to call upon foot soldiers supplied by the Dorgerist 'Committee of Peasant Defence' and the PSF. The ACEA clearly intended to provoke a conflict. It declared a 'total rupture' with the FNTA on 30 April, announcing that there would be no renewal of collective contracts and that farmers would no longer accept the right of prefects or sub-prefects to arbitrate disputes.[247] Attempts were also made to provoke divisions within the workforce and isolate supporters of the union. In the region north-east of Paris, farmers offered a wage increase and organised a ballot 'to consult' workers, by-passing the union.[248] A new contract was drawn up, which workers were asked to sign on an individual basis; union activists refusing to do so were sacked.[249]

The approach of the FNTA leadership towards the movement is summed up by the resolution passed at the union's executive on 7 June. Significantly, the meeting took place after the Communist Party's Political Bureau had discussed the strikes and demanded a full report from Parsal and Rius.[250] The minutes record:

> Position to take in face of the current situation. Win the strikes currently in progress. Show caution in relation to launching new strikes. Organise solidarity.[251]

The decision indicates the union's reluctance to generalise the movement. But also demonstrates its preparedness to mobilise resources in support of the conflicts that had already broken out. Union officials were drafted into strike-bound areas from around the country, including from the Languedoc wine region. Attempts were made to publicise the conflict in Parisian factories. In the engineering industry, unions sent significant donations and a 'solidarity rally' in Paris was organised by the CGT, addressed by communist union officials including Parsal.[252] The position adopted by the communists led to further conflict with socialist activists within the FNTA. Chaussy wrote a letter to the Executive attacking the decision to support strike action in his constituency of Brie-Compte-Robert. In the Cambrai, communists criticised the moderate approach and organisational ineptitude displayed by socialists in the regional leadership – some of whom were close to Trotskyism – and took the opportunity to remove them from the regional committee.[253] As in the previous year, communists utilised a strike movement to strengthen their hold on the union.

Attempts to build solidarity for striking farm workers were, however, hampered by the general retreat of the workers' movement. In some regions, there was even the tendency by some industrial workers to take seasonal work in agriculture, thus acting as strikebreakers in a fashion that would have been unacceptable in the towns. In the Oise, the FNTA passed a resolution condemning 'certain employees' of the Nord railways whose actions were 'harmful to the moral and material interests of agricultural workers and who impede their action against their employers'.[254] In the Cambrai region, members of the Communist Party were amongst those who participated in such activity; the regional party noting that 'some industrial workers either partly or wholly unemployed, including some "communists", have contributed to breaking the agricultural strikes in this region (disciplinary action will be taken)'.[255]

Violence was a recurrent feature of the conflict. Many individual workers complained of harassment and assault by farmers. In June, at Vaux-le-Pénil (Seine-et-Marne), 36-year-old Anna Buczak claimed:

I was home with my husband when I heard someone kicking at my front door. I opened it and it was my employer, M. Maurice Jean. He said to us: 'you can bugger off out of here straight away [Il faut foutre le camp].' We told him: 'We pay our rent. We will leave as soon as the strike finishes.' He grabbed a bucket. . . and threw it at the window. . . Next, he grabbed me and hit me in the head, on the back and on the left side of my body. My husband tried to defend me but he got a punch in the right eye and his jacket was ripped.[256]

It was not uncommon for farmers to intimidate strikers with guns and, on occasions, shots were fired. Maurice Legras, a farmer at Lieusaint (Seine-et-Marne) became a hero of the agrarian movement after wounding seven Polish strikers, one seriously on 3 July 1937. The criminal investigation found that after discharging his weapon, Legras had also proceeded to vandalise the bicycles abandoned by the fleeing strikers.[257] He eventually received a six-month suspended prison sentence. At Beuzeville (Seine-Inférieure) on 22 June, a farmer, Albéric Vanneste, shot dead a union delegate called Fernand Resse, who had been attempting to spread the strike amongst his workers. Within two days, an investigation by the public prosecutor [Procureur Général] had decided that the matter was not worth pursuing, classifying Vanneste's action as one of 'legitimate defence'.[258] In the same region, at Saint-Martin-aux-Buneaux, a farmer accelerated his lorry and ploughed into a crowd of strikers, seriously injuring Alphonse Lemonnier. On this occasion, the public prosecutor criticised the leniency displayed by the judge – a three-month suspended prison sentence.[259] Other shooting incidents took place on 29 June at Goussainville (Seine-et-Oise) and on 15 June at Estrées-Saint-Denis (Oise).[260] In the Brie, the Special Commissioner received intelligence from a 'very reliable source' that a 'certain M. Gervais, landed proprietor at Moissy-Cramayel (Noisement Farm), a PSF militant and very dangerous agitator, has just bought a dozen automatic pistols with a view to arming his workers against the strikers'. A list of eight local farmers, 'all of them activists of the PSF' was also supplied.[261] In face of the inherent violence, communist leaders of the FNTA took to arming themselves. When Rius was arrested on 2 June after a confrontation between strikers and strikebreakers at Tremblay-lès-Gonesse, he was found to be carrying a loaded revolver, an offense for which he received a fine and a six-month suspended prison sentence.[262]

Clashes involving strikers, strikebreakers and police led to arrests and court cases. While the authorities showed leniency towards violence perpetrated by farmers, a number of agricultural workers were imprisoned. At Louvres, on 1 July, a Polish woman was arrested for shouting the following words at a gendarme trying to prevent her from approaching a group of strikebreakers: 'You bunch of cows. You will not prevent me coming through. You cowards and murderers, do you want our children to starve of hunger? What ever you do, I'm coming through.' Her comments earned her eight days' imprisonment.[263] Some strikers received longer terms. The authorities took an incident at Mesnil-Amelot on 17 July particularly seriously. A group of 50 strikebreakers working in a field had been confronted by around two hundred and fifty strikers. According to the police, the strikers attacked the workers with 'batons and truncheons'. Three groups of mobile gardes entered the fray but failed to make arrests.[264] Later enquiries, however, led to the prosecution of six ring leaders, who were eventually sentenced to serve between three and six months' imprisonment.[265]

The summer of 1937 represented a major reversal for agricultural workers' unionism. The collective contracts were generally lost and workers were again forced to reach arrangements with farmers on an individual or village basis. In some cases, farmers introduced wage rates linked to the price of wheat.[266] In the region surrounding Mitry-Mory and Tremblay-lès-Gonesse, one of the cradles of the 1936 strike movement, the employers rubbed salt into the wounds by negotiating a contract with the Syndicats professionels français.[267] Union membership went into steep decline. In July 1938, a report to a communist peasant conference in the Nord recorded FNTA membership in the region at 2000, compared to 8000 in 1936; facing repression, many of the 'best militants' had sought work elsewhere, 'in factories or on the railways'.[268] A report to the union's Federal Bureau on activities in the Oise (November 1937) was summarised in the minutes: 'situation bad – absence of organisation.'[269] The party's Regional Committee in the Aisne (February 1938) received a report from the secretary of the Montescourt section: 'Comrade Demoulin says that the farm workers' unions are disappearing and that seven or eight agricultural workers have not retaken their party cards.'[270] Repression in the Aisne was particularly fierce following the strike: figures from 11 villages recorded 59 sackings of union militants, often fathers and sons.[271] The response of a farmer to a union meeting held in Réau

7. FNTA fundraising event held in Melun (June 1937)
as the strikes became increasingly bitter

(Seine-et-Marne) in October 1937 indicates not only the retreat of farm workers' organisation, but also the depth of employers' vengeance: out of only seven workers in attendance, four of them were immediately sacked. The prefect reported:

> These four workers are three Frenchmen and a Pole: Marcel Breugnot, 37-years old, married with three children, in the service of M. Garnot for 17 years; Armand Blot, 65-years old, has been in the service of M. Garnot for 30 years; Raymond Viox, 26-years old, single, has been with this employer since leaving school; Joseph Napirala, Polish, aged 20, has worked at M. Garnot's for seven years.[272]

The defeat, however, cannot be considered total. The union still managed to maintain a significant structure and network of activists. The national congress at Saint-Quentin in February 1939 was attended by 204 delegates representing 620 local sections.[273] Strikes continued to break out on a localised and sporadic basis.[274] In addition, local elections in October 1937 signalled another shift towards the left by agricultural workers in large-scale farming regions. The Communist Party showed a particularly marked progression in many areas touched by strikes. In six rural villages in the Magny-en-Vexin canton, for example, its vote grew from 106 to 441, overtaking the socialists.[275] Enthusiasm for the party amongst agricultural workers was often noted by party propagandists. A report filed from the Aisne in September 1937 reads: 'Chevresis-Montreau. . . exclusively agricultural area with strong influence of the party. Meeting of 40 people (large majority of the commune's agricultural workers). . . friendly atmosphere with the possibility of forming a cell which does not yet exist, although the agricultural workers' union distributes the party's material.'[276] Elsewhere, there were the first signs that agricultural workers were challenging farmers' inviolable position on municipal councils. In La-Ville-aux-Bois-lès-Dizy, Louis Marécal was elected to the council in January 1938 and immediately stood for the position of mayor against Jules Drapier, president of the farmers' syndicate, losing seven votes to three.[277] Despite the defeat during the summer of 1937, workers were seeking alternative, more political, methods of maintaining their movement.

*****

The agricultural workers' movement of 1936–37 signalled the political and social awakening of a super-exploited and marginalised section of French society – one not only considered docile but whose existence as a group with specific interests and rights was denied by the prevalent agrarian outlook. The political context of the Popular Front gave a significant section of farm workers the confidence and opportunity to break through the cultural and social barriers that had restrained them and to fuse their particular demands with those of a wider social movement. Pouring into the CGT-affiliated agricultural workers' union they attempted to fashion, in the words of Shorter and Tilly, 'a new political deal'.[278] The attachment to the CGT displayed not dependency on an 'external power' but a political resolve to be viewed as part of wider society, as well as an understanding that they shared common interests with other social groups.

The identity of a social group is always rooted in lived experience, but it is also politically and culturally constructed. In the case of agricultural workers, a major influence was the discourse of the Communist Party, particularly through its influence in the agricultural workers' union. The communist representation portrayed farm labourers as disciplined, class conscious workers who 'understood the importance of the union movement'.[279] A group of people often previously described in a negative manner as 'the pariahs of the soil' [les pariahs de la terre] were now referred to positively as 'les agricoles' – in the same manner that railworkers became 'cheminots' and metallurgical workers, 'métallos'. In this way, communists challenged the conventional image of farm workers as uncouth and uncultured, with an inclination to abuse alcohol – a view that had been popularised on the left by Compère-Morel.[280] The central demand of the farm workers' movement – social and legal parity with workers in industry and commerce – challenged the paternalistic relationships on the farms, the long and unregulated working hours, the expectations of deference and obedience. It called into question one of the principal tenets of agrarianism by expressing an identity with a wider interest group than the peasantry: the organised working class.

Agricultural workers were, however, attempting both to define their relationship with the working class and to clarify their position within the peasantry. When the FNTA launched a national weekly newspaper on 14 August 1936, it was titled *Le Paysan*, and the name was carefully chosen, reflecting workers' aspirations to be accepted as a legitimate and valued component of the countryside. As Parsal explained: 'The Larousse dictionary gives the definition of *paysan* as "man, woman of the countryside". . . Agricultural workers are men of the countryside. They are the most authentic peasants that there are.'[281] By trying to wrestle the meaning of 'paysan' from its narrow definition, agricultural workers were challenging their exclusion from the peasantry. Their identity was, in fact, a dynamic interaction between two experiences – that of being a wage worker but also that of living and working in the countryside. They were demanding recognition as a social group in their own right. This sentiment arose from agricultural workers' persistent exclusion from reforms applicable to the working class and the simultaneous marginalisation of their interests in the formulation of policy relating to the peasantry – a feeling reinforced by the Popular Front government's sidelining of their interests in both the Matignon accord and its measures designed to benefit agriculture.

The Popular Front marks the point at which the Communist Party fashioned a representation of the French working class that would condition its politics well into the post-war era. It constructed an image of a proletariat, employed in heavy industry, which was male and indigenous to France.[282] Although achieving recognition through their movement, agricultural workers would consequently remain a peripheral section of the working class within the communist vision. Moreover, and as the next chapter will discuss, two components of the agricultural workforce were marginalised within the constructed identity of 'agricultural worker'. As seen in the quotation above, Parsal specifically reduced agricultural workers to the 'men of the countryside', thus ignoring women. In the same manner, the specific problems faced by immigrant workers remained unrecognised. Agricultural workers during 1936–37 had, nevertheless, emerged as a social agent. It was one that left a deep impression on rural politics and society and, particularly, on the politics of the French left.

6

CHARACTERISTICS OF THE FARM STRIKES

'The birth, life and death of a strike could be said to be a classic piece of urban theatre,' writes Michelle Perrot in her study of the French strike as it emerged at the end of the nineteenth century.[1] Her comment is particularly pertinent to the Popular Front social explosion, a high drama in every sense of the words. But while the characteristics of the conflict in the towns have been explored from almost every angle, the tendency to focus on strikes as exclusively urban experiences – of which Perrot's study provides a good example – has meant that those in agriculture have rarely come under scrutiny. After the sketch of its evolution in the preceding chapter, some of the agricultural movement's features will now be examined in greater detail: firstly, the manner in which the conflict in the countryside tended to focus on the village community, rather than on the workplace (as in the towns); secondly, the role of farm occupations, the aspect of the movement that most excited the right-wing press and agrarian organisations; and finally, the participation of immigrant workers.

The Farm Strikes as Community Struggles

Communists participating in the farm workers' movement often commented on the particularities of the farm strikes. At the regional conference of the party in the Seine-et-Marne, a 'special intervention' by Marcel Depernet stressed the differences in organising 'union action amongst workers in the countryside compared with the methods to be employed amongst workers in the great industrial towns'.[2] Much of this contrast arose from the far greater social and political power possessed by farmers over the lives of workers and their families.

At La-Ville-aux-Bois-lès-Dizy, it was almost impossible for agricultural workers to escape the omnipotence, as well as the omnipresence, of the employers' group and those attached to it through personal and social ties. Whereas, in nearby towns, factory workers could generally return from work to a home situated in a community of similar workers, thereby escaping the surveillance of their employers or their representatives, in the village employers and workers lived in close proximity, in some cases the employer owning the workers' home. At La-Ville-aux-Bois, farmers' control of the local administration guaranteed further intrusions. In the case of applications for unemployment and other means-tested allowances, a family's personal circumstances would be extensively picked over by farmers at a council meeting. The limited controls over employment conditions on the farms were also overseen by the Mayor.[3] Everything from the grand architecture of farm buildings to the imposing family tombs in the small cemetery was designed to demonstrate the authority of the farmers over village society.

Situated in the square at the centre of the village, the enterprise run by Louis Marécal was one of the few spaces in which workers could escape the social dominance of the farmers. A shop to buy food and provisions, a café and bar in which to socialise (particularly for male workers), a source of information and advice, a centre of debate and discussion: *l'Économie Moderne* became the focus of the agricultural workers' community and, during 1936, the organising centre of their social movement. Jules Drapier, the farmers' representative in the village, would complain: 'Each time we need to deal with a question of any sort with our workers, I am never allowed to meet with any one of them. Instead, I have always found myself in the presence of an outsider to the profession in the person of M. Louis Marécal.'[4] In response, Marécal ingeniously turned the agrarian argument on its head. Quoting extensively from the law of 1884, he argued that the agricultural profession included 'everyone who cultivates the land or directly receives its produce, whether a large proprietor. . . or a man maintaining his modest vegetable garden'. Referring to his own garden, he declared: 'I am a land owner and I cultivate my land. I belong to the same profession.'[5]

Scott Haine has traced the evolution of the French café owner in the period before the First World War, describing him as 'an intermediary and social entrepreneur' who offered services such as witnessing passports, weddings and baptisms, as well as an 'immediate, open and neutral space' in which workers could meet.[6] At La-Ville-aux-Bois, Marécal became far more than a 'social entrepreneur'. Influenced by the political climate of the Popular Front, he put his resources and skills at the disposal of workers in the village out of conviction, rather than for entrepreneurial gain. Marécal organised the union in the same meticulous manner in which he ran his business, became an expert on employment law and constantly checked that farmers were applying the conditions agreed in the collective contract. Throughout 1936 and 1937, his influence extended into villages beyond La-Ville-aux-Bois as he became general secretary of the farm workers' union covering the region to the east of Laon.

Marécal was not the only café owner involved in the agricultural workers' movement. In the Écaillon Valley (Nord), police reported that 'on 18 August

1936, around fifty agricultural workers suddenly stopped work at the instigation of a certain Obin, general secretary of the agricultural workers' union section, a retired former brigade major in the Gendarmerie who now runs a bar'.[7] School teachers formed another group to play an important role at village level. At the January 1937 FNTA conference, a teacher, Georges Vanderbanken reported how he had become the secretary of the 175-strong agricultural workers' union at Villers-Outréaux (Nord). As he finished speaking, another delegate jumped to his feet and announced, to great applause, 'in the name of my 70 comrades. . . we too have our comrade teacher with us, here by our side to give us his assistance'.[8]

How is the role of these 'étrangers à la profession' explained? Are they examples of an 'external power', proving a lack of autonomy amongst agricultural workers? In the summer of 1937, the farmers' syndicate in La-Ville-aux-Bois attempted to sue Marécal 'for constraint upon the freedom of labour' [pour entrave à la liberté du travail] and the court papers reveal a great deal about the conflict in the village.[9] It is, of course, impossible to know in what form the agricultural workers' movement would have developed in La-Ville-aux-Bois without the assistance of Marécal; undoubtedly, it was enormously strengthened by his participation. What is apparent from the statements taken from inhabitants by the police, however, is the reciprocity of the relationship between the café owner and other activists amongst the agricultural workers. The mayor described village troublemakers: 'Louis Dhénin has lived in the locality for around twenty-four years: he is one of the leaders stirring up conflicts between employers and workers. Albert Bricout was born in the area: he is thought to be of dubious morality and is a driving force [grand animateur] behind these types of conflict.' The activities of Bricout's wife, Albertine, also warranted a mention.[10] In other words, amongst the farm workers, there were clearly discernible leaders of the strike movement. Significantly, many of these workers could not read or write. The 'grand animateur', Albert Bricout, was described by police as '32 years old, four children, illiterate, knows how to sign'.[11] So while Marécal had skills that could be drawn on by the workers' movement, simultaneously the movement presented him with an opportunity to act on his political and social beliefs.

Mutuality was also a feature in the relationship between farm workers and the teacher at Villers-Outréaux. Vanderbanken explained that he had not sought the position of union secretary or approached the workers in any way: 'It was the workers themselves who last July asked me to put them on the right track, asked me to support them in their struggle, to lead them in their trade union organisation.'[12] Describing the abuse and insults received from farmers, he added another important point: 'They have not been able to do me any harm. . . It would have been different if I had been an agricultural worker. I would have certainly been thrown out on to the stones, like many good comrades who have had the courage to try to create union organisation in their small village.'[13] In other words, workers had sought out a prominent member of the local community not only for the assistance he could lend to their movement but also to maintain a certain anonymity in the face of victimisation by farmers.

Sometimes, kinship ties were important in the development of relations between an 'outsider' and the agricultural workers' movement. At Ennemain (Somme), a village dominated by two large farms (population 219), the 'étranger à la profession' who initiated the strike was 32-year-old quarry worker, Prosper Lescuyer. According to police, at 6.15 a.m. on the morning of 20 July 1936 he turned up at the Duclaux farm while workers were arriving at the stables. After a few words from the visitor, 'the workers left and took up a position at the entrance to the farm'.[14] A quarter-of-an-hour later, together with two workers, Raymond Longuet and Jules Marchand, Lescuyer turned his attention to the farm run by M. Champault, where he successfully appealed to the workers to stop work.[15] Born locally into a family of agricultural day labourers, Lescuyer would have intimately known workers on the Champault farm, having previously worked there with his father. Even more significant were the ties of his wife, Marguerite Longuet. Her father and brother (the same Raymond, who had accompanied Lescuyer to launch the strike) both still worked on the farm and other relatives were employed on the Duclaux farm.[16] Lescuyer's experience on the farms, combined with an independence from the farmers, meant that he was an ideal conduit for workers' demands.

Kinship ties help also to explain how the communist, Alexandre Baptiste, functioned as secretary of the agricultural workers' section in Silly-le-Long and emerged as the most prominent leader of agricultural workers in the Valois. The 61-year-old Baptiste worked in insurance, but he had been long established at Silly and his connections with the agricultural workers' movement were not new.[17] Most importantly, his 69-year-old wife, Louise Canivet, had been born in the village and was part of a large family, most of whose members were agricultural workers. During the 1930s, Louise Canivet had three cousins, a brother and a number of nephews working on the local farms, a ready-made network for the agricultural workers' union secretary.[18]

The historian should avoid judging strike struggles against a template based on a view, often idealised, of the twentieth-century urban experience. It should be remembered that the involvement of café owners, teachers and other intermediary groups, to use Marxist terminology, in social struggles was not particular to the farm workers' movement – and it is rare for such participation to be held up as an example of a lack of autonomy by other groups of workers. In fact, in the large majority of cases, local branches of the agricultural workers' union were administered by agricultural workers. Nevertheless, it is undoubtedly the case that involvement by 'outsiders' was more prevalent in the farm conflict than in more 'conventional' strikes. The phenomenon can only be fully understood by considering the wider context of agricultural strike conflicts.

*****

The modern strike evolved during the late-nineteenth century, alongside the rise of large-scale industrial production, as essentially a phenomenon centred on the workplace. It was likewise with the emergence of modern trade unionism, which focussed on organisation at the place of production rather than in the neighbourhood. Previously, the preferred method of industrial protest (and forerunner of the modern strike) was the 'turnout'. During the earlier part of the nineteenth century, as Charles Tilly has described, workers with grievances against employers went from shop to shop in a locality. They called on other 'workers to join them in a march through the town, voted to make a certain set of demands, sent a delegation to the employers, declared a work stoppage, and enforced it as best they could'. Essentially, the turnout was a movement aimed not at specific employers, but 'owners of the trade as a whole' and aimed to put pressure on 'both the employers and the local authorities'.[19] The turnout was a more inclusive form of struggle than the type of workplace-based conflict that emerged towards the end of the century. It was highly dependent on networks based on families, extended families and communities to spread news and build the struggle.

Many elements of this pre-industrial form of conflict can be found within the farm strike movement. At Oye-Plage (Pas-de-Calais), for example, an embryonic union committee presented a list of demands at the mairie before touring the farms and calling out the workers. Around a hundred strikers then paraded through the village, before going to the mairie to find out the response of the employers.[20] This type of event was repeated in other villages across northern France, particularly those with a relatively large number of middling farmers. It was rooted in the economic position of farm labourers who, while often attached to one particular employer, were not exclusively so. It was further reinforced by the presence of many women and children in the seasonal workforce, as well as other local people who might work on the farms at harvest times. The focus on the mairie arose partly from its symbolism of the social and political power in the village, normally in the hands of farmers; and partly from its role in the state administration, the mayor being officially the arbiter to resolve a conflict between two social groups within the village community. In some regions it was common for the farm workers' movement to occupy the mairie. During the Calais strike movement, occupations took place at Marck, Saint-Tricat, Andres, Quelmes and elsewhere; in the Artois, at Croisilles and Inchy-en-Artois; in the Nord department, at Esnes.[21] At the mairie in Tincourt-Boucly (Somme), agricultural workers presented demands relating to pay and working conditions to Monsieur Obert, the local mayor and farmer. They refused to leave, or to allow him to leave, until they received a positive response. According to the misogynist account by a local journalist, when police arrived they found 'around sixty agricultural workers, frenzied [échevelées] women and children occupying the offices and access to the mairie, protesting and screaming'.[22] Meanwhile, another section of the community was also engaged in activity. The mayor's son had combed the village and surrounding farms in order to assemble a group of friends and associates. Armed with truncheons, they soon arrived at the town hall, determined to free the mayor and break the occupation by force.[23]

In many agricultural villages, the Popular Front strikes are consequently best seen as community struggles, in which the arena of the conflict was the village rather than workplace. They symbolise the breaking of the farmers' hegemony over village politics and society. In such situations, class identities and community identities become intrinsically linked. While farmers viewed an 'outsider' in strictly defined economic terms – that is, whether or not an individual was involved in working the land – agricultural workers considered the question quite differently. For farm workers at La-Ville-aux-Bois, Ennemain and Villers-Outréaux, Marécal, Lescuyer and Vanderbanken were part of their community: their education, skills and economic independence from the employers could be drawn on for the benefit of the community's cause. Within the polarised situation arising from the farm workers' movement, it was, in fact, difficult for any member of the village community not to take sides.[24]

The community character of the conflict encouraged attempts by agricultural workers' unions to become a focus of village life. Football teams and theatre groups were established for young members; dances and concerts organised.[25] Often, a newly established union would stage a public demonstration to announce its presence within civil society, simultaneously challenging the monopoly of the farmers over local institutions and rituals. At Bouquehault (Pas-de-Calais), a ceremony was organised to commission the union banner, including 'a procession through the village and homage at the cemetery'.[26] Such assertions of social identity by agricultural workers could lead to conflicts within village society, often involving the Church. Funerals of agricultural workers were one source of tension. At Longperrier (Seine-et-Marne), the local priest refused permission for a large wreath of red roses with the message, 'The Agricultural Workers' Union of Longperrier', to be placed on the coffin of a union member, declaring it a 'revolutionary inscription'.[27]

The community nature of the agricultural conflict also helps to explain the prominent participation of women, who are ever-present in contemporary photographs and police reports. Women played, in fact, a dual role in the movement. Firstly, their position as workers, particularly seasonal workers, ensured they made up a significant proportion of the strikers. On a few occasions, women led strikes. At Arleux (Nord), in May 1937, a strike of mainly women seasonal workers, planting garlic, was led by female members of the Communist Party.[28] Following the conflict, a union section was established with a membership of 31 women and 6 men; all the officers were women.[29] That same month, in the Neuilly region (Oise), local Dorgerists mobilised to break a strike involving 200 workers in five villages. The agrarians were not only disturbed at the role of 'communist agitators' but particularly vexed by the fact that the pickets were organised by a 'rather young woman'.[30] Secondly, women participated through their role in the village community. Maintaining kinship ties, developing relationships between families and establishing local networks, women possessed a certain authority as the community's moral guardians. Often, they took the initiative against strikebreakers who disregarded communal solidarity. A report of an occurrence in the commune of Saint-Méry (Seine-et-Marne) during June 1937 is typical. André Bailly, a local farmer was working in a field with a number of strikebreakers while a group of 150 strikers patrolled the vicinity. A man broke off from the demonstration and approached him to talk. While the farmer's attention was diverted, several women also entered the field. Led by Catherine Chovan, who had been employed on his farm the previous year, they directly confronted the strikebreakers. 'They jostled my workers,' claimed Bailly. One strikebreaker told how 'Catherine snatched the pitchfork from my hands and broke it'.[31] Women's traditional role within the community, coupled with the element of surprise, meant that such actions were particularly effective.

Communists were aware of the propaganda value of highlighting the appalling conditions faced by female agricultural workers in order to illustrate the general legitimacy of the union's case. Photographs in *Le Paysan* and *L'Humanité* showed groups of women in back-breaking positions harvesting potatoes and cauliflowers.[32] But despite their prominent participation on demonstrations and pickets, women had little influence over decisions relating to the strikes' demands or the terms of their settlement. The union's claim for 'equal pay for equal work' was an ambiguous formulation that challenged neither the gendering of agricultural roles nor the traditional outlook that linked the value of manual work to assumptions about physical strength. Nevertheless, given that farmers were particularly insistent on preserving women's pay at around half the rate of men's, the demand could have provided the basis for some improvements.[33] But often in negotiations the first compromise to be made was over women's wages. At Guînes in July 1936 the union demanded 18 francs-a-day for women but quickly accepted the employers' 12 francs offer, a figure less than half the agreed male rate.[34] At Saint-Tricat, the contract agreed for the harvest stipulated '28 francs per day plus two litres of beer for the men, 18 to 22 francs for the old and partially disabled'. However, the agreement infantilised women, granting them only 14 francs – the same rate as 'boys and girls [gamins ou gamines] under 16'.[35] The overall impact of the agricultural strike movement in the Paris basin on women's wages compared with male workers can be surmised by generalising figures from the Lagny region of the Brie. Between May 1936 and September 1937, male wages increased from 20 francs to 30 francs per day; wages of young men between sixteen and eighteen rose from 10 francs to 25 francs. Women, however, only saw their wages increase from 12 francs to 18 francs. In other words, they had moved from a position of being paid

8. Agricultural workers on strike in the village of Mory (Pas-de-Calais) in July 1936

more than young men to that of being paid substantially less.[36] The union attempted to appeal to women through introducing a column in *Le Paysan*. Combining reports of female working conditions with articles on cooking and knitting, it was based on the belief that women would be best attracted by references to their traditional role as consumers and housewives.[37] But the union's acceptance of the gendering of the workforce and women's role as casual and seasonal workers meant demands recognising women's specific interests, either as workers or members of the community, were not pursued.

There is one further characteristic of the agricultural conflict that suggests elements of pre-industrial protest: the propensity for attacks on property and crops. In June 1936, communists emphasised the 'respect' accorded to factory equipment by workers participating in workplace occupations. 'Our workers love their machines. . . love their trade and are proud of their production in the same way a great artist is proud of his masterpiece', declared Maurice Thorez.[38] Rather than representing reality, such statements were designed to emphasise the communists' new attachment to the nation and to reassure the middle class of their desire for propriety and order. Pronouncements made by communist leaders of the FNTA, stressing that farm strikers should care for the animals and maintain 'discipline', had similar motives. Against this background, the number of cases of arson, on farm buildings and agricultural produce, coinciding with the strikes is quite remarkable. At La-Ville-aux-Bois-lès-Dizy, a barn belonging to Jules Drapier was razed to the ground on the night of 11 September 1936, destroying the harvest 'in a flash'.[39] At nearby Neuville-Bosmont (Aisne), union activists were blamed for a fire during a strike in June 1936.[40] In the Andelys region (Eure), in October, there were fires at Vesly, Frenelles, Provemont, and Mezières, coinciding with a major strike movement.[41] In October 1936, at Louvres (Seine-et-Marne), there were three fires on the same night (8 October), the Dorgerists and communists blaming each other.[42] The following year, arson attacks were even more prevalent. Around Silly-le-Long (Oise), there were three fires during a two-week period in August 1937, just after the defeat of a strike.[43] During a conflict at Gouy (Aisne), a fire broke out on the night of 1 August 1937, leading to fights between strikers and police when firefighters arrived.[44] The following night, in nearby Dury, the police reported that 'several individuals' had damaged 2000 sheaves of wheat stacked in the fields following the harvest.[45] During the strike at Saint-Rémy-en-l'Eau (Oise) in August 1937, it was claimed that 'strikers had each night cut 7000 bundles of wheat'.[46] While the number and scale of these incidents are not sufficient to characterise the farm strikes as examples of 'the violent strike', a prominent feature of labour protest before the First World War,[47] they nevertheless raise the question of whether in 1936–37 such traditional forms of action against farmers were still viewed as a legitimate and effective method of protest by farm workers' communities.[48]

Farm Occupations

The significance of workplace occupations has been contentious in Popular Front historiography. For some, they have symbolised the 'social explosion' as a festival, with the 'joy of not working. . . manifesting itself in dancing and singing in the factories'.[49] Others have stressed the assertion of workers' power and rights, as well as the potentially revolutionary challenge to the property rights of the employers.[50] Whatever the 'meaning' of the phenomenon, it would seem irrefutable that occupations began as a defensive tactic to prevent employers sacking workers and employing replacement labour against the background of widespread unemployment – but their character quickly changed as the strike movement became more generalised, at which point, as Danos and Gibelin note, they 'seemed an almost unnecessary precaution'.[51]

Some important differences arise when turning to the position in agriculture. Firstly, occupations were not a general feature of the farm strike conflict. They were more localised: a central aspect of the movement in some regions, but absent in others; in contrast to the position in industry, where there were occupations in 74 per cent of strikes.[52] Occupations were most prevalent in the Aisne, where between mid-June and mid-July 1936 out of 75 reports of strikes in the archives there were occupations in 53 cases and no occupations in 13 (information is unavailable in nine cases).[53] In the Seine-et-Oise, there were occupations during the strikes centred on Boissy-Saint-Léger and Corbeil.[54] In the Oise, occupations took place in the villages surrounding Méru and in the French Vexin at Flavacourt. Farm occupations were most common in situations where one or two large farms employed the majority of agricultural workers in a village and on large farms based in semi-rural/semi-industrial areas. The average number of strikers on the farms in the Corbeil region was, for example, 24.[55] Where agriculture was less concentrated, farm occupations were not a general feature. No occupations were reported during the movements in the Pas-de-Calais and Nord departments, in the Caux and in most villages (but not all) touched by the first wave of strikes in the Somme. In these regions there were, however, a number of cases in which strikers occupied the local mairie (see above).

Secondly, farm occupations, as Robert Paxton notes, had none of the 'conviviality' that marked the disputes in industry and commerce, 'none of the festive dancing of shopgirls in the aisles of the Bon Marché department store'. Increased friction derived from the fact that farm occupations targeted not only a place of work but also encroached on the living space of the farmer and his family. This created a 'sense of invasion and injury [that] went even deeper among the owners of occupied farms than among owners of factories'.[56] Further emotions were aroused by the perceived challenge to peasant property rights. An article in *La Santerre*, a paper covering a large-scale farming region and politically inclined towards the Radicals, discussed the 'essential difference' between industrial property – often owned anonymously by shareholders – and rural property, 'born in the majority of cases out of the accumulated labour of generations of peasants'. In the case of industry, the 'workforce's rights over the means of production can, up to a certain point, be accepted' but, the paper argued, in agriculture 'the measures of occupation take a revolutionary character which goes beyond the immediate objectives, giving rise to violent antagonisms'.[57] It would, nonetheless, be wrong to imagine that the festive element was completely missing from farm occupations. At Vrély (Somme), there were reports of 'specifically nocturnal demonstrations and gatherings' taking place in farm buildings making 'life unbearable for farmers and their families'.[58]

Thirdly, compared with those in industry, a far higher percentage of farm occupations seem to have held a concrete objective linked to the needs of the strike they were part of. A good example is the occupation that received the most publicity – that on the Schlumberger farm near Guebwiller, Alsace (Haut-Rhin).[59] During July 1936, the Guebwiller occupation became a national *cause célèbre* for right-wing agrarians. National and regional newspapers used it as an example of the 'measures of terror' that the farm workers' movement was inflicting on the peasantry.[60] Around the country, farmers' associations voted resolutions saluting the 'resistance' of the Alsatian peasantry, whose 'resolute action' had supposedly succeeded in breaking the occupation. A thousand farmers meeting in the Cambrai region sent 'a message of sympathy and admiration' to their 'Alsatian brothers'.[61] Schlumberger took legal action against the public authorities, claiming damages for their 'negligence' in not preventing the occupation. The documents of the case provide some rare source material to trace the evolution of a farm occupation.[62]

Rather than a typical peasant holding, Schlumberger operated a huge enterprise, farming a range of agricultural produce, as well as producing wine. Polish families made up the greater proportion of the permanent staff; many seasonal workers were recruited from the town. Starting on Saturday 13 June, the strike involved 70 workers, including around twenty-five women and a contingent of young people under eighteen. While the issue was officially pay rates, described by the Sub-Prefect as 'very bad', the grievance centred on Schlumberger's insistence on 'the right to pay each worker not only according to his age and speciality but also according to his capabilities and performance'.[63] The strike leader was the prominent local communist and CGT secretary, Louis Bréchot. He claimed to have been alerted to the situation on the farm by building workers employed as seasonal workers. For Schlumberger and the Alsatian agricultural associations, his involvement proved a clear case of 'revolutionary action' instigated by 'outsiders'.[64] The communists were accused of organising 'violence', fermenting 'a state of siege' and instigating 'riots'. Accordingly to Schlumberger's lawyer, the occupation had been organised by a 'revolutionary committee. . . all armed with iron bars and clubs', who were refusing to allow the supervisory staff 'the right to feed and attend the animals'.[65] The Guebwiller Sub-Prefect gave an alternative version of events. He rejected claims of criminal activity and, in relation to the occupiers, stressed that 'the large majority' were regular employees.[66]

The occupation emerged from the dynamic of the strike movement itself. For the first two days (13 and 14 June), there was no occupation: workers maintained a picket outside the main gates and, on one occasion, left the farm's vicinity to march through the streets of Guebwiller.[67] What Schlumberger referred to as the 'state of siege' began on 16 June. Firstly, strikers reinforced 'the blockade with cars and various objects and raised the red flag over the farm's gate'.[68] Two days later (18 June), they moved into the entrance courtyard of the farm. Then, on Friday 19 June they took over a barn.[69] In other words, there was a progressive intensification of the workers' action: a demonstration outside the gates was in stages transformed into an occupation of part of the premises.

Although farmers' associations complained that the occupation proved the dispute had political aims, the action was guided by more practical concerns. Following unsuccessful negotiations at the Sub-Prefecture on Monday 15 June, Schlumberger demanded police support 'in order to ensure free movement' of labour.[70] For the strikers, this was a clear signal that he was preparing an attempt to break the strike. The Sub-Prefect later reported: 'Bréchot explained that the farm's entrance had been occupied to put pressure on the employer. It seems, above all, that the decision was taken to prevent M. Schlumberger intimidating certain workers to return to work, which would have been relatively easy given the high percentage of foreign workers he employed.'[71] The occupation began, therefore, as a 'necessary precaution': workers took over the courtyard to ensure they had a full view of farm operations. According to Schlumberger, 'they organised permanent patrols' to check on the activities of the farm management.[72] At one point, strikers prevented milk leaving for distribution in Guebwiller, although they always allowed the managers to feed and care for the animals.[73] The move into the barn also had a utilitarian purpose: it was a place for workers to sleep, as well as acting as a headquarters from which the strike could be organised.

The occupation continued until Sunday morning (21 June). The much vaunted 'resistance' of the Alsatian peasantry amounted to little more than a delegation of representatives of farmers' associations, accompanied by regional parliamentarians, arriving at the Colmar Prefecture the previous evening. They insisted that the Prefect take action to end the occupation, 'threatening to take responsibility themselves in the event of a refusal'.[74] When the Prefect visited the farm the following morning, the strikers displayed a deferential attitude towards the state's representative, agreeing to lift the occupation in return for a promise of intercession in negotiations with Schlumberger.

While the occupation at Guebwiller was primarily a defensive measure by workers (hindering attempts at strikebreaking), other farm occupations combined defensive and offensive objectives. The Ferme des Anglais near Reims was occupied in July 1936 by 24 men and 50 women employed on the pea harvest. The action was a response to the threat by the farmer 'that if workers do not return to work, he would bring in 50 men to carry out the harvest'.[75] But by effectively guarding the peas, the occupation also maximised pressure on an employer faced with the urgent need of completing the harvest before it became over-ripe. Similar tactics were used in the Champagne wine region, where workers specifically targeted the grape presses, occupying them to prevent wine production.[76]

Most farm occupations took place between the second week of June and the second week of July 1936. After Salengro's statement in the Senate (7 July), the FNTA followed the CGT's directive and pledged to use its influence to prevent further occupations, though in reality it had been attempting to restrict their development from the end of June.[77] After mid-July, there were only a few isolated cases, for example on a number of farms in the Marne.[78] During the 20 July 'general strike' in the Île-de-France region, workers were instructed by the union to enter the farms to feed the animals, but to leave immediately afterwards to form pickets outside. On the few occasions when farms were occupied, interventions by the union and, in some cases, by communist deputies rapidly brought the action to an end.[79]

The strikebreaking operations organised by farmers ensured, however, that farm occupations remained a contentious item on the FNTA's agenda. The lodging of contingents of police on farms to protect strikebreakers, as during the dispute in the Artois, confirmed in a negative fashion the advantages of a tactic that had been relinquished. Rank-and-file communists in the union section at Bailleul-le-Soc were amongst those who demanded 'strikes with occupations' during the autumn of 1936.[80] Although Parsal conceded that the union might have to review its position,[81] there was no attempt to occupy farms during the strikes in the Paris basin during the spring and summer of 1937 – farms were again garrisoned by police and strikebreaking 'volunteers', rather than workers. In early September 1937, however, the union established a commission, made up almost exclusively of communists, to consider the lessons of the summer's strikes and to draw up tactics to deal with future strikebreaking. The report recommended a radical shift in approach concerning occupations: 'In recent strikes, the extent of protection guaranteed by the public authorities to professional strikebreakers meant that workers were practically denied the right to strike. . . The commission considers *the Federation must withdraw its recommendation of not occupying the farms*. . . On the large farms, the tactic of occupation can produce excellent results [emphasis in original].'[82] By this time, however, the union had suffered a serious defeat, one conditioned by the changed political and social climate, but one to which constraints placed upon the union's tactics – including the renouncement of farm occupations – had also contributed.

Immigrant Workers: the 'Spearhead of the Movement'?

Right-wing agrarians highlighted the participation of immigrants in the farm strikes to allude that the roots of the conflict could be found outside French rural society. 'A curious aspect of the agricultural strike at Gonesse – of 28 strikers, 25 are foreigners', headlined *Le Journal* in June 1937. The article quoted a farmer: 'My French workers understand the heavy expenses we are burdened with and have accepted the offer. The foreigners, as a group, are refusing.'[83] Some historians have also viewed the strikes as essentially a movement of immigrant workers. Farcy describes immigrants as the 'spearhead of the social movement of 1936–37 in the Paris Basin'.[84] In relation to the Seine-et-Marne, Ponchelet contends that the strikes 'could never have happened without the massive participation of foreigners'.[85] In contrast, Lynch argues that the role of immigrant workers was 'most probably exaggerated by the police and administrative sources'.[86] This section attempts, firstly, to draw up a balance sheet of the role of immigrant workers in the strike movement before examining the communists' approach towards the immigrant workforce during the Popular Front period.

An assessment of the participation of immigrant workers in the conflict requires comparison between regions and a consideration of the position at different stages of the movement's evolution. A birds-eye view of the first stage would reveal that most workers participating were of French origin. An examination of the population of fifteen communes hit by the Calais-Guînes conflict finds only 18 Polish men and 45 Polish women, an average of only 4 per commune.[87] The majority of Polish agricultural workers in the region were young female farm servants, who faced extreme isolation and played no role in the disputes. In the Artois, the strike at Marquion involved 50 permanent workers and 30 local seasonal workers (15 women and 15 children), but there were only 10 immigrant agricultural workers living in the commune (nine Poles and one Belgian). At Inchy-en-Artois, only 3 of the 86 agricultural workers living in the commune were Polish.[88] Typical of the position in the Somme is Vrély, the first village to join the movement. Out of a population of 495, there were only 36 immigrants.[89] In the strikes to break out in the Beauce, Caux and Nord department, the participants were also almost exclusively French.[90] In the Vermand region, not only did French workers make up a majority of strikers, but there are also several reports of strikebreaking by Polish workers.[91] In the first strikes in the Oise, French workers were also predominant, although here significant groups of immigrant workers were involved.[92] Polish and other immigrant workers were more prominent during the strike at Tremblay-lès-Gonesse and during the initial stage of the movement in the Brie, Multien and around Soissons, regions in which they formed around 50 per cent of strikers.[93] But, even in these cases, it is noticeable that the first farms and villages to join the movement were those in which there were significant numbers of French workers, while villages and farms in which immigrant workers formed the overwhelming majority remained, often, outside the movement's early stages.[94] Villages such as Réau (Seine-et-Marne), where 73 per cent of farm workers were immigrants (predominantly Polish) did not join the movement until its second stage. In short, there seems to have been some hesitancy amongst immigrant workers before joining the conflict.

At La-Ville-aux-Bois, the large majority of strikers were indigenous to the locality.[95] Although farmers recruited some outside labour, primarily Belgian workers, most seasonal workers were drawn from the families of permanent agricultural workers. The breakdown of workers employed on the Drapier farm during the summer of 1936 was 17 local French workers on a yearly contract, 4 Polish workers also on a yearly contract, 2 Belgian seasonal workers and a seventy-year-old labourer, who had worked on the farm for most of his life – 'mon vieil ouvrier', as his employer paternalistically described him. The Polish workers and the old labourer continued to work throughout the strike.[96]

Immigrant workers were more prominent during the movement's second stage. In the two weeks following 20 July 1936, 2536 strikers in the Seine-et-Marne were recorded as being of immigrant origin, 1778 as French.[97] Immigrants also formed the largest proportion of strikers in the Valois and around Soissons. Likewise, there was greater participation by immigrant workers during this stage of the conflict in the Artois, though it can be estimated that, here, indigenous workers made up around 70–75 per cent of strikers.[98] In other regions, French workers also remained in a majority. This was the case in the Santerre (on the strike-hit SIAS farm at Matigny, there were 34 French and 7 Polish/Yugoslavian workers), in the French Vexin (where 74 per cent of workers were French), and on the Picardy plain (at Bailleul-le-Soc, only 19 per cent of agricultural workers were immigrants).[99]

The ethnic make-up of strikers was broadly similar during the movement's final stage – the spring and summer of 1937. The national press gave prominence to conflicts close to Paris, in which immigrants formed the majority of strikers, but virtually ignored those in the Caux, the Cambrésis and Artois, where most of the strikers were French. Indigenous workers also dominated the important dispute in the Saint-Quentin region: out of 59 workers victimised by farmers following the dispute, only 2 had an obviously non-French name.[100] Nevertheless, it is incontestable that the longest and most violent strikes during this period were those in which immigrants were most prominent. In the conflict in the Melun region, beginning on 28 May 1937, 496 (88 per cent) of the 565 participants were recorded as 'étrangers'; while in the Moissy-Cramayel region during June-July 1937, 873 out of 1,050 strikers were of immigrant origin.[101] During these strikes, in which some workers stayed out for more than 60 days, immigrants made up around 90 per cent of those participating in demonstrations and provided the majority of those arrested.[102] Even if likely exaggerations are taken into account, their tenacity is evident from police reports.[103] According to a Republican Guard commander: 'At the entry to the village of Aubigny, the platoon confronted a group of strikers who were trying to prevent ploughs and carts leaving the farms. . . The group (around sixty in all) was comprised mainly of foreigners, and the number of women stood out. The strikers were very aggressive and threatening and greeted the platoon with loud shouts (probably insults), but we were not able to translate them.'[104]

It would seem possible to sketch a general process. The movement's first stage was marked by a certain wait-and-see attitude by immigrant workers. Nevertheless, during these weeks, they were signing up in large numbers to the agricultural workers' union. As Janice Ponty notes, Polish workers were not willing to 'step into full view' by striking, but they wanted to 'take out insurance' by joining the CGT.[105] When the FNTA – a recognised part of French society – sanctioned strike action, immigrants had more confidence to act and, once roused, were particularly determined. The small immigrant (mainly Polish) communities that had emerged in rural and semi-rural areas to the north and east of Paris provided an important cohesion to strikes in these regions. Excluded by French society, their members were firmly bound by national sentiment and the practice of mutual solidarity, with networks largely maintained by women. During the Popular Front, immigrant communities were able to express their grievances openly for the first time. Conversely, the authorities and the farmers responded in a particularly uncompromising fashion to demands from a section of society expected to be obedient and deferential. So, while the description of immigrants as 'the spearhead of the movement' would appear an overstatement, the participation of immigrant communities certainly gave the agricultural conflict some of its most distinctive characteristics.

The hesitancy in joining the conflict and the resolve demonstrated once committed were both rooted in the severe restrictions on immigrants' civil and legal rights. Today, the obstacles would be characterised as forms of institutionalised state racism. Numerous examples can be given of the way in which police specifically targeted immigrant workers. After strikers had blocked the path of workers and horses going into the fields in August 1936 at Barenton-Cel (Aisne), police warned Polish workers that 'they risked possible expulsion because of their attitude'.[106] During the strikes in the Multien, the police captain at Villeneuve-sous-Dammartin reported that 'the brigade is ensuring the maintenance of order. . . the foreign strikers are under particular surveillance'.[107] Throughout the Popular Front period, the Ministry of Labour continued to warn immigrants of grave sanctions if they failed to abide by the conditions of their contract of employment. The Minister wrote to prefects in May 1937: 'It goes without saying that foreign workers must be held. . . strictly to conform to the obligations of their contract and that there are grounds to take severe action against offenders. . . up to the withdrawal of their right to stay.'[108]

The Popular Front government also tightened previous regulations faced by immigrant agricultural workers. A particularly firm line was taken in relation to young workers (under 21) who after spending three years working as agricultural labourers wanted to join their father or mother working in industry. The Ministries of Agriculture and Labour stipulated that 'whatever may be the special circumstances of the worker concerned', there could be no authorisation that would cause 'disruption' to the agricultural labour market or 'serious harm to the farm on which he was employed'.[109] In relation to young women, the government made little attempt to honour agreements with the Polish government designed to ensure basic levels of protection against unscrupulous employers.[110]

The extensive police surveillance of immigrant farm workers allows some insight into those playing a prominent role in the agitation. Most strike leaders amongst the Polish community were relatively young and had put down roots in a particular area over a period of years. In the Seine-et-Oise, a major investigation was conducted into the activities of Pawel Matezak after the French Ambassador in Poland had reported him as a 'communist agent' charged with conducting 'propaganda amongst Polish workers'.[111] A 32-year-old married man with two children, Matezak had worked at the Préaumont farm since March 1930. He first emerged as the principal spokesperson of the Polish farm workers, before becoming union delegate. Sacked together with other union activists in January 1937, he helped to organise a strike at the Préaumont farm in March that (unsuccessfully) sought reinstatement of the workers. The Prefect admitted: 'He has a good reputation as a worker. . . besides his extremist activities, Matezak is not badly thought of at Goussainville.'[112]

Another noticeable category of activists was that of immigrant workers taking refuge in the countryside because of the economic crisis or threat of expulsion. In the Somme, a dossier was prepared on the activities of Albert Jungling, an inhabitant of Sancourt, a small agricultural village of 261 people.[113] Jungling had lived in France since the mid-1920s, but only moved to Sancourt in 1935. A metal worker, he had previously lived in the industrial region of Tergnier-La Fère (Aisne).[114] Police recorded accusations that Jungling had visited inhabitants of Sancourt and neighbouring villages in order to incite them to strike: 'According to several trustworthy people in the commune. . . he is suspected of spreading communist propaganda. . . It is equally likely he is involved in contraband. He has a suspicious appearance and his way of life is dubious.'[115] A link between left-wing activity and criminality was a common thought in the minds of the authorities monitoring the behaviour of immigrant workers.

There was undoubtedly a national dimension to the agricultural conflict. While in many regions the strike movement manifested a unity in action between French and immigrant workers, anti-immigrant sentiments continued to persist amongst important sections of French agricultural workers – sentiments that became more pronounced as the movement waned and disappointment set in with the Popular Front government. Many cases can be found in which French workers refused to support protests by immigrant workers against their conditions. In the Ardres region (Pas-de-Calais), a Polish couple complained that they were being paid a monthly joint-wage of six hundred francs for approximately 168 hours-a-week, while local French male workers were being paid thirty francs-a-day. The police investigator found: 'It is true that these two employees begin work at 6 in the morning and, in the evening, the husband finishes at 6 and his wife at 8. On Sunday, they go to church in the morning and in the afternoon have only a few hours free.' But their complaint was rejected after police interviewed French domestics who told of their satisfaction with conditions on the farm and the high esteem in which they held their employer.[116]

On a number of big farms in the Oise and in the Soissons region, the division between French and immigrant workers provided the basis for the establishment of branches of Colonel de la Rocque's Syndicats professionnels français. In the commune of Mont-l'Évêque (population 376), near Senlis (Oise), a strike broke out on 21 July 1936 involving 39 workers, the majority of whom were immigrants.[117] The SPF section claimed 31 members, the precise number of non-strikers, and was made up of French workers in supervisory positions, members of their families, and relatives of the employer.[118] On the other hand, the immigrant workers formed the backbone of the local FNTA section.

Immigrant workers demanded equality of wages and conditions on the farms but they also began to resist other aspects of their oppression, including discriminatory practices and the open racism to which they were subjected. 'Incidents' arising from workers' refusal to tolerate verbal abuse became more common. At Pargny-les-Bois (Aisne), a farmer 'made some observations' to a Polish worker who was unloading a truck of fertiliser. When the worker replied 'with a word', the employer 'grabbed the Pole by the neck' and sacked him on the spot.[119] Elsewhere in the Aisne, 'M. Petit, the Mayor of Prouvais and local farmer, complained to the gendarmerie that he had been sworn at and threatened by one of his workers, the Pole Antoine Boruta, after he had made "an observation" to the worker while he was reaping the wheat'.[120]

Bonds within some immigrant communities supporting the movement were strengthened when – as in the Brie and Multien during the summer of 1937 – they were confronted by police, farmers and strikebreakers, all drawn from the dominant national group. On 27 May 1937, at Aubigny (Seine-et-Marne), three Polish women accompanied by their children and a 16-year-old Czechoslovakian boy approached a carter, Ladislaw Joc, who was working in a field of sugar beet. Born in Poland, Joc had married a local French woman and was now a naturalised French citizen. The previous summer, he had been the agricultural workers' union representative but was now breaking the strike. The women denounced Joc as a 'dirty Frenchman' [un sale français] and told him that 'the French will eat shit' when the strike finishes. His wife was denounced as 'a piece of French filth' [une saloperie de française].[121] Mirroring the consistent racist abuse endured by immigrants, the insults arose from a double sense of betrayal: Joc's previous role as union leader and his flouting of communal solidarity. They indicate the manner in which the community closed ranks during the conflict and illustrate the importance of the national aspect of Polish farm workers' identity.

The impact of the defeats suffered by the farm workers' movement during the spring and summer of 1937 was greatest for immigrant workers. Repression from farmers and the authorities, the disappearance of the hope of fundamental changes in their social and civil position, led many to abandon union activity, with a corresponding impact on Communist Party membership. Typical is a report on the situation at Saint-Eu (Oise): 'The peasants are supporting Dorgères. The agricultural workers are Polish and not opposed to union organisation but they are foreigners and so – difficulties.'[122] In the market gardening region of Achères, the communist section reported: 'The very large majority of agricultural workers are Polish and Czechoslovakian immigrants and. . . they particularly fear the repression.' In June 1936, communists had helped to build a large union on local farms; two major strikes unfolded during the summer. Within two years, the membership was 'greatly reduced' with the result that the party cell on the farms, 'made up entirely of immigrants', had disintegrated.[123] At Achères, however, some immigrant activists found other ways to continue the struggle, seven of them volunteering for the International Brigades in Spain.[124]

*****

Immigration into agriculture continued to be a contentious issue within agricultural workers' unionism throughout the Popular Front period. While established immigrant rural communities tended to support the movement, more recent arrivals and those living in more isolated situations generally remained subservient to farmers' demands and could be relied upon to break strikes.[125] The practice of using immigrants as cheap, non-unionised labour prevailed and there remained a widespread sentiment amongst agricultural workers that, in order to protect jobs and conditions, immigration into agriculture should be stopped. During the spring of 1937, demonstrations against immigration were held at a number of hiring fairs. At Issoudun, in the Berry, agricultural workers unable to find work protested against 'the recent arrival of contingents of workers into France', rather than against the farmers as they had the previous year.[126] The agricultural associations, on the other hand, placed continuous pressure on the Popular Front government to increase quotas of immigration into agriculture.

Prominent socialists in and close to the agricultural workers' union maintained their previous position that immigration should be restricted into
agriculture, now frequently adding calls for the repatriation of immigrant farm
workers. In the Valois, where Polish workers had played an important role in the
strikes, the deputy Jean Vassal promised (August 1936): 'Since French workers
are being got at [brimer], we are going to take up the issue of regulating the
employment of foreign labour on the farms and have a good number of foreign
labourers sent back to their countries of origin.'[127] At the 1937 FNTA Congress,
Chaussy argued for 'a measure of expulsion' against 'foreign labourers without
ten years' presence in France and who face unemployment'.[128]

The communists' position during the summer of 1936 was very different.
Parsal's arguments during the FNTA's reunification congress against socialist
demands for immigration controls had been adopted as union policy. The
emphasis of propaganda during the strikes centred on the right of immigrant
workers to the same conditions and wages as French workers, a clause that was
enshrined in many collective contracts. Communists made special efforts to draw
immigrant workers into the movement. In the Oise, the Procureur Général
reported in June 1936 that 'the gendarmerie is looking for a foreigner by the
name of Orszulack who is reported to be carrying out strike propaganda amongst
agricultural workers'.[129] The reference was to the 35-year-old Kazimierz
Orszulak, who had lived in France since 1925, and was leader of the communist
faction within the Fédération des émigrés polonais.[130] Orszulak became the
principal leader amongst the Polish agricultural workers and would play an
important role in the functioning of the FNTA at national level. Throughout
1936 and into 1937, the participation of immigrant workers within the FNTA's
activities was, in effect, quite remarkable. Reports noted the enthusiasm
generated by the 'Polish speaker', often Orszulak, at union meetings and
rallies.[131] A section of Le Paysan was given over to material published in Polish.
Beginning as translations of routine notices, directives and information for
activists, the Polish columns were soon receiving reports written by and
reflecting the lives of Polish agricultural workers. At a national level, Orszulak
attended the union's bureau and sometimes presided over its executive, despite
the fact that he was not formally elected to either body.[132] The approach helped
the party to secure considerable support amongst immigrant workers within the
agricultural workers' movement.

The communists' position on immigration began, however, to change. By
fusing the interests of the nation with those of the working class, the party's
Popular Front discourse increasingly championed the 'national workforce' and
inevitably sidelined the position of the immigrant.[133] By November 1936, Parsal
was telling the union executive that it was 'impossible not to oppose a new round
of immigration' in agriculture.[134] An attack on agricultural associations for
attempting to recruit fresh immigrant workers, while workers within France

remained unemployed, became an increasingly consistent theme of communist propaganda.[135] It was not unusual for union activists during strikes to chastise recently arrived immigrant workers for their 'lack of guts and trade union education'.[136] The communists were, however, more conscious than the socialists of the need to formulate a programme that took account of the sensibilities of immigrant workers within the farm workers' movement. They made no calls for repatriation and injected a large dose of class rhetoric by arguing that measures to limit the employment of immigrant labour should be particularly applied to farmers who had victimised trade unionists. This was another instance of communists embracing the national interest while seeking to maintain the symbiosis with their base, in this case the support they were gaining amongst immigrant farm workers. Nevertheless, at no time during the Popular Front period did communists criticise the government for sustaining discriminatory legislation and regulations faced by immigrant workers. As the movement declined during 1937, they argued more frequently for controls on immigration, sometimes linking the question with the needs of national defence.[137] When the government agreed in May 1938 to tighten regulations on immigration into agriculture, it was one of the few occasions when the union would claim that the government had listened to its demands.

Throughout the farm strikes, reports in *l'Humanité* and other sections of the communist press gave little indication of the significant participation of immigrant workers within the conflict. Strikes were viewed strictly in conventional class terms: a struggle between workers and 'large farmers and proprietors'. The communist vision ignored not only the community aspect of the movement but also the specific interests of a large section of its participants, immigrants as well as women. The perception of a conflict exclusively involving 'large farmers' also misrepresented another essential characteristic of the movement – the way in which it touched a significant section of the small and middling peasantry.

7

THE FARM STRIKES AND THE PROBLEM OF 'PEASANT UNITY'

No, I refuse to have anything more to do with these workers. They want to be masters of my farm and no longer obey my wife or myself. I'm not going to take them back at any price. And yet I'm radical-socialist and a supporter of the Popular Front.

M. Delcroix, farmer at Saint-Rémy-en-l'Eau (Oise),
during a strike involving his six workers, August 1937.[1]

There was a poignant moment during the Communist Party's first national conference following the Popular Front election, held on 10–11 July 1936 in Paris. The 'representative of the agricultural region of Clay-Dammartin' (Seine-et-Marne), as he described himself, came to the rostrum. Reporting that his region had just established 17 new cells with a total of 300 members, mostly farm workers, he turned towards Maurice Thorez and Marcel Cachin, the editor of *l'Humanité*, and presented them with a sheaf of wheat and poppies: the wheat representing his region's identity, the poppies symbolising 'the colour of our hopes'.[2] Earlier, in his general secretary's address, Thorez had proposed a package of measures for agricultural workers, including the regulation of working hours, a mandatory day-off each week, the extension of social legislation, and a proposal for an Agricultural Labour Code.[3] Significantly, and in marked contrast to the priorities outlined in his pre-election radio address, Thorez had articulated the demands of farm workers before turning to issues relating to the wider peasantry. When Waldeck Rochet came to the podium shortly after the general secretary, he also acknowledged the importance of the farm strike movement – but his emphasis was on its problematic aspects, particularly its negative consequences for peasant unity: 'Our policy. . . is not a policy that aims to set agricultural workers against small and middling farmers but, on the contrary, which attempts to make them partners [les associer] in a common effort. . . It is even necessary to find the means to reconcile their interests and not encourage conflicts between agricultural workers and small and middling farmers.'[4]

Taken together, the two speeches well illustrate the contradictory impact of the agricultural workers' movement on communist agrarian strategy. While the party recognised and championed workers' demands, its vision of peasant unity meant it simultaneously sought to reconcile the conflict between workers and peasant employers. The difficulties faced by communists in translating this policy into political practice along with the inevitable tensions it created are the principal themes of this chapter.

Waldeck Rochet and the Strike Movement

An abridged version of Rochet's speech was published in *l'Humanité* under the headline, 'Agricultural workers and farmers have common interests'.[5] The article, which supplied the template for propaganda by communists in many rural areas,[6] outlined the essential problem:

> On the one hand, agricultural workers quite rightly do not want to be treated as second-class citizens and are demanding a limit on the working day, better wages and the general benefits of the social legislation introduced for workers in industry. On the other hand, amongst farmers employing wage labour are tens of thousands of farmers working for themselves and with their family and also employing one, two, three, four or five agricultural workers. These small and middling farms have been hit hard by the crisis and the collapse in the price of agricultural produce. So, when speaking of reducing hours and raising wages for agricultural workers, we cannot ignore the difficult situation of these small and middling farms. The question posed is how to satisfy the legitimate demands of agricultural workers without worsening the situation of these small and middling farmers.[7]

The proposed solution was a 'comprehensive agricultural policy' that would equally benefit farmers and agricultural workers. By increasing agricultural prices, reducing costs and providing cheap loans, farmers' economic position could be improved: they would be able to pay better wages and grant shorter working hours to workers, without any detrimental affect on income.[8]

Rochet's argument, though consistent with that outlined in Moscow the previous year (see Chapter 4), had evolved to make further concessions to agrarianism. Firstly, the category of small and middling farmers, against whom strikes should be avoided, had been extended to cover farmers employing up to five workers (in reality more, if seasonal labour was included). Secondly, the notion that an improved economic position for farmers would be translated into improvements in wages and conditions, as an almost automatic process, now came close to justifying farmers' arguments that wages of agricultural workers should be tied to the price of agricultural produce. On this point, communists within the FNTA took a very different approach. Trade unionists had always opposed the traditional practice in large-scale farming regions to link workers' wages to the price of bread, which was still common during the 1920s, and now resisted the agrarian argument that wage increases should be dependant on increases in the price of wheat.[9] In some regions, however, farmers managed to insist that clauses linking wages to agricultural prices be included in collective contracts and were sometimes surprised to receive support from local communists.[10] 'For several weeks, agricultural workers have been stirred by agitation and, justifiably, have demanded an increase in their wages', wrote Serge Lefranc, a prominent activist in the Étampes region. 'What do the farmers say? Simply this: "We would like to meet the demands of our workers, but on the sole condition that we are able to sell our produce at prices which allows us to meet our expenses." These farmers are absolutely right. We are not amongst those who attempt to bring agricultural workers into conflict with small and middling farmers.'[11] Such arguments, consistent with Rochet's reasoning, precluded any consideration of an exploitative element in the relationship between small and middling farmers and their workers.

A major problem for Rochet's argument was that legislation to alleviate the position of farmers could only be introduced at government level, and at some point in the future. Yet the social movement of agricultural workers was evolving in an increasingly profound fashion in the present. It was, therefore, difficult to avoid taking a position on the strikes. Nevertheless, Rochet managed to avoid giving explicit support to the agricultural workers' movement, a remarkable position for the party's rural policymaker to take.[12] Others in the Agrarian Section were less equivocal. As we have noted (Chapter 5), Mioch demanded that farm workers should 'only direct their blows' against 'big capitalist farmers' and should not disrupt the small and middling holdings in any way.[13] The extent to which this policy was followed will be returned to shortly.

The Strikes and the Small and Middling Farmers

Historians drawing a balance sheet of the period have noted the 'paradox' that farmers were 'the section of society that gained most from the Popular Front'.[14] Yet, in late 1936 and early 1937, evidence indicates a widespread disillusionment in rural communities with the actions of government. Although the price of wheat had almost doubled – fixed at 140 francs a quintal for 1936 by the Wheat Office, compared with around eighty francs in 1935 – many of the potential benefits had been wiped out by inflation. 'At every country fair, in every rural café and shop', observed Renaud Jean, 'it's the same refrain: "How do price rises help us if the produce we buy undergoes an increase which is identical, if not more?".'[15] With the exception of the revision of the hated law on peasant debts, which had permitted the public seizure of peasant property, little else had changed. One of the biggest disappointments for tenant farmers was the government's failure to introduce a promised law on 'cultural property', which would have recognised rights of farmers over improvements to land and buildings rented from a landlord. Peasants are resentful, argued Renaud Jean, because they feel that 'they did not get their share' of the 'enormous legislative package' carried out by the Popular Front in June and July. 'They have the impression that the actions of the Popular Front were pursued solely on behalf of workers and public servants.'[16]

As 1936 continued, the communist leadership became increasingly concerned with the mood of the peasantry. Maurice Thorez opened the October meeting of the Central Committee by commenting on the way in which, 'the development of the workers' movement has frightened elements of the petite bourgeoisie' in both town and country. He was followed by a parade of speakers giving examples of 'the fear amongst the peasants': a delegate from Normandy spoke of the growing influence of the PSF amongst farmers; another from Alsace noted that reaction against the Popular Front had become bolder following the farm occupation at Guebwiller; Benoît Frachon, the party's principal trade union leader, remarked that 'the slightest strike is considered by peasants as something abnormal' and urged the party to do more to avoid conflicts.[17] This, of course, applied particularly to strikes by agricultural workers.

Articles commenting on the farm strikes in l'Humanité, La Voix Paysanne and, after January, La Terre – the new peasant paper, edited by Rochet – attempted to reassure peasant readers. The common theme was that the strikes were exclusively affecting the big farmers. Reports of advances by the union into new regions were accompanied with promises that 'contrary to what is being said. . . we have no intention of plundering our small farmer comrades'.[18] Small employers were portrayed as treating their workers fairly and honouring contracts. This is true because 'often the small and middling proprietor is a former agricultural worker who has known their hardship and suffering. . . he loves them and wants to improve their lot in life as much as we do', wrote Mioch, overlooking the fact that the small employer was often the most demanding.[19] 'Where the farmer works with one, two or three agricultural workers', reported Parsal, 'there are no conflicts.'[20] Sometimes, though, articles intimated that relations between workers and smaller farmers were far from harmonious. Le Paysan reported that union activists in the Auneau region (Eure-et-Loir) had concluded that 'small farmers have not yet sufficiently realised that the big employer is their irreconcilable enemy'.[21] In the Caux, Fernand Legagneux, a member of the party's Regional Bureau, described how 'the big proprietors' had incited smaller farmers 'against agricultural trade unionists, in such a way that throughout the department the normally peaceful rural population is divided into two camps'.[22]

What, then, was the direct impact of the strikes on small and middling farmers? The position varied between regions. In the Brie, during the strike starting on 20 July, the average number of strikers on each farm was 14. Some affected farms were extremely large: 71 workers walked off the Garnier farm at May-en-Multien, 51 off the Dewulf farm at Soignolles.[23] In the Soissons region, during June 1936, the average number of strikers per farm was 24.[24] In the Nanteuil canton in the Valois on 21 July, the Sub-Prefect reported 1138 strikers on 38 farms, an average of 30 per farm.[25] The communists had no problem in supporting disputes on such farms: the only consideration was the impact of agrarian anti-strike propaganda on the wider peasantry. Yet, even in regions where agricultural holdings were most concentrated, the number of small and middling farms drawn into the movement was significant. In relation to the Brie, the Seine-et-Marne Prefecture recorded 320 farms touched by the 20 July movement. While the largest 62 provided 1913 strikers, 83 farms employed five or fewer workers, and there were an unspecified number of 'small farms' employing only ones and twos. Small and middling farms made up 30 per cent of strike-bound farms, although providing only a small percentage of the total number of strikers (around 6 per cent).[26]

On the fringes of Paris, market gardening posed particular problems for communists. In the 'red suburb' of Bobigny, between 120 and 130 small enterprises each employed and lodged between one and three workers.[27] In the period before the Popular Front elections, the party had conducted propaganda amongst the gardeners, whose livelihood had been hit hard by the economic crisis. But, as Annie Fourcaut notes, events in June 1936 ensured that any possibility of accruing positive results from this activity evaporated. When, between 15 and 20 June, a strike mobilised almost all 200 agricultural workers in Bobigny, the communist-controlled municipality offered support, including premises and food, to the participants. For the communists, the contradictions of a broad class alliance now 'burst open' and it was 'impossible to demonstrate class solidarity with the workers and also hope to conserve the neutrality of the employers'.[28] The outcome was the political radicalisation of the market gardeners, many of whom by the autumn were firm followers of Dorgères.

The process outlined by Fourcaut was replicated in many other regions of the Paris basin and northern France. The position in the Calais and Artois conflicts has already been outlined.[29] In the Somme, strike-hit villages included Épéhy, where, in August 1936 the movement involved 104 strikers on 30 farms.[30] In the Vermand region (Aisne), although the strike touched many large farms, the position at Bohain – 49 striking workers on 13 farms – was not untypical.[31] In the Thelle region (Oise), where 644 workers stopped work on 1 July 1936, the average number of strikers per farm was 4.5 per cent.[32] In the Beauce, at Béville-le-Compte (Eure-et-Loir), the strike involved 65 workers on 13 farms. While the four largest employed 15, 14, 12 and 12 workers, the majority of farms affected employed five or less.[33]

During 1937, communists made even greater attempts to present the strikes as involving only 'a handful' of 'big capitalist farmers'.[34] In the Brie and Multien, the union took a decision not to include small farms in the strike, on condition that farmers signed a pledge to abide by its outcome. But this approach was the exception rather than rule. Throughout the Paris basin and north, cases abound in which party activists working in or supporting the agricultural workers' union conspicuously pursued a policy contrary to that outlined by party.

The strikes in the Cambrésis during the spring of 1937 were led by communists and involved over a thousand workers. Although a statistical breakdown is not available for the entire region, police in Arleux diligently listed the strikers in the villages they covered. At Bugnicourt, they recorded 40 strikers on 25 farms; at Dechy, 58 on 25 farms; and at Lécluse, 12 on 8 farms.[35] The workers were defeated after 'small farmers, faced with the urgency of carrying out the work, appealed to parents and friends in neighbouring villages to come to help them'.[36] The following year, the regional party organised a 'peasant conference' and reviewed the lessons of the farm strikes. The report sent to party head-quarters criticised the agricultural workers' movement for adopting 'an attitude that was a bit too violent towards the farmers and small proprietors employing wage workers'. It concluded: 'In the aftermath of the victory of 1936. . . many farmers joined the party or were sympathising with it. The agricultural workers' strike has lost us a section of sympathisers.'[37]

Communist activists in the Aisne were also criticised from within the party. Here, the first farms hit during the strikes of July 1937 were the large farms at Ollezy and Dury, operated by the SIAS. But, once again, many small and middling farms were drawn into the conflict. The strike involved 39 out of the 43 workers on ten farms at Wiège-Faty; 60 out of 75 workers on seventeen farms at Puisieux-et-Canlieu; 32 out of 42 workers on nine farms at Aisonville-et-Bernoville; 26 out of 36 workers on eight farms at Gricourt.[38] In the Saint-Quentin region, the police reported that 150 workers on 'farms of little import-ance employing only one or two workers' had joined the strike.[39] A party propagandist complained that the Aisne communists had behaved as if the only social groups within agriculture were 'big country squires' [gros hobereaux] and wage workers and had, consequently, refused to defend the interests of small farmers 'for fear of losing influence amongst agricultural workers'.[40]

In the Caux, communists also pursued an approach at variance to that advocated by Rochet. Support for the party amongst agricultural workers had grown substantially in the year following the Popular Front elections and communists topped the poll in a number of villages at the cantonal elections in April 1937.[41] With enhanced confidence, workers began formulating demands and in May and June a wave of strikes swept the region.[42] This was a conflict in which the vast majority of farmers would have been officially classed by communists as paysans travailleurs: the average number of workers employed on strike-hit farms was just below four, and around 80 per cent of farms employed five or fewer workers.[43] Local communists rejected any suggestion that the relationship between peasant employers and workers was anything but restrictive and oppressive. An article in the regional party newspaper commented: 'On our farms we are the subject of suffocating supervision. By every means possible, our employers are preventing their workers to broaden and enlighten their minds. And that is relatively easy in these farms in which two, three or four workers are in permanent contact with their boss.'[44] For the Caux communists, it was out of the question that peasant employers and workers should become 'partners in a common effort'.

The peasant policy pursued by communists in the Paris basin and parts of northern France was influenced by the fact that agriculture was often relatively close to urban centres with big concentrations of the industrial working class. Offering leadership to the farm workers' movement was viewed as a bigger political priority than any consideration of the conflict's potential impact on the wider peasantry. Moreover, in many regions, there remained a legacy of hostility towards farmers on account of their traditional support for the political right and attachment to clericalism. Even when party activists were urged to pay more attention to the 'peasant question', as they had been at the Pas-de-Calais regional conference held in June 1936, it did not fundamentally alter their approach. After an Information Conference in the Pas-de-Calais in February 1937, the Central Committee's representative complained 'that not a single delegate [had] dealt with the question of the peasantry which is, it seems, almost ignored [by the party] in the region, despite its significant size within the department'.[45] In regions dominated socially by the peasantry and politically by agrarianism, the party's approach could, however, be decidedly different. 'Peasant unity' was more likely to become the centrality of political practice. Communists were likely to be more sensitive to the fact that support for the agricultural workers' movement would pose serious problems for their relations with small and middling farmers.

Uniting Workers and Farmers in the Auvergne

Farming in the western party of the Cantal was dominated by dairy production and cattle rearing. The agricultural cycle was underpinned by the region's geography – shaped by an extinct volcano – and extreme variations in climate. During the summer months, cattle were taken to graze on the high plateaux, the accompanying agricultural workers living in *burons* (stone huts) in which they made cheese. As frosty mornings approached, the animals returned to farms based in villages nestling in the valleys.[46] Although outlets to markets had created a relatively prosperous agriculture in this part of the Auvergne, farms did not recruit large numbers of workers.[47] In March 1936, a Communist Party report noted that those 'employing more than three workers are rare and it is almost impossible to imagine action by workers against their employers'.[48] Workers were generally recruited on yearly contracts negotiated personally with farmers, leading to wide variations in pay and conditions. Summer life in the *burons* was particularly hard – a seven-day working week from dawn to dusk, often combined with solitude.

A radicalisation amongst farm workers in the months preceding the election of the Popular Front government is indicated by the numbers joining the Communist Party. In March 1936, membership was reported as showing a 'very noticeable increase', with agricultural workers forming 'a higher percentage of new recruits during the last five weeks'.[49] In the Mauriac region, a cell was created made up totally of agricultural workers.[50] Along with building workers, agricultural workers were described as forming 'the active strength of the party in rural villages'.[51] Although during 1934 communists had temporarily succeeded in establishing an agricultural trade union of 50 members,[52] at the time of the Popular Front elections the regional leadership was fully committed to a position of peasant unity and considered that a unionisation campaign would be disruptive to this aim. In any case, while conflicts swept through the wheat and sugar-beet fields in the north of the country, the herdsmen were leaving their farms to spend the summer in the mountains. It was not until they returned in the autumn that Cantal farm workers began to demand the kind of improvements in wages and conditions accorded in other regions.

As discontent amongst agricultural workers began to grow during the autumn, the Cantal communists continued to dismiss the idea that they should organise in support of workers' independent demands. A commentary in the regional party newspaper declared:

> The peasant class must be united if it wants to triumph. The enemies of the working class, who are also those of the peasant class, think only of divide and rule. We, communists, say that peasants in the Cantal must be careful and not fall into a trap set by their clever ploy. At the present time, they are trying to set agricultural workers against small and middling farmers. Keep a cool head.[53]

The pressure to take up the cause of farm workers was not, however, coming from 'the enemies of the working class' but from agricultural workers turning up in increasing numbers to party meetings. In late November, a propagandist touring the region reported to party headquarters that 'in several meetings, agricultural workers have demanded to get organised, astonished that nothing has been done for them'.[54]

Two weeks later, the Cantal CGT, led by communists, agreed to launch a unionisation drive on the farms. Whether or not pressure to do so was exerted on the regional leadership from the national party, following the report from the propagandist, is not clear. The new orientation was, however, quite consistent with the party's attempt to balance pressures emanating from the agricultural workers' movement with those arising from the strategy of peasant unity. Throughout the winter, enthusiastic meetings were held in villages in the valleys and on the Trizac and Cheylade plains. By the spring, 40 sections of the agricultural workers' union had been established, with between fifteen hundred and two thousand members.[55] A number of teachers, including the party's regional secretary, Michel Leymarie, participated in the campaign. Emerging as the union's principal spokesperson and organiser was another party member, Jean Hilaire, a herdsman from Thiézac. Leymarie expressed satisfaction at the union's progress, particularly as 'the multiplicity of small farms [and] the absence of big domains in which country squires lay down the law. . . create psychological conditions resistant to the spirit of trade unionism'.[56] Doubts about whether the party should be making a turn towards agricultural workers nevertheless persisted within the regional party and Leymarie directly addressed them: 'I hear the pessimists declaring: "are you not going to clash with our small proprietors and farmers? They will not understand the claims of the domestics. As a consequence, they will be tempted to go over to the camp of the bourgeois".'[57] Although he recognised that such a risk existed, Leymarie argued that it could be minimised through a skilfully applied policy ensuring solidarity between 'all labouring classes of the soil'.[58]

Yet, the growth of the agricultural workers' union did, indeed, provoke a reaction. Farmers and their sons turned up at union public meetings, shouting down speakers and threatening workers signing up.[59] What most concerned regional party leaders was the character of the opposition. Not only had the farm workers' movement inflamed, quite expectedly, the fury of the 'reactionary and fascist big farmers', it had also induced 'violent and unfair criticisms from small farmers and proprietors'.[60] By February, a campaign was well underway to break the farm workers' movement: 'The zeal of certain farmers – unfortunately not the biggest! – is worthy of a better cause', declared the communist paper.[61]

The Cantal communists began a desperate attempt to resolve the tensions between workers and farmers. Following a discussion at the Regional Committee, Leymarie requested advice from the CGPT headquarters in Paris: 'The organisation of agricultural workers is antagonising the small and middling proprietors and farmers. It is necessary that we bridge the gap between them, otherwise we risk pushing many paysans travailleurs, sympathetic to the Popular Front, towards the fascist organisations.'[62] He was surprised to receive a reply not from the CGPT but from the party secretariat simply repeating the need to build agricultural workers' unions whilst not antagonising small farmers.[63]

There were three aspects to the position now adopted by the Cantal communists. Firstly, propaganda argued that 'sharecroppers, farmers, and small proprietors', together with agricultural workers, were 'all proletarians' who needed to unite together against the 'common enemy of capitalism'.[64] One article argued:

> In the towns, the worker slaves away in the grime, the smoke and noise, and on mind-numbing production lines, and does not know his employer. . . With the majority earning a pittance to provide profits for a minority, is it any wonder that these conditions give rise to feelings of hatred between employers and workers? In the countryside, it is quite different. More often than not. . . the employer lives with his workers; he shares their work, while overseeing it; he shares their meal. . . There needs to be not conflict but understanding between employers and employees, whose interests are interconnected.[65]

The points are, of course, identical to those put forward by Renaud Jean in the early 1920s: a 'proletarian' peasant class, an idealisation of agricultural work, an idyllic view of the relationship between employer and worker. The problem for the communists was that the agricultural workers' movement was increasingly challenging this vision.

Conditions faced by farm workers in the Cantal are indicated by the *cahier* formulated by the union in early 1937. The claim included a maximum 15-hour-day during the four summer months and a single day-off per month for herdsmen and their assistants.[66] Workers also demanded the 'freedom of expression' and other basic rights, including the end to 'political, religious and other pressures on agricultural workers and farm servants'.[67] Such demands, of course, contradicted the notion of a harmonious employer-worker relationship presented by communist agrarianism in the Cantal.[68]

The communists argued, secondly, that farmers should respond to the organisation of their workers by creating an organisation to fight for their own interests. The proposed 'peasants' syndicate' would campaign for legislation, including the establishment of Milk and Meat Offices to regulate prices (on the same lines as the Wheat Office) and for controls on imports. The introduction of these measures could then allow farmers to 'earn more money' and 'by mutual agreement' resolve the demands of agricultural workers.[69] Peasant organisation did indeed begin to develop in the Cantal, but its primary focus was to resist workers' demands and undermine their union. In early 1937, Dorgères began activity in the department and his supporters soon established a network of 'Syndicats mixtes professionnels', uniting proprietors, farmers and agricultural workers within the same association.[70] Although communists complained that Dorgères was 'stirring up trouble', the party found itself politically disarmed in the face of the 'mixed unions', which were, in effect, the logical organisational conclusion to draw from its own assessment of the worker/employer relationship in the countryside.

Thirdly, noticing that attempts to calm the wrath of farmers were meeting little success, Leymarie suggested agricultural workers take an initiative in order to reassure employers. He argued that the union should propose that their wages be tied to the price of agricultural produce:

> Wages, in the way they are assessed, are currently a dupery for the worker, if the market rises, and for the employer, if the market falls. A relationship should be established between the earnings of the employer and the pay of the agricultural worker. Since the Cantal is made up of a majority of cattle rearers, it should be possible to base wages on the average market price of the main products: cheese and livestock. Each month, the average price of cheese and cattle should be established and a scale of coefficients drawn up applicable to each category of worker. A departmental commission, comprised of delegates from the Chamber of Agriculture, the Syndicate of the Paysans Travailleurs and the agricultural workers' union should be created for this purpose. What do you think of this suggestion, comrades? It's your turn to speak![71]

His proposal amounted to a form of agrarian corporatism that was, in some respects, even more pronounced than that embraced by the farmers' associations.

Linking the worker's cause to the functioning of the farmer's business neither assisted the building of the farm workers' movement nor succeeded in appeasing peasant employers. As Leymarie had noted at the outset of the campaign, 'workers will not join the union simply to have a membership card in their pocket'.[72] Unions were a means not only to improve wages, but also workers' general conditions and social position. They were unlikely to attract members and activists if prospects of real change were limited, particularly when membership invited severe repression from the employers. By late 1937, even prominent communist activists in the farm workers' movement had become disillusioned with the lack of progress.[73] On the other hand, the communists' strategy failed to halt employers' drift towards right-wing reaction. By 1938, the Dorgerist-inspired peasant organisation had reached 150 sections and 5727 members, constituting a 'very dangerous movement', according to a communist report.[74] At the party's regional conference in May 1938, Leymarie could only lament on 'the outcome of errors. . . which have set small peasants against agricultural workers and pushed them towards the Dorgerists'.[75]

The Cantal is one of the most striking examples of the way in which contradictory social pressures conditioned communist peasant policy. The party lurched within a matter of months from a rather passive position of peasant unity to an active campaign to build agricultural workers' unions to, finally, the advocacy of an explicitly agrarian argument in a vain attempt to reconcile class antagonisms in the rural world. Although the party supported and associated with the agricultural workers' movement, the social weight of the peasantry induced it to adopt a more accommodating position towards employers than that generally pursued by activists in the Paris basin and north. In some regions, communists adopted a third model of political behaviour – one that refused completely to recognise the legitimacy of an agricultural workers' movement. Such was the position in the Calvados.

A 'Fascist Provocation' in the Calvados

In terms of the social structure of agriculture, the position in the Calvados was, if anything, more favourable to the development of an agricultural workers' movement than that in the Cantal.[76] Wage workers made up 42 per cent of the peasantry, a higher ratio than some strike-hit departments in the Paris basin and north.[77] There were, however, no strikes in the department and the FNTA failed to establish any local sections, even in embryonic form.[78]

A number of factors contributed to the movement's absence. Overwhelmingly rural without a radical tradition, the Calvados was one of an enclave of departments in north-west France in which more than half of the votes were cast for the right at the 1936 elections.[79] While the relatively small amount of large-scale industry limited the scale of the June 'social explosion' in the towns, the weakness of the labour movement did little to restrain the development of right-wing reaction in the countryside.[80] Dorgerism had, notes Paxton, by the mid-1930s already 'penetrated established agrarian organisations more deeply in the Calvados than in any other department'.[81] Moreover, the process of structural change in social relations in agriculture of the kind witnessed in the Paris basin had proceeded extremely slowly. Important sections of agricultural workers still identified with the interests of their employers and became politically attached to Dorgerism and other trends of right-wing agrarianism. When dairy workers staged a strike at Isigny in late 1936, the regional CGT was horrified to find that many of those mobilised by farmers to break the strike were 'authentic agricultural workers'.[82]

The regional right-wing press widely reported the strikes on farms in the Paris basin and north. Similar actions in the Calvados, it was announced, would face severe repression. 'The communists are playing with fire. But we warn them, it's a futile and dangerous game', warned one article, before adding that farmers were preparing their rifles.[83] Communists in the Calvados, however, not only had little intention of organising agricultural workers, but they were also quick to condemn those who attempted to do so.

The position of the Calvados communists has to be viewed against the background of their general response to strikes involving small employers. In the big cities and industrial regions, many small firms were drawn into the 'social explosion'; in Paris, for example, strikes took place in cafés and even hairdressers. Communist support for such movements was conditioned by the city's political and social climate: the overwhelming sympathy of the population for the strikes. In the Calvados, however, the workers' movement and the left functioned in a more politically hostile environment. Not only was the rural–urban balance of the population markedly different, but within the towns the social weight of small employers was much higher: 60 per cent of non-agricultural workers were employed in firms employing less than ten workers (compared with 43 per cent nationally and 24 per cent in Paris).[84] Consequently, communists reacted defensively to a press campaign highlighting the impact of the strike movement on small employers and accusing the communists of 'seeking to ruin small artisans'. When three workers stopped work at a sawmill in Balleroy, raising a red flag over the establishment, the local communist cell attempted to disassociate itself from the strike, which it claimed had been staged by fascists.[85]

The approach in relation to potential movements amongst farm workers was even more cautious. After a new recruit to the party proposed that a campaign be waged to organise agricultural workers' unions, he was declared an 'agent provocateur' for wanting to 'incite workers against their employers'.[86] Reporting the incident, local communists explained that his 'over eagerness' had given him away:

> Considering the difficulties against which farmers and small proprietors, who are the large majority here, are struggling; and seeing the campaign waged by fascists claiming that we want to ruin the peasants by jeopardising their harvests, it is clear what the Dorgerists were up to. Unfortunately for them, we did not fall into the trap.[87]

In another incident, in the village of Neuilly-la-Forêt, a local resident, this time not a party member, applied for a room in the mairie for a meeting to establish an agricultural workers' union. When he asked local communists to assist in publicising the meeting, the activity was again denounced as a 'fascist provocation'. On the day of the meeting, a convoy of 500 Greenshirts arrived in the locality. Armed with 'pitchforks, scythes and large stones, they assembled in the courtyard of a farm, where a speaker spewed out threats of death against trade unionists and communists'.[88] For the communists, this was proof that the initiative had been a 'crude manoeuvre' rather than a genuine attempt to organise a union, an assumption accepted at face value by the editors of *La Voix Paysanne*.[89]

The attempt to blame farm strikes on 'fascists' was not isolated to the Calvados. During the summer of 1937 in the Issoudun region (Indre), the local communist leader Robert Habert, who the previous year had led a strike by agricultural workers, associated the idea of renewing the conflict with the

extreme right. According to police, he urged workers at the Issoudun hiring fair
to demand 'the highest wages possible, but to be wary of giving any credence to
certain agitators (for example, the Dorgerists) who are encouraging strikes in
agricultural regions'.[90] Around the same time, in the Étampes region, an article
in the party newspaper (by the aforementioned Lefranc) praised local farmers for
awarding pay rises at the recent hiring fairs. Simultaneously, it criticised an
unsuccessful attempt by the local agricultural workers' union to launch a strike
in support of a new collective contract, condemning those who 'wanted the strike
and resulting unrest amongst agricultural workers' of 'admirably serving fascist
demagogy'.[91]

Two Ideas on 'Peasant Unity'

The above survey illustrates the way in which the agricultural workers' movement not only brought the two traditional trends on agrarian strategy to the
surface but also sharpened the antagonism between them. Some communist
activists gave uncompromising support to workers, showing little concern for
the impact on paysan travailleurs. Others reserved their empathy for peasant
employers and viewed workers' demands as, at best, an unwelcome complication
for the project of peasant unity. The attempt by the party to synthesise the two
trends by supporting agricultural workers' demands while seeking to limit their
impact on small and middling employers was unsuccessful. Tensions within the
party provoked by the agricultural workers' movement were, however, not all
directly related to workers' demands and strikes. Perhaps inevitably, the workers'
struggle was also at the root of differences over how the policy of the Peasant
Popular Front should practically be pursued.

In September 1936, the communists supported a conference held at Châteauroux
under the grandiose title of General Estates of the Peasantry [États Généraux de
la Paysannerie]. The event was jointly organised by the CGPT and the socialist-
inspired CNP. Waldeck Rochet and others in the Agrarian Section had argued
for its aims to be ambitious, the beginning of a 'vast peasant assembly' [vaste
rassemblement paysan], unifying all major organisations in the rural world. In
contrast, the socialists insisted that attendance should be limited to autonomous
regional peasant organisations, along with members from the CGPT and CNP.[92]
Despite losing out in this debate, the communists placed considerable
significance on the event, announcing that it would be a step towards 'a great
peasant organisation' that would be established within the subsequent six
months.[93]

Rochet's speech, updating the party's strategy for peasant unity, was reproduced in the national and regional communist press. Stressing again a common
peasant interest, one transcending political and class divisions, Rochet argued for
'a single national peasant confederation', representing 'all members of the same

profession', and fulfilling the same role as does the CGT in relation to workers in the towns:

> Whatever their political or religious opinions. . . whether on the left or the right, the peasant wants to sell his produce at a fair price to be able to live through his work. . . Whether Catholic, agrarian or socialist, the peasant aspires to loosen the extortion of the trusts, giant distributors and middlemen, as well as crushing taxation. The agricultural syndicates and various organisations created with the aim of defending the interests of the profession. . . should be neither right nor left. They must be unions nothing more, nothing less, having only one aim: to defend peasant interests.[94]

To emphasis his point, Rochet appropriated the slogan of the right-wing agrarians: 'neither right nor left, but peasant' [ni droite, ni gauche, rien que paysan]. He insisted, however, that it be applied in an inclusive fashion, criticising those 'agrarians with a fascist tendency', who utilised it to organise only right-wing peasants and to create 'conflict and even fratricidal struggles' in the villages.[95]

While the last point was a veiled reference to events surrounding the farm strikes, any direct reference to agricultural workers, or their demands and struggles, was conspicuously absent from Rochet's speech. A movement whose ramifications did not fit into the schema of uniting 'all members of a profession' and 'common peasant interests' was simply ignored. Rochet's use of the word 'paysan' to signify a 'profession' aiming to 'sell its produce' – a definition that implicitly excluded those who sold their labour – was another concession to agrarianism. Despite the claim that the General Estates represented 'all categories of workers of the land and all regions of France', representatives of agricultural workers had not been invited to participate, or even to observe.

The General Estates, and particularly Rochet's speech, immediately created unease amongst leading communists within the FNTA. Their first complaint was over the omission of agricultural workers from the conference.[96] In an article in Le Paysan, Parsal barely hid his contempt: 'All attempts to create a Peasant Assembly [Rassemblement Paysan] have failed. . . because agricultural workers' organisations have been either disregarded [dédaignées] or excluded [éliminées] and insofar as there has been an appeal to agricultural workers, it has been to have them serve as hostages.'[97] But Parsal's second criticism went deeper and touched on how the party should interpret the concept of peasant unity. As an alternative to Rochet's proposals, he proposed a 'new idea' of uniting 'all true peasants' within a Peasant Cartel [Cartel Paysan].[98]

There would, on the surface, appear little divergence between this proposal and that put forward by the secretary of the Agrarian Section, but Parsal's approach was fundamentally different. Rather than being sidelined from the project of creating a peasant organisation, agricultural workers' unions would become one of its major components. Within the 'cartel', agricultural workers would unite with working farmers and campaign for measures such as the revalorisation of agricultural produce and the stabilisation of prices. But, crucially, their own demands would neither be sidelined nor subordinated to the need for peasant unity. Instead, they would become a condition around which peasant unity would be built: 'We are ready to collaborate with all organisations that accept the just demands of agricultural workers', wrote Parsal.[99]

Proposals for the new organisation, which would affiliate to the CGT under the name Confédération Paysanne, were drawn up and presented to the party in late 1936. The component sections of the confederation were to be the FNTA, a new federation to organise small sharecroppers, a federation of small and midd-ling proprietors or tenant farmers (to be formed by the CGPT and other autonomous peasant organisations), and a federation of agricultural technicians.[100] When the proposals were discussed at the Agrarian Section in early 1937, it was conceded that such a peasant confederation would permit 'a very wide recruitment amongst the poorest and most politically advanced peasants'. But the idea was resolutely rejected. If adopted, it would provoke the hostility of middling and comfortably well-off peasants, as well as 'more politically backward small proprietors who consider their class interests to be closer to the big landed proprietors than to wageworkers'. According to the Agrarian Section:

> The constitution of a peasant federation. . . would encourage the creation and consolidation of a reactionary rural bloc under the control of the Dorgerist extremists. Two blocs would confront each other in the countryside, the bloc of poor peasants with the CGT and that of the peasants hostile to the CGT who would more easily fall prey to fascism. It would therefore be contrary to our policy of unity of the French peasantry.[101]

While Parsal's language was coloured by the rhetoric of the Popular Front (at the January 1937 congress, where he repeated his proposition, he spoke of 'united peasant action. . . on the rich and beautiful land of France'),[102] his position on peasant unity remained in the tradition of the orthodox approach within French Marxism and the thesis of the Third International's Second Congress. It continued to place agricultural workers at the centre of communist policy in the countryside, including within the campaign for peasant unity. The centrality of the interests of agricultural workers meant that attitudes towards the interests of wage labourers would be the essential dividing line around which communist policy in the countryside should be based. His proposal for a new peasant confederation recognised this dividing line by proposing to organise not the entire peasantry but that section of the small and middling peasantry prepared to support demands of agricultural workers and ally itself to the CGT. The debate illustrates that, even during the Popular Front period, two essentially conflicting approaches to social relations in the countryside – one that stressed the common interests and unity of the 'peasant class' and another based on recognition of social differentiation in the countryside – continued to be expressed amongst French communists.

CONCLUSION

The nature of the French Communist Party has meant that its historiography has always been contentious. Communists took 'history' very seriously. The party drew on references from the past to justify its politics and to activate its members, imbuing them with the idea that they were bearers of a historical mission. It would organise pageants to commemorate the French Revolution, celebrate the bolshevik uprising and establish (in 1939) a 'Museum of Living History' to the east of Paris. Maurice Thorez, the General Secretary, was proclaimed during the 1950s to be nothing less than 'un historien de type nouveau'.[1] The PCF's leaders believed that Marxism – or more precisely the increasingly vulgarised version disseminated through the Communist International – proffered a privileged insight not only into historical trends and happenings but also into the party's own history. They diligently constructed an official version of events, expunging embarrassing moments, distorting the role of former members and glossing over the twists and turns in the party's evolution. The relationship between the Communist Party and 'history' meant that for many years it was difficult to separate the historical study of French communism from the political polemic between the party and its opponents.

After it re-emerged as a mass force at the Liberation, the party drew particularly on two historical reference points. The first was its role in the Resistance. The sacrifice of thousands of resistant fighters was utilised to stress the party's patriotism and republicanism, while the image of a heroic party provided a useful weapon against political opponents. The second was the Popular Front. References from 1936 emphasised the party's democratic credentials but, critically, also helped to construct its identity as 'the party of the working class'. After the dark years of occupation and war, the 'social explosion', with its mass strikes, factory occupations and, above all, victories – particularly, paid holidays and the 40-hour week – was for many the memory of a joyous experience. The Popular Front became, in the words of Gérard Noiriel, 'a founding institution relating more to commemorative practice than historical analysis'.[2] This helps to explain, at least partly, why farm workers' struggles during the period remained only a footnote in the historical record. The exclusion of an important section of workers from the Matignon accord, the successes of well-organised groups of extreme right-wing strikebreakers, conflicts between peasants and workers (and between immigrants and indigenous workers), industrial workers (including communists) breaking agricultural workers' strikes, destruction of crops and property: these are just some of the movement's characteristics that contradict the mythology of the Popular Front as a disciplined and unified workers' action leading to successful and lasting outcomes.

The party's reputation in the Resistance enabled it to broaden its influence into rural regions in southern and central France and, generally, the countryside took on renewed importance as an area of activity. *La Terre*, a weekly paper launched in 1937 and edited by Waldeck Rochet, became France's best-selling agricultural journal.[3] As in the towns, the Popular Front played the role of 'a founding institution' in the creation, or recreation, of the party's identity in the countryside. Commemorative articles in *La Terre* drew up a totally positive balance sheet of the Popular Front's agrarian policy. 'The harvest of success reaped in 1936 was extraordinary', declared an article on the thirtieth anniversary.[4] The main example to illustrate this assertion was the establishment of the Wheat Office, a reform, though initially controversial, that had succeeded in alleviating peasant anxiety following years of falling prices. It is, however, striking that most commemorative articles about the rural aspect of the Popular Front failed to mention the agricultural workers' movement.[5] And on those occasions when references to it were made, readers were presented with a version of events possessing only a partial relationship with historical reality. The article in 1966, for example, not only ignored the fact that farm workers had taken strike action but disingenuously stated that the Popular Front government had introduced 'a good many laws and decrees. . . for the benefit of agricultural workers'.[6]

Today, although the PCF is only a fringe element within politics and no longer guards its history in the manner it did previously, debate continues to rage over the role of communism in French twentieth-century history.[7] At the root of the historiographical conflict is the contradiction which (until the late 1980s) lay at the heart of the party's character: the tension between its 'implantation' within French society and politics and its subservience to the interests of the political system in the Soviet Union. One trend, organised around the revue *Le Communisme* and responsible for the publication of *Le Livre Noir du Communisme* [The Black Book of Communism], emphasises the latter aspect of the party's character.[8] Its roots can be found in Annie Kriegel's thesis, put forward over 40 years ago, that communism was a bolshevik branch 'grafted' on to the trunk of the French workers' movement.[9] This analysis inevitably prioritises an investigation into the influence of the Soviet state on the party's functioning and politics, a project for which the opening of the Soviet archives has opened up many possibilities. The second trend is symbolised by the publication of *Le Siècle des Communismes* [The Century of Communisms].[10] It includes historians from a range of traditions – some connected to the PCF, others politically opposed to it – but united by a refusal to view communism as an essentially 'criminal' or 'totalitarian' project, reduced to the methods ruthlessly deployed in Stalin's Russia. Moreover, it argues, a study of the undoubted subservience of the French party to the interests of Moscow does not explain its relationship with French politics and society and particularly with the social movements to which it was intrinsically linked.

An understanding of the evolution of the party's agrarian strategy depends on recognising both the influence of Moscow and the impact of indigenous forces. The first turn towards peasant unity during the mid-1920s, the prioritisation of the agricultural proletariat during the 'class against class' period and the idea of the Peasant Popular Front were political zigzags connected to Soviet politics – particularly the drift away from the promotion of 'world revolution' towards the building of 'socialism in one country' – and the resulting influence on the policy and functioning of the Communist International. But like all political parties rooted or seeking to root themselves within a society, the PCF was, to borrow an analogy from Antonio Gramsci, a 'living organism' conditioned by its immediate environment; that is, the social, political, cultural and economic contexts in which it operated.[11]

The complex reality of French rural society – with the small peasantry dominating in many regions, large numbers of wage workers existing in others, the diversity within regions and the complexities of the agricultural proletariat – ensured that a sophisticated and flexible agrarian strategy was certain to present a severe challenge for French communists. Activists in different regions adapted policy in varying ways to take account of the social make-up, as well as the political and cultural traditions, of their audiences. A peasantist wing had roots in the small-scale farming regions where peasants had strong attachments to property and where potential class differences were submerged by an array of personal and social ties between workers and employers. Those who viewed relationships in the countryside through the prism of class gained sustenance from the growing social differentiation in the most advanced sectors of agriculture, a process that evolved significantly during the inter-war period. In short, peasant politics in the French Communist Party – particularly during the inter-war years – were far from monolithic.[12]

The scale of the debate (the discussion at the Marseille congress, the number of articles in *Les Cahiers du Bolchevisme*, the debate at the 1933 Central Committee and the critical role accorded to the peasantry in the Popular Front strategy) indicates, in fact, that in the inter-war years the party accorded more significance to the peasant question than is often recognised. While the contributions of Renaud Jean and Marius Vazeilles to the party's peasant politics have been rightly emphasised in the historical record, those of leaders such as André Parsal and Jean Desnots have been virtually forgotten. The vibrancy of the controversy between two contrasting approaches to agrarian strategy demonstrates that party functioning was far more complicated than being that of a simple transmission belt for Moscow.

It is also necessary to emphasise the continuity between communist approaches and earlier traditions within pre-war French socialism, particularly those expressed by Compère-Morel. Renaud Jean's general outlook, the position adopted during the mid-1920s and Rochet's attempts to regulate relations between workers and peasant employers during the Popular Front period were all rooted in the principles adopted by French socialism at the Nantes Congress. Viewed in this light, the aim of a Peasant Popular Front in 1935 appears not so much as innovatory politics but as a continuation of the agrarian strand within French Marxism that had been present from the end of the nineteenth century. Similarly, a line can be drawn between the position of Longuet in pre-war socialism and the politics exposed by Dunois and others in early communism, before the baton of class politics was taken up by Parsal during the 'class against class' period. The orthodox Marxist approach to politics in the countryside was then given practical application by communist activists in a number of large-scale farming regions during the Popular Front strike movement. The continuities between trends in pre-1914 socialism and post-war communism should be sufficient to contradict any suggestion that in relation to agrarian strategy the communist approach was 'grafted on' from the outside.

One aspect of these continuums is the significance they impart to communist policy from 1929 to 1933. In relation to agrarian policy, the 'class against class' period can be viewed as a dramatic shift away from a developing trend within the party during the mid-1920s towards peasant unity against fascism, which was to re-emerge and reach fruition during the Popular Front period. But equally, without the turn towards the agricultural proletariat during 1929 and 1933, which convinced an important layer of communist activists of the importance of conducting work amongst agricultural workers, it would have been inconceivable for the party to play such an important role within the Popular Front farm strike movement and unionisation campaign.

During the Popular Front, communists emerged as leaders of the striking farm workers, partly because of their orientation towards agricultural workers in the preceding period, partly because they showed sensitivity to pressures emanating from the movement. Although attempting to restrain its demands and careful to avoid the development of a generalised conflict, they championed the farm workers' cause, were sufficiently flexible to organise and support strikes, and succeeded in constructing a vibrant trade union. The outcome was that large numbers of farm workers formed a political attachment to the Communist Party.

The awakening of agricultural workers in 1936 can be viewed as the first stage in a process that reached its apogee in the years following the Liberation. After 1945, agricultural workers once again poured into the FNTA, which remained firmly in communist hands. The union's influence became broader, reaching regions barely touched during the Popular Front period. During 1947 and 1948, major strikes again broke out in the Paris basin, the Languedoc wine regions and elsewhere. According to Hubscher, FNTA membership reached 350,000, organised in 3000 sections; in other words, around twice the size of the position in 1936–37.[13]

In this period, the 'symbiosis' between the Communist Party and agricultural workers was significantly strengthened. The party's post-war base within the peasantry relied disproportionately on agricultural workers. In 1952, agricultural workers provided 8 per cent of the communist electorate compared to 5 per cent drawn from the self-employed peasantry. In 1956, the percentage of agricultural workers supporting the Communist Party was 28.5 per cent, compared to 14.9 per cent of self-employed peasants.[14] Before the war, in the Paris basin and north, agricultural workers were rarely appointed as party election candidates or elected to serve on regional party committees. After 1945, in some departments it became obligatory that an agricultural worker appear on the list of communist candidates for the National Assembly. In 1946, FNTA activists were on the lists in the Seine-Inférieure, Seine-et-Marne and Oise. In the Eure-et-Loir, two of the four communist candidates were farm workers.[15] In many of these regions, communists received their highest votes in the agricultural sectors; winning, for example, 39.5 per cent in the Betz canton and 36.2 per cent in Nanteuil, both centres of the 1936 strike movement in the Oise. In the Paris basin and Picardy, a number of agricultural workers' union activists took up important positions in the party at regional level. In the Oise, the FNTA secretary, Henri Desmaret, became a leading member of the communist federation and departmental secretary of the CGT.[16] In the Estrées-Saint-Denis canton, Marceau Truquin, a communist agricultural worker, was elected Conseiller Général.

Perhaps most significant was the transformation of the local authorities. Following the war, mayoral dynasties of farming families often came to an end, both communists and socialists making remarkable gains. On new admini-strations, agricultural workers were prominent, including many leaders of the Popular Front strike movement. In the Oise, of 568 communists elected to local councils in 1945, 120 were agricultural workers. Amongst individuals met earlier, Alexandre Baptiste became mayor of Silly-le-Long. In the Aisne, the café owner, Louis Marécal became mayor of La-Ville-aux-Bois-lès-Dizy and was joined on the council by three activists from the agricultural workers' strike movement. One of his first decisions was to propose that the traditional street names in the village be changed to commemorate 'the heroes of the Resistance', a ceremony at which Maurice Thorez officiated.[17]

The party's activity and support amongst agricultural workers during the post-war period ensured that potentially conflicting interests within the peasantry remained a topic of debate. The issue arose at the Political Bureau and Central Committee towards the end of 1955. At the Political Bureau, Maurice Thorez attacked an 'opportunist tendency' that, amongst other things, tended to defend the interests of agriculture as a 'bloc'. He criticised a document drawn up by Waldeck Rochet for only demanding a reduction of hours for agricultural workers on the big farms. 'Is it not known that the small capitalist farmer is often more tight-fisted than the large?', he asked.[18] At the October Central Committee, a number of speakers spoke of conflicts between middling peasants and workers and argued that the party was 'defending the middling peasants too much'. Waldeck Rochet was forced to make 'a bit of a self-criticism', as Thorez put it in his notes of the meeting, by accepting that the Agrarian Section was too oriented towards farmers and 'not enough towards agricultural workers'.[19] The contradiction in party strategy would be largely resolved by the rapid decline in the number of agricultural workers and small peasants during the 1960s as a result of the further mechanisation of farming.

Today, the social complexion of villages that were centres of the farm strike movement has fundamentally changed: bustling agricultural communities have disappeared; fields are worked by tractors and harvesters, not teams of men and women; cafés and shops have long closed; middle-class refugees from the towns sometimes occupy what were once workers' cottages; agricultural centres closest to Paris and other big towns have been swallowed up by the extension of the urban sprawl. In any case, the influence of the agricultural workers' movement on local administrations was short-lived – political influence waning simultaneously with the numerical decline of the workforce.

By the 1950s, a member of the Bertrand family was again mayor of La-Ville-aux-Bois-lès-Dizy. The decision to give the streets back their traditional names was quick in coming. And after Marécal left the village, his café – the meeting place and symbol of the agricultural workers' movement – was razed to the ground. Perhaps the demolition of *l'Économie Moderne* should be viewed as just one of a series of acts that managed to cloud the popular memory of the agricultural conflict during the Popular Front years.

NOTES AND REFERENCES

Introduction

1 Enquête statistique, May 1942, Archives Départementales (AD) Aisne, 1030W 20.
2 Brigade de Montcornet, 'Procès-verbal des renseignements sur des entraves à la liberté du travail', 20 July 1936, AD Aisne, 1M 22.
3 Ibid.
4 An important collection of essays exploring the Popular Front's place in both the collective memory and history is X. Vigna, J. Vigreux, S. Wolikow (eds), *Le Pain, La Paix, La Liberté: Expériences et territoires du Front Populaire*, La Dispute-Éditions Sociales, Paris, 2006.
5 L. Bodin and J. Touchard, *Front Populaire 1936*, A. Colin, Paris, 1961, p. 146.
6 See, for example, the illustrated popular history, D. Tartakowsky, *Le Front Populaire: La Vie est à nous*, Gallimard, Paris, 1996. The rural world is better covered in a more recent popular history: J. Girault, *Au-devant du bonheur: Les français et le Front Populaire*, CIDE, Paris, 2005.
7 J. Jackson, *The Popular Front in France: Defending Democracy, 1934–38*, Cambridge University Press, Cambridge, 1988. Jacques Kergoat's *La France du Front Populaire*, La Découverte, Paris, 1986, remains the general account of the Popular Front years with the most serious focus on rural developments.
8 *Le Temps*, 12 July 1936.
9 There is an extensive literature on movements in the Languedoc wine region. See L.L. Frader, *Peasants and Protest: Agricultural Workers, Politics, and Unions in the Aude, 1850–1914*, University of California Press, Berkeley, 1991; J. Sagnes, *Le Mouvement ouvrier en Languedoc: Syndicalistes et socialistes de l'Hérault de la fondation des bourses du travail à la naissance du Parti communiste*, Privat, Toulouse, 1980; J. Sagnes, *Politique et syndicalisme en Languedoc: L'Hérault durant l'entre-deux-guerres*, Université Paul Valéry, Montpellier, 1986; M. Cadé, *Le Parti des campagnes rouges: Histoire du Parti communiste dans les Pyrénées-Orientales, 1920–49*, Éditions du Chiendent, Vinça, 1988; J. Sagnes, 'Le Syndicalisme des ouvriers agricoles du Languedoc Méditerranéen-Roussillon', in R. Hubscher & J.-C. Farcy (eds), *La Moisson des autres: Les Salariés agricoles aux XIXème et XX siècles*, Éditions Créaphis, Paris, 1996, pp. 327–40; Y. Rinaudo, 'Ouvriers agricoles provencaux en grève 1890–1939', in Hubscher & Farcy (eds), *La Moisson des autres*, pp. 282–301. For strikes in the Roussillon during 1937–38, see G. Gavignaud, 'Un mouvement de grève roussillonnais, 1937–38', Colloque, 'Le Front Populaire et la vie quotidienne des Français', Centre de

recherches d'histoire des mouvements sociaux et du syndicalisme (CRHMSS), 15–16 September 1986. For the early history of the 'bûcherons' (forestry workers) see P. & M. Pigenet et al, *Terre de luttes (précurseurs 1848–1939): Histoire du mouvement ouvrier dans le Cher*, Éditions Sociales, Paris, 1977, pp. 34–46.

10   G. Wright, *Rural Revolution in France: The Peasantry in the Twentieth Century*, Stanford University Press, Stanford Cal, 1964, p. 68.

11   Farmers' leader quoted in S. Berger, *Peasants against Politics, Rural Organization in Brittany, 1911–67*, Harvard University Press, Cambridge MA, 1972, p. 73.

12   R. Hubscher, 'Introduction', in Hubscher & Farcy (eds), *La Moisson des autres*, p. 5.

13   H. Newby, *The Deferential Worker: A Study of Farm Workers in East Anglia*, Allen Lane, London 1977, p. 23.

14   D. Pretty; *The Rural Revolt that Failed: Farm Workers' Trade Unions in Wales, 1899–1950*, University of Wales Press, Cardiff, 1989, p. xi.

15   This tendency was identified by Philippe Gratton in the 1970s. A good example is the four-volume, *Histoire de la France rurale*, which devotes only seven pages to 'un sous-prolétariat ignoré' and just one paragraph to the strikes of 1936. More recently, attention has begun to be paid to agricultural workers as a social category. The title of an important collection of essays, *La Moisson des autres*, summarises well their exclusion from the historical record. P. Gratton, *Les Luttes de classes dans les campagnes*, Éditions Anthropos, Paris, 1971, p. 18; P. Gratton, *Les Paysans français contre l'agrarisme*, F. Maspero, Paris, 1972, pp. 9–12; G. Duby and A Wallon (eds), *Histoire de la France Rurale*, vol 4, Seuil, Paris, 1977, pp. 412–19; Hubscher & Farcy, *La Moisson des autres*, 1996.

16   See, for example, G. Welter, *La France d'aujourd'hui: agriculture-industrie-commerce*, Payot, Paris, 1927, p. 23.

17   R. Tombs, *France 1814–1914*, Longman, London, pp. 297–98.

18   On the evolution of peasant identity in France, see R. Hubscher, 'Réflexions sur l'identité paysanne au XIX siècle: identité réelle ou supposée', *Ruralia*, 1, 1997, pp. 65–80.

19   Congrès national des syndicats agricoles (Lyons, 1894); quoted in M. Cleary, *Peasants, Politicians and Producers:The Organisation of Agriculture in France since 1918*, Cambridge University Press, Cambridge, 1989, pp. 152–53.

20   R. Paxton, *French Peasant Fascism: Henry Dorgères's Greenshirts and the Crises of French Agriculture, 1929–39*, Oxford University Press, New York, 1997, pp. 169–70 and 175–76.

21   M. Augé-Laribé, *La Politique agricole de la France de 1880 à 1940*, Presses Universitaires de France, Paris, 1950, p. 89.

22   Ibid., p. 36 and p. 87. Figures from 1892 agricultural enquiry.

23   G. Garrier, 'L'Apport des récits de vie et des romans "paysans"', in Hubscher & Farcy, *La Moisson des autres*, pp. 15–27.

24   The exception is the character of Jacqueline, the farm servant used to illustrate sexual immorality.

25   M. Cleary, *Peasants, Politicians and Producers*, p. 150.

26   J. Moquay, *L'Évolution sociale en Agriculture: La Condition des ouvriers agricoles depuis juin 1936*, Niort, Imprimerie Saint-Denis, 1939, p. 14.

27   Ministère de l'Économie Nationale, *Résultats statistiques du recensement général de la population, mars 1936*, vol. 1, part 1, Paris, 1938, p. 76. The category 'ouvrier agricole' covered workers producing cereals, industrial crops, such as sugar beet, chicory and flax, and a range of vegetables and fruit. It also included those occupied in livestock rearing, dairy farming, horticulture, the vineyards and forestry.

28 A. Prost, *La CGT à l'époque du Front Populaire, 1934–39*, A. Colin, Paris, 1964, p. 207.

29 *Résultats statistiques du recensement général*, vol. 1, part 1, pp. 81–83.

30 Hubscher, 'Introduction', in Hubscher & Farcy, *La Moisson des autres,* pp. 5–11.

31 J.-C. Farcy, *Les Paysans beaucerons au XIX siècle*, 2 vols, Société archéologique d'Eure et Loir, Chartres, 1988, p. 1050.

32 S. W. Mintz, 'The Rural Proletariat and the Problem of Rural Proletarian Consciousness', *Journal of Peasant Studies*, vol. 1, 3 (pp. 291–325), p. 319.

33 T. Leroux & A. Gaud, *Nos ouvriers agricoles*, Rapports présentés à la Société des Agriculteurs et au Syndicat de Défense Agricole de l'Oise, Beauvais, 1907.

34 *Le Temps*, 4 July 1936 and 13 June 1937; *La Somme*, 10 July 1936.

35 *Cahiers du Bolchevisme*, 15 June 1936, p. 752; Décisions du Bureau politique, 25 June 1936. Parti communiste français archives (PCF), microfilm 786.

36 Prost, *La CGT*, pp. 74–76.

37 S. Courtois & M. Lazar, *Histoire du Parti communiste français*, Presses Universitaires de France, Paris, 1995, p. 148.

38 *Résultats statistiques du recensement général de la population*, vol. 1, part 1, p. 33.

39 J. Buschbaum, *Cinema Engagé: Film in the Popular Front*, University of Illinois Press, Chicago, 1988, pp. 89–90 and p. 142.

40 D. Brower, *The New Jacobins: The French Communist Party and the Popular Front*, Cornell University Press, New York, 1968, pp. 113–14.

41 See R. M. Lagrave, 'Le Marteau contre la Faucille' (pp. 9–26) and the collection of essays in 'Les "petites Russies" des campagnes françaises', *Études Rurales*, 171–72, July-December 2004. For the communists' relationship with rural movements during the Popular Front period, see J. Vigreux, 'Regards européens sur les mobilisations rurales', Vigna et al (eds), *Le Paix, La Paix, La Liberté*, pp. 69–81.

42 J. Vigreux, *Waldeck Rochet, Une biographie politique*, La Dispute, Paris, 2000; J. Vigreux, 'Le PCF, garant de l'héritage agrarien progressiste', in S. Wolikow & A. Bleton-Ruget (eds) *Antifascisme et nation: les gauches européennes au temps du Front Populaire*, Publications de l'Université Contemporaine-CNRS, 1998, pp. 163–71; J. Vigreux, 'Paysans et responsables du travail paysan dans la direction du parti communiste', in Dreyfus, Michel *et al*, *La part des militants, biographie et mouvement ouvrier: Autour du Maitron, dictionnaire biographique du mouvement ouvrier français*, Les Éditions de l'Atelier/Éditions Ouvrières, Paris 1996, pp. 205–18.

43 L. Boswell, 'Le Communisme et la Défense de la Petite Propriété en Limousin et en Dordogne', *Communisme*, 51–52, 1997, pp. 7–27; L. Boswell, *Rural Communism in France, 1920–39*, Cornell University Press, London, 1998.

44 See the review of the historiography of communist agrarian policy in J. Vigreux, 'Le Parti communiste français à la campagne, 1920–64. Bilan historiographique et perspectives de recherche', *Ruralia*, 3, 1998, pp. 43–66.

45 Only one of 19 essays in the issue of *Études Rurales* devoted to the agrarian policy of the Communist Party (July-December 2004) makes reference to the party's relationship with agricultural workers. I. Bruneau & E. Le Doeuff, 'Les Paysans du "Maitron": militants de l'entre-deux-guerres', pp. 161–74. An example of misunderstandings of communist strategy towards agricultural workers is the article by Vigreux, 'Paysans et responsables'. Amongst other mistakes, it conflates the FUA, the communist-dominated agricultural workers' union, with the FPT (Fédération des Paysans Travailleurs), the organisation of peasant proprietors led by Marius Vazeilles (see also note 16, Chapter 3).

46 Boswell, *Rural Communism,* p. 41; Vigreux, 'Paysans et responsables', p. 206.

47   J.-C. Farcy, 'Les Grèves agricoles de 1936–1937 dans le Basin parisien' in Hubscher
     & Farcy, *La Moisson des autres,* p. 322. See also D. Ponchelet, 'Ouvriers nomades et
     patrons briards: les grandes exploitations agricoles dans la Brie 1848–1938', thèse
     du IIIe cycle, Institut national de la recherche agronomique économie et sociologie
     rurales, 1987.

48   É. Lynch, *Moissons rouges, Les Socialistes français et la société paysanne dans l'entre-deux-
     guerres (1918–40),* Presses Universitaires du Septentrion, Villeneuve d'Ascq, 2002,
     pp. 333–75.

49   Paxton, *French Peasant Fascism.*

50   O. Marchand & C. Thélot, *Deux siècles de travail en France; Population active et structure
     sociale, durée et productivité du travail de 1800 à 1990,* INSEE, Paris, 1991, p. 90.

Chapter 1

1   Correspondance, Engels-Lafargue, 10 October 1893. Cited in C. Willard, *Les
     Guesdistes: Le Mouvement socialiste en France 1893–1905,* Éditions Sociales, Paris,
     1965, p. 363.

2   K. Marx, *Capital,* vol. 1, Lawrence & Wishart, London, 1954, p. 474.

3   F. Engels, 'The Peasant War in Germany. Preface to the Second Edition', 1870,
     Marxists Internet Archive: http://www.marxists.org/archive/marx/works/1850/
     peasant-war-germany/ch0a.htm

4   A. Hussain & K. Tribe, *Marxism and the Agrarian Question (Vol. 1), German Social
     Democracy and the Peasantry 1890–1907,* Humanities Press, Atlantic Highlands NJ,
     1981, pp. 93–97.

5   K. Kautsky, *La Question agraire: Étude sur les tendances de l'agriculture moderne,* V. Giard
     & E. Brière, Paris, 1900.

6   One exception was in Italy. John Davis notes that 'the militancy and strength of the
     labourers' unions in the Po Valley was interpreted [by the socialists] as evidence that
     the capitalist transformation of the countryside was advanced and irreversible.'
     J. Davis, 'Socialism and the Working Classes in Italy before 1914', in D. Geary (ed.),
     Labour and Socialist Movements in Europe before 1914, Berg, Oxford, 1989, p. 216.

7   C. Landauer, 'The Guesdists and the Small Farmer: Early Erosion of French
     Marxism', *International Review of Social History,* vol 6, 2, 1961, pp. 212–25.

8   Gratton, *Les Luttes,* pp. 40–41.

9   Only one proposal directly affected the pockets of peasant employers: the
     establishment of a minimum wage. A pension system would be financed through
     the taxation of rich landlords and an arbitration system established to resolve
     disputes, which, while possibly leading to improvements for workers, could also
     encourage an outlook of social partnership between workers and peasant employers.

10   F. Engels, 'The Peasant Question in France and Germany', first published in Die
     Neue Zeit, 1894–95, *Marxists Internet Archive*: http://www.marxists.org/archive/
     marx/works/1894/peasant-question/index.htm

11   L. L. Frader, 'Grapes of Wrath: Vineyard workers, Labour Unions, and Strike
     Activity in the Aude, 1860–1913', in L. Tilly & C. Tilly (eds), *Class Conflict and
     Collective Action,* Sage Publications, London, 1981, p. 201.

12   E. Lynch, 'Compère-Morel et la Politique Agraire de la SFIO: L'Élaboration d'une
     doctrine entre socialisme et agrarisme, 1900–21', DEA Mémoire, IEP Paris, 1990–
     91; P. Barral, *Les Agrariens français de Méline à Pisani,* A. Colin, Paris, 1968,
     pp. 157–64.

13   Speaking at the 1906 SFIO National Congress. Cited in Lynch, 'Compère-Morel', p. 59.

14   L. L. Frader, *Peasants and Protest: Agricultural Workers, Politics, and Unions in the Aude, 1850–1914,* University of California Press, Berkeley, 1991, pp. 103–04.

15   J.-P. Besse, *Le Mouvement ouvrier dans l'Oise, 1890–1914*, Centre Départemental de Documentation Pédagogique de l'Oise, Beauvais, 1982, p. 116.

16   *Le Travailleur de l'Oise*, 23 March 1907. Cited in Ibid.

17   Ibid.

18   F. Engels, 'On the Dissolution of the Lassallean Workers' Association', *Demokratisches Wochenblatte*, 3 October 1868, available at Marxists Internet Archive: http://www.marxists.org/history/international/iwma/documents/1868/dissolution

19   *Le Socialiste*, 26 October 1902; cited in Lynch, 'Compère-Morel', p. 57.

20   Parti socialiste, 6e Congrès national, Saint-Étienne, 11–14 Avril 1909, Compte-rendu sténographique, Au Siège du Conseil national, Paris, 1909, p. 191.

21   C. Langlois, *Léonne, Bonne de ferme à 12 ans, une vie en Beauce au début du XX siècle*, Éditions Tirésias, Paris, 2002, p. 116.

22   Parti socialiste, 6e Congrès national, pp. 193, 196–7.

23   D. Pick, *Faces of Degeneration: A European Disorder, c.1848– c.1918*, Cambridge University Press, Cambridge, 1989.

24   Compère-Morel, 'Le Prolétariat agricole', *Le Semeur*, 11 June 1910.

25   The 1892 survey recorded this category as making up 49 per cent of day labourers.

26   J. Moquay, *L'Évolution sociale en Agriculture*, p. 21.

27   M.-C. Allart, 'Les Femmes de trois villages de l'Artois : travail et vécu quotidien (1919–39)' *Revue du Nord*, vol. 63, 250, pp. 703–24.

28   Langlois, *Léonne*, p. 109.

29   Farcy, *Les Paysans beaucerons,* pp. 1046–54.

30   Langlois, *Léonne*, p. 105.

31   *Le Démocrate Soissonnais*, 30 June 1907.

32   G. Postel-Vinay, *La Rente foncière dans le capitalisme agricole, analyse de la voie 'classique' du développement du capitalisme dans l'agriculture à partir de l'exemple du Soissonnais'*, François Maspero, Paris, 1974, pp. 191–95.

33   'Listes nominatives', Dammard, 1F1, AD Aisne.

34   J.-P. Jessenne, *Pouvoir au village et Révolution: Artois 1760–1848*, Presses Universitaires de Lille, 1987, pp. 185–89.

35   Farcy, *Les Paysans beaucerons,* pp. 1004–05

36   Postel-Vinay, *La Rente foncière*, pp. 145–48, 175–77.

37   *Le Démocrate Soissonnais*, 10 June 1906.

38   Postel-Vinay, *La Rente foncière*, p. 176.

39   *Le Démocrate Soissonnais*, 21 November 1906.

40   C. Willard, *Les Guesdistes,* p. 372.

41   Frader, 'Grapes of Wrath', p. 194.

42   The movement has been given little attention by historians. For a sketch see Gratton, *Les Luttes*, pp 246–52. For the Seine-et-Marne see D. Ponchelet, 'Ouvriers nomades', pp. 197–224. For the Aisne, J. Bulaitis, 'Les Luttes agricoles de 1906–8: premier conflit social du XXe siècle dans les campagnes de l'Aisne', *La Vie rurale dans l'Aisne, Mémoires*, vol. XLVIII, 2003, Fédération des Sociétés d'Histoire et d'Archéologie de l'Aisne, pp. 191–205.

43   A. Joppé, 'Conditions de salaire et de travail des ouvriers agricoles (1910)', in J. Borgé & N. Viarnoff (eds), *Archives du Nord*, Éditions Balland, 1979, pp. 161–63.

44   See dossier, 'Grèves des ouvriers agricoles 1910', AD Pas-de-Calais, M1781.

45   Besse, *Le Mouvement ouvrier*, p. 139.
46   *Le Démocrate Soissonnais*, 18 October 1907.
47   *L'Humanité*, 13 June 1907.
48   *Le Combat,* 4 April 1908.
49   Statement by H. Leroux and L. Beauquesne, *Le Démocrate Soissonnais*, 15 September 1907.
50   *L'Indépendant de Seine-et-Marne*, 11 April 1907, AD Seine-et-Marne, M3216.
51   *Argus Soissonnais*, 22 March 1907.
52   At Tartiers (Aisne), a family who had recently been recruited and housed was sacked after the farmer discovered that 'the father and several sons were members of the union'. *Le Démocrate Soissonnais,* 16 and 30 June 1907.
53   *Le Démocrate Soissonnais*, 18 October 1907.
54   *L'Humanité,* 15 and 16 June 1907.
55   *Le Socialiste*, 28 July 1907.
56   Préfet de l'Aisne, 7 April 1908, Archives Nationales (AN) F7 12787.
57   *L'Humanité,* 6 April, 1908.
58   Commissaire spécial de police (Saint-Quentin), 9 April 1908, AN F7 12787.
59   Parti socialiste, 6e Congrès national, pp. 331–35.
60   Ibid., p. 333.
61   Ibid., p. 193.
62   Ibid., pp. 359–60.
63   Ibid., p. 231.
64   Barral, *Les Agrariens*, p. 162.
65   Intervention by Fernand Corcos, Parti socialiste, 6e Congrès national, p. 346.
66   Intervention by Jean Longuet, Ibid., p. 335.
67   An invitation to Compère-Morel probably indicates that socialists were involved in establishing a union in the Forez region (Loire) in 1910. J. Vercherand, *Un Siècle de syndicalisme agricole, la vie locale et nationale à travers le cas du département de la Loire*, Publications de l'Université de Saint-Étienne, 1994, p. 75.
68   J. Sagnes, *Jean Jaurès et le Languedoc viticole*, Presses du Languedoc, Montpellier, p. 70.

Chapter 2

1   A. Kriegel, *Aux Origines du communisme français, 1914–20: Contribution à l'histoire du mouvement ouvrier français*, 2 vols, Mouton & Co, Paris, 1964, pp. 834–38.
2   'Resolution of the ECCI on the French Communist Party (2 March, 1922)', L. Trotsky, *The First Five Years of the Communist International*, vol. 2, New Park Publications, London, 1974, pp. 110–12.
3   *L'Humanité*, 15 January 1922 and 22 May 1922.
4   G. Belloin, *Renaud Jean: Le Tribun des paysans*, Les Éditions de l'Atelier/Éditions Ouvrières, Paris, 1993.
5   'Resolution of the French Commission, 2 December 1922', in *Theses, Resolutions & Manifestos of the First Four Congresses of the Third International*, A. Adler (ed.), Humanities Press, Atlantic Highlands, 1980, pp. 354–57.
6   L. Trotsky, 'The Communists and the Peasantry in France', in *The First Five Years*, pp. 113–18.
7   L. Trotsky, 'To Comrade Treint, 28 July 1922', in *The First Five Years*, pp. 152–55.
8   *L'Émancipateur*, 7 November 1920.

9   *La Voix Paysanne*, 15 January 1921. The fact that such an article could appear in a journal officially edited by Renaud Jean is explained, firstly, by its timing – it appeared in the first issue following Tours and before Renaud Jean had practically taken over as editor – and, secondly, by the party's assignment of another member of the left, Paul Vaillant-Couturier, to assist in the editorship.

10 A. L. Cardoza, *Agrarian Elites and Italian Fascism*, Princeton University Press, Princeton NJ, 1982, pp. 245–94.

11 J.-B. Holt, *German Agricultural Policy 1918–34: The development of a national philosophy towards agriculture in post-war Germany*, University of North Carolina Press, Chapel Hill, 1936, p. 28.

12 J. Riddell (ed.), *The German Revolution and the Debate on Soviet Power, documents 1918– 19, preparing the founding conference*, Anchor Foundation, New York, 1986, p. 224; C. Harman, *The Lost Revolution, Germany 1918 to 1923*, Bookmarks, London, pp. 169–70.

13 K. Kautsky, 'Die Sozialisierung der Landwirtschaft', cited in Riddell (ed.), *The German Revolution*, p. 223.

14 Gratton, *Les Luttes de Classes*, pp. 338–43.

15 Report of Hodée. Premier congrès de la FNTA, 4–6 avril 1920, Compte-rendu sténographique, Villeneuve-St-Georges, p. 320, AD Seine-Saint-Denis 35J 1.

16 *La Voix Paysanne*, 22 January 1921.

17 'Union régionale terrienne de la Brie et du Gâtinais. Convention collective, 8 August 1919', AD Seine-Saint-Denis, 35J 40.

18 'Preliminary Draft Theses on the Agrarian Question', in *Theses, Resolutions & Manifestos*, pp. 113–23. Longuet was now leader of what communists described as the 'opportunist' and 'centrist' wing of the SFIO. While enthusiastic about the Russian Revolution, he argued that it was possible and desirable to 'reconstruct' the Second International, rather than building a new one. At the Congress of Tours, he was in favour of affiliation to the Communist International but was unwilling to accept the 21 Conditions imposed by the Moscow leadership.

19 Report of Hodée. 'Premier congrès de la FNTA', p. 317.

20 'Preliminary Draft Theses', pp. 114–19.

21 *La Voix Paysanne*, 19 February 1921.

22 *L'Émancipateur*, 20 May 1921.

23 *La Voix Paysanne*, 10 September 1921.

24 Belloin, *Renaud Jean*, p. 60.

25 *La Voix Paysanne*, 7 January 1922.

26 Renaud Jean, 'Le Communisme et les Paysans en France', *Bulletin Communiste*, 7 December 1922.

27 *L'Humanité*, 1 August 1923.

28 Ibid.

29 Vigreux, *Waldeck Rochet*, p. 55.

30 'Thèses adoptées par le premier congrès national, Marseille, 25–30 Décembre 1921', *Bulletin Communiste*, 14 February 1922.

31 Congrès de Marseille, PCF 14. Sally Sokoloff is mistaken in thinking that the thesis was adopted at Marseille 'with scarcely any debate'. The transcript shows that a full session, involving 24 speakers, was devoted to the peasant question. S. Sokoloff, 'Peasant Leadership and the French Communist Party, 1921–40', *Historical Reflections*, vol 4, 2, 1977, (pp. 153–70), p. 157.

32 *Le Populaire*, 2 October 1921; cited in Lynch, *Moissons rouges*, p. 231.

33 Gratton, *Les Luttes de classes*, pp. 330–44.
34 R. Hubscher, 'Révolution aux champs: La Fédération national des travailleurs de l'agriculture (1920–81)', in Hubscher & Farcy, *La Moisson des autres,* pp. 343–59.
35 *L'Humanité*, 2 November 1924.
36 At the end of 1922, the FNTA claimed 387 affiliated unions, undoubtedly an exaggeration but nevertheless some indication of the superior position of the socialist-influenced union. *Le Travailleur de la Terre*, January–March 1923. For the life of the socialist agricultural workers' leader, Arthur Chaussy, see M. Pruvot, *Arthur Chaussy 1880–1945*, Collection La Fresnaye, Combs-la-Ville, 1983.
37 *L'Humanité*, 24 October 1922.
38 Ibid., 20 March 1923.
39 The FNTA faced similar problems. An article in *Le Travailleur de la Terre* (June–July 1923) complained: 'People only come to the union during strikes and, whatever the results achieved, they do not persevere with their participation.'
40 J. Girault, *Sur l'implantation du Parti communiste français dans l'entre-deux-guerres,* Éditions Sociales, Paris, 1977, p. 35.
41 Préfet de l'Eure-et-Loir, 3 April 1920, AN F7 12983.
42 *Le Travailleur de l'Eure et Loir*, 17 April 1920, 18 November 1920 and 25 October 1921.
43 *Le Travailleur de la Terre*, January 1923.
44 The Midi wine region also witnessed a rapid shift from internal to external migration, mostly through an influx of Spanish workers. Communist policy towards immigration in agriculture is examined in Chapter 4.
45 *La Voix Paysanne*, 22 January 1922.
46 *L'Humanité*, 1 August 1923.
47 M. Vazeilles, *La Voix Paysanne*, 7 June 1924.
48 *La Voix Paysanne*, 21 October 1922.
49 Ibid., 1 July 1922.
50 Trotsky, 'The Communists and the Peasantry', p. 116.
51 Marcel Munier, *La Voix Paysanne*, 10 March 1923.
52 *La Voix Paysanne*, 25 February 1922 and 15 April 1922.
53 An edited version of the text was published in the party members' bulletin. J. Castel, 'Le Prolétariat et les paysans', *Les Cahiers du Militant*, July 1925, pp. 3–23.
54 'Resolution on the Question of the Agricultural Workers and of the Peasantry', *Resolutions and Decisions of the Third World Congress of the Red International of Labour Unions*, Moscow, July 1924, The National Minority Movement, London, 1924, pp. 49–51.
55 Castel, 'Le Prolétariat et les paysans', p. 5.
56 J. Castel, 'La Question agraire en France', *Le Communisme du Nord Ouest*, 11 October 1924.
57 Castel, 'Le Prolétariat et les paysans', p. 22.
58 'Les Cellules communistes d'entreprises', *Les Cahiers du Militant*, September 1924, p. 22.
59 G. D. Jackson, *Comintern and Peasant in East Europe, 1919–30*, Columbia University Press, New York, 1966, pp. 78–115.
60 Bukharin's report was reprinted in a special issue of *Cahiers du Bolchevisme*, 22 May 1925.
61 By 1925, the party was not only more centralised and organisationally tied to Moscow but also less tolerant of differences within its ranks. Dunois was removed from his responsibilities for voicing opposition to the suppression of 'criticism and

self-criticism' and, particularly, the expulsion of members of the party's left. He resigned from the party in 1927.

62 A. Marty, 'Le Parti français et les paysans', *Cahiers du Bolchevisme*, 15 November 1925.
63 J. Desnots, 'Projet de thèse sur la question agraire', *Cahiers du Bolchevisme*, 15 June 1926; J. Desnots, 'Le Bouleversement de l'économie rurale', *Cahiers du Bolchevisme*, May 1928.
64 'Circulaire de la section d'agit prop de la région parisienne sur le travail paysan', 25 October 1926, PCF 193.
65 Marty, 'Le Parti français et les paysans', p. 2102 and p. 2105.
66 'Circulaire no 43 sur le travail paysan', 20 August 1924, PCF 66.
67 *Cahiers du Bolchevisme*, 2 January 1925, pp. 483–85.
68 *L'Humanité*, 26 January 1926.
69 'Résolution de la Commission sur le travail paysan, adopté par le BP, 24 mai 1925', PCF 112.
70 Préfet du Cantal, 10 October 1927, AN F7 12977.
71 *La Voix Paysanne*, 28 August 1926.
72 The strikes mainly touched the Brie. They involved 50 workers on four farms at Vinantes in April 1925 and 105 workers on four farms at Villeroy, Charnentroy and Charny in August 1926. Sous-préfet de Meaux, 10 April 1925, 12 and 17 August 1926, AD Seine-et-Marne, 1Mp 96.
73 'Circulaire de la section d'agit prop de la région parisienne sur le travail paysan', 25 October 1926, PCF 193.
74 Commission syndicale centrale, Réunion du 25 mars 1926, PCF 169.
75 Desnots, 'Projet de thèse', 15 June 1926, p. 1380.
76 'Aperçu de la situation économique et des taches immédiates du parti à la campagne', 12 May 1928, PCF 292.
77 Courtois & Lazar, *Histoire du Parti communiste*, pp. 96–98
78 A. Cardoza, *Agrarian elites*, pp. 274–327.
79 Renaudet, 'Nos Alliés les paysans', *Cahiers du Bolchevisme*, 15 December 1926.
80 'Notes et rapports sur l'évolution de l'agriculture et sa situation en 1932', AD Oise, Mp 4514.
81 Direction des Services Agricoles de Seine-et-Oise, 19 March 1930, AD Yvelines, 13M 242.
82 'Rapport de la Section Agraire', 25 August–25 September 1926, PCF 175.
83 *La Voix Paysanne*, 29 May 1926.
84 Lettre de la Fédération de l'agriculture, 26 October 1926, PCF 169.
85 *La Voix Paysanne*, 1 October, 1927.
86 Ibid., 30 July 1927.

Chapter 3

1 Jackson, *Comintern and Peasant*, p. 116 and p. 128.
2 M. Worley (ed.), *In Search of Revolution: International Communist Parties in the Third Period*, I B Tauris, London, 2004. See, in particular, M. Worley, 'Courting Disaster? The Communist International in the Third Period', pp. 1–17.
3 *L'Humanité*, 1 February 1930.
4 J. Berlioz, 'Les Paysans Travailleurs créent leur confédération générale', *Cahiers du Bolchevisme*, April-May 1929, p. 297. The 'prolétariat mixte' was a term used to characterise peasants who worked partly in factories and partly on the land.

5   A. Puech, 'Politique paysanne marxiste et politique paysanne petite-bourgeoisie', *Cahiers du Bolchevisme*, June 1929.

6   Notice by G. Bourgeois and C. Pennetier, *Dictionnaire biographique du mouvement ouvrier français (Le Maitron)*, CD-Rom, Les Éditions de l'Atelier, Paris, 1997.

7   Commissaire central de police, Ville d'Orléans, 26 November 1932. Dossier, 'Puech André dit Parsal', Centre des Archives Contemporaines (CAC) 19940469 415.

8   A Puech, 'Politique paysanne', p. 420. Parsal used the term 'kulak', which now entered the vocabulary of the French party, to describe peasants who employed wage labour and engaged in some small-scale business activity. Kulaks were differentiated from 'capitalist farmers' and 'gros propriétaires' in that, though employers, they also participated personally in agricultural work. Consequently, they included many farmers previously characterised as 'paysans travailleurs'.

9   Ibid., p. 423.

10   J. Desnots, 'Le redressement de la politique paysanne du PCF à travers la crise agricole', *Cahiers du Bolchevisme*, December 1929.

11   Ibid., p. 900.

12   Ibid., p. 892.

13   Ibid., p. 897.

14   Ibid., p. 892.

15   'Au Bureau Politique du PCF', n.d. (probably April 1930), PCF 389.

16   Ibid. It is necessary to clear up a misunderstanding over what Parsal and his supporters were arguing. According to Vigreux, 'an article by Ramier [a supporter of Parsal's arguments – JB] denounced the principles of the agrarian programme of the PC, considered much too indulgent towards peasant proprietors. It advocated collectivisation of all those employing paysans travailleurs!' There was, in fact, no challenge to the party's position on collectivisation and peasant property in either Ramier's article or in texts by Parsal. The critique centred on the party's class analysis of the agrarian population, the question of what social groups the party should prioritise and the position to take in relation to conflicts between agricultural workers and peasant employers, rather than the programmatic question of collectivisation. Vigreux is also confused in his use of the term 'paysans travailleurs'. While the meaning of the concept evolved, in the period under discussion the party was using it to describe self-employed peasants. Vigreux, 'Paysans et responsables', p. 208; See G. Ramier, 'La Question de l'alliance révolutionnaire du Prolétariat et de la Paysannerie et les classes à la campagne', *Cahiers du Bolchevisme*, October 1930.

17   J. Desnots, 'Quelques objectifs immédiats parmi le prolétariat agricole', *Cahiers du Bolchevisme*, May 1930.

18   Comité central, 27 October 1930, PCF 381.

19   Desnots, 'Quelques objectifs', p. 483.

20   Letter from Renaud Jean, 22 February 1930, PCF 389. Renaud Jean continued the theme throughout 1931. See letter, 26 June 1931, PCF 464.

21   Parsal broke with the party in January 1940. During the occupation, he flirted with Jacques Doriot's Parti populaire français (PPF), before joining the collaborationist Parti ouvrier et paysan français (POPF). He also organised the French Federation of Agricultural Labourers [Fédération française des travailleurs de l'agriculture] which openly co-operated with the German authorities. A number of texts issued by this organisation can be found in the archives of the FNTA. In 1944, communists in the Resistance condemned him to death as a 'spy' and 'traitor'. Several attempts were

made on his life. In 1945, Parsal served one year in prison for collaboration with the Nazis. Archives Départementales (AD) de Seine-Saint-Denis, 35J 39. G. Bourgeois & C. Pennetier, 'André Parsal', *Dictionnaire biographique (Le Maitron)*, CD-Rom.

22   For example, they criticised Parsal for characterising the small peasantry as those working primarily for their own subsistence, whereas, they noted, virtually all peasants worked to some extent for the market. *L'Humanité*, 1 February 1930 and 17 March 1932.

23   G. Fouilloux, 'Projets de thèse sur la question agraire', *Cahiers du Bolchevisme*, August 1932.

24   J.-P. Guillerot, 'La Politique Agraire et Paysanne du PCF de 1920 à 1934', Mémoire de Maîtrise, Université de Paris VIII, 1973, p. 401.

25   *L'Humanité*, 20 June 1931.

26   Ibid.

27   *Le Travailleur Agricole*, July 1928.

28   Ibid., April 1929.

29   'Rapport sur l'activité et sur les perspectives de la Fédération', November 1928, PCF 294.

30   *Le Travailleur Agricole*, April 1929.

31   Ibid.

32   'Section agraire. Réunion du mardi 18 nov 1930', PCF 401.

33   *Le Travailleur Agricole*, June 1931 and August 1930.

34   When a farmer sacked an activist at Pannes (Loiret) in August 1931, '8 of the 11 workers on the farm stopped work'. The following spring at Solterre (Loiret), farmers were forced to accept the union's wage claim for work on the sugar beet after workers 'refused to go into the fields'. *Le Travailleur Agricole*, Sept 1931 and May-June 1932.

35   For example, at Nogent-sur-Vernisson (Loiret) in June 1931. *L'Humanité*. 20 June 1931.

36   *La Vie Ouvrière*, 10 June 1932.

37   *Le Travailleur Agricole*, June 1931.

38   Ibid., May-June 1932; P. Fromont & F. Bourgeois, 'Les Grèves agricoles de Tremblay-lès-Gonesse en 1936', *Revue d'Économie Politique*, September-October 1937, pp. 1417–19.

39   It was represented at the CGTU National Congress in September 1933. 'Congrès national, Paris 23–29 septembre 1933', Imprimerie de la Maison des syndicats, Paris.

40   *Le Travailleur Agricole*, June 1930.

41   Comité central, 10–14 February 1933, PCF 583.

42   See dossiers in AN BB18 2849, AN BB18 2864 and AN BB18 2880.

43   *Le Travailleur Agricole*, August 1930. Problems in maintaining organisation were also experienced in the Versailles region following the establishment of a union at a conference of 50 delegates in early 1930. Desnots, 'Quelques objectifs', pp. 486–87.

44   *Le Travailleur Agricole*, June 1930.

45   Desnots, 'Quelques objectifs', pp. 486–87.

46   *La Vie Ouvrière*, 4, 18 November and 9 December 1932.

47   L'Inspecteur principal Thiebaud, 13 February 1933, AD Yvelines, 4M 2/76.

48   Report by Étienne Fajon, Comité central, 10–14 February 1933, PCF 583.

49   'Appréciation de la section agraire sur les thèses agraires du 2ème Congrès et les thèses du 7ème du PCF' (n.d.), PCF 543.

50   Comité central, October 1930, PCF 381.

51   *Le Populaire*, 24 March 1929.

52   Lynch, *Moissons Rouges*, pp. 192–94. Compère-Morel wrote in 1929: 'What can be done from a socialist point of view with these poor people [agricultural workers], victims of excessive labour, bad food and detestable hygiene. . .? But the farmers, sharecroppers and small proprietors enjoy a greater liberty. They observe, they understand, they chat, they discuss, they analyse, they compare, they judge. . . They have understood that socialism is a system of both liberty and justice.' *Le Populaire*, 24 March 1929.

53   H. Desvaux, 'Encore sur le projet de thèses agraires', *Cahiers du Bolchevisme*, 15 September 1932.

54   This occurred, for example, at Saulx-lès-Chartreux (Seine-et-Oise), part of the market gardening region to the south of Paris. *La Voix Paysanne*, 12 April 1930.

55   Section Agraire, 'Rapport 1 avril 1933', PCF 630.

56   Rapport de Bourneton, 'Situation de la Fédération de l'Agriculture en France', 16 October 1932, PCF 543.

57   'Projet de résolution sur la politique du Parti à la campagne', 20 October 1930, PCF 439.

58   'Rapport sur le travail paysan du PCF', n.d. (around June 1933), PCF 613; Section Agraire, 'Rapport du 1 avril 1933', PCF 630.

59   Ibid.

60   'Appréciation de la section agraire réunie le 18 mai 1932', PCF 543.

61   'Rapport de Bourneton', 16 October 1932, PCF 543.

62   P. Semard, 'La Conquête et l'organisation du prolétariat agricole', *Les Cahiers du Bolchevisme*, 1 February 1933.

63   *Le Prolétaire Normand*, 20 January 1933.

64   *L'Humanité*, 26 November 1932.

65   'Rapport de Bourneton', 16 October 1932, PCF 543.

66   Semard, 'La Conquête', pp. 167–68.

67   Soupé, Comité central, 10–14 February 1933, PCF 583.

68   Parsal, Ibid.

69   Fouilloux, Bureau Politique, 18 January 1933, PCF 596.

70   Paxton, *French Peasant Fascism*, pp. 12–27.

71   Ibid., pp. 154–64.

72   'Frachon, pour le Secrétariat, aux bureaux régionaux', 30 August 1932, PCF 629.

73   *L'Humanité*, 15 October 1932. A similar position was adopted by the FUA and by the region of the party that covered the Beauce. 'Procès-verbal du Comité régional de la région Orléanaise', 20 November 1932, PCF 561.

74   Bureau Politique, 18 and 26 January 1933, PCF 596.

75   'Les Problèmes agraires en France et l'activité du Parti communiste', 26 January 1933, PCF 627.

76   M. Romier, 'La Crise agraire en France et le mouvement paysan', *Cahiers du Bolchevisme*, 1 February 1933, pp. 159–60.

77   Bureau Politique, 17 November 1932, PCF 519.

78   Comité central, 10–14 February 1933, PCF 583.

79   Ibid.

80   'Circulaire sur la question paysanne', 12 December 1933, PCF 606.

81   'Rapport sur le travail paysan du PCF.' n.d. (mid-1933), PCF 613.

82   Renaud Jean, Comité central, January 1934, PCF 683.

83   Ibid.
84   'Rapport sur le travail paysan du PCF.' n.d. (mid-1933), PCF 613.
85   After claiming to be 'frozen out' by the leadership in 1933, Desnots broke with the
     party at the time of Jacques Doriot's expulsion in 1934. He then passed through
     the Front social of Gaston Bergery, the Trotskyist PCI and Marceau Pivert's PSOP
     before moving towards fascism, joining Marcel Déat's Rassemblement national
     populaire during the Nazi occupation. See notice: J.-M. Brabant & C. Pennetier,
     Dictionnaire biographique (Le Maitron), CD-Rom.
86   Romier, 'La Crise agraire en France', p. 157.
87   Semard, 'La Conquête', p. 165.
88   Ibid.
89   *La Vie Ouvrière*, 20 October 1933.
90   F. Mioch, 'Rapport sur la conférence paysanne de la région Tourangelle',
     21 November 1933, PCF 628.
91   *Le Travailleur de Somme et Oise*, 14 October 1933.
92   Ibid., 30 July, 9 September 1933 and 17 November 1934.
93   Ibid.
94   'Matériaux pour les agitateurs sur la question agraire, 6 mars 1934', PCF 699.

Chapter 4

1   The Minister of the Interior asked for information on the Federation's activities in
     February 1933. Ministre de l'Intérieur, 14 February 1933, AD Yvelines, 4M 2/78.
     See reports in AN F7 13628.
2   CAC 20010216 art 74 1890.
3   T. Kemp, *The French Economy 1913–39, The History of a Decline*, Longman, London,
     1972, p. 137; H. Clout, *After the Ruins; Restoring the Countryside of Northern France
     after the Great War*, University of Exeter Press, Exeter, 1996.
4   In the Arras arrondissement, 150 out of 211 communes suffered over 90 per cent
     damage during the war. N. Gilbert, 'La Restauration des structures agricoles', in *'La
     Grande Reconstruction': Reconstruire le Pas-de-Calais après la grande guerre*, Actes du
     colloque 8 au 10 novembre 2000, Archives Départementales du Pas-de-Calais,
     2002, pp. 159–77.
5   L. Dubois, *Lafarge Coppée, 150 ans d'industrie, une Mémoire pour demain*, Pierre
     Belfond, Paris 1988, p. 209.
6   Pigenet et al, *Terre de Luttes,* p. 114. Kevin Passmore identifies the same trend in
     the Rhône. K. Passmore, *From Liberalism to Fascism, The Right in a French Province,
     1928–39*, Cambridge University Press, Cambridge, 1997, pp. 90–91.
7   'Notes et rapports sur l'évolution de l'agriculture et sa situation en 1932', AD Oise,
     Mp4514.
8   Ibid.
9   Listes nominatives, Dammard, 1F1, AD Aisne.
10   Ibid.
11   A. Langlet, 'Une Exploitation agricole dans la Santerre', Thèse agricole, Institut
     supérieur agricole de Beauvais, 1928, p. 18
12   J. Derocquigny, 'Modifications à apporter au mode d'exploitation actuelle de la Ferme
     de Dercy', Thèse agricole, Institut supérieur agricole de Beauvais, 1930, p. 19.
13   J. Grandel, 'Une Ferme de grande culture dans le Soissonnais', Thèse agricole,
     Institut supérieur agricole de Beauvais, 1925, p. 36.

14   Directeur des services agricoles, 8 June 1931, AD Pas-de-Calais, M/DSA 276.

15   In 1930, police investigated the well-meaning individuals running the organisation 'Le Travail aux Champs', based in Rouen, after it supplied a worker to one of the region's farms. The Special Commissioner reported: 'A man called Raymond Saillard, an unskilled worker who has been, in turn, docker, day labourer and carter, reported for work at Le Travail aux Champs. He was sent to fill the position of carter on the farm run by M. and Mde. Tinel at Pissy-Poville. As soon as he arrived, he started to remonstrate about the work he was asked to do, about the food, and his sleeping arrangements. . . During the course of these conversations he expressed extremist aims, encouraging his workmates to join him in taking strike action. Saillard is above all a lazy good-for-nothing and, in fact, declared himself to be a communist.' Le Commissaire spécial de Rouen, 8 July 1930, CAC 20010216 art 135 3937.

16   'Notes et rapports sur l'évolution de l'agriculture et sa situation en 1932', AD Oise, Mp 4514.

17   Maire de Compans, n.d. (1936), AD Seine-et-Marne M1190.

18   Sous-préfet de Douai, 23 January 1935, AD Nord M149/89.

19   *L'Agriculture de la Région du Nord*, 22 September 1934.

20   *La Vie Ouvrière*, 17 March 1933.

21   P. Leroy, 'Monographie agricole de la commune de Marck', September 1947. AD Pas-de-Calais, M/MONOAGRIC109.

22   Enquête agricole de 1929, questionnaires communaux. AD Pas-de-Calais, M/DSA 10

23   Listes nominatives 1936, Marck, AD Pas-de-Calais.

24   *L'Unité d'Action*, February 1935/2.

25   Commissaire spécial de Calais, 11 June 1934, AD Pas-de-Calais, 2Z 249.

26   Ibid., 19 January 1935, AD Pas-de-Calais, 2Z 254.

27   Listes nominatives 1926, 1931 & 1936, Campagne-lès-Guînes, AD Pas-de-Calais.

28   These included Saint-Tricat, Nielles-lès-Calais, Hames-Boucres, Vieille-Église, Guemps, Oye-Plage and Balinghem. *L'Unité d'Action*, February 1935/1, p. 4.

29   Listes nominatives 1936, Saint-Tricat, AD Pas-de-Calais.

30   *L'Unité d'Action*, December 1935/1.

31   Commissaire spécial de Calais, 7 July 1934; Sous-préfet de Boulogne, 7 July 1934; Préfet du Pas-de-Calais, 17 July 1934, AD Pas-de-Calais, M5323.

32   Commissariat spécial de Calais, 14 September 1934, AD Pas-de-Calais, 4Z 791.

33   See, for example, *L'Unité d'Action*, February 1936.

34   *Le Prolétaire Normand*, 29 March 1935.

35   *L'Exploité*, 9 June 1934.

36   Seven workers joined the Communist Party at Ambleny, a 'region where the majority of workers are exploited on the farms'. *L'Exploité*, 4 August 1934.

37   *L'Exploité*, 16 March 1935.

38   Including at Patay, Auneau, Terminiers, Châteauneuf-en-Thymerais. *Le Travailleur, Loiret-Eure et Loir-Loir et Cher*, 14 July 1934.

39   Dossier, 'Étampes – ouvriers agricoles', AD Yvelines, 4M 2/76.

40   Le Commissaire de police de la Ville d'Étampes, 24 September 1933, AD Yvelines, 4M 2/76.

41   Ibid., 22 September 1933.

42   Ibid., 24 September 1933.

43   *L'Humanité*, 9 September 1933.

44   Comité central, 17–19 October 1935, PCF 727.

45   Ibid.

46   Rapport du Capitaine Marnier sur un mouvement d'ouvriers agricoles à Pelves,
     4 October 1934; Rapport du Capitaine Marnier sur un mouvement d'ouvriers
     agricoles à Quéant, 4 October 1934, AD Pas-de-Calais, M5323.

47   Arthur Ramette, Comité central, January 1934, PCF 683.

48   In 1935, the Sub-Prefect reported five sections: Avesnes-les-Aubert (400 members),
     Avesnes-le-Sec (106), Iwuy (100), Naves and Ramillies (200). There were also
     groups in Rumilly, Villers-en-Cauthies and a number of other villages. Sous-préfet
     de Cambrai, 2 April 1935, AD Nord, M149/86.

49   L'Enchaîné, 22 November 1935 and 6 December 1935.

50   Le Commissaire Spécial Adjoint Marcel Rigal, 24 February and 25 March 1935, AD
     Nord M149/86.

51   Préfet du Nord, 3 June 1935, CAC 20010216 art 74 1894; L'Enchaîné, 7 February
     1936.

52   'Ordre du Jour', AD Nord M149/86.

53   'Rapport pour la Conférence régionale des 9 et 10 mars 1935 (Clichy)', Brochure
     éditée par la Région Paris-Ouest, PCF 745.

54   'La Lutte pour la conquête des ouvriers agricoles et des petits paysans de Seine-&-
     Marne', Cahiers du Bolchevisme, 15 May 1935.

55   L'Exploité, 12 October 1935.

56   Ibid.

57   Enquête statistique, May 1942, AD Aisne 1030W 21.

58   The union began at Prémont with 28 members and then spread into Beaurevoir,
     Gouy, Seboncourt, Villeret, Fonsommes and Montbrehin. L'Exploité, 30 November,
     14 December 1935, 11 and 18 January 1936.

59   L'Exploité, 29 February 1936.

60   Ibid., 14 December 1935.

61   Ibid., 8 February 1936.

62   Ibid., 11 April 1936.

63   R Schor, L'Opinion française et les étrangers, 1919–39, La Sorbonne, Paris, 1985, p. 35.

64   For immigration into the French countryside see R. Hubscher, L'Immigration dans
     les campagnes françaises (XIXe–XXe siècles), Paris, Odile Jacob, 2005.

65   Cited in J. Ponty, Polonais méconnus. Histoire des travailleurs immigrés en France dans
     l'entre-deux-guerres, Publications de la Sorbonne, Paris, 1988, p. 88.

66   Schor, L'Opinion française, p. 213.

67   Grandel, 'Une Ferme de grande culture', p. 38.

68   G. Mauco, 'Les Étrangers dans l'agriculture française' in A. Demangeon & G.
     Mauco, Documents pour servir à l'étude des étrangers dans l'agriculture française, Hermann
     & Cie, Paris, 1939, p. 40.

69   A. Papault, 'Le rôle de l'immigration agricole étrangère dans l'économie française',
     Thèse, Université de Paris, Faculté de Droit, 1933, p. 170.

70   Ministre de l'Agriculture à MM les Présidents des Chambres d'Agriculture, 3 and
     7 February 1930. AD Marne 135M ter109.

71   Préfet de l'Eure-et-Loir, 2 January 1925, AD Eure-et-Loir, 4M 232.

72   Préfet de l'Oise, January 1928, AD Oise, Mp 4383; Echo républicain du Valois,
     17 December 1927.

73   R. Justiniart, 'Le Marlois agricole', Thèse agricole, Institut supérieur agricole de
     Beauvais, 1924, p. 40.

74   Before the split in agricultural workers' unionism, the demand to limit the number

of immigrant workers in the workforce to 10 per cent had been widely accepted within the FNTA. It was included, for example, in the contract signed between the union and employers in horticulture in the Paris region in 1920. 'Premier congrès de la FNTA', p. 314.

75   *Le Travailleur de la Terre*, August-September 1923.

76   *La Voix Paysanne*, 27 February 1926.

77   Ibid., 25 July 1925.

78   Ibid., 30 January 1926.

79   Marcel Cachin, *l'Humanité*, 17 July 1923; cited in Schor, *L'Opinion française*, p. 248.

80   'Compte-rendu, 4e Congrès national, tenu à Clichy', 17–21 January 1925, Paris 1925, p. 418.

81   Ministère de l'Agriculture, 'Les Questions agricoles au Conseil national de la Main d'œuvre, 1926–7', Paris, 1927, p. 6.

82   A survey conducted in 1927 found that out of 600,000 immigrant workers introduced into agriculture between 1918 and 1926, only 253,000 still remained on the farms. Schor, *L'Opinion française*, p. 227.

83   Assemblée générale et réunion de propagande organisée par le Syndicat agricole de la région de Paris et la Fédération régionale des associations agricoles de l'Île de France, 17 December 1931, AN F7 13628.

84   Of the 105 workers involved in the strikes (August 1926) at Villeroy, Charnentroy and Charny (Seine-et-Marne), 28 were immigrant workers. Sous-préfet de Meaux, 12 August 1926, AD Seine-et-Marne, 1Mp 96.

85   Schor, *L'Opinion française*, pp. 275–79. Significant numbers of Spanish and Italian workers also joined the FUA in the Languedoc wine regions, in some areas forming around half the union's membership. A report noted that 'although a great deal of work still needs to be done, the French workers are getting used to seeing a Spaniard as a work comrade and not as an enemy'. *La Voix Paysanne*, 30 July 1927.

86   *La Voix Paysanne*, 1 October 1927.

87   *Le Travailleur Agricole*, March 1930.

88   J. Desnots, Comité central, October 1930, PCF 381,

89   *Le Travailleur Agricole*, April 1930.

90   Other conflicts took place at Mormant, Moussy-le-Neuf and Survilliers.

91   *La Voix Paysanne*, 21 July 1934.

92   *Les Communistes défendent les paysans*, Les Publications Révolutionnaires, Paris, 1935, p. 14.

93   *L'Humanité*, 13 June 1935.

94   Ibid., 8 June 1935.

95   *Le Travailleur de la Terre*, December 1931.

96   Ibid., September 1931.

97   Cited in Schor, *L'Opinion française*, p. 556 and pp. 562–66.

98   FNTA, 'Compte-rendu du Congrès national d'Unité', p. 27.

99   Ibid, p. 25.

100 Ponty, *Polonnais méconnus*, p. 294 and p. 321.

101 Mauco, 'Les 'Étrangers dans l'agriculture française', p. 7.

102 In April, a train deported sacked Polish and Czechoslovakian workers. On 15 October, 529 Polish and 152 Yugoslavs were expelled, followed on 30 October by 502 Polish workers from mines around Marles, Bruay, Courrières and Dourges. (Reports from Prefect du Pas-de-Calais, April and October 1934, AN F7 13027.

103 Courtois & Lazar, *Histoire du Parti communiste français*, p.122.

104 For a summary of the process by which the French communists adopted the Popular Front policy, see Jackson, *The Popular Front*, pp. 22–51.

105 Pierre Viansson-Ponté, cited in Vigreux, *Waldeck Rochet*, p.13.

106 W. Rochet, 'Le Travail des communistes à la campagne', *Cahiers du Bolchevisme*, 15 October 1934, p. 1228.

107 *La Voix Paysanne*, 3 November 1934.

108 'Section agraire du 2 juin 1935', PCF 738.

109 W. Rochet, 'La Crise agraire', 22 June 1935, PCF 738.

110 Ibid.

111 W. Rochet, 'Pour un front paysan qui défendre nos intérêts', *La Voix Paysanne*, 19 October 1935.

112 Rochet, 'La Crise agraire'.

113 *Cahiers du Bolchevisme*, 1 October 1935, pp. 1163–69.

114 W. Rochet, 'Les Importants problèmes du Front populaire à la campagne', *Cahiers du Bolchevisme*, 15 November 1935, p. 1405.

115 Ibid, p. 1406.

116 W. Rochet, 'Le Travail des communistes à la campagne', p. 1229.

117 W. Rochet, 'A la tête des luttes paysannes', *Cahiers du Bolchevisme*, 1 March 1935, pp. 271–72.

118 'Au secours de l'agriculture français', *L'Humanité*, 25 August 1935.

119 'Programme de sauvetage de l'agriculture française', *Cahiers du Bolchevisme*, 1 October 1935. p. 1167.

120 See excerpt from Rochet's Comintern speech in Vigreux, 'Regards européens', p. 77.

121 W. Rochet, 'L'Action communiste à la campagne', *Cahiers du Bolchevisme*, 15 October 1935.

122 Ibid, p. 1271.

123 Renaud Jean, 'Le Programme agricole', *La Voix Paysanne*, 2 November 1935.

124 Direction des Services Agricoles de la Somme, 12 August 1935, AD Somme, 1M KZ1140.

125 *L'Humanité*, 13 August 1935.

126 *Le Travailleur de Somme et Oise*, 17 August 1935.

127 *L'Humanité*, 16 August 1935.

128 W. Rochet, 'Les Importants problèmes du Front populaire à la campagne', p. 1406.

129 R. Jean & W. Rochet, 'L'Union des paysans de France', Rapport présenté au VIIIème Congrès national du Parti communiste, Villeurbanne 22–25 janvier 1936, p. 59.

130 *L'Exploité*, 24 August 1935.

131 *Bulletin des agriculteurs de l'Oise*, 17 August 1935.

132 See his speech at Dourdon (Seine-et-Oise) in February 1936. Commissariat spécial de Versailles, 23 February 1936, AD Yvelines 4M2/81.

133 'Rapport de Seinforin sur sa délégation à Compiègne pour la préparation d'éléctions', 29 October 1935, PCF 744.

134 'Rapport de H. Gourdeaux sur le Comité régional de la Région Aude-Hérault du 24 février 1935', PCF 740.

135 Direction générale de la Sûreté nationale, 20 May 1935, CAC 20010216 art 74 1890.

136 W. Rochet, 'La situation viticole et nos taches pour gagner les petits vignerons du Midi', 3 June 1935, PCF 738.

137 Ibid.

138 'Matériaux pour les agitateurs sur la question agraire, 6 mars 1934', PCF 699.
139 Ramette, Comité central, January 1934, PCF 683.
140 *L'Enchaîné*, 30 August 1935.
141 Ibid., 20 September 1935.
142 *L'Étampois*, February-April 1936.
143 *Le Prolétaire Normand*, 24 April 1936.
144 The figure was given by Parsal at the Comité central. The prefects estimated 30,000 strikers. Comité central, 17–19 October 1935, PCF 728; Sagnes, *Politique et syndicalisme*, p. 327.
145 *L'Humanité*, 8 September 1935.
146 Ibid, 11 September 1935. For Michel Rius, see: A. Balent, *Dictionnaire biographique (Le Maitron)*, CD-Rom.
147 *L'Humanité*, 11 September 1935.
148 Comité central, 17–19 October 1935, PCF 727.
149 CGTU, 'VIIIe Congrès national ordinaire, 24–27 septembre 1935', Imprimerie de la Maison des syndicats, Paris, pp. 108–09.
150 *Le Travailleur, Loiret, Loir-et-Cher, Eure-et-Loir*, 14 March 1936.
151 FNTA, 'Compte-rendu du Congrès national d'unité, Narbonne 29 février–1 Mars', CGT-FSI, Paris 1936, p. 1, AD Seine-Saint-Denis, 35J 1.
152 Ibid., p. 8 and p. 11.
153 Ibid., p. 29.

Chapter 5

1   J. Kergoat, *La France du Popular Front*, p.163.
2   Farcy, 'Les Grèves agricoles', pp. 306–11.
3   B. Badie, *Stratégie de la grève: pour une approche fonctionnaliste du Parti communiste français*, Presses de la Fondation Nationale des Sciences Politiques, Paris, 1976, pp. 68–70.
4   G. Lavau, *A Quoi sert le parti communiste français?*, Fayard, Paris, 1982.
5   *Cahiers du Bolchevisme*, 15 June 1936, p. 752.
6   'Décisions du Bureau politique', 25 June 1936; 'Décisions du Secrétariat', 20 July 1936, PCF 786.
7   *La Voix Paysanne*, 18 July 1937.
8   *L'Argus Soissonnais*, 27 April 1936.
9   *L'Écho Républicain*, 9 May 1936.
10 *L'Étampois*, 30 May 1936.
11 J. Valengin, 'Les Répercussions de la crise des années trente sur le syndicalisme agricole dans l'Aisne', Mémoire de maîtrise, Université de Lille III, 1994, pp. 182–84; P. Bréemersch & J-M. Decelle, *1936, Le Front Populaire dans le Pas-de-Calais*, Archives du Pas-de-Calais, Arras, 1997, p. 54.
12 P. Bernard, *Économie et Sociologie de la Seine-et-Marne, 1850–1950*, Cahiers de la Fondation Nationale des Sciences Politiques, Paris, 1953, p. 235.
13 Chaussy lost his seat in 1928 but was re-elected in 1932 and 1936.
14 *L'Humanité*, 15 May 1936.
15 'Cahier de revendications des ouvriers agricoles, Offranville', *Le Prolétaire Normand*, 10 July 1936.
16 *L'Humanité*, 7 April 1936.
17 Ibid., 18 May 1936

18   Procureur général, Amiens, 20 May 1936, AN BB18 3008; *L'Humanité*, 18 May 1936.
19   *L'Exploité*, 23 May 1936.
20   *L'Humanité*, 30 May; Procureur général, Amiens, 20 and 23 May 1936, AN BB18 3008.
21   *L'Argus Soissonnais*, 21 May 1936.
22   Procureur général, Amiens, 29 May 1936, AN BB18 3008.
23   Fromont & Bourgeois, 'Les Grèves agricoles'; Gratton, *Les Paysans français*, pp. 183–86.
24   *L'Humanité*, 17 May 1936.
25   *L'Humanité* (30 May 1936) reported 150 strikers at Tremblay. Unless indicated otherwise, numbers cited in the text are from police and administrative reports. They are often an underestimate, one reason being the tendency to exclude seasonal workers, often local women, from the calculations.
26   Communes touched in the Seine-et-Oise included Villepinte, Sevran, Roissy-en-France, Aulnay-sous-Bois. Parquet de Pontoise, 20 and 30 May 1936, AN BB18 3011.
27   Service de la police, AD Yvelines, 300W117; Sous-préfet de Meaux, 20 June 1936, AD Seine-et-Marne, M4947.
28   *L'Argus Soissonnais*, 30 May 1936.
29   Préfet de la Seine-et-Oise, 1 June 1936, AD Yvelines, 13M 241.
30   *L'Aube Sociale Mantaise*, 1 July 1936.
31   *L'Humanité*, 10 June 1936; Directeur des services agricoles de Seine et Seine-et-Oise, 11 July 1936, AD Yvelines, 13M 241; Police générale, AD Yvelines, 300W117.
32   *L'Éveil de Seine et Oise*, 15 July 1936; Parquet de Corbeil, 12, 13, 15, 17 and 23 June 1936, AN BB18 3011; Police générale, AD Yvelines, 300W117.
33   Chambre d'agriculture d'Eure-et-Loir, 23 June 1936, 10M 34.
34   'Premières grèves agricoles', AD Seine-et-Marne, M4947.
35   AD Aisne, 1M 22.
36   'Rapport du Capitaine Le Dall sur des grèves agricoles dans la région de Marle', 18 July 1936, AD Ainse, 1M 22.
37   'Situation de l'agriculture au 16 June 1936', AD Oise, Mp4285. Other communes hit in the region included Rosoy-en-Multien and Morienval.
38   Procureur de la République de Beauvais, 15, 17, 18, 19, 20, 22 and 26 June 1936, AN BB18 3008.
39   Préfet de l'Oise, 1 July 1936, AD Oise, Mp4285.
40   Procureur de la République de Clermont de l'Oise, 23, 27 June 1936, AN BB18 3008.
41   The first strike was at Vrély, starting 19 June. The agitation spread to other villages and in some cases settlements took place without a stoppage (including at Bouchoir, Méharicourt, Caix, Rosières). Where farmers did not accept workers' demands, strikes took place, such as at Harbonnières (50 workers, starting on 25 June), Villers-Bretonneux (27 June), Marcelcave (1 July). Procureur de la République de Montdidier, 22, 26 and 27 June 1936, AN BB18 3008; *Le Progrès de la Somme*, 3 and 18 July 1936. There was also a strike involving over 125 workers in a large fruit and vegetable enterprise on the coast at Saint-Quentin-en-Tournant. *Le Progrès de la Somme*, 2 and 5 July 1936.
42   In relation to the Caux, Paxton is mistaken to say that 'the first agricultural strikes broke out. . . only in the summer of 1937'. *French Peasant Fascism*, p. 99. Police reported strikes in the summer of 1936 at Daubeuf-Serville, Tocqueville, Ypreville-Biville, Criquebeuf, Saint-Léonard, Gervilles, Fonguesemare, Goderville and Les

Loges. Commissaire divisionnaire de Police spécial, 7 and 8 July 1936; Rapport du Capitaine Brunet, 7 July 1936, AD Seine-Maritime, 10M 380.

43   Commissaire spécial de Dunkerque, 18 and 19 June 1936, AD Nord, 5Z 562; Rapport du Capitaine Ansel, 20 June 1936, AD Nord, 5Z 563.

44   Capitaine Werquin, 16, 19, 21, 23, 25, 27 June and 8 July 1936, AD Nord, M619/104a.

45   Commissaire divisionnaire de police spéciale à Reims, 15 June 1936; Commissaire de police Chef de la Sûrete, 3 and 6 July 1936, AD Marne, 3Z 447.

46   The strike touched Ay, Cumières, Hautvillers, Chamillion, Dizy, Mailly-Champagne, Bouzy, Avize and Verzenay. Le Commissaire divisionnaire de police spéciale à Reims, 13 and 16 June 1936. Gendarmerie national, section de Reims, 'Rapport sur les grèves des ouvriers vignerons', 17 June 1936, AD Marne, 3Z 447. Le Commissaire divisionnaire de police spéciale, Arrondissement d'Épernay, 22 June 1936, AD Marne, 194M 28.

47   *L'Émancipateur*, 18 July 1936.

48   *L'Humanité*, 22 June 1936.

49   An important survey of the Popular Front strike movement in the department fails to mention the strikes in agriculture. M. Gillet, 'Le Nord/Pas-de-Calais en grève: 36–38', in M. Gillet & Y-M Hilaire (eds), *De Blum à Daladier: Le Nord/Pas-de-Calais 1936–1939*, Presses Universitaires de Lille, Villeneuve-d'Ascq, 1979, pp. 125–60.

50   P. Vandamme, *L'Agriculture du Pas-de-Calais*, Centre National de la Recherche Scientifique, Paris, 1951, p. 5.

51   R. Hubscher, *L'Agriculture et la société rurale dans le Pas de Calais du milieu du XIX siècle à 1914*, 2 vols, Mémoires de la Commission départementale des monuments historiques du Pas-de-Calais, Arras, 1979, vol. 2, p. 897.

52   *L'Agriculture de la Région du Nord*, 27 July 1936.

53   *Le Paysan*, 30 July 1937.

54   Jessenne, *Pouvoir au village et révolution*.

55   Hubscher, *L'Agriculture et la société rurale*, vol 2, p. 899.

56   Chambre d'agriculture du département du Pas-de-Calais, 6 July 1936, AD Pas-de-Calais, M2386.

57   Dossier of letters from farmers complaining about disturbances, particularly from M. Breton, 27 June 1936, AD Pas-de-Calis, M2386. There were similar 'regrettable incidents' involving agricultural workers at the market in Goderville (in the Caux region). Bernard Lefebvre, Conseiller général du Canton de Goderville, AD Seine-Maritime, 10M 380.

58   Commissariat de police, Aniche-Auberchicourt, 16 June 1936, AD Nord, 4Z 111.

59   The most prominent manifestation of the worker/peasant confrontation during the 'social explosion' took place in Avignon. Several fruit and vegetable farmers were 'arrested' by strike pickets who, according to an internal communist report, 'were applying their instructions too mechanically'. Lettre d'Arnal sur la grève générale en Avignon, 12 July 1936, PCF 796a.

60   'Cahier revendicatif', AD Pas-de-Calais, 2Z93.

61   'Rapport sur le mouvement gréviste des travailleurs agricoles dans le Pas de Calais', 15 July 1936, AD Pas-de-Calais, M/DSA286; Gendarme Nationale (Boulogne-sur-Mer), 22 June 1936, AD Pas-de-Calais, 2Z 151; *L'Humanité*, 23 June 1936.

62   Reports from Mayors of Nielles-lès-Calais and Saint-Tricat, AD Pas-de-Calais, M4456.

63   Commissariat spécial de Calais, 15 June 1936, AD Pas-de-Calais, 2Z 152.

64   *Le Petit Calaisien*, 17 June 1936; Commissariat spécial de Calais, 17 June 1936, AD
     Pas-de-Calais, 2Z 152.

65   Sous-préfet de Boulogne-sur-Mer, 16 June 1936, AD Pas-de-Calais, 2Z 93.

66   *L'Humanité*, 22 June and 1 July 1936.

67   'Avis aux populations agricoles', 18 June 1936, AD Pas-de-Calais, 2Z 93.

68   Sous-préfet de Boulogne-sur-Mer, 19 June 1936, AD Pas-de-Calais, 2Z 93.

69   Ibid.

70   'Avis aux ouvriers agricoles du canton de Guînes et du canton Sud-ouest de Calais',
     AD Pas-de-Calais, 2Z 93.

71   Sous-préfet de Boulogne-sur-Mer, 19 June 1936, AD Pas-de-Calais, 2Z 93.

72   Sous-préfet de Saint-Omer, 23 June 1936, AD Pas-de-Calais, M2385.

73   'Tarif proposé des salaires pour la région de Marck', 20 June 1936. AD Pas-de-
     Calais, 2Z 93.

74   'Accord du 7 juillet 1936', AD Pas-de-Calais, 2Z 93.

75   'Rapport de Léon Mauvais sur la conférence constitutive de la région du Pas-de-
     Calais du 28 juin', 2 July 1936, PCF 799.

76   *L'Enchaîné*, 3 July 1936.

77   In the Pas-de-Calais, police reports indicate many instances of dual membership.
     AD Pas-de-Calais, 4Z 807.

78   P. Ory, 'Le Dorgérisme: Institution et discours d'une colère paysanne, 1929–39',
     Revue d'histoire moderne et contemporaine, 22, 1975, p. 170.

79   It is no accident that Ory's study finds that the two Pas-de-Calais Dorgerist com-
     mittees sending the greatest number of subscriptions to the movement's head office
     in 1936 were those in Marquise and Arras, the former adjacent to the Calais/Guînes
     strike movement, the latter, the centre of operations against the strikes in the Artois.
     Ibid, p. 189.

80   Dorgères wrote: 'The new law on the 40-hour week will not be applicable to
     agriculture. Why are peasants and their workers treated as the poor relations? I hope
     that a peasant deputy will see it necessary to put an amendment extending the new
     law to the whole of agriculture, for both workers and employers.' *Le Progrès Agricole
     de l'Ouest*, 14 June 1936.

81   *L'Agriculture de la Région du Nord*, 4 July 1936.

82   'Extrait du registre des délibérations du Conseil municipal de Violaines', 31 July
     1936, AD Pas-de-Calais, M2386.

83   *Le Phare de Calais et du Pas-de-Calais*, 6 August 1936.

84   See, for example, R. Hainsworth, 'Les grèves du Front Populaire de mai et juin
     1936. Une nouvelle analyse fondée sur l'étude de ces grèves dans le basin houiller
     du Nord et du Pas-de-Calais', *Le Mouvement Social*, 96, 1976, pp. 3–30; J.-P.
     Depretto & S. V. Schweitzer, *Le Communisme à l'usine: vie ouvrière et mouvement ouvrier
     chez Renault 1920–39*, EDIRES, Roubaix, 1984.

85   Kergoat, *La France du Front Populaire*, p. 148 and pp. 150–51. An article by Prost
     has attempted to find a synthesis, arguing that the strikes were 'spontaneous' in the
     sense that they were a movement from below: 'No national political or trade union
     forces wanted these strikes', but, rather, the initial movements were the result of
     'local initiatives. . . often taken by militants'. But this only repeats the argument of
     the first camp, except that Prost has now redefined the term 'spontaneous'. A. Prost,
     'Les grèves de mai–juin 1936 revisitées', *Le Mouvement social*, July-August 2002,
     p. 37. See the more convincing argument by Jackson, *The Popular Front*, pp. 88–92.

86   Ponchelet, 'Ouvriers nomades', p. 417.

87   E. Wolf, *Peasant Wars in the Twentieth Century*, Faber and Faber, London, 1973, pp. 290–91.
88   Lynch, *Les Moissons rouges*, p. 338.
89   Préfet de l'Oise, 17 June 1936, AD Oise, Mp4285.
90   *La Somme*, 10 July 1936, AD Somme, M149/1.
91   Préfet de l'Oise, 17 July 1936, AD Oise, Mp 4285.
92   Maréchal des logis, Chef Bleux, 17 July 1936, AD Oise, Mp 4285.
93   Comité central, 10–14 February 1933, PCF 583.
94   D. Tartakowsky & C. Willard, *Des Lendemains qui chantent, La France des années folles et du Front populaire*, Messidor/Éditions Sociales, 1996, p. 185.
95   Lynch, *Les Moissons rouges*, p. 338.
96   *L'Étampois*, 30 May 1936. Although generally more cautious, socialists also joined the agitation. In the Valois, the socialist paper declared: 'Stand up to these employers. . . Demand an increase in wages from them. . . We will help you. . . Agricultural workers, stop being slaves. Raise your heads. Your time has come!' *L'Écho Républicain*, 9 May 1936.
97   Lynch, *Les Moissons rouges*, p. 337.
98   *Le Travailleur, Loiret, Loir-et-Cher, Eure et Loir*, 11 July 1936.
99   *Le Journal d'Issoudun*, 23 June and 28 June 1936.
100 Their most prominent local representative, Georges Monnet, the soon to be appointed Minister of Agriculture, was subjected to severe criticism from local communists for failing to support the demands of the strike movement in the Vermandois. *L'Exploité*, 23 May 1936.
101 Transcription of a discussion between Michel Leroux and Guy Marival, 27 March 1996, Programme Mémoire 2000, Chambre d'Agriculture de l'Aisne.
102 'Liste du bureau du syndicat Saint-Pierre-Aigle et Dommiers', 22 June 1936, Archives Communales, Saint-Pierre-Aigle, 2I4. AD Aisne.
103 Listes nominatives, Dommiers, 1F1, AD Aisne.
104 'Liste du bureau du syndicat Saint-Pierre-Aigle et Dommiers', 22 June 1936, Archives Communales, Saint-Pierre-Aigle, 2I4, AD Aisne.
105 Listes nominatives 1936, Silly-le-Long, AD Oise.
106 Sous-préfet de Senlis, 16 May 1906, AD Oise, Mp 4292.
107 Rapport du Préfet, 15 July 1936, AD Pas-de-Calais, M2386.
108 Listes nominatives, Quéant 1936, AD Pas-de-Calais.
109 For the 1911 revolt, see J. Saillet & J. Girault, 'Les Mouvements vignerons de Champagne', *Le Mouvement social*, 67, 1969, pp. 79–88.
110 Le Commissaire de police d'Ay-Champagne, 26 June 1936, AD Marne, 194M 30.
111 Archives Communales, Saint-Pierre-Aigle, 2 I4, AD Aisne.
112 FNTA Congrès national, 17–19 février 1939, Compte-rendu sténographique, p. 25, AD Seine-Saint-Denis, 35J 1.
113 Ponchelet, 'Ouvriers nomades', p. 359.
114 F. Langlois, *Les Salariés agricoles en France*, A. Colin, Paris, 1962, pp. 162–66.
115 Some historians underestimate the extent of the exclusion. Lynch, for example, believes that the Minister of Agriculture wrote to prefects on 20 July 1936 urging them to intervene as 'certain employers were refusing to implement the law on paid holidays in agriculture, arguing practical difficulties' (Lynch, 'Le Parti socialiste', p. 718). The circular concerned was, in fact, only setting out guidelines for a consultation process. See 'Avis relatif à la consultation des syndicats agricoles en vue de l'application de la loi du 20 juillet', AD Eure-et-Loir, 10M 26.

116 'Projet d'accord provisoire entre la Fédération régionale des associations agricoles de l'Île de France et la Fédération nationale des travailleurs de l'agriculture (CGT)', 19 June 1936, AD Seine-et-Marne, M4951.

117 Fédération régionale des associations agricoles de l'Île de France, 'Une Mise au point à propos des grèves agricoles', 15 July 1936, AD Yvelines, 13M 241.

118 Sous-préfet de Meaux, 20 June 1936.

119 Ibid.

120 The evolution of the ACEA can be traced through its newspaper, duplicitously titled *La Paix des campagnes,* an incomplete collection of which is conserved at the Bibliothèque Nationale.

121 *L'Humanité,* 27 June and 21 July 1936.

122 XXIème Congrès de l'Union départementale des syndicats confédérés de l'Aisne, 27–28 February 1937.

123 J.-P. Besse, 'Le Front Populaire dans l'Oise (1936–1938)', *Annales Historiques Compiègnoises,* 36, 1986, pp. 12–13.

124 Préfet de l'Oise, 1 July 1936, AD Oise, Mp 4285.

125 *L'Humanité,* 25 June 1936.

126 Ibid., 22 June 1936.

127 Communiqué de la FNTA, *Le Populaire,* 10 July 1936.

128 Directeur des services agricoles de la Seine-et-Oise, 11 July 1936, AD Yvelines, 13M 241.

129 A copy of the contract can be found in AD Aisne, 10M 62.

130 *L'Humanité,* 27 June 1936 and 6 July 1936.

131 *Le Temps,* 14 July 1936.

132 Ministre de l'Agriculture, 2 July 1936, AD Pas-de-Calais, M2386.

133 *Le Populaire,* 17 July 1936.

134 'A certain agitation has been noted amongst agricultural workers in several regions. At a time when harvests are about to begin, it is important to follow the evolution of this movement very closely. . . [and] hold an enquiry in view of informing me as quickly as possible about the mood of agricultural workers in your department and on the possibility of a strike movement amongst this category of workers.' Ministre de l'Intérieur, 7 July 1936, AD Pas-de-Calais, M2386.

135 *Pour les travailleurs de la terre, projets de lois et propositions du groupe parlementaire communiste,* Éditions du Comité Populaire de Propagande, Paris, 1936.

136 Ibid, p. 6.

137 *Écho Républicain,* 4 July 1936.

138 J. Vassal au Préfet de l'Oise, 11 July 1936, AD Oise, Mp4285.

139 Out of 21 meetings of the Secrétariat in 1936, Chaussy only attended 4 and Guillon (the other socialist member) 3. *Le Paysan,* 18 December 1936.

140 'Examen général de la situation en ce qui concerne les grèves agricoles, et les négociations entre la CGT et les employeurs de l'Île de France', 18 July 1936, AD Yvelines, 13M 241.

141 Ibid.

142 The Communiqué reads: 'After long debates held at the Ministry of Agriculture chaired by M. Monnet, the Union of Agricultural Employers and Fédération Nationale des Travailleurs de l'Agriculture (CGT) have agreed in principle on the majority of questions under discussion, notably working hours, a weekly break, overtime payments, notice of dismissal, paid holidays, family allowances, union rights, workers' delegates and arbitration commissions. As the parties have been

unable to reach agreement on a uniform wage covering all regions, they have decided to ask workers and employers to get immediately in touch with each other in order to conclude local or regional agreements.' *Le Temps*, 20 July 1936.

143 *Le Populaire*, 20 July 1936.

144 AD Seine-et-Marne, M4957.

145 Grèves agricoles, enquêtes auprès des communes, Seine et Marne, M1190. The reports from mayors (M4957) also indicate a number of villages and farms not included on the Prefect's list of strikes; for example, the village of Montévrain and two additional farms at Iverny.

146 *L'Humanité*, 22 July 1936

147 Préfet de l'Oise, 23 July 1936, AD Oise, Mp4285.

148 Procureur général, Abbeville, 8 October 1936, AN BB18 3008.

149 L'Adjudant Guérin, 22 and 24 July 1936; *L'Humanité*, 22 July 1936.

150 Undated written report, AD Aisne, 1M 22.

151 Commissaire de police de la Ville de Soissons, 27 July 1936, AD Aisne, 7M 20.

152 AD Aisne, 1M 22; F. Stévenot, '"Débout les damnés de la terre", Les grèves agricoles dans l'Aisne 1936–37', *Bullétin de la Fédération des Sociétés d'Histoire et d'Archéologie de l'Aisne*, 36, 1991, (pp. 145–68) p. 161.

153 Ross uses the term to describe strikes that allow workers to vent discontent without the danger that they become serious movements. G. Ross, *Workers and Communists in France: From Popular Front to Eurocommunism*, University of California Press, Berkeley, 1982, pp. 33 and 46.

154 *L'Humanité*, 20 July 1936.

155 Télégramme, 21 July 1936, AD Aisne, 1M 22.

156 Later, however, the haste with which agreements were signed would be the subject of criticism from activists. At the FNTA National Congress (January 1937), the delegate from Provins complained that the region's contract had been 'finalised too quickly', leaving open many questions. The delegate from Roissy-en-France also complained of the lack of consultation, which had enabled employers to 'give with one hand and take back with the other'. Congrès national extraordinaire, FNTA, 24/25 janvier 1937, Compte-rendu sténographique, p. 38 and p. 170, AD Seine-Saint-Denis, 35J 1.

157 Sous-préfet de l'Oise, 30 July 1936. AD Oise, Mp4285.

158 'Rapport sur la tournée dans la Région Basse-Seine-Picardie', 25–26 July 1936, PCF 796a.

159 Sous-préfet de Compiègne, 2 October 1936, AD Oise, Mp4285; Listes nominatives, Bailleul-le-Soc, AD Oise.

160 Commissaire divisionnaire de police spéciale, 22 July 1936, AD Seine-Maritime, 10M 380.

161 *L'Humanité*, 22 July 1936.

162 *Le Travailleur, Eure et Loir, Loiret, Loir et Cher*, 8 August 1936; *Le Journal d'Issoudun*, July, August 1936; *L'Émancipateur*, 25 July, 1 and 29 August 1936.

163 For example, in the Saint-Just-en-Chaussée/Maignelay region (Oise), where 2000 workers threatened to stop work. *Le Temps*, 26 July 1936.

164 Ministère de l'Agriculture, 23 July 1936, AD Yvelines, 13M 241.

165 Union départementale des syndicats unifiés du Pas de Calais, 25 July 1936, AD Pas-de-Calais, M2386.

166 'Accord de Marquion du 26 juin 1936', AD Pas-de-Calais, M2386.

167 *Le Grand Écho du Nord de France*, 21 July 1936.

168 Communiqué préfectorale, Département du Nord, 20 July 1936; *Le Réveil du Nord*, 21 July 1936.

169 'Procès-verbal de la réunion du 18 juillet 1936', AD Pas-de-Calais, M/DSA 286.

170 Préfet de l'Hérault au Ministre de l'Intérieur, 30 July 1936, AD Pas-de-Calais, M2386.

171 Handwritten note, AD Pas-de-Calais, M2386.

172 Ibid.

173 Commissariat de police de la Ville d'Arras, 2 August 1936, AD Pas-de-Calais, M2386.

174 *La Dépêche*, 30 July 1936.

175 Handwritten note, n.d., AD Pas-de-Calais, M2386.

176 Maire de Boiry-Becquerelle, 30 July 1936, AD Pas-de-Calais, M2386.

177 *Le Réveil du Nord*, 2 August 1936; *L'Enchaîné*, 14 August 1936.

178 Police questioning of the volunteers on 5 August found that out of 152 from whom details were taken, 71 were from the Paris region. They included four office workers, three commercial representatives, two bakers, an architect, an actor, a private teacher and only one agricultural worker. 'Rapport du Chef d'Escadron Éloy', 5 August 1936, AD Pas-de-Calais, M2386.

179 Listes nominatives, 1936, AD Pas-de-Calais.

180 'Rapport d'Adjudant Chef Dupois sur les incidents de grève à St-Léger', 3 August 1936, AD Pas-de-Calais, M2386.

181 'Rapport de l'Adjudant Chef Dupois', 5 August, AD Pas-de-Calais, M2386.

182 *Le Populaire* did not comment on the dispute until 12 August.

183 *L'Humanité*, 27 July 1936.

184 Ibid.

185 Rapport de l'Adjudant Chef Dupois, 5 August, AD Pas-de-Calais, M2386.

186 *L'Humanité* 13 August 1936.

187 Ibid.; A similar statement was carried in *L'Enchaîné*, 28 August 1936.

188 At Mory, workers accepted around four per cent, at La Herlière ten per cent.

189 'Accord patronaux, ouvriers de Mory', n.d., (August 1936), AD Pas-de-Calais, M/DSA 286.

190 *L'Enchaîné*, 28 August 1936.

191 Préfet du Nord, 4, 6 and 18 August, AD Nord, M619/103a.

192 Chef d'escadron Pierron, 20 August 1936, AD Nord, M619/104a.

193 Commissaire spéciale de Dunkerque, 19 August 1936, AD Nord, 5Z 563.

194 See reports in AN BB18 3008; AD Nord, M619/103b and M619/104a; *Le Paysan*, 16 October 1936; *L'Humanité*, 28 October 1936; *Le Paysan*, 20 November 1936.

195 *L'Avenir du Vexin et des Andelys*, 9 October 1936.

196 'Aux Ouvriers et Ouvrières agricoles de Marck', n.d., AD Pas-de-Calais, 2Z 93.

197 Letter from René Gaston Vattement, 3 August 1936, AD Seine-Maritime, 10M 380.

198 AD Ainse, 7M 20.

199 Sous-préfet de Meaux, 10 July 1936, AD Seine-et-Marne, M4947.

200 Letter from Agricultural Workers' Union, Coulommiers, 13 July 1936, AD Seine-et-Marne, M4957.

201 Sous-préfet de Saint-Quentin, 6 March 1937, AD Aisne, 7M 20.

202 Sous-préfet de Saint-Omer, 24 June 1936, AD Pas-de-Calais, M2385.

203 Préfet de Seine-et-Oise, 3 August 1936, AD Yvelines, 4M 2/81. Paxton (*French Peasant Fascism*, p. 92) remarks that the PSF 'began a major effort to enlist farmers

in 1937'. But the party's campaign began one year earlier and can be directly linked to the farm strike movement.

204 Letters from George Mathy, délégué agricole du Syndicat professionnel français, 24 July 1936 and 24 August 1936, AD Aisne, 7M 19.

205 'Listes des syndicats déclarés', n.d. (late 1936), AD Oise, Mp 4911.

206 In some regions, farmers encouraged their workers to join the Fédération des Travailleurs de la Terre (FTT), the agricultural workers' union established by the Christian trade union confederation (CFTC).

207 L'Écho Républicain, 22 August 1936.

208 Letter from Elie Bloncourt, 2 November 1936, AD Aisne, 7M 20.

209 Commission paritaire mixte agricole de l'Arrondissement de Melun, 22 September 1936, AD Seine-et-Marne, M4947.

210 L'Humanité, 23 and 27 August 1936.

211 Letter from M. Bertout, n.d. (August 1936), AD Oise, Mp4285.

212 Courrier de l'Aisne, 3 December 1936.

213 P. Dutton, Origins of the French Welfare State, Cambridge University Press, 2002, p. 146.

214 Ibid., p. 161.

215 'Rapport de Sautel sur la section de Romorentin', 11 April 1937, PCF 827.

216 'Le Ministre de l'Agriculture à Messieurs les Préfets', 7 October 1936, AD Somme, 1M KZ1765.

217 'Arrête de 31 October 1936', AD Somme, 1M KZ 1765.

218 Secrétaire du Syndicat des ouvriers d'agriculture, Proyart, 31 October 1936, AD Somme, 1M KZ1765.

219 Letter from Louis Marécal, 9 December 1936, AD Aisne, 7M 20.

220 L'Écho Républicain, 5 December 1936.

221 Le Progrès de la Somme, 15 December 1936.

222 Le Paysan, 11 September 1936.

223 Ibid., 11 December 1936; L'Humanité, 26 December 1936.

224 Lynch, 'Le Parti socialiste', pp. 777–78.

225 A. Parsal, 'Pour le bien-être des travailleurs de la terre dans une agriculture riche et prospère', 24/25 January 1937, pp. 18–19, AD Seine-Saint-Denis, 35J 39.

226 Intervention of Blotteau, FNTA, Congrès national extraordinaire, 1937, p. 113.

227 Le Prolétaire Normand, 29 January 1936.

228 Although still joint general secretary with Parsal, Chaussy was only a fringe figure in the union's functioning. Seeking an alternative base, he established 'le Groupe parlementaire de défense des ouvriers agricoles', significantly without consultation with communists in the FNTA leadership. FNTA, Bureau fédéral, 23 April 1937, AD Seine-Saint-Denis, 35J 5.

229 FNTA Bullétin fédéral, February 1937. Archives Saint-Saint-Denis, 35J 38.

230 Maréchal des logis-chef Gallet, 2 and 27 April 1937, Mp 4280; Commissariat spécial de Versailles, 5 April 1937; Sous-préfet de Dreux, 6, 10 April 1937 AD Eure-et-Loir, 10M 28.

231 In other regions the strikes also drew in villages not previously touched: in the Beauce, 17 farms around Dreux and Saint-Rémy-sur-Avre; in the Pas-de-Calais at Le Transloy and Sainte-Marie-Kerque. Le Sous-préfet de Dreux, 19 June 1936, AD Eure-et-Loir, 10M28; Le Préfet du Pas-de-Calais, AD Pas-de-Calais, 13 April and 7 May 1937, M2406.

232 Sous-préfet de Dreux, 19 June 1936, AD Eure-et-Loir, 10M28; Accord du Travail, 17 June 1937, AD Eure-et-Loir, 10M34.

233 Sous-préfet de Senlis, 6 July 1937, AD Oise, Mp4300.

234 The union claimed a victory after a bitter conflict at Arles in May 1937, despite an attempt to break the strike by Colonel de la Roque's 'Syndicats professionals'. *L'Humanité*, 30 May 1937.

235 Le Commissaire de police de la Ville d'Étampes, 19 July 1937, AD Yvelines, 4M 2/83.

236 Préfet de l'Oise, 20, 22 and 27 July 1937, AD Oise, Mp4300.

237 Leclercq, the organiser of the strikebreaking in the Artois the previous summer, played an important role in the operation. Valengin, 'Les Répercussions de la crise', pp. 277–79.

238 Brigade de Montcornet, 'Procès-verbal des renseignements sur des entraves à la liberté du travail', 20 July 1936, AD Aisne, 1M 22.

239 Procès-verbal, Pierre Mortelette & Abel Lancelle, Gendarmes à pied, 14 June 1937, AD Aisne, 51U 30.

240 Ponchelet, 'Ouvriers nomades', p. 417.

241 Sous-préfet de Boulogne-sur-Mer, 5 August 1936, AD Pas-de-Calais, M2386.

242 FNTA, 'Résolution de la Commission fédérale des grèves', 4 September 1937, AD Seine-Saint-Denis, 35J 39.

243 'Rapport du Capitaine de gendarmerie d'Yvot', 24 May 1937, AD Seine-Maritime, 2Z 94.

244 *Le Réveil du Nord*, 7 June 1937.

245 *Le Populaire*, 2 August 1937.

246 Sous-préfet de Compiègne, 19 July 1937, AD Oise, Mp 4300

247 *Le Temps*, 4 May 1937.

248 On a very low poll, it was endorsed by 1234 votes to 843.

249 Sous-préfet de Pontoise, 3 May 1937, AD Yvelines, 13M 241.

250 'Décisions du BP du 27/5/37', PCF 817.

251 FNTA, Commission exécutive, 7 June 1937, AD Seine-Saint-Denis, 35J 5.

252 *L'Humanité*, 18 and 21 June 1937.

253 FNTA, Commission éxécutive, 7 June 1937, AD Seine-Saint-Denis, 35J 5; AD Oise, Mp4300; Commissaire central de police, 14 June, AD Nord, M598/98.

254 FNTA, Section de Noailles, 20 June 1937, AD Oise, Mp4300.

255 'Rapport sur la Conférence paysanne de la region du Nord (Lille, 3 Juillet 1938)', PCF 844.

256 Procès-verbal, 9 June 1937, AD Seine-et-Marne, M4958

257 Parquet du Procureur de la République Melun, 4 July 1937, AN BB18 3064. See also dossier Affaire Legras, AD Seine-Saint-Denis 35J 53.

258 Procureur général, Rouen, 24 June 1937, AN BB18 3064.

259 Ibid., 16 December 1937.

260 *L'Humanité*, 30 June 1937; Maréchal des logis Chef Beaurain, 15 June 1937, AD Oise, Mp4300.

261 Commissaire spécial de Melun, 9 June 1937, AD Seine-et-Marne, M 4957.

262 Capitaine Le Magny, 15 June 1937, AN BB18 3064. The incident raises the question of whether or not prominent communists tended to carry weapons during this period.

263 Procureur de la Republique à Pontoise 14 October, 1937, AN BB18 3064.

264 Procureur general, Paris, 20 July 1937, AN BB18 3064.

265 Parquet de la Court d'appel de Paris, 6 June 1938, AN BB18 3064.

266 *L'Écho Républicain*, 7 August 1937.

267 'Accord', AD Pas-de-Calais, M/DSA 318.

268 'Rapport sur la Conférence paysanne de la region du Nord (Lille, 3 Juillet 1938)', PCF 844.

269 Bureau fédéral, 2 November 1937, AD Seine-Saint-Denis, 35J 5.

270 'Rapport de Decaux sur le Comité régional de l'Aisne (26–27 février 1938)', PCF 840.

271 Sous-préfet de Saint-Quentin, 'Ouvriers licenciés suites des grèves', 12 August 1937, AD Aisne, 1M 22.

272 Préfet, 29 October 1937, AD Seine-et-Marne, M4955.

273 FNTA, 'VIII Congrès national (17–19 février 1939), Compte-rendu sténographique', pp. 254–65, AD Seine-Saint-Denis, 35J 1.

274 In the Oise during the autumn of 1937 there were strikes led by communists at Tricot and Méry-la-Bataille. In 1938, there was a new conflict at Tricot (involving 109 workers) and a strike at Wariville. In the Pas-de-Calais strikes broke out during 1938 at Metz-en-Couture (April), Quéant (August) and Saint-Léger (October). In the Aisne, there was a strike of 35 workers out of the 50 employed on 16 farms in the village of Montloué (August 1938). A number of isolated conflicts continued during 1939; for example, at Cuirieux in the Laon region (Aisne). Sous-préfet de Compiègne, 24 October 1937, 17 May and 10 June 1938, AD Oise, Mp4300; Directeur des services agricoles, 22 April, 4 August and 28 November 1938, Pas-de-Calais M/DSA 286; Secrétaire général, 13 and 17 August 1938, AD Aisne, 1M 22; Brigade de Marle, 'Rapport sur une grève agricole à Cuirieux', 28 May 1939, AD Aisne, 1M 22.

275 'VI Conférence de la région Paris-Ouest du Parti communiste français, 4–5 décembre 1937', AD Yvelines, 4M 269

276 'Rapport de O Rabaté sur les réunions. . . dans l'Aisne du 13 au 26 septembre 1937'. PCF 825.

277 Procès-verbaux du Conseil municipal, 28 January 1938, Archives communales, La-Ville-aux-Bois-lès-Dizy.

278 E. Shorter & C. Tilly, *Strikes in France 1830–1968*, Cambridge University Press, London, 1974, p. 362.

279 *L'Humanité*, 1 June 1936.

280 Sometimes, however, union officials saw it necessary to remind activists of their responsibilities. The FNTA secretary at Fontenay-Trésigny issued instructions: 'Our union comrades must maintain their dignity – and not drink to excess; our union comrades must be clean and spread the word that hygiene is healthy; all union members must be an example to their work comrades.' (Syndicat ouvrier agricole de Fontenay-Trésigny, 'Règlement disciplinaire du Syndicat', non-dated, AD Seine-et-Marne, M4947.) Propriety and sobriety were deemed important not only for the public image but also for the maintenance of discipline within the workers' movement.

281 Parsal, 'Pour le bien-être des travailleurs de la terre', p. 40.

282 M. Lazar, 'Damné de la terre et homme de marbre. L'ouvrier dans l'imaginaire du PCF du milieu des années trente à la fin des années cinquante', *Annales ESC*, September-October 1990, pp. 1082–83.

Chapter 6

1 M. Perrot, *Workers on Strike, France 1871–1890* (trans. C. Turner), Berge, Leamington Spa, 1987, p. 12.

2 'Rapport de A. Vassart sur la conference d'information de la Seine et Marne', 18 October 1936, PCF 801.

3 'Procès-verbaux du Conseil municipal à partir de l'année 1930', Archives Communales, La-Ville-aux-Bois-lès-Dizy.

4 'Procès-verbal de Jules Drapier', 11 June 1937, AD Aisne, 51U 30.

5 'Procès-verbal de Louis Marécal', 11 June 1937, AD Aisne, 51U 30.

6 S. W. Haine, *The World of the Paris Café, Sociability among the French Working Class, 1789–1914*, John Hopkins University Press, Baltimore, 1996, pp. 130–34, p. 237 and p. 139.

7 Rapport du Capitaine Meurs, 20 August 1936, AD Nord, M619/104.

8 FNTA, Congrès national extraordinaire, 1937, p. 128.

9 Tribunal de première instance, Laon, 7 August 1937, AD Aisne, 51U 30.

10 Procès-verbal d'Henri Bertrand, 14 June 1937, AD Aisne, 51U 30.

11 Procès-verbal, Pierre Mortelette & Abel Lancelle, Gendarmes à pied, 14 June 1937, AD Aisne, 51U 30.

12 FNTA, Congrès national extraordinaire 1937, p. 128.

13 Ibid.

14 Procureur général d'Amiens, 29 July 1936, AN BB18 3008.

15 Procureur de la République, Péronne, 23 July 1936, AN BB18 3008.

16 Listes nominatives, Ennemain, AD Somme.

17 In 1927, a union had been formed in a number of Valois villages and some strikes took place. Baptiste spoke at a meeting in Silly. *Écho Républicain du Valois*, 9 July, 13 August and 17 December 1927

18 Listes nominatives, Silly-le-Long, AD Oise.

19 C. Tilly, *The Contentious French*, Belknap Press, Cambridge MA, 1986, p. 394.

20 *Le Petit Calaisien*, 20 June 1936.

21 Préfet du Nord, 27 May 1937, AD Nord, M619/103c.

22 *La Somme*, 10 July 1936, AD Somme, M149/1.

23 Ibid.

24 While teachers, café owners and others would usually be found on the side of the agricultural workers, it was not always the case. During a strike at Brunvillers (Oise) in July 1937, Rius sent a letter to the Prefect saying that strikers were surprised to see 'the village teacher working in the fields'. M Rius, 29 July 1937, AD Oise, Mp4300.

25 For example, at Lehaucourt and Chouy (Aisne). *Le Paysan*, 12 March, 24 September 1937 and 24 December 1937.

26 *Le Paysan*, 6 August 1937.

27 Ibid., 23 October 1936.

28 Rapport du Chef Petit, 1 June 1937; Rapport du Capitaine Dubois, 3 June 1937, AD Nord, 4Z 110.

29 Rapports au Ministère du Travail, January 1938, AD Nord, 4Z 96.

30 Le Préfet de l'Oise, 14 June 1937, AD Oise, Mp 4300. Le Réveil de l'Oise, 5 July 1937.

31 'Procès-verbal constatant des entraves à la liberté du travail et coups et blessures sur Bailly à St Méry.' 10 June 1937, AD Seine-et-Oise, M4958

32 *Le Paysan*, 20 November 1936.

33 'Cahier revendicatif', AD Pas-de-Calais, 2Z93.

34 'Revendications des ouvriers agricoles' & 'Accord du 7 juillet 1936', AD Pas-de-Calais, 2Z 93.

35 'Accord Provisoire de Travail', 20 June 1936, AD Pas-de-Calais, 2Z 93.
36 Moquay, *L'Évolution sociale en agriculture*, pp. 48–49.
37 *Le Paysan*, January 1937.
38 Quoted in Lazar, 'Damné de la Terre', p. 1077.
39 *Les Tablettes de l'Aisne*, 16 September 1936.
40 Les Présidents des syndicats d'ouvriers et d'ouvrières agricoles de Marle-Cilly et communes environnantes, 6 July 1936, AD Aisne, 1M 22.
41 *L'Avenir du Vexin et des Andelys*, 2, 9, 16 October and 6 November 1936.
42 *Le Paysan*, 13 November 1936.
43 *L'Écho Républicain*, 4 September 1937.
44 Procureur de la République, Saint-Quentin, 15 October 1937, AN BB18 3062.
45 Gendarmerie nationale, Saint-Quentin, 'Rapport sur des grèves agricoles', 4 August 1937, AD Aisne, 1M 22.
46 Sous-préfet de Compiègne, 11 September 1937, AD Oise Mp4300.
47 E. Shorter & C. Tilly, 'Le déclin de la grève violente en France de 1890 à 1935', *Le Mouvement Social*, 76, July-September, 1971.
48 It is, of course, impossible to know who was directly responsible for these actions, or even how many of them were deliberate. In some cases, the perpetrators were found. In the Dreux region (Eure-et-Loir), Auguste Boyer, 48-years-old 'without fixed address', set fire to a stack of wheat belonging to his employer, destroying 34,000 francs worth of produce. 'My employer had sacked me without paying me the 60 francs he owed me and I decided to take revenge,' he explained. *Le Populaire*, 20 September 1936.
49 M. Seidman, 'Towards a History of Workers' Resistance to Work: Paris and Barcelona during the French Popular Front and the Spanish Revolution, 1936–8', *Journal of Contemporary History*, 23, 1988, pp. 191–220.
50 Kergoat, *La France du Front Populaire*, pp. 154–56.
51 J. Danos & M. Gibelin, *June '36: Class Struggle and the Popular Front in France*, Bookmarks, London, 1986, p. 132.
52 S. Wolikow, *Le Front Populaire en France*, Complexe, Bruxelles, p. 152.
53 'Conflits de grève survenus au cours du mois de juin 1936', 24 July 1936, AD Aisne, 10M 44.
54 *L'Éveil de Seine et Oise*, 15 July 1936; Parquet de Corbeil, 15 June and 8 July 1936, AN BB18 3011.
55 Police générale, AD Yvelines, 300W 117.
56 Paxton, *French Peasant Fascism*, p. 89.
57 *La Santerre*, 24 July 1936.
58 Procureur général d'Amiens, 22 June 1936, AN BB18 3008.
59 *Le Figaro*, 23 June 1936.
60 *Le Temps*, 21 July 1936; *L'Avenir d'Arras et du Pas de Calais*, 9 July 1936.
61 Préfet du Nord, 3 July, CAC 20010216 art 74 1894.
62 AD Haut-Rhin, Purgatoire 201763.
63 Sous-préfet de Guebwiller, 20 December 1938, AD Haut-Rhin, Purgatoire 201763.
64 Ibid.
65 Paul J. Kalb, Avocat au Tribunal de première instance, Colmar, 4 November 1938, AD Haut-Rhin, Purgatoire 201763.
66 Sous-préfet de Guebwiller, 20 December 1938, AD Haut-Rhin, Purgatoire 201763.
67 Ibid.
68 Paul J. Kalb, 4 November 1938. AD Haut-Rhin, Purgatoire 201763.

69   Sous-préfet de Guebwiller, 20 December 1938, AD Haut-Rhin, Purgatoire 201763.
70   Paul J. Kalb, 4 November 1938. AD Haut-Rhin, Purgatoire 201763.
71   Sous-préfet de Guebwiller, 20 December 1938, AD Haut-Rhin, Purgatoire 201763.
72   Paul J. Kalb, 4 November 1938. AD Haut-Rhin, Purgatoire 201763.
73   Sous-préfet de Guebwiller, 20 December 1938, AD Haut-Rhin, Purgatoire 201763.
74   *Le Figaro*, 23 June 1936.
75   Commissaire de police, Chef de la Sûreté, Reims, 3 and 6 July 1936, AD Marne 3Z 447.
76   Commissaire divisionnaire de police spéciale, Épernay, 16 June 1936, AD Marne 194M 28.
77   *Le Paysan*, 30 October 1936.
78   Directeur des services agricoles (Marne), 29 July 1936; Gendarmerie nationale, Reims, 'Rapport sur la grève des ouvriers agricoles de la Ferme Gauthier', 10 August 1936, AD Marne 3Z 447.
79   Préfet de la Seine-et-Marne, Télégramme officielle, 23 July 1936, AD Seine-et-Marne, M4947.
80   Sous-préfet de Compiègne, 2 October 1936, AD Oise, Mp 4285.
81   Parsal, 'Pour le bien-être des travailleurs de la terre', p. 40.
82   'Résolution de la Commission fédérale des grèves', 4 September 1936, AD Seine-Saint-Denis, 35J 39.
83   *Le Journal*, 17 June 1937.
84   Farcy, 'Les Grèves Agricoles', p. 322.
85   Ponchelet, 'Ouvriers nomades', p. 366.
86   Lynch, *Les Moissons rouges*, p. 337; Lynch, 'Le Parti socialiste et la société paysanne', pp. 715–16.
87   The communes of Campagnes-lès-Guînes, Marck, Sangatte, Fréthun, Nielles-lès-Calais, Saint-Tricat, Coquelles, Campagnes-lès-Guînes, Andres, Pihen-lès-Guînes, Hamres-Boucres, Les Attaques, Bonnigues-lès-Calais, Vieille-Église, Bonnigues-lès-Calais, Nouvelle-Église, Quelmes. 'Situation numérique des étrangers au 31 Décembre 1936', AD Pas-de-Calais, M6757.
88   Mayors' comments on questionnaires, AD Pas-de-Calais, AD M4456.
89   Listes nominatives, Vrély, AD Somme.
90   During the strike at Béville (Eure-et-Loir), the police noted: 'Les ouvriers qui ont cessé le travail sont en majeure partie originaires de Béville.' Rapport de l'Adjudant Guérin, 24 July 1936, AD Eure-et-Loir, 10M 26.
91   *Le Grand Écho de l'Aisne*, 30 May 1936.
92   At Amblainville, the breakdown of the workforce on the five farms impacted was 60 French workers, 15 Polish, three Czechoslovakian and one Swiss worker. At Lierville, the strike hit the Boissy farm, where there were fourteen French workers and seven Polish. Listes nominatives, Amblainville, Lierville, AD Oise.
93   Le Commissaire de police de Mitry-Mory, 31 May 1937, AD Seine-et-Marne, M4955.
94   At Mitry-Mory, the workforce on the farms was made up of 148 French and 163 immigrant workers (including workers of Belgian origin). Le Commissaire de police de Mitry-Mory, 31 May 1937, AD Seine-et-Marne, M4955.
95   The register of immigrants in the village for the year 1937 indicates a total of fifteen living in the commune, including a group of Polish workers. Archives Communales, La Ville-aux-Bois-lès-Dizy.
96   Gendarmerie nationale. Brigade de Montcornet, 'Procès-verbal des renseignements sur des entraves à la liberté du travail', 20 July 1936. AD Aisne 1M 22.

97   Ponchelet, 'Ouvriers nomades', p. 368.

98   'Situation numérique des étrangers au 31 décembre 1936', AD Pas-de-Calais, M6757.

99   Listes nominatives, Matigny, AD Somme; 'Notes et rapports sur l'évolution de l'agriculture et sa situation en 1932', AD Oise, Mp 4514; Listes nominatives, Bailleul-le-Soc, AD Oise.

100 Sous-préfet de Saint-Quentin, 'Ouvriers licenciés suites des grèves', 12 August 1937, AD Aisne, 1M 22.

101 Ponchelet, 'Ouvriers nomades', p. 402.

102 Rapport du Capitaine Le Magny, 15 June 1937; Procureur de la République, Pontoise, 14 October 1937, AN BB18 3064.

103 See particularly, AD Seine-et-Marne, M4958.

104 Rapport de l'adjudant chef Dupuy, 10 June 1937, AD Seine-et-Marne, M4958.

105 Ponty, Les Polonnais méconnus, p. 327.

106 Gendarmerie national, section de Laon, 'Rapport sur des entraves à la liberté du travail relevées à Barenton-Cel contre des ouvriers grévistes', 13 August 1936, AD Aisne 1M22.

107 Rapport du Capitaine Duhanel, 28 May 1936, AD Seine-et-Marne, M4947. At Luçay-le-Libre (Indre), the union protested that 'gendarmes have visited a certain number of workers, principally foreigners, with the intention of putting individual pressure on them and making them return to work.' Le Journal d'Issoudun, 16 August 1936.

108 Ministre du Travail, J. Lebas, à Messieurs les Préfets, 21 May 1937, AD Indre, M5716. Expulsions of immigrant farm workers found without appropriate papers were not uncommon. At Clermont-les-Fermes (Aisne), a Polish worker was arrested in October 1936 and served with an 'arrête d'expulsion'. Les Tablettes de l'Aisne, 21 October 1936.

109 Sous-secrétaire d'État au Travail, 24 September 1937; Le Ministre de l'Agriculture, 26 October 1937, AD Marne, 135M ter109.

110 In the Marne, the Conseil général (May 1937) refused to reappoint the female inspector employed to oversee the conditions of female immigrant workers for 'financial reasons'. Préfecture de la Marne, Extrait du procès-verbal des délibérations du Conseil général, AD Marne 135M 42.

111 Ministre de l'Intérieur, 8 March 1937, CAC 20010216 art 36 922.

112 Préfet de Seine et Oise, 7 April 1937. CAC 20010216 art 36 922.

113 Procureur général, Amiens, 'Propagande active dans les exploitations agricoles en vue de provoquer la cessation du travail', AN BB18 3008.

114 Listes nominatives, Sancourt, AD Somme.

115 Rapport du Capitaine Gueydan sur les agissements du sujet Polonais Jungling, 9 July 1936. AN BB18 3008.

116 'Rapport de l'Inspecteur de police spéciale Auzuret', 8 December 1937, AD Pas-de-Calais, 4Z 631.

117 Sous-préfet de Senlis, 21 July 1936, AD Oise, Mp4285.

118 'Listes des syndicats déclarés', n.d. (late 1936). AD Oise, Mp4911; Listes nominatives, Mont-l'Évêque, AD Oise.

119 Les Tablettes de l'Aisne, 25 July 1936.

120 Ibid., 8 July 1936.

121 Procès-verbal, 2 June 1937, AD Seine-et-Marne, M4958.

122 'Comité régional élargi de Picardie', 11 June 1939, PCF 854.

123 Parti communiste, 'Rapport d'activité local d'Achères, le 16 avril 1939'. AD Yvelines, 4M 2/69.

124 Ibid.

125 For example, there were reports of Polish workers breaking the strike at Lehaucourt (Aisne) during July 1937. *Le Paysan*, 30 July 1937.

126 Commissaire spéciale, Châteauroux, 28 June 1937, AD Indre, M5716.

127 *Écho Républicain*, 1 August 1936. A few months later, Vassal added: 'Agriculture has too many hands. . . We are going to ask the public authorities to repatriate unemployed foreign labour.' *Écho Républicain*, 9 January 1937.

128 FNTA, Congrès national extraordinaire, 1937, p. 46

129 Procureur de la République, Beauvais, 20 June 1936, AN BB18 3008

130 The police dossier on Orszulak is conserved at CAC 20010216 art 155.

131 Préfet de l'Aisne, 13 July 1937. AD Ainse, 4Z 70.

132 FNTA Bureau fédéral, 12 March 1937, AD Seine-Saint-Denis, 35J 5.

133 Lazar, 'Damné de la terre', pp. 1082–83.

134 FNTA, Commission éxecutive, 4 November 1936, AD Seine-Saint-Denis, 35J 5.

135 *L'Humanité*, 17 February 1937.

136 As was the case during a dispute in July 1937 at Valenton (south-east of Paris), after a group of immigrants returned to work on receiving threats from the employer. *Le Paysan*, 27 August 1937.

137 'In the circumstances in which we live, at a time when the problem of national defence is posed. . . it is inadmissible that a category of employers can deprive a section of the rural population of work by bringing in foreign labour.' Letter from Chiquois, Secrétaire de la Section fédérale de l'Île de France, 29 March 1939, AD Yvelines, 13M 241.

Chapter 7

1 Sous-préfet de Compiègne, 11 Sept 1937, AD Oise, Mp 4300.

2 Conférence national, 10 July 1936, PCF 777–78.

3 Ibid.

4 Ibid.

5 *L'Humanité*, 25 July 1936.

6 See, for example, the report from Selles-sur-Cher in *Le Travailleur (Loiret, Loir-et-Cher, Eure et Loir)*, 8 August 1936.

7 *L'Humanité*, 25 July 1936.

8 Ibid.

9 In December 1927, the Oise Prefect reported that in the Valois, 'the wage of workers follows the price of bread. . . a rise of 0.5 francs prompts an increase of 5 francs per month, and a similar decrease in price an equal fall.' Le Préfet de l'Oise, December 1927, AD Oise, M4383.

10 At Marle, the agreement stipulated that wages 'will be established taking account of the average price of wheat'. Accord, Mairie de Marle, 19 July 1936, AD Aisne, 1M 22

11 *L'Étampois*, 4 July 1936.

12 Vigreux claims, on the contrary, that Rochet 'showed complete solidarity' with the strikes of agricultural workers. But the evidence he gives does not support the assertion. It refers to Fourcaut's account of Rochet's participation in an attempt to organise market gardeners and their workers in a Committee for the Defence of

Agriculture at Bobigny. Vigreux, *Waldeck Rochet*, p. 74; A. Fourcaut, *Bobigny, Banlieue Rouge*, Les Éditions Ouvrières, Paris, 1986, p. 174.

13   *La Voix Paysanne*, 18 July 1937. It is interesting that Renaud Jean, by now effectively elbowed out of the party's agrarian policy-making, put more emphasis on peasant employers taking a benevolent approach to workers' demands than the team around Rochet. He urged that 'regional secretaries in peasant regions ask our militants to explain to self-employed peasants that it is necessary rapidly to give wage workers the same social benefits as those obtained by workers in commerce and industry'. He argued that the government's reforms were not specifically 'workers' legislation' but equally essential in agriculture as 'if agricultural workers were kept outside the reforms, before long the countryside would completely empty'. 'Rapport de Renaud Jean sur le travail à la campagne', Conférence des secrétaires régionaux (Gentilly, 27 April 1937), PCF 822.

14   M. Larkin, *France Since The Popular Front: Government and People, 1936–96*, Oxford University Press, 1997, p.60.

15   Renaud Jean, 'Le Front Populaire et les Paysans', *Cahiers du Bolchevisme*, 20 February 1937, p. 150.

16   Ibid, pp. 150–51.

17   Maurice Thorez, Georges Désiré, Marcel Rosenblatt and Benoît Frachon. Comité central, 16 October 1936, PCF 783 & 784.

18   As in the Nogent-sur-Seine (Aube) region, *Le Paysan*, 28 August 1936.

19   *La Voix Paysanne*, 18 July 1936.

20   *L'Humanité*, 17 July 1936.

21   *Le Paysan*, 16 October 1936.

22   *Le Prolétaire Normand*, 6 November 1936.

23   Report on strikes drawn up by Prefect, n.d., (August 1936), AD Seine-et-Marne, M4947.

24   'Réponses aux questionnaires du Ministère du Travail relatifs aux grèves de 1936', AD Ainse, 10M 44a.

25   Sous-préfet de Senlis, 21 July 1936, AD Oise, Mp4285.

26   See reports in AD Seine-et-Marne, M4947.

27   Fourcaut, *Bobigny, Banlieue Rouge*, p. 172.

28   Ibid, pp. 173–74.

29   See Chapter 5.

30   Procureur Géneral, Amiens, AN BB18 3008.

31   The number of workers on each farm was: 10/10/8/6/4/2/2/2/1/1/1/1/1. AD Aisne, 10M44a.

32   Préfet de l'Oise, AD Oise, Mp4285.

33   Rapport de l'Adjudant Guérin, 24 July 1936, AD Eure-et-Loir, 10M 26.

34   *L'Humanité*, 1 and 19 June 1937.

35   Rapport du Chef Petit, 1 June 1937; Rapport du Capitaine Dubois, 3 June 1937, AD Nord, 4Z 110.

36   Rapport du Capitaine Dubois, 21 June 1937, AD Nord, 4Z 110.

37   'Rapport sur la Conférence paysanne de la region du Nord (Lille, 3 Juillet 1938)', PCF 844.

38   Other examples are 15 workers out of 22 on six farms at Vendhuile and 62 of the 80 workers on 14 farms at Lesquielles-Saint-Germain. Rapport du Capitaine Noeuveglise, 29 July 1937, AD Aisne, 4Z 70.

39   Police compagnie de l'Aisne, Section de Saint-Quentin (August 1937), AD Aisne, 10M 45.

40 'Rapport de O. Rabaté sur les réunions dans l'Aisne du 13 au 26 septembre 1937', PCF 825.

41 In the elections in April 1937 in Bacqueville-en-Caux canton, communist votes increased from 130 (April 1936) to 408, with the party topping the poll in villages that would become bases of the 1937 strike, including Luneray and Greville. *Le Prolétaire Normand*, 16 April 1937.

42 The strike began at the end of May in the Ourville-en-Caux, Valmont and Ouainville regions, involving 600 workers in 28 villages (*L'Avenir Normand*, 12 June 1937). On 18 June, it spread to Luneray, Bacqueville, Sotteville-sur-Mer, Gueures, Bourg-Dun, La Chapelle-sur-Dun and surrounding villages, involving another 500 workers (*L'Avenir Normand*, 25 June 1937).

43 Information compiled from mayors' reports. AD Seine-Maritime, 1Z 16.

44 *L'Avenir Normand*, 4 June 1937.

45 'Rapport de J Berlioz sur la conférence d'information de la région du Pas-de-Calais', 14 February 1937, PCF 827.

46 A. Durand, *La Vie rurale dans les massifs volcaniques; des Dores, du Cézallier, du Cantal et de l'Aubrac*, Laffitte, Marseille, 1980.

47 According to the 1936 census, there were 17,755 farms in the Cantal, of which 9,553 did not employ any workers. Of the others, 7,886 employed between one and five workers, 291 between six and ten and only 25 between 11 and 20.

48 Rapport sur l'organisation de la région du Cantal, March 1936, PCF 796b.

49 Ibid.

50 'Sur la situation du parti dans la région du Cantal', 25 February 1936, PCF 796b.

51 'Rapport sur l'organisation de la région du Cantal', March 1936, PCF 796b.

52 *L'Humanité*, 4 May 1934.

53 *Le Cantal Ouvrier et Paysan*, 1 November 1936, p. 3.

54 'Rapport d'Adrien Langumier sur sa tournée de propagande dans le Cantal', 30 November 1936, PCF 796b.

55 In October 1938, when the movement was in decline, an internal communist report gave the membership as 1200. 'Rapport de Bourdarias sur la tournée effectuée dans le Cantal du 16 au 31 octobre 1938', s.d., PCF 841.

56 *Le Cantal Ouvrier et Paysan*, 27 December 1936.

57 Ibid.

58 Ibid.

59 Ibid., 7 February 1937.

60 Ibid., 3 January 1937.

61 Ibid., 13 February 1937.

62 'Compte-rendu du Comité régional de la région du Cantal', 10 January 1937, PCF 825.

63 Ibid. As well as an indication of the party's relationship with its front organisations, the provenance of the reply is explained by the fact that the party was moving to wind up the CGPT. The 'peasant unity' strategy placed emphasis on working within agricultural associations, whatever their political persuasion, rather than building a specifically communist-influenced organisation amongst the peasantry.

64 *Le Cantal Ouvrier et Paysan*, 10 January 1937.

65 Ibid., 7 February 1937.

66 Ibid., 21 February 1937.

67 Ibid.

68 Ibid.

69 Ibid., 7 February 1937.

70 'Intervention by Leymarie, Conférence des secrétaires régionaux (Gentilly, 27 avril 1937)', PCF 822.

71 *Le Cantal Ouvrier et Paysan*, 3 January 1937.

72 Ibid., 27 December 1936.

73 Hilaire remained a party member but was 'not active'. 'Rapport de Bourdarias sur la tournée effectuée dans le Cantal du 19 juin au 3 juillet 1938', PCF 841.

74 'Rapport de Bourdarias sur la tournée effectuée dans le Cantal du 16 au 31 octobre 1938', PCF 841.

75 'Compte-rendu du Comité régional Cantal', 8 May 1938, PCF 841.

76 In the Cantal, only 1.95 per cent of workers were employed on farms with over ten employees, in the Calvados, the figure was 4.8 per cent. *Recensement général de la population*, 1936.

77 Workers formed 42 per cent of the peasantry in the Somme, 39 per cent in the Nord, 38 per cent in the Pas-de-Calais. They made up 32 per cent in the Cantal. *Recensement général de la population*, 1936.

78 The Christian CFTC managed to establish a union in horticulture.

79 See chart in R. Vinen, *France 1934–1970*, MacMillan Press, London, p. xv.

80 J. Quellien, *Le Calvados au temps du Front Populaire*, Édition du Lys, Caen, 1996.

81 Paxton, *French Peasant Fascism*, p. 109 .

82 *Le Réveil des Travailleurs*, 12 December 1936, cited in Quellien, *Le Calvados*, pp. 195–96.

83 *L'Indicateur de Bayeux*, 10 July 1936, Cited in Ibid., p. 193.

84 *Recensement général de la population*, 1936.

85 *La Voix Paysanne*, 22 August 1936.

86 Ibid.

87 Ibid.

88 Ibid.

89 It is striking that later reports from communist propagandists touring the region indicate significant numbers of agricultural workers attracted to the political left and seeking to participate in agricultural workers' unionism. In early 1938 reports describe how agricultural workers attended communist meetings in significant numbers in small rural villages. At Fierville-la-Campagne, a village of 263 inhabitants, 14 agricultural workers attended a public meeting, 6 joined the party. At Vieux-Fumé, farm workers complained of the repression of local farmers and 12 workers joined the party. 'Rapport de Le Troadec sur la tournée de propagande effectuée dans la région du Calvados', 13 February 1938, PCF 841.

90 Commissaire spécial, Châteauroux, 25 June 1937, AD Indre, M5716.

91 *L'Étampois*, 7 August 1937.

92 G. Belloin, *Renaud Jean, le tribun des paysans*, Éditions de l'Atelier/Éditions Ouvrières, Paris, 1993, p. 241.

93 *La Voix Paysanne*, 25 September 1936.

94 *L'Enchaîné*, 9 October 1936.

95 Ibid.

96 FNTA Bureau fédéral, 12 October 1936, AD Seine-Saint-Denis, 35J 5.

97 *Le Paysan*, 2 October 1936.

98 FNTA Bureau fédéral, 12 October 1936; *Le Paysan*, 2 October 1936.

99 Ibid.

100 Section agraire, n.d. (early 1937), PCF 821.

101 Ibid.

102 Parsal, 'Pour le bien-être des travailleurs de la terre', p. 41.

Conclusion

1 Jean Bruhat, 'L'Apport de Maurice Thorez à l'histoire', *Cahiers du Communisme*, April 1950, pp. 33–48. Cited in M-C. Lavabre, *Le Fil Rouge: Sociologie de la mémoire communiste*, Presses de la Fondation Nationale des Sciences Politiques, Paris, 1994, p. 57.

2 G. Noiriel, *Workers in French Society in the Nineteenth and Twentieth Centuries*, Berg, New York, 1990, p. 141.

3 Boswell, *Rural Communism*, p. 34 and p. 39.

4 *La Terre*, 30 June 1966.

5 See, for example, *La Terre*, 28 May 1986.

6 Ibid., 30 June 1966.

7 For an outline of this debate, see M. Lazar, *Le Communisme: une passion française*, Éditions Perrin, Paris, 2005, pp. 7–25; L. Boswell, 'L'Historiographie du communisme français, est-elle dans une impasse?', *Revue française de science politique*, vol. 55, 5–6 (2005), pp. 919–33; S. Courtois, 'Chronique de l'Historiographie du Parti Communiste Francais' in S. Courtois (ed) *Communisme en France, De la révolution documentaire au renouveau historiographique*, Paris, Éditions Cujas, Paris, 2007, pp. 5–43.

8 S. Courtois (ed), *Le Livre noir du communisme: Crimes, terreur et répression*, Paris, Robert Laffont, Paris, 1997.

9 A. Kriegel, *Aux Origines du communisme français*.

10 M. Dreyfus, B. Groppo, C. Ingerflom, R. Lew, C. Pennetier, B. Pudal, S. Wolikow (eds), *Le Siècle des communismes*, Éditions de l'Atelier, Paris, 2000.

11 A. Gramsci, *The Modern Prince and Other Writings*, Lawrence and Wishart, London, 1957, p. 137.

12 This is graphically illustrated by the regional studies by Boswell and Cadé. Boswell, 'Le Communisme et la Défense de la Petite Propriété en Limousin et en Dordogne'; Cadé, *Le Parti des campagnes rouges*.

13 R. Hubscher, 'Révolution aux champs', p. 351.

14 Boswell, *Rural Communism*, p 27.

15 'Élections générales à l'Assemblée nationale du 2 juin 1946. Recul de tracts électoraux, listes, programmes, professions de fois et engagements des candidats.' BN microfiche M-17589.

16 Rapports des renseignements généraux, AD Oise, 89W 10913. I thank Jean-Pierre Besse for information relating to the Oise.

17 La-Ville-aux-Bois-lès-Dizy, Procès-verbaux du Conseil municipal, 26 December 1945, 27 March 1946 and 1 September 1946.

18 Maurice Thorez, 'Intervention au BP sur la Question paysanne', 29 September 1955, Archives de Maurice Thorez, 626 AP13.

19 Maurice Thorez, Notes on Central Committee 19–20 October 1955, Archives de Maurice Thorez, 626 AP5.

SOURCES

ARCHIVES NATIONALES

Correspondance de la Division Criminelle du Ministère de la Justice

BB18 2849   Grèves dans différents ressorts (Montpellier: grève agricole de Courson), 1931.

BB18 2864   Grèves dans divers ressorts (Nîmes: ouvriers agricoles à Calvisson), 1932.

BB18 2880   Grève agricole de Capestang, 1933.

BB18 2914   Agitation crée par M. d'Halluin dit Dorgères. Articles, réunions, poursuites, 1935–37.

BB18 2915   Agitation crée par Dorgères. Agitation du Front paysan, 1935–37.

BB18 2954   Refus de l'impôt, Parti agraire, Comité d'Action paysan, 1935.

BB18 3005   Grèves dossier général et quelques pièces concernant la cour d'appel de Paris (poursuites pour entraves à la liberté du travail), 1936.

BB18 3006–3012   Grèves dans les différents ressorts de cour d'appel, 1936.

BB18 3048   Dissolution des groupements Croix de feu; Activité du Parti social français, 1936–39.

BB18 3058   Communisme, 1937.

BB18 3062–3064   Grèves, classement par cour d'appel, 1937.

Série F7 (Ministre de l'Intérieur)

F7 12735   Rapports des préfets et des commissions spéciales sur la situation générale des départements, 1924–28.

F7 12787   Grèves: renseignements généraux; grèves agricoles (classement départemental), 1908.

F7 12970, F7 12977,
F7 12983, F7 13010,
F7 13027   Rapports sur la situation générale dans les départements, 1920–36.

F7 13090   Parti communiste, 1921–30.

F7 13628   Notes générales et presse sur le mouvement agricole, 1926–36.

CENTRE DES ARCHIVES CONTEMPORAINES (CAC)

Archives de la Direction Générale de la Sécurité Nationale de la France

Seized by the Germans, these documents were taken to Moscow following the war and have now returned to France.

19940469 415   Dossier, 'Puech André dit Parsal'.

940500 art 202   Inspection générale du service de la police administrative. Les grèves en France d'après les documents de la police française. Renseignements relatifs à la surveillance policière des activités des syndicats des travailleurs agricoles.

20010216 art 36   Renseignements relatifs à la surveillance policière des activités des communistes en France.

20010216 art 73   Les Syndicats de l'agriculture.

20010216 art 74   Rapports des préfets des départements de France au sujet de la surveillance policière des réunions, meetings, congrès organisés par les syndicats des travailleurs de l'agriculture dans les départements.

20010216 art 135   Renseignements relatifs à la surveillance policière des activités des organisations des travailleurs de l'agriculture.

20010216 art 155   Surveillance policière des activités des Associations, des Sociétés, des Ligues françaises et étrangères.

ARCHIVES DÉPARTEMENTALES

Archives Départementales de l'Aisne

1M 12   Parti communiste: agitation politique, 1921–34.

1M 16   Compte-rendu de réunions, manifestations, meetings, enquête de police sur des personnes suspectées de sentiments communistes, 1936–39.

1M 18   Autres partis et groupes politiques de gauche, activité du Parti radical socialiste, de la SFIO, de la Ligue des droits de l'homme, du syndicat des paysans travailleurs, 1934–40.

1M 22   Grèves agricoles: rapports de sous-préfets, police et gendarmerie, 1936–38.

1M 23   Enquêtes administratives sur l'unité syndicale, 1935–39.

7M 15   Dossier sur la main d'œuvre agricole; conflits du travail et conflits syndicaux, 1935–40.

7M 19   Main d'œuvre agricole: Commissions paritaires départementales et d'arrondissement: désignations des délégués patronaux et ouvriers, procès-verbaux des séances.

7M 20   Licenciements d'ouvriers agricoles pour activités syndicales; petits conflits entre employeurs et salariés, 1936–39.

7M 21   Congés payés en agriculture, 1936–39.

7M 22   Travaux betteraviers: fixation du prix des binages et arrachages, discussion sur les salaires entre les syndicats patronaux et ouvriers, 1936–37.

10M 10   Conseil supérieur du travail: élections; liste des syndicats votant avec leurs membres; correspondance, 1924–37.

10M 32	Chômage: Réclamations et conflits divers soumis au directeur de l'office départemental de placement à Laon. . . surtout au sujet de l'emploi de la main d'œuvre étrangère alors que la main d'œuvre local chôme, 1932–38.
10M 44	Grèves: Réponses aux questionnaires du Ministère du travail relatifs aux grèves de 1936.
10M 45	Grèves, 1936.
10M 61	Syndicats professionnels – Correspondance. Listes et renseignements divers, 1931–37.
10M 62	Conventions Collectives.
3Z 155	Sous-préfecture de Soissons. Conflits du travail: rapports mensuels du Sous-préfet de Soissons, 1936–39.
4Z 70	Sous-préfecture de Vervins. Conflits agricoles commissions paritaires de l'Arrondissement de Vervins 1936–37.
1030W 20 & 1030W 21	Enquête statistique (agriculture), May 1942.
51U 30	Tribunal de première instance, Laon. Marécal – Procès.

Archives Communales

Dammard
Dommiers
Saint-Pierre-Aigle
Saint-Pierremont
La-Ville-aux Bois-lès-Dizy (conserved at Mairie).

Archives Départementales de l'Eure

1M 139	Rapports des préfets et sous-préfets, janvier–juin 1936.
1M 153	Administration générale. Rapports des sous-préfets des Andelys et de Bernay, 1936–37.
10M 47	Main d'œuvre étrangère. Protection de la main d'œuvre étrangère: instructions, correspondance, 1924–40.
10M 67	Conflits du travail, 1936–39.

Archives Départementales de l'Eure-et-Loir

4M 232	Mouvements politiques, syndicaux 1923–38.
10M 26	Travail et main d'œuvre. Grèves diverses – instructions, rapports, correspondance, 1936.
10M 27	Grève sucrerie (Toury), 1936.
10M28	Grèves diverses; instructions, rapports, correspondance. Dossier: Grève des ouvriers agricoles de Boutigny, 1937.
10M 34	Convention collective du travail en agriculture, 1937.

Archives Départementales du Haut-Rhin

| Purgatoire 201763 | Action en justice contre la commune de Guebwiller par le propriétaire |

du domaine viticole et agricole Schlumberger, suite à la grève de 1936.

Archives Départementales de l'Indre

M5711	Main d'œuvre, secours aux ouvriers agricoles en chômage, correspondance, décisions, 1937.
M5716	Main d'œuvre, demandes d'ouvriers agricoles, réglementation pour embaucher des ouvriers étrangers 1937–40.

Listes Nominatives: Lizeray, Choudray, Ségry.

Archives Départementales de la Marne

135M 42	Comité des femmes immigrantes: désignation des membres du comité, instructions, circulaires, main-d'œuvre agricole étrangère, réquisitions, correspondence, 1937–45.
135M ter109	Main-d'œuvre étrangère, femmes immigrantes, 1929–41.
194M 28	Protestations des sections agraires contre les grèves des ouvriers agricoles, listes des établissements atteints par la grève, rapports de police, situation journalière, 1936.
194M 30/1 & 2	Rapports, 1936.
194M 33	Conflits du travail. Renseignements concernant les conflits survenus dans le département, 1936–39.
195M 29	Enquête relative à la situation de la main d'œuvre agricole, 1937.
2Z 398	Sous-préfecture d'Épernay. Grèves agricoles, 1936.
3Z 447	Sous-préfecture de Reims. Rapports du Commissaire central et du Chef de la sûreté sur le mouvement de grèves, 1936.

Archives Départementales du Nord

M149/15	États d'esprit, rapport généraux, 1936.
M149/16	Idem, 1937.
M149/86	Agriculture: Front paysan, Parti agraire (1930–36), Syndicats agricoles unitaires, 1933–37.
M149/89	Agriculture: agitation paysanne, 1935.
M154/304	Défense paysanne, 1936.
M595/35	Listes des syndicats (1938); listes des dirigeants (mars 1939).
M595/98	Syndicats 1891–1939. Corporations et syndicats divers: agriculture, ouvriers agricoles, 1936–39.
M619/103	Grèves, occupation d'usines. Rapports quotidiens du préfet, juin–octobre, 1936–37.
M619/104	Grèves, occupations d'usines Rapports des sous-préfets: Avesnes, Cambrai, Douai, Dunkerque, Valenciennes, 1936–37.
3Z 152	Sous-préfecture de Cambrai. Agriculture, 1919–36.
4Z 83	Sous-préfecture de Douai. Syndicats professionnels, 1913–38.
4Z 84	Sous-préfecture de Douai. Syndicats divers. Situation des syndicats professionnels au regard du décret du 26/9/39.

4Z 95	Sous-préfecture de Douai. Syndicats agricoles: activités, rapports de police, 1932–35, 1937.
4Z 96	Sous-préfecture de Douai. Syndicats agricoles: rapports au Ministère du Travail, 1937–38.
4Z 110	Sous-préfecture de Douai. Grèves 1934–39.
4Z 111	Sous-préfecture de Douai. Événements de 1936.
5Z 552	Sous-préfecture de Dunkerque. Chômage. Ouvriers agricoles saisonniers, 1932.
5Z 562–5Z 563	Sous-préfecture de Dunkerque. Grèves et conflits de travail, rapports de police, juin–novembre 1936.

Archives Départementales de l'Oise

Mp 1448	Grèves, conflits du travail: arbitration, conventions collectives, 1936–38.
Mp 3696	Services agricoles: affaires diverses, 1929–39.
Mp 3760	Main d'œuvre agricole, 1923–37.
Mp 4280	Conflits du travail. Arrondissement de Beauvais, 1936–37.
Mp 4281	Conflits du travail. Arrondissement de Compiègne, 1936–37.
Mp 4282	Conflits du travail. Instructions, renouvellement conventions collectives, 1936–39.
Mp 4284	Conflits du travail, 1937–39.
Mp 4285	Grèves. Conflits relatifs à l'agriculture. Accords intervenus. 1936.
Mp 4292	Grèves dans l'arrondissement de Senlis, 1894 –1914.
Mp 4294	Conflits du travail. Arrondissement de Beauvais, 1936–38.
Mp 4300	Conflits du travail relatifs à l'agriculture, 1937–39.
Mp 4301	Conflits du travail. Arrondissement de Senlis, 1938.
Mp 4383	Grèves: questionnaires, affaires diverses, 1919–36.
Mp 4514	Notes et rapports sur l'évolution de l'agriculture et sa situation en 1932.
Mp 4515	Enquête 1929: monographies de ferme.
Mp 4706	Agriculture: affaires diverses, 1913–39.
Mp 4909	Syndicats dissous, 1936–39.
Mp 4911	Syndicats: statistiques diverses, 1873–1939.

Listes Nominatives (various communes).

Archives Départementales du Pas-de-Calais

M1781	Grève des ouvriers agricoles, 1910.
M2380	Grèves 1936–38. Instructions, télégrammes. Statistiques des occupations d'usine.
M2385	Grèves 1936–37. Listes et rapports journaliers.
M2386	Grèves, 1936–37.
M2405	Grèves, situations, 1936.
M2406	Grèves, situations, 1937.
M2407	Grèves, situations, 1938.
M2460	Grèves questionnaires mensuels, 1908–21.
M4456	Grèves de 1936, questionnaires.
M5304	CGT-CGTU enquêtes, 1934–35.

M4690	Ouvriers agricoles, 1930.
M5323	Conflits du travail, grèves 1929–38.
M5466	Parti communiste français, région du Pas-de-Calais (1930s).
M6757	Situation numérique des étrangers au 31 décembre 1936.
M7181	Dossiers des syndicats dissous, 1936.

Listes Nominatives (various communes).

Monographies agricoles rédigées par des instituteurs du Pas de Calais pour obtenir le brevet agricole (Série M/MONOAGRIC).

Directeur des Services Agricoles

M/DSA 10–20	Enquête Agricole de 1929: questionnaires communaux.
M/DSA 276	Ouvriers saisonniers et travailleurs étrangers, c1925–c1934.
M/DSA 286	Main d'œuvre, salaires, 1936–38.
M/DSA 318	Main d'œuvre, salaires, 1936–37.

Sous-préfecture de Béthune
| 1Z 210 | Rapports de police, 1936 |

Sous-préfecture de Boulogne-sur-Mer
2Z 93	Mouvements ouvriers agricoles: correspondance, rapports de police, rapports du Sous-préfet, 1936.
2Z 151	Grèves, correspondence, 1936.
2Z 152	Grèves, rapports de police, situations, 1936.
2Z 249	Activité syndicale et des partis politiques de gauche. Rapports de police, 1934.
2Z 254	Activité syndicale et politique. Rapports de police, 1935.

Sous-préfecture de Saint-Omer
4Z 631	Main d'œuvre agricole étrangère.
4Z 660	Grèves de 1936–37; rapports, enquêtes, correspondance, renseignements statistiques.
4Z 791	Police, rapports 1934–38.
4Z 807	Fichier relatif à l'activité politique dans les communes, cellules, syndicats, 1933–44.

Archives Départementales de la Seine-Maritime

1M 304	Parti communiste: organisation, 1924–38.
7M 139	Main d'œuvre agricole 1853–1939.
10M 380	Conflits du travail, contrats de travail, agitation ouvrière agricole, juillet–septembre 1936.
10M 392	Conflits du travail, contrats de travail, 1937.
1Z 16	Sous-préfecture de Dieppe. Grèves des ouvriers agricoles, 1920–38.
2Z 41	Sous-préfecture du Havre. Activités du PC à Bolbec, Fécamp, Lillebonne, Sanvic, 1921–38.
2Z 94	Sous-préfecture du Havre. Grèves et conflits du travail par profession et secteur d'activité, 1934–38.

Archives Départementales de la Seine-et-Marne

1Mp 96	Grèves. Comptes-rendus des grèves dans les diverses branches de l'industrie, des communes et de l'agriculture, 1919–24.
1Mp 97	Mouvements ouvriers, grèves agricoles et dans l'industrie, comptes-rendus, 1920–36.
M1190	Grèves agricoles. Enquêtes auprès des communes, 1936.
M3216	Grèves agricoles, 1906–07.
M4947	Grèves agricoles. Rapports et états relatifs aux exploitations agricoles touchées par les conflits sociaux. Interventions des syndicats ouvriers et patronaux des parlementaires, des autorités préfectorales, 1936.
M4950	Rapports de sous-préfets et gendarmerie, correspondance, maires et agriculteurs, 1936.
M4951	Circulaires diverses ayant trait aux grèves et conditions, 1936.
M4952	Grèves agricoles, 1937.
M4955	Grèves agricoles. Rapports des sous-préfets, des maires, des commissaires de police. Correspondance, 1937.
M4956	Grèves agricoles. Rapports de la Gendarmerie sur l'évolution des conflits sociaux agricoles. P.-V. d'incidents et états des exploitations touchées par les grèves, 1937.
M4957	Grèves agricoles. Comptes-rendus de la gendarmerie sur les incidents, 1937.
M4958	Préparation des contrats collectifs dans l'agriculture, 1924–36.

Archives Départementales de la Somme

1M KZ1140	Vie politique, Manifestations agricoles, 1930s.
1M KZ1765	Congés payés dans l'agriculture, 1936–37.
99M 83	Front Populaire, manifestations publiques, grèves, rapports de police, 1928–36.

Listes Nominatives (various communes).

Archives Départementales des Yvelines

These archives conserve most of the archives of the former Seine-et-Oise Department.

4M 2/59	Rapports mensuels du Préfet et des Sous-préfets, 1923–39.
4M 2/68–4M 2/69	Communistes, organisation et militants. Rapports sur les cellules et rayons, listes de militants, notices individuelles, 1917–38.
4M 2/71–4M 2/76	Activités communiste et syndicaliste. Réunions, tracts, affiches, presse, fêtes: rapports de police et du Préfet, 1919–38.
4M 2/77–4M 2/80	Réunions et manifestations, tracts et affiches. Rapports de police, 1916–35.
4M 2/81–4M 2/83	Idem, 1936.
4M 2/84–4M 2/87	Idem, 1937.
4M 2/88	Idem. Tableaux quotidiens 1936–39.
4M 2/89	Idem. Rapports d'ensemble de la Police d'État, 1936–39.
4M 2/98–4M 2/100	Grèves: instructions, rapports. 1926–39.

13M 241	Conflits du travail dans l'agriculture. Grèves: rapports de police, renseignements (1937); conventions collectives chez les horticulteurs, les maraîchers, les jardiniers, 1936–37.
13M 242	Agriculture. Logements des ouvriers agricoles, 1920–30.
300W 117	Grèves dans diverses professions et entreprises, 1932–37.

PRIVATE ARCHIVES

Archives of the Fédération Nationale des Travailleurs de l'Agriculture (FNTA)

35J 1	Congrès (1920, 1936, 1937, 1939).
35J 5	Procès-verbaux du secrétariat de la Fédération (10 septembre 1936 au 7 septembre 1939).
35J 6	Le Paysan, 1936–37.
35J 38	Autres publications: Le Bulletin fédéral, Le Cahier du militant agricole.
35J 39	Autres publications: Parsal, André, 'Pour le bien-être des travailleurs de la terre dans une agriculture riche et prospère', 1937; Parsal, André, 'Une puissante organisation des travailleurs de la terre pour assurer leur victoire', 1937; Rius, Michel, 'Rapport sur l'organisation, les taches et le fonctionnement des Syndicats, fait au Congrès fédéral de Paris', 24 et 25 janvier 1937; Rius, Michel, 'Histoire du mouvement syndical des ouvriers agricoles forestiers et similaires', 1952.
35J 40	Mouvements de grève, 1904–80; conventions collectives, 1919–72.
35J 45–35J 46	Activités des régions et syndicats, 1903–77.
35J 53	Documentation, 1930–48; Affaire Legras, 1937.

Archives of the French Communist Party

The Communist Party's inter-war archives are microfilm copies of originals conserved in Moscow. The numbers relate to bobbins.

12–15	Congrès de Marseille, 1921.
66	Circulaire no. 43 sur le travail paysan, 20 août 1924.
112	Question paysanne: résolution, rapports, 1925.
155	Correspondance: Commission paysanne, agit-prop, divers, 1926.
169	Commission syndicale, 1926.
175–76	Commission paysanne, 1926.
192–93	Régions du PCF: rapports, correspondances, compte-rendus, 1925–26.
246	Commission paysanne: rapports, 1927.
292	Commission paysanne: rapports, divers, 1928.
294	Commission syndicale: procès-verbaux, rapports, correspondances, 1928.
344	Commission paysanne, 1929.
381	Comité central, 1930.
389	Correspondance, 1930, Rapport sur l'activité paysanne, 1929.
398	Commission agraire: procès-verbaux, correspondances, 1930.

401	Commission agraire: procès-verbaux, rapports, 1930.
439	Résolutions, projets; Projet de résolution sur la politique du parti à la campagne, 1930–31.
443	Rapports; Rapport sur la paysannerie, 1931.
464	Commission paysanne, 1931.
543	Commission paysanne, 1932.
561	Régions du Parti communiste: rapports, 1932.
583–84	Comité central: procès-verbal, février 1933.
596–97	Bureau politique, 1933.
606	Circulaires. Section agraire, 1933.
608	Secrétariat: correspondances, rapports, 1933.
613	Section d'organisation: rapports, 1929–33.
627–30	Commission paysanne, 1933.
683	Comité central (janvier) 1934.
688	Comité central (novembre) 1934.
698	Correspondances, effectifs, rapports; documentation sur la question paysanne, 1934.
699	Matériaux pour les agitateurs sur la question agraire, 6 mars 1934.
727–28	Comité central: procès verbal, 1935.
738	Commission paysanne, 1935.
740	Régions du PCF: Procès-verbaux des comités régionaux, correspondances, rapports, 1934–35.
744	Régions du PCF: Rapports sur les conférences régionales et les comités régionaux, correspondances, résolutions, 1935.
745	Région parisienne: Rapports sur les conférences régionales, correspondances, résolutions, brochures, 1934–36.
777–78	Conférence nationale, 10–11 Juillet 1936.
780–85	Comité central, 1936.
786	Décisions du Bureau politique, 1936.
787	Décisions du Secrétariat, 1936.
796 (a&b)	Régions du PCF: correspondances, rapports sur les conférences régionales et les comités régionaux, tracts, résolutions, 1935–36.
798–799	Régions du PCF: correspondances, rapports sur les conférences régionales, résolutions, 1935–36.
801	Régions du PCF: correspondances, résolutions, rapports, écoles du Parti, 1936.
817	Décisions du Bureau politique, 1937.
818	Secrétariat: décisions, 1937.
821	*La Voix Paysanne*, 1937.
822	Conférence des secrétaires régionaux (Gentilly, 27 avril 1937).
825–827	Régions du PCF: rapports, correspondances, résolutions, 1937.
840–848	Régions du PCF, 1938.
853–854	Régions du PCF: composition des comités régionaux, rapports, correspondances, 1939.

Archives of Maurice Thorez and Jeanette Vermeersch

| 626 AP5 | Réunions du CC, convocations, correspondance, rapports, 1953–57. |
| 626 AP13 | Réunions du BP: notes, manuscrites, 1934–64. |

Chambre d'Agriculture de l'Aisne

Project Mémoire 2000, Guy Marival.

Musée Social

Press dossier on 1906–07 agricultural strike movement.

CONTEMPORARY PRINTED MATERIAL

Communist Pamphlets

'3ème Congrès national, tenu à Lyon, 20–23 janvier 1924, adresses et résolutions', Librairie de l'Humanité, Paris, 1924.
'4ème Congrès national, tenu à Clichy, 17–21 Janvier 1925', Paris, 1925.
'5ème Congrès national, tenu à Lille 20–26 juin 1926, compte-rendu sténographique', Bureau d'éditions, Paris, 1927.
'6ème Congrès National, Saint-Denis 31 mars–7 avril 1929, compte-rendu, manifeste, thèses et résolutions', Bureau d'éditions, Paris.
'7ème Congrès, Paris 11–19 mars 1932, thèses et résolutions', *Cahiers du Bolchevisme*, numéro spécial (mai 1932), Bureau d'éditions, Paris.
'Dix-huit mois d'activité de la Région communiste (Pas-de-Calais), mesurés par des chiffres', Imp. Moderne, Avion, 1937.
'First International Peasant Conference, Theses, Messages, Addresses', 10–15 October 1923, International Peasant Union Documents, no 19, New York, 1956.
'L'Union des paysans de France', Rapport présenté au 8ème Congrès national du Parti communiste par Renaud Jean, Villeurbanne, 22–25 Janvier 1936.
'Les Communistes défendent les Paysans', Les Publications Révolutionnaires, 1935.
'Pour les travailleurs de la terre; Projets de lois et propositions du Groupe parlementaire communiste', Éditions du Comité Populaire de Propagande, Paris 1936
Racamond, Julien & Marius Vazeilles, 'La CGTU et les Paysans', CGTU Paris, sd, (1934)
Ramette, Arthur, 'La Crise à la campagne. La Situation tragique des ouvriers agricoles. Discours prononcé à la Chambre des Députés le 1er février 1935', CDLP, Paris.
Renaud Jean, Waldeck Rochet & André Parsal, 'Les devoirs du Front Populaire envers les Paysans de France', IX Congrès du Parti Communistes Français, Arles 25–29 décembre 1937. Éditions du Comité Populaire de Propagande, 1938.
'Report of the Fourth Congress of the R.I.L.U., 1928', Minority Movement, London, 1928.
'Resolutions and Decisions of the Third World Congress of the Red International of Labour Unions, Moscow', July 1924', The National Minority Movement, London, 1924.
Thorez, Maurice, 'Un an du Front Populaire', Supplément de *l'Humanité*, 18 juin 1937.

CGTU Documents

'Congrès National, 5e Congrès, Paris, 15–21 septembre 1929', Imprimerie de la Maison des syndicats, Paris.
'Congrès National, 8–14 novembre 1931', Imprimerie de la Maison des syndicats, Paris.
'Congrès National, VII Congrès, 23–29 septembre 1933', Imprimerie de la Maison des syndicats.

'Congrès National, VIII Congrès, 24–27 septembre 1935', Imprimerie de la Maison des syndicats, Paris.

Socialist Party Documents

Compère-Morel, Adéodat, 'La Question agraire en France, Rapport déposé sur le Bureau du Congrès de Toulouse en 1908 au nom de la Commission agraire et imprimée par ordre de ce Congrès', Librairie du Parti socialiste (SFIO).

Compère-Morel, Adéodat, 'Les Paysans et le Socialisme à la Chambre', Librairie du Parti socialiste (SFIO), 1909.

Parti Socialiste (Section Française de l'Internationale Ouvrière), '6ème Congrès national, Saint-Étienne, 11–14 Avril 1909', Compte-rendu sténographique, Au Siège du Conseil national, Paris.

Agricultural Theses

Butruille, Benoît, 'Une ferme au nord de l'Artois', Thèse agricole, L'Institut agricole de Beauvais, 1927.

Cardon, L, *Une Société d'exploitation agricole aux environs de Soissons*, Thèse agricole, l'Institut agricole de Beauvais, Imprimerie Centrale, Chateaudun, 1928

De Chevigny, Philippe, 'Grèves et sociologie à la Campagne', Thèse agricole, L'Institut supérieur agricole de Beauvais, 1938.

Derocquigny, Jean, 'Modifications à apporter au mode d'exploitation actuelle de la Ferme de Dercy', Thèse agricole, Institut supérieur agricole de Beauvais, 1930.

Grandel, Jean; *Une ferme de Grande Culture dans le Soissonnais*, Thèse agricole, Institut supérieur agricole de Beauvais, Imprimerie de l'Ouest-Éclair, Rennes, 1925.

Justiniart, R, 'Le Marlois agricole', Thèse agricole, Institut supérieur agricole de Beauvais, 1924.

Langlet, André, 'Une exploitation agricole dans la Santerre', Thèse agricole, Institut supérieur agricole de Beauvais, 1928.

Other Contemporary Publications

'Élections générales à l'Assemblée nationale du 2 juin 1946. Recul de tracts électoraux, listes, programmes, professions de fois et engagements des candidats.' BN microfiche M-17589.

Apchié, M, 'L'Évolution des salaires agricoles en France depuis 1924', *Études Agricoles d'Économie Corporative*, 1, July–August 1941, pp. 6–39.

Bailly, Pierre, *L'Agriculture du département de Seine-et-Marne*, Imprimerie de la République, Melun, 1937.

Demangeon Albert & Georges Mauco, *Documents pour servir à l'étude des Étrangers dans l'Agriculture française*, Hermann & Cie, Paris, 1939.

Duval, Alexandre, 'Le Visage agricole de la France: La Normandie', *La Vie agricole et Rural*, Paris, 1934.

Fromont, Pierre & François Bourgeois, 'Les Grèves agricoles de Tremblay-lès-Gonesse en 1936', *Revue d'Économie Politique*, September–October 1937, pp. 1413–51.

Leroux, Th. & Auguste Gaud, 'Nos Ouvriers agricoles', Rapports présentés à la Société des agriculteurs et au Syndicat de défense agricole de l'Oise, Beauvais, 1907.

Ministère de l'Agriculture, 'Les Questions agricoles au Conseil national de la Main d'œuvre', Paris, 1927.

Ministère de l'Agriculture, 'Statistique agricole de la France, Résultats généraux de l'Enquête de 1929', Paris, 1936.

Ministère de l'Économie Nationale, 'Résultats statistiques du recensement général de la population, mars 1936', vols 1 & 2, Paris, 1938 & 1941.

Moquay, Jean, *L'Évolution sociale en Agriculture: La condition des ouvriers agricoles depuis juin 1936*, Imp. Saint-Denis, Niort, 1939.

Papault, André, 'Le Rôle de l'immigration agricole étrangère dans l'Économie française,' Thèse, Université de Paris, Faculté de Droit, Paris, 1933.

Ratineau, Jacques & Maurice Gaillot, *L'Agriculture dans l'Aisne en 1928*, Office Agricole Départemental de l'Aisne, 1928.

Risler, Georges, *Le Travailleur agricole français*, Paris, 1923.

Sochon, A, *La Crise de la main d'œuvre agricole en France*, A. Rousseau, Paris, 1914.

Welter, Gustave, *La France d'aujourd'hui: Agriculture-Industrie-Commerce*, Payot, Paris, 1927.

Wlocevski, S, *L'Établissement des Polonais en France*, Travaux du Centre de Documentation de l'École Normale Supérieure, Paris, 1936.

NEWSPAPERS

Communist Press

L'Aube Social Mantaise, 1935–37.

L'Avenir Normand, 1937–38.

La Bretagne Ouvrière-Paysanne- Maritime, 1935–37.

Bulletin Communiste, 1920–23.

Les Cahiers du Bolchevisme.

Les Cahiers du Militant.

Le Cantal Ouvrier et Paysan, 1936–38.

La Champagne Ouvrière et Paysanne, 1937–38.

Le Communiste du Nord Ouest, 1923.

Le Cri du Gard, 1935–36.

Le Cri du Peuple (Loire & Haute-Loire), 1936–37

L'Émancipateur (Centre) 1919–23, 1929–37.

L'Enchaîné (Nord-Pas-de-Calais), 1933–38.

L'Étampois, 1936–37.

L'Éveil de Seine et Oise, 1936–37.

L'Exploité, Aisne, Ardennes, Marne, 1934–36.

L'Humanité, 1919–38.

Le Prolétaire Normand, 1933–37.

La Terre, 1937–38.

Le Travailleur d'Eure et Loir, 1919–23.

Le Travailleur de l'Yonne, Cote d'Or, 1937.

Le Travailleur de Somme et Oise, 1933–38.

Le Travailleur du Languedoc, 1931–33, 1936–37.

Le Travailleur, Eure et Loir, Loiret, Loir et Cher, 1926–27, 1934–37.

L'Unité d'Action (Calais), 1934–36.

La Voix du Peuple (Seine-et-Marne), 1936–37.

La Voix Paysanne, 1920–37.

Union Press

Oise Sociale (CFTC), 1936.
Ouvrier Agricole (CFTC), 1936–39.
Le Paysan (FNTA), 1936–39.
Le Syndicalisme (CFTC), 1936–39.
Le Travailleur Agricole (FUA), 1928–32.
Le Travailleur de la Terre (FNTA), 1923–24, 1931–32.
Le Travailleur de la Terre (CFTC, Pas de Calais), 1936.
La Vie Ouvrière (CGTU), 1933–34.

Agricultural Press

L'Agriculture de la Région du Nord, 1921–24, 1931–37.
La Paix des Campagnes (ACEA), 1938–39.
Le Progrès Agricole de l'Ouest (Dorgerist), 1936.

Socialist Press

L'Aurore de Seine et Marne, 1936–37.
Le Cri du Peuple (Somme), 1936.
L'Écho Républicain (Crépy-en-Valois), 1926–38.
Le Socialiste, 1900–08.
Le Travailleur de l'Oise (Oise) 1902–07.

National Newspapers

Le Figaro, 1935–37.
Le Temps, 1935–37.

Regional Newspapers

L'Avenir d'Arras et du Pas de Calais, 1936–37.
L'Avenir du Vexin et des Andelys, 1936.
Centre Éclair, 1936–37.
Courrier de l'Aisne, 1936.
La Dépêche (Pas de Calais), 1936.
Le Grand Écho du Nord de France, 1935–37.
Le Journal d'Issoudun, 1936–37.
Le Petit Calaisien, 1936.
Le Phare de Calais et du Pas-de-Calais, 1936.
Le Progrès de la Somme, 1936–37.
Le Réveil du Nord, 1936–37.
La Santerre, 1936.
Les Tablettes de l'Aisne, 1936–37.

BIBLIOGRAPHY

Books

Adler, Alan (ed.), *Theses, Resolutions & Manifestos of the First Four Congresses of the Third International*, Humanities Press, Atlantic Highlands, 1980.

Alexander, Martin S. & Helen Graham (eds), *The French and Spanish Popular Fronts, Comparative Perspectives*, Cambridge University Press, Cambridge, 1988.

Augé-Laribé, Michel, *La Politique agricole de la France de 1880 à 1940*, Presses Universitaires de France, Paris, 1950.

Badie, Bertrand, *Stratégie de la grève: Pour une approche fonctionnaliste du Parti communiste français*, Presses de la Fondation Nationale des Sciences Politiques, Paris, 1976.

Barral, Pierre, *Les Agrariens français de Méline à Pisani*, A. Colin, Paris, 1968.

Belloin, Gérard, *Renaud Jean, le Tribun des paysans*, Les Éditions de l'Atelier/Éditions Ouvrières, Paris, 1993.

Berger, Suzanne, *Peasants against Politics, Rural Organization in Brittany, 1911–1967*, Harvard University Press, Cambridge MA, 1972.

Bernard, Philippe, *Économie et sociologie de la Seine-et-Marne, 1850–1950*, Cahiers de la Fondation Nationale des Sciences Politiques, Paris, 1953.

Besse, Jean-Pierre, *Le Mouvement ouvrier dans l'Oise 1890–1914*, Centre Départemental de Documentation Pédagogique de l'Oise, Beauvais, 1982.

Bloch, Pierre, *Jusqu'au dernier jour, Mémoires*, Albin Michel, Paris, 1983.

Bodin, Louis & Jean Touchard, *Front Populaire, 1936*, A. Colin, Paris, 1961.

Boswell, Laird, *Rural Communism in France, 1920–1939*, Cornell University Press, London, 1998.

Bourdé, Guy, *La Défaite du Front Populaire*, F. Maspero, Paris, 1977.

Bouvier, Jean (ed.), *La France en mouvement (1934–38)*, Champ Vallon, Paris, 1986.

Bradley, Dan, *Farm Labourers, Irish Struggle 1900–1976*, Athol, Belfast, 1988.

Branciard, Michel, *Histoire de la CFDT: Soixante-dix ans d'action syndicale*, Éditions la Découverte, Paris, 1990.

Bréemersch, Pascale & Jean-Michel Decelle, *1936, Le Front Populaire dans le Pas-de-Calais*, Archives du Pas-de-Calais, Arras, 1997.

Brot, Michel, *Le Front Populaire dans les Alpes-Maritimes, 1934–37*, Éditions Serre, Nice, 1988.

Brower, Daniel R., *The New Jacobins, The French Communist Party and the Popular Front*, Cornell University Press, New York, 1968.

Brunet, Pierre, *Structure agraire et économie rurale des plateaux tertiaires entre la Seine et l'Oise*, Caron & Cie, Caen, 1960.

Bur, Michel, *Histoire de Laon et du Laonnois*, Éditions Privat, Toulouse, 1987.

Buschbaum, Jonathon, *Cinema Engagé: Film in the Popular Front*, University of Illinois Press, Urbana, 1988.

Cadé, Michel, *Le Parti des campagnes rouges: Histoire du Parti communiste dans les Pyrénées-Orientales 1920–49*, Éditions du Chiendent, Vinça, 1988.

Cardoza, Anthony, *Agrarian Elites and Italian Fascism*, Princeton University Press, Princeton NJ, 1982.

Chevallier, J-M., D. Debouis, A. Hu & M. Royer, *Les Moissons Rouges: 1936 en Soissonnais*, Corps 9 Éditions, Troesnes, 1986.

Cleary, Mark, *Peasants, Politicians and Producers: The Organisation of Agriculture in France since 1918*, Cambridge University Press, Cambridge, 1989.

Clout, Hugh, *After the Ruins; Restoring the Countryside of Northern France after the Great War*, University of Exeter Press, Exeter, 1996.

Clout, Hugh, *The Land of France 1815–1914*, Allen & Unwin, London, 1983.

Colton, Joel, *Compulsory Labor Arbitration in France, 1936–1939*, King's Crown Press, New York, 1951.

Courtois, Stéphane (ed.), *Le Livre noir du communisme: Crimes, terreur et répression*, Robert Laffont, Paris, 1997.

Courtois, Stéphane & Marc Lazar, *Histoire du Parti communiste français*, Presses Universitaires de France, Paris, 1995.

Danos, Jacques & Marcel Gibelin (trans. Peter Fysh & Christine Bourry), *June '36: Class Struggle and the Popular Front in France*, Bookmarks, London, 1986.

Depretto, Jean-Paul & Sylvie V. Schweitzer, *Le Communisme à l'usine: vie ouvrière et mouvement ouvrier chez Renault 1920–39*, EDIRES, Roubaix, 1984

Dreyfus, Michel, Bruno Groppo, Claudio Ingerflom, Roland Lew, Claude Pennetier, Bernard Pudal & Serge Wolikow, *Le Siècle des communismes*, Éditions de l'Atelier, Paris, 2000.

Dubois, Léon, *Lafarge Coppée, 150 ans d'industrie, une mémoire pour demain*, Pierre Belfond, Paris, 1988.

Duby, Georges & Armand Wallon, *Histoire de la France rurale*, vols 3 and 4, Seuil, Paris, 1976, 1977.

Dupeux, Georges, *Le Front Populaire et les élections de 1936*, Cahiers de la Fondation Nationale des Sciences Politiques, Paris, 1959.

Durand, Alfred, *La Vie rurale dans les massifs volcaniques; des Dores, du Cézallier, du Cantal et de l'Aubrac*, Laffitte, Marseille, 1980.

Dutton, Paul V., *Origins of the French Welfare State*, Cambridge University Press, Cambridge, 2002.

Farcy, Jean-Claude, *Les Paysans beaucerons au XIXème siècle*, 2 vols, Société Archéologique d'Eure-et-Loir, Chartres, 1988.

Fauvet, Jacques & Henri Mendras (eds), *Les Paysans et la politique dans la France contemporaine*, A. Colin, Paris, 1958.

Fourcaut, Annie, *Bobigny, banlieue rouge*, Les Éditions Ouvrières, Paris, 1986.

Frader, Laura, L., *Peasants and Protest: Agricultural Workers, Politics, and Unions in the Aude, 1850–1914*, University of California Press, Berkeley, 1991.

Funffrock, Gérard, *Les Grèves ouvrières dans le Nord (1919–1935): Conjoncture économique, catégories ouvrières, organisations syndicales et partisanes*, EDIRES, Roubaix, 1988.

Geary, Dick (ed.), *Labour and Socialist Movements in Europe before 1914*, Berg, Oxford, 1989.

George, Pierre & Pierre Randet, *La Région parisienne*, Presses Universitaires de France, Paris 1959.

Gillet, Marcel & Yves-Marie Hilaire (eds), *De Blum à Daladier: Le Nord/Pas-de-Calais 1936–1939*, Presses Universitaires de Lille, Villeneuve-d'Ascq, 1979.

Girault, Jacques, *Au-devant du bonheur: Les français et le Front Populaire*, CIDE, Paris, 2005.

Girault, Jacques, *Sur l'implantation du Parti communiste français dans l'entre-deux-guerres*, Éditions Sociales, Paris, 1977.

Grafteaux, Serge, *Mémé Santerre*, Éditions du Jour, Paris, 1975.

Gramsci, Antonio, *The Modern Prince and Other Writings*, Lawrence and Wishart, London, 1957.

Gratton, Philippe, *Les Luttes de classes dans les campagnes*, Éditions Anthropos, Paris, 1971.

Gratton, Phillipe, *Les Paysans français contre l'agrarisme*, F. Maspero, Paris, 1972.

Guérin, Daniel, *Front populaire, révolution manquée: témoignage militant*, Rév. éd., Paris, 1970.

Haine, Scott W., *The World of the Paris Café; Sociability among the French Working Class 1789–1914*, John Hopkins University Press, Baltimore, 1996.

Hobsbawm, Eric J. & George Rudé, *Captain Swing*, Lawrence & Wishart, London, 1969.

Holt, John Bradshaw, *German Agricultural Policy, 1918–1934. The Development of a National Philosophy toward Agriculture in Post-war Germany*, University of North Carolina Press, Chapel Hill, 1936.

Hubscher, Ronald & Jean-Claude Farcy (eds), *La Moisson des autres: Les Salariés agricoles aux XIXème et XXème siècles*, Éditions Créaphis, Paris, 1996.

Hubscher, Ronald, *L'Agriculture et la société rurale dans le Pas de Calais du milieu du XIX siècle à 1914*, 2 vols, Mémoires de la commission départementale des monuments historiques du Pas-de-Calais, Arras, 1979.

Hubscher, Ronald, *L'Immigration dans les campagnes françaises (XIXᵉ–XXᵉ siècles)*, Paris, Odile Jacob, 2005.

Hussain, Athar & Keith Tribe, *Marxism and the Agrarian Question, Volume One, German Social Democracy and the Peasantry, 1890–1907*, Humanities Press, Atlantic Highlands NJ, 1981.

Hussain, Athar & Keith Tribe, *Paths of Development in Capitalist Agriculture: Readings from German Social Democracy, 1891–99*, MacMillan Press, London, 1984.

Jackson, George D. Jr., *Comintern and Peasant in East Europe, 1919–1930*, Columbia University Press, New York, 1966.

Jackson, Julian, *The Popular Front in France: Defending Democracy, 1934–38* Cambridge University Press, Cambridge, 1988.

Jessenne, Jean-Pierre, *Pouvoir au village et Révolution, Artois 1760–1848*, Presses Universitaires de Lille, Lille, 1987.

Kautsky, Karl, *La Question agraire: Étude sur les tendances de l'agriculture moderne*, V. Giard & E. Brière, Paris, 1900.

Kemp, Tom, *The French Economy 1913–39: The History of a Decline*, Longman, London, 1972.

Kergoat, Jacques, *La France du Front Populaire*, La Découverte, Paris, 1986.

Kriegel, Annie, *Aux Origines du communisme français, 1914–20: Contribution à l'histoire du mouvement ouvrier français*, 2 vols, Mouton & Co, Paris, 1964.

Kriegel, Annie, *The French Communists: Profile of a People*, University of Chicago Press, Chicago, 1972.

Lagarrigue, Max, *Renaud Jean, Carnets d'un paysan député communiste*, Atlantica, Anglet, 2001.

Lagrave, Rose-Marie (ed.), 'Les "petites Russies" des campagnes françaises', *Études Rurales*, 171–72, July–December 2004.

Langlois, Caroline, *Léonne, Bonne de ferme à 12 ans, une vie en Beauce au début du XX siècle*, Éditions Tirésias, Paris, 2002.

Langlois, François, *Les Salariés agricoles en France*, A. Colin, Paris, 1962.

Larkin, Maurice, *France since the Popular Front, Government and People, 1936–39*, Clarendon, Oxford, 1997.

Launay, Michel, *La CFTC: Origines et développement 1919–1940*, Publications de la Sorbonne, Paris, 1986.

Lavabre, Marie-Claire, *Le Fil Rouge: Sociologie de la mémoire communiste*, Presses de la Fondation Nationale des Sciences Politiques, Paris, 1994.

Lavau, Georges, *À quoi sert le Parti communiste français?*, Fayard, Paris, 1982.

Lazar, Marc, *Le Communisme: Une passion française*, Éditions Perrin, Paris, 2005.

Le Coadic, Ronan, *Les Campagnes rouges de Bretagne*, Skol Vreizh, Montroules, 1991.

Le Maner, Yves, *Histoire du Pas-de-Calais 1815–1945*, Mémoires de la Commission départementale d'histoire et d'archéologie du Pas-de-Calais, Arras, 1993.

Lefranc, Georges, (Montreuil), *Histoire du mouvement ouvrier en France, des origines à nos jours*, Aubier, Paris, 1946.

Lefranc, Georges, *Juin '36: L'Explosion sociale*, Julliard, Paris, 1966.

Lynch, Édouard, *Moissons rouges, Les Socialistes français et la société paysanne durant l'entre-deux-guerres (1918–1940)*, Presses Universitaires du Septentrion, Villeneuve d'Ascq, 2002.

Magraw, Roger, *A History of the French Working Class*, 2 vols, Blackwell, Oxford, 1992.

Marchand, Olivier & Claude Thélot, *Deux siècles de travail en France, Population active et structure sociale, durée et productivité du travail de 1800 à 1990*, INSEE Études, Paris, 1997.

Martelli, Roger, *Le Rouge et le bleu: Essai sur le communisme dans l'histoire française*, Éditions de l'Atelier, 1995.

Marx, Karl, *Capital*, Vol. One, Lawrence & Wishart, London, 1954.

Mendras, Henri, *The Vanishing Peasant: Innovation and Change in French Agriculture*, The MIT Press, Cambridge MA, 1970.

Mitrany, David, *Marx against the Peasant*, Weidenfeld & Nicolson, London, 1951.

Molinari, Jean-Paul, *Les Ouvriers communistes: Sociologie de l'adhésion ouvrière au PCF*, Albaron, Thonon-les-Bains, 1991.

Mortimer, Edward, *The Rise of the French Communist Party, 1920–47*, Faber and Faber, London, 1984.

Muchembled, Robert & Gérard Sivéry, *Nos Ancêtres, les paysans: Aspects du monde rural dans le Nord-Pas-de-Calais des origines à nos jours*, Centre d'histoire de la Région du Nord, Lille, 1981.

Newby, Howard, *The Deferential Worker: A Study of Farm Workers in East Anglia*, Allen Lane, London, 1977.

Noguères, Henri, *La Vie quotidienne en France au temps du Front Populaire, 1935–38*, Hachette, Paris, 1977.

Noiriel, Gérard, *Workers in French Society in the Nineteenth and Twentieth Centuries*, Berg, New York, 1990.

Paige, Jeffery M, *Agrarian Revolution, Social Movements and Export Agriculture in the Underdeveloped World*, Collier Macmillan, London, 1975.

Passmore, Kevin, *From Liberalism to Fascism, The Right in a French Province, 1928–39*, Cambridge University Press, Cambridge, 1997.

Paxton, Robert O., *French Peasant Fascism, Henry Dorgères's Greenshirts and the Crises of French Agriculture, 1929–1939*, Oxford University Press, New York, 1997.

Perrot, Michelle (trans. C. Turner), *Workers on Strike, France 1871–1890*, Berg, Leamington Spa, 1987.

Pennetier, Claude (ed.), *Dictionnaire biographique du mouvement ouvrier français (Le Maitron)*, CD-Rom, Les Éditions de l'Atelier, 1997.

Philipponneau, Michel, *La Vie rurale de la banlieue parisienne: Étude de géographie humaine*, Centre d'Études Économiques, Paris, 1955.

Pick, Daniel, *Faces of Degeneration: A European Disorder, c. 1848–c. 1918,* Cambridge University Press, Cambridge, 1989.

Pigenet, Phryné & Michel, Robert Rygiel & Michel Picard, *Terre de luttes (précurseurs 1848–1939): Histoire du mouvement ouvrier dans le Cher*, Éditions Sociales, Paris, 1977.

Pinchemel, Philippe, *Structures sociales et dépopulation rurale dans les campagnes picardes de 1836 a 1936*, Librairie Armand Colin, Paris, 1957.

Ponty, Janine, *Polonais méconnus. Histoire des travailleurs immigrés en France dans l'entre-deux-guerres*, Publications de la Sorbonne, Paris, 1988.

Postel-Vinay, Gilles, *La Rente foncière dans le capitalisme agricole, analyse de la voie 'classique' du développement du capitalisme dans l'agriculture à partir de l'exemple du Soissonnais'*, François Maspero, Paris, 1974.

Pretty, David, *The Rural Revolt that Failed: Farm workers' Trade Unions in Wales, 1899–1950*, University of Wales Press, Cardiff, 1989.

Price, Roger, *The Modernization of Rural France: Communication Networks and Agricultural Market Structures in Nineteenth Century France*, Hutchinson, London, 1983.

Prost, Antoine, *La CGT à l'époque du Front Populaire, 1934–1939: Essai de description numérique*, A. Colin, Paris, 1964.

Pruvot, Monique, *Arthur Chaussy 1880–1945*, Collection La Fresnaye, Combs-la-Ville, 1983.

Quellien, Jean, *Le Calvados au temps du Front Populaire*, Édition du Lys, Caen, 1996.

Rémond, René & Janine Bourdin (eds), *Édouard Daladier, chef du gouvernement, avril 1938–septembre 1939*, Presse de la Fondation Nationale des Sciences Politiques, Paris 1977.

Riddell, John (ed.), *The German Revolution and the Debate on Soviet Power, Documents 1918–19, Preparing the Founding Conference*, Anchor Foundation, New York, 1986.

Robrieux, Philippe, *Histoire Intérieure du Parti communiste française*, Fayard, Paris, 4 vols, 1980–84.

Ross, George, *Workers and Communists in France: From Popular Front to Eurocommunism*, University of California Press, Berkeley, 1982.

Sagnes, Jean, *Jean Jaurès et le Languedoc Viticole*, Presses du Languedoc, Montpellier, 1988.

Sagnes, Jean, *Le Mouvement ouvrier en Languedoc. Syndicalistes et socialistes de l'Hérault de la fondation des Bourses du travail à la naissance du Parti communiste*, Privat, Toulouse, 1980.

Sagnes, Jean, *Politique et syndicalisme en Languedoc: L'Hérault durant l'entre-deux-guerres*, Université Paul Valéry, Montpellier, 1986.

Schor, Ralph, *L'Opinion française et les étrangers, 1919–1939,* La Sorbonne, Paris, 1985.

Sellier, François, *La Confrontation sociale en France 1936–1981*, Presses Universitaires de France, Paris, 1984.

Shorter, Edward & Charles Tilly, *Strikes in France 1830–1968*, Cambridge University Press, London, 1974.

Tartakowsky, Danielle, *Le Front Populaire: La Vie est à nous*, Gallimard, Paris, 1996.

Tartakowsky, Danielle, *Une Histoire du PCF*, Presses Universitaires de France, Paris, 1982.

Tartakowsky, Danielle & Claude Willard, *Des Lendemains qui chantent. La France des années folles et du Front populaire*, Messidor/Éditions Sociales, Paris, 1986.

Terrier, Didier, *Les Deux ages de la proto-industrie. Les Tisserands du Cambrésis et du Saint-Quentinois, 1730–1880*, Éditions de l'École des Hautes Études en Sciences Sociales, Paris, 1996.

Tilly, Charles, *The Contentious French*, Belknap Press, Cambridge MA, 1986.

Tombs, Robert, *France 1814–1914*, Longman, London, 1996.

Torigian, Michael, *Every Factory a Fortress, The French Labour Movement in the Age of Ford and Hitler*, Ohio University Press, Athens, 1999.

Trotsky, Leon, *The First Five Years of the Communist International*, 2 vols, New Park Publications, London, 1974.

Vandamme, P., *L'Agriculture du Pas-de-Calais*, Centre National de la Recherche Scientifique, Paris, 1951.

Vercherand, Jean, *Un Siècle de syndicalisme agricole, la vie locale et nationale à travers le cas du département de la Loire*, Publications de l'Université de Saint-Étienne, 1994.

Vigna, Xavier, Jean Vigreux and Serge Wolikow (eds), *Le Pain, la Paix, La Liberté: Expériences et territoires du Front Populaire*, La Dispute-Éditions Sociales, Paris, 2006.

Vigreux, Jean, *Waldeck Rochet, Une Biographie politique*, La Dispute, Paris, 2000.

Vinen, Richard, *France 1934–1970*, MacMillan Press, London.

Warwick, Paul, *The French Popular Front: a Legislative Analysis*, University of Chicago Press, Chicago, 1977.

Weber, Eugen, *The Hollow Years, France in the 1930s*, Sinclair-Stevenson, London, 1995.

Willard, Claude (ed.), *Histoire de la classe ouvrière et du mouvement ouvrier français*, 2 vols, Éditions Sociales, Paris, 1993 & Éditions de l'Atelier, Paris, 1995.

Willard, Claude, Jacques Chambaz, Jean Bruhat, Georges Cogniot & Claude Gindin, *Le Front Populaire (la France de 1934 à 1939)*, Éditions Sociales, Paris, 1972.

Willard, Claude, *Les Guesdistes: Le Mouvement socialiste en France 1893–1905*, Éditions Sociales, Paris, 1965.

Wolf, Eric R., *Peasant Wars of the Twentieth Century*, Faber and Faber, London, 1973.

Wolikow, Serge, *Le Front Populaire en France*, Complexe, Bruxelles, 1996.

Worley, Matthew (ed.), *In Search of Revolution: International Communist Parties in the Third Period*, I.B. Tauris, London, 2004.

Wright, Gordon, *France in Modern Times*, W.W. Norton, New York, 1995.

Wright, Gordon, *Rural Revolution in France: The Peasantry in the Twentieth Century*, Stanford University Press, Stanford Cal., 1964.

Zola, Émile, *The Earth*, Penguin, London, 1980.

Articles and Conference Papers

Allart, Marie-Christine, 'Les Femmes de trois villages de l'Artois: travail et vécu quotidien (1919–39)' *Revue du Nord*, vol. 63, 250, pp. 703–724.

Barral, Pierre, 'Note historique sur l'emploi du terme "paysan"', *Études Rurales*, 21, April–June 1966, pp. 72–80.

Besse, Jean-Pierre, 'Le Front Populaire dans l'Oise (1936–1938), *Annales Historiques Compiègnoises*, 36, 1986.

Boswell, Laird, 'Le Communisme et la défense de la petite propriété en Limousin et en Dordogne', *Communisme*, 51–52, 1997, pp. 7–27.

Boswell, Laird, 'The French Rural Communist Electorate', *Journal of Interdisciplinary History*, vol. 23, 4 (1993), pp. 719–49.

Boswell, Laird, 'L'Historiographie du communisme français, est-elle dans une impasse?', *Revue française de science politique*, vol. 55, 5–6 (2005), pp. 919–33.

Bulaitis, John, 'Les Luttes agricoles de 1906–08: premier conflit social du XXe siècle dans les campagnes de l'Aisne', in *La Vie rurale dans l'Aisne, Mémoires*, vol. XLVIII (2003), Fédération des Sociétés d'Histoire et d'Archéologie de l'Aisne, pp. 191–205.

Cadé, Michel, 'La Grève des ouvriers agricoles de Rivesaltes en 1928: un épisode de la lutte des classes dans les campagnes', *Annales du Midi*, 94, 1982, pp. 403–39.

Chambaz, B, 'Petite bibliographie critique sur le Front Populaire', *Cahiers d'Histoire de l'Institut Maurice Thorez*, July–Sept 1973, pp. 186–91.

Charvet, Jean-Paul, 'Les régions de '"grande culture" en France', *Historiens et Géographes*, 370, May–June 2000, pp. 335–40.

Cogniot, Georges, 'La Question Paysanne devant le mouvement ouvrier français de 1892 à 1921', *Cahiers de l'Institut Maurice Thorez*, 24, 1971, pp. 5–21.

Courtois, Stéphane, 'Chronique de l'Historiographie du Parti Communiste Francais', in S. Courtois (ed.) *Communisme en France, De la revolution documentaire au renouveau historiographique*, Actes du colloque organise par le Centre de recherches Hannah Arendt le 11 Mai 2006, Éditions Cujas, Paris, 2007, pp. 5–43.

Ehrmann, Henry W., 'The French Peasant and Communism', *American Political Science Review*, vol. XLVI, 1952, pp. 19–42.

Engels, Frederick, 'On the Dissolution of the Lassallean Workers' Association', *Demokratisches Wochenblatte*, 3 October 1868, available at Marxists Internet Archive: http://www.marxists.org/history/international/iwma/documents/1868/dissolution

Engels, Frederick, 'The Peasant Question in France and Germany', first published in *Die Neue Zeit*, 1894–95; Marxists Internet Archive, http://www.marxists.org/archive/marx/works/1894/peasant-question/index.htm

Engels, Frederick, 'The Peasant War in Germany. Preface to the Second Edition', 1870, Marxists Internet Archive, http://www.marxists.org/archive/marx/works/1850/peasant-war-germany/ch0a.htm

Frader, Laura L, 'Grapes of Wrath: Vineyard workers, Labour Unions, and Strike Activity in the Aude, 1860–1913' in Tilly, Louise A. & Charles Tilly (eds), *Class Conflict and Collective Action*, Sage Publications, London 1981, pp. 185–206.

Fremont, Armand, 'L'Exploitation du sol et les productions agricoles dans la partie occidentale du Pays de Caux', *Études Normandes*, 80, 1957.

Gaçon, Jean, 'La Politique paysanne du Parti communiste français de 1921 à 1939', *Cahiers de l'Institut Maurice Thorez*, 24, 1971, pp. 33–44.

Gavignaud, Geneviève, 'Un mouvement de grève roussillonnais, 1937–38', Colloque, 'Le Front Populaire et la vie quotidienne des Français', Centre de recherches d'histoire des mouvements sociaux et du syndicalisme (CRHMSS), 15–16 September 1986.

Gilbert, Noël, 'La Restauration des structures agricoles', in *'La Grande Reconstruction': Reconstruire le Pas-de-Calais après la grande guerre*, Actes du colloque, 8–10 novembre 2000, Archives Départementales du Pas-de-Calais, 2002, pp. 159–77.

Gogolewski, Edmond, 'Les Polonais en France avant la seconde guerre mondiale', *La Revue du Nord*, vol. 61, July–Sept 1979, pp. 649–69.

Goldberg, Harvey, 'Jaurès and the Formation of a Socialist Peasant Policy, 1885–1898', *International Review of Social History*, vol. 2, 1957, pp. 372–91.

Greaves, Thomas C., 'The Andean Rural Proletarians', in Nash, June (ed.), *Ideology and Social Change in Latin America*, Gordon & Breach, New York, 1977.

Hainer, Paul, 'The Rural Proletariat: The Everyday Life of Rural Labourers in the Magdeburg Region, 1830–1880', in Evans, Richard J. & W. R. Lee (eds) *The German Peasantry, Conflict and Community in Rural Society from the Eighteenth to the Twentieth Centuries*, Croom Helm, London, 1986, pp. 102–28.

Hainsworth, Raymond, 'Les Grèves du Front Populaire de mai et juin 1936. Une Nouvelle analyse fondée sur l'étude de ces grèves dans le basin houiller du Nord et du Pas-de-Calais', *Le Mouvement Social*, 96, 1976, pp. 3–30.

Howkins, Alun, 'Structural Conflict and the Farmworker, Norfolk, 1900–20', *Journal of Peasant Studies*, vol. 4, no. 3, April 1977, pp. 217–29.

Hubscher, Ronald, 'Réflexions sur l'identité paysanne au XIXe siècle: identité réelle ou supposée?', *Ruralia*, 1, 1997, pp. 65–80.

Joppé, A., 'Conditions de salaire et de travail des ouvriers agricoles (1910)', in J. Borgé & N. Viarnoff (eds), *Archives du Nord*, Éditions Balland, 1979, pp. 161–63.

Landauer, Carl, 'The Guesdists and the Small Farmer: Early Erosion of French Marxism', *International Review of Social History*, vol. VI, 2, 1961, pp. 212–25.

Lazar, Marc, 'Damné de la terre et homme de marbre. L'Ouvrier dans l'imaginaire du PCF du milieu des années trente à la fin des années cinquante', *Annales ESC*, September-October 1990, pp. 1071–96.

Lynch, Édouard, 'Toury: une grève à la campagne sous le Front Populaire', *Vingtième Siècle*, 67, July-September 2000, pp. 79–93.

Mintz, Sidney W., 'The Rural Proletariat and the Problem of Rural Proletarian Consciousness', *Journal of Peasant Studies*, vol. 1, 3, pp. 291–325.

Molinari, Jean-Paul, 'Les Paysans du Parti communiste français', *Politix*, Presses de la Fondation Nationale des Sciences Politiques, 14, 1991, pp. 87–94.

Ory, Pascal, 'Le Dorgérisme: Institution et discours d'une colère paysanne, 1929–39', *Revue d'histoire moderne et contemporaine*, 22, 1975, pp. 168–90.

Perkins, J. A., 'The German Agricultural Worker, 1815–1914', *Journal of Peasant Studies*, vol. 11, 3, April 1984, pp. 3–25.

Prost, Antoine, 'Les Grèves de mai-juin revisitées', *Le Mouvement Social*, 200, 2002, pp. 33–54.

Prost, Antoine, 'Les Grèves de Juin 36, essai d'interprétation' in Bourdin, J, (ed.) *Léon Blum, chef de gouvernement, 1936–37*, A. Colin, Paris, 1967, pp. 49–68.

Ragache, Gilles, 'Les Grèves d'ouvriers agricoles été 1936', *Le Peuple Français*, nouvelle série 1, 1978, pp. 21–23.

Saillet, Jacqueline & Jacques Girault, 'Les Mouvements vignerons de Champagne', *Le Mouvement Social*, 67, 1969, pp. 79–88.

Sandrin, Jean, 'La Grande colère des Maraîchers, Séptembre 1936,' *Gavroche*, 7–8, December 1982 & February 1983.

Schwarz, Salomon 'Les Occupations d'usines de mai et juin 1936', *International Review for Social History*, vol. 2, 1937, pp. 50–104.

Seidman, Michael, 'Towards a History of Workers' Resistance to Work: Paris and Barcelona during the French Popular Front and the Spanish Revolution, 1936–38', *Journal of Contemporary History*, vol. 23, 1988, pp. 191–220.

Sénéchal, Jean-Paul, 'Images du Front Populaire Finistère: 1934–38', *Skol Vreizh*, 7, Brest, 1987.

Shorter, Edward & Charles Tilly, 'Le Déclin de la grève violente en France de 1890 à 1935', *Le Mouvement Social*, 76, 1971, pp. 95–118.

Sokoloff, Sally, 'Peasant Leadership and the French Communist Party, 1921–1940', *Historical Reflections*, vol. IV, 2, 1977, pp. 153–70.

Vigreux, Jean, 'Le Parti communiste français à la campagne, 1920–1964. Bilan historiographique et perspectives de recherché', *Ruralia*, 3, 1998, pp. 43–66.

Vigreux, Jean, 'Le PCF garant de l'heritage agrarien progressiste' in Wolikow, Serge & Annie Bleton-Ruget (eds), *Antifascisme et nation: les gauches européennes au temps du Front Populaire*, Publications de l'Université Contemporaine-CNRS, 1998, pp. 164–71.

Vigreux, Jean, 'Paysans et responsables du travail paysan dans la direction du parti communiste', in Dreyfus, Michel (ed.), *La Part des militants, biographie et mouvement ouvrier: Autour du Maitron, dictionnaire biographique du mouvement ouvrier français*, Les Éditions de l'Atelier/Éditions Ouvrières, Paris 1996, pp. 205–18.

Wolikow, Serge, 'Le PCF et la Nation au temps du Front Populaire', in Wolikow, Serge & Annie Bleton-Ruget (eds), *Antifascisme et nation: les gauches européennes au temps du Front Populaire*, Publications de l'Université Contemporaine-CNRS, 1998, pp. 129–40.

Wright, Gordon, 'Four Red Villages in France', *The Yale Review*, spring 1952, pp. 361–72.

Theses and 'Mémoires de Maîtrise'

Arnoux, José, 'Milieux ruraux et urbains dans le Pas de Calais dans la tourmente nationaliste de l'entre deux guerres: le Dorgérisme et le PSF', Mémoire de maîtrise, Université Charles de Gaulle Lille III, 1990–91.

Caron, Marianne, 'Le Front Populaire dans le Bas-Languedoc et le Roussillon', Thèse, Université Paul Valéry de Montpellier, 1972.

Chaudeurge, Emmanuel, 'Les Paysans et le Front Populaire dans l'Orne', Mémoire de maîtrise, Paris I, 1971.

Dubois, Martine & Gilbert Grassi, 'Le Front Populaire dans l'Aisne 1934–38', Mémoire d'histoire contemporaine, UER, Reims, 1974.

Guillerot, Jean-Pierre, 'La Politique Agraire et Paysanne du PCF de 1920 à 1934', Mémoire de maîtrise, Université de Paris VIII, 1973.

Happe, Danièle, 'La Vie agricole dans l'ancien arrondissement d'Arras', Mémoire, École de Hautes Études Commerciales du Nord, 1961.

Lynch, Édouard, 'Compère-Morel et la politique agraire de la SFIO. L'Élaboration d'une doctrine entre socialisme et agrarisme, 1900–1921', DEA Mémoire, IEP Paris, 1990–91.

Lynch, Édouard, 'Le Parti socialiste (SFIO) et la société paysanne durant l'entre-deux-guerres. Idéologie, politique agricole et sociabilité politique (1914–1940)'. Thèse, Institut d'études politiques, Paris, 1998.

Petit, Odile, 'La Naissance et le développement du syndicalisme et de la mutualité agricole dans le département de l'Aisne entre les deux guerres', Thèse de doctorat, Université Paris IV, 1986.

Ponchelet, Danielle, 'Ouvriers nomades et patrons briards: Les Grandes exploitations agricoles dans la Brie, 1848–1938', Thèse, Institut national de la recherche agronomique économie et sociologie rurales, 1987.

Sokoloff, Sally, 'Communism and the French Peasantry, with a special reference to the Allier, 1919–39', Phd. Thesis, University of London, 1975.

Valengin, Jean, 'Les Répercussions de la crise des années trente sur le syndicalisme agricole dans l'Aisne', Mémoire de maîtrise d'histoire contemporaine, Université de Lille III, 1994.

Vigreux, Jean, 'Waldeck Rochet, du militant paysan au dirigeant ouvrier', Thèse, Institut d'études politiques, Paris, 1997.

INDEX